PIONEER FAMILIES
OF
FRANKLIN COUNTY
VIRGINIA

Marshall Wingfield

CLEARFIELD

Reprinted for
Clearfield Company, Inc. by
Genealogical Publishing Co., Inc.
Baltimore, Maryland
1992
with the permission of
The Virginia Book Company

Reprinted for
Clearfield Company, Inc. by
Genealogical Publishing Co., Inc.
Baltimore, Maryland
1996, 2000

International Standard Book Number: 0-8063-4631-0

Made in the United States of America

Preface

In 1924, Dr. Marshall Wingfield published <u>A History</u> <u>of Caroline County, Virginia</u>.

Then focusing his attention upon his native Franklin County, he published, in 1939, <u>Marriage Bonds of Franklin</u> <u>County, Virginia. 1796-1858</u>, which was followed, in 1948, by <u>An Old Virginia Court. Being a Transcription of the Records</u> <u>of the First Court of Franklin County, Virginia 1786-1789</u>.

The manuscript for the present volume was completed by Dr. Wingfeild in 1936, and is published through the courtesy of Dr. Wingfield's widow, Marie Gregson Wingfield. It will be followed shortly by the publication of Dr. Wingfield's history of Franklin County.

Chesapeake Book Company

CONTENTS - FAMILIES

THE AKERS FAMILY

      William Akers purchased land in West New Jersey about 1698, at which time he and others were granted 100 acres by the West Jersey Company "for a meeting house, burial ground and school house in Maiden Township, above the falls of the Delaware".

      Simon Akers, son of William Akers, had three sons: Simon, Robert and John. He died in Hunterdon County, New Jersey, in 1722.

      Robert Akers, second son of Simon Akers, was born in New Jersey in 1703. He married Sarah, of Welch descent, who was born March 13, 1706. To this union a son, William, was born.

      William Akers, son of Robert and Sarah, was born in 1730, and died in 1810. He married Elizabeth Martye (or Marte) of Pennsylvania. She was of Holland-Dutch extration of Heinrich Martye from the Palatinate, Germany, who sailed from Rotterdam in the "Alexander and Ann", and landed at Philadelphia, October 1730. William Akers patented 175 acres in Nelson County, Virginia, in 1751. He later moved to what is now Campbell County, Virgina. He is buried in the second burial ground of Old Concord Presbyterian Church. His tombstone still stands in a grove, near the Church. It is of dark coloured native rock, and the lettering is still quite distinct.

      William and Elizabeth (Martye) Akers were the parents of eleven children, four sons and seven daughters. Three sons served in the Revolutionary War. They were the oldest sons, who settled in Franklin County; Peter, the second son; and John, a younger son, nicknamed "Bunker John", because he was in the battle of Bunker Hill. "Bunker John" was a maker of "Slays" for weaving, and lived at Concord, Virginia.

      Their cousin, James Akers, also saw service at Bunker Hill, and was afterwards called "Bunker Jim". He lived at the foot of Clemen's Bald Knob, in Franklin County.

      William Akers, oldest son of William and Elizabeth (Martye) Akers, was born in 1752. He served as Corporal in the Revolutionary War, in Capt. Russell's company, Col. Charles Scott's Fifth Regiment, Virginia Continental Line. He married Dolly Blackburn. They established their home in Franklin County, near Blackwater River. They were the parents of six sons as follows:

      (1) James Akers, who was married on January 13, 1792 (by Rev. Randolph Hall) to Lucy Webster, daughter of Luke and Sarah Webster. They lived on Blackwater River near Dillon's Mill in

Franklin County. (2) Samuel Akers, who married Mary Brown, and lived in Franklin County. (3) Daniel Akers, who married Rebecca Webster and lived in Franklin County. (4) John Akers, who married Sarah Brown, and removed to Georgia in 1830. (5) Blackburn Akers, who married Elizabeth Lashores, and removed to Floyd County, Virginia. (6) Nathaniel Akers, who married Elizabeth Akers, daughter of John Akers and Nancy (Jeffs) Akers, and lived in Franklin County.

James Akers, oldest son of William and Elizabeth (Martye) Akers, was born in 1774. He served in the War of 1812. His father and two of his uncles served in the War of the Revolution. He was a lifelong resident of Franklin County. He settled about one mile north of Dillon's Mill in Franklin County on the north fork of Blackwater River where he became a well-to-do planter , and owned many slaves and much land. He was a man of high moral character, and greatly esteemed by his neighbors. He and his wife were Separate Baptists. His wife's father was a wealthy planter who owned many slaves and much land on Blackwater River, and who gave each of his children a farm, slaves and other property.

William Akers, son of James and Lucy, was born in Franklin County, October 3, 1802. He married Lavinia Capper, and they established their home near Dillon's Mill.

Jennie Akers, daughter of James and Lucy, was born in Franklin County, September 15, 1804, and was married to Joe Hickman, in 1825, by Rev. Wilson Turner. They established their home near the headwaters of Little Creek, a short distance west of Bethlehem Dunkard Church, of which they were members. Here they lived for many years, and reared a large family. Their residence was of brick and was built by John R. Webster. It is still standing, and is owned and occupied by Mrs. Danie Flora.

Betsy Akers, daughter of James and Lucy, married John B. Webster. They lived on the headwaters of Blackwater River. John B. Webster, the progenitor and pioneer of the Websters in Franklin, was known as "Daddy" Webster.

Fibbie Akers, daughter of James and Lucy, married David S. Webster, son of John Robbin Webster. They were members of the Fairmont Baptist Church, having united with it in October 1856. They moved to Wabash, Indiana, in 1864 or 1865. They had no children, but reared Betty and James, the children of her sister, Mrs. Fannie Kinsey. They never returned to Virginia.

Henry Akers, son of James and Lucy moved to Indiana when a young man.

Fannie Akers, daughter of James and Lucy, married George Kinsey, and removed to Wabash Indiana and reared a large family.

Early in life, William Akers, first of the children of James and Lucy Webster, purchased a plantation adjoining that of his father, near the foot of Kahay's Knob. On this he established his home, when he married Lavinia Capper in 1820. She was born January 14, 1802, and died August 25, 1871. Her father came from Lincolnshire England. Her mother was of Scotch-Irish descent. Mrs. Akers was high spirited and witty, and was an exceptionally good housekeeper. Mr. Akers was rather stout. He wore a Van Dyke beard, had blue eyes, fair complexion. He was mild mannered, unassuming, thoughtful of others, and extremely hospitable. He owned a large plantation and many slaves. He was kind to them, and both master and slaves were contented, hence he was convinced that slavery was not an evil institution. When they were set free, he felt a great injustice had been done him. His slaves loved him and remained with him as long as he lived, working his farm as tenants and attending to the household duties as before. He died March 25, 1867. His widow died in 1871. Both are buried at the John Jamison burial ground, near his old homestead. The Akers family were members of Fairmont Baptist Church.

Mr. and Mrs. William Akers were the parents of four Children:
(1) John Akers, their only son, was born June 29, 1822. At the outbreak of the War between the States, he volunteered for service in the Confederate Army, and died in Norfolk, April 12, 1862, being buried in the Jamison burial ground.

Elizabeth Akers, their eldest daughter, was born July 2, 1824, and died of diptheria January 14, 1859. She married John Jamison August 2, 1844. They were the parents of seven children, two sons and five daughters: Martha Jane, Sarah Elizabeth, John William, Lucy Ann, Hannah Katherine, Sue Lavinia and Samuel Henry.

Elizabeth Akers Jamison was an attractive and accomplished woman who exerted a remarkable influence over her children. Though a firm believer in the Baptist faith, and deeply religious, she never united with any church. She is buried just south of, and in full view of her father's old homestead in the Jamison burial ground.

Hannah Akers, the second daughter, was born December 24, 1826. She moved to Texas about 1875 and never returned, dying there unmarried on May 17, 1892.

Lucy Ann Akers, the third daughter, was born December 28, 1828, and married Jessie Young. She was a member of Fairmount Baptist Church. She died August 5, 1874 and is buried at the Jamison burial ground.

THE BERNARD FAMILY

The Franklin County Bernards are descended from Benjamin Bernard, who was born February 20, 1757, in Powhatan County.

While residing in that county he enlisted and served with the
Virginia troops, as follows: One and one-half months in Capt.
Richard Crump's Company; one and one-half months in Capt. Robert
Hughes's Company; he was in the Battle of Guilford Court House;
three months guarding the boats at Jud's Ferry in Powhatan County;
and, one and one-half months in guarding the boats at a ferry in
Chesterfield County. He was out on several other tours, but no
dates are given for any of them.

He was allowed pension on his application executed
September 18, 1832, at which time he was living in Chesterfield
County.

The son of this Benjamin Bernard, also named Benjamin,
married a Miss Betz, came to Franklin County, and settled soon
after the Revolution. Their children were:
(1) Benjamin Bernard, who married Emeline Hutchinson.
(2) John A. Bernard (Jack) never married.
(3) Joseph Bernard, who married first, Martha Wells, second,
Sally Hamlet (widow).
(4) Polly Bernard, who married a Mr. Wells.
(5) Elizabeth Bernard, who moved to Texas and married John
Bowe.
(6) Sally Bernard, who married Spottswood Belcher.
(7) Silas G. Bernard, born August 20, 1809, died August 9,
1884. He married Lucinda Pullen who was born June 6, 1813, and
died May 2, 1888.

Silas G. Bernard was surveyor of Franklin County. He
was also a talented cabinet maker, and pursued this hobby in his
spare time. He represented the county of Franklin in the General
Assembly for the sessions of 1871-72 and 1872-73. His portrait
how hangs in the hall of the House of Delegates.

The children of Silas G. Bernard as follows:
(1) Thomas, who married Susan Williamson.
(2) John, who married Julia Williamson.
(3) Frank, who married Julia Williamson.
(4) Matilda, who married Jason Hundley.
(5) Julia, who married John Semones.
(6) Nannie, who married George K. Cooper.
(7) Mary Lucinda, who married William S. Williamson.

Of these children of Silas G. Bernard, Thomas Bernard,
John Bernard, Nannie (Bernard) Cooper and Mary Lucinda (Bernard)
Williamson, spent their lives in Franklin County. Of their descendants, only William Bernard, son of Thomas and Susan Williamson Bernard, and the children of Nannie Bernard Cooper, now live
in Franklin.

The children of William S. and Mary Lucinda (Bernard)
Williamson were:
(1) Lawson Williamson, who married Charmian Hamilton of
Bristol.
(2) Richard Silas Williamson, who married Maggie Prunty of

Franklin County, and had six children.
 (3) Loula Williamson, who married O. Parker of Henry County, and had three children.
 (4) Julia Williamson, who married John H. Dyer of Martinsville, and had four children.
 (5) William Thomas Williamson, who married Margaret Scott of Winston-Salem, and had four children.
 (6) Chapman S. Williamson, who married Julia Tench of Waynesboro.
 (7) Jason Hundley Williamson, who married Winifred Burnett of Roanoke, and had two children.
 (8) Nannie Williamson, who never married.
 (9) Essie Williamson, who married Dr. W. L. Lyle of Bedford, and has one child.

Issue of Richard Silas and Maggie (Prunty) Williamson:
 ((1) Doris Williamson, who married H. Clay Turner, Martinsville.
 (2) Mary Williamson, who married B. Clifford Goode, living at Centralia.
 (3) Charmian Williamson, teacher, Martinsville.
 (4) Mildren Williamson, teacher, Martinsville.
 (5) Bernard Williamson, clerk with William Asssett Furniture Company, Martinsville.
 (6) Nancy Williamson, secretary, Martinsville.

Issue of Loula (Williamson) and O. Parker:
 (1) Paul Parker, Schuyler.
 (2) Reginald Parker, who married Frances Tuggle of Greensboro, North Carolina.
 (3) T. O. Parker, who married Alice Price, Luray.

Issue of Julia (Williamson) and John H. Dyer:
 (1) Lilliam Dyer, employed by First National Bank, Martinsville.
 (2) John Lawson Dyer, employed by a Martinsville Furniture factory.
 (3) James W. Dyer, employed by Service Printing Company, Martinsville.
 (4) Mary Lyle Dyer, Martinsville.

Issue of William T. and Margaret (Scott) Williamson:
 (1) William T. Williamson.
 (2) Daniel Scott Williamson.
 (3) Mary (Patsy) Williamson.
 (4) Margaret (Peggy) Williamson.

Issue of Jason H., and Winifred (Burnett) Williamson:
 (1) Colleen Williamson.
 (2) Jason Henry Williamson, Jr.

Issue of Essie (Williamson) and Dr. W. L. Lyle:
 (1) Mary Lydia Lyle.

THE BOONE FAMILY

A branch of the Boone family lived in Devonshire, near Exeter, where George Boone, III, progenitor of the Franklin County family, was born.

George Boone III, son of George II, and Sarah Uppey his wife, was born in 1666. He was married in 1689 to Mary Maugridge, (born 1669) daughter of John Maugridge and Mary Milton of Bradnich, Devonshire. They had nine children: (1) George IV, (2) Sarah, (3) Squire, (4) Mary (5) John, (6) Joseph, (7) Benjamin, (8) James and (9) Samuel, all born in Bradnich.

George Boone IV, Sarah and Squire were in America as early as 1716. Their parents, with their younger sister and brothers, arrived at Philadelphia October 10, 1717, and settled in Pennsylvania.

Squire Boone was the father of Daniel Boone of pioneer fame.

Joseph Boone, fourth son of George and Sarah (Uppey) was born April 5th 1704 and died January 30, 1776. He married, Catherine who died January 31, 1778. They were the parents of John Boone and Jacob Boone who settled in Virginia prior to 1786. Both John and Jacob served in the Revolutionary War, John receiving a pension 1835, and Jacob receiving 36 pounds on March 17, 1782, for his services.

Jacob Boone settled about 1775 in the beautiful valley on Maggoty Creek. He was the grandfather of Catherine Boone who married John Jamison in 1806.

The mill and homestead which Jacob Boone built at Boone Mill remained in his family for many years. Nearby is the burial ground, known as Boone-Hardy graveyard, where he and many of his descendants are buried. He was born in 1749, and died in 1815. He and his brother John both began paying taxes in Bedford County which later became a part of Franklin County, as early as 1782 and 1783. The first record of Jacob's permanent residence in Franklin is in connection with the purchase of land on Maggoty Creek on May 1, 1786. This land was doubtless used for the establishment of a mill. In the same year, he purchased more land and probably established his home. John Boone owned land on Glade Creek, a branch of Roanoke River, in January 1769. His land adjoined that of John Thompson and John Mills (see Deed Book 16, page 80, Abstracts of Augusta County, later Botetourt County, and now Roanoke County.) Whether he lived there or in Bedford, which is now Franklin, is unknown. He later lived between Little Creek and Blackwater River about four miles south of the town of Boone Mill. His children were John, Mary, Elizabeth, Catherine, Jacob, Abram, Joseph and Nancy.

Jacob Boone, son of John and Elizabeth Boone, married, first, Rachael Kesler, and second, her sister, Barbara Kesler. They were daughters of Mary (Boone) and Ludowich Kesler, and they and Jacob were cousins. The children of the first marriage were:

(1) John Boone, married Martha Turner.
(2) Elizabeth Boone, married Nathaniel S. Akers.
(3) Susan Boone, married Robert Patterson.
(4) Ludowich Boone, married Emily Ross.
(5) Joseph Boone, married first, Keziah Wray, second, Mary (Flora) Bowman, widow of Jacob Bowman.
(6) Stephen Boone married Mahaley Oyler.
(7) Benjamin Boone, married Susan Oyler.
(8) Levi Boone, married _____, and moved to the West.

Andrew Boone married, first, Lucy Ann Fralin, second, Clemmy Mason. He was a Methodist minister, and served in Franklin County. The second marriage was childless.

Abram Boone married Nancy Gearhart, and had issue: Jacob, Isaac, Daniel, Benjamin, Polly, Laura, Susan, Sallie, and Martha.

Of Abram Boone's children:

Jacob Boone lived in Floyd County.
Daniel Boone was born April 10, 1828, and died June 20, 1865. His son, Joshua Lee Boone lived at Inglewood, California. Daniel Boone was buried at Peters Grave Yard at Dillon's Mill.
Benjamin Boone married Margaret Fisher and had issue: William Boone of Floyd County; Ben Boone of McDowell, West Virginia; John Boone of Roanoke; Charles Milton Boone of Boone Mill; and Sallie Boone, who married J. W. Spangler of Roanoke.
Polly Boone married _____ Weaver.
Susan Boone married Joseph Noftsinger.
Martha Boone married Wilson Weaver, and moved to Indiana in 1867.
John Boone, son of Jacob, married Martha Turner and had issue: John Oat Boone, a Brethren minister; George Boone; Josiah Boone; and Richard Boone.

Elizabeth Boone married Nathaniel Akers, and had issue: Jacob Akers married Martha Overfelt; Sarah Akers married Charles Akers; Emaline Akers married Rev. George Bowman; Cora Akers married Edward Willis; Chesley Akers married Jennie Fralin; Henry Akers married Elizabeth Hickman; Kance Akers married Kittie Hickman.

Susan Boone married Robert Patterson.

Ludowich Boone married Emily Ross and had issue: (1) Anne Boone; (2) Dosia Boone, who married William Peters; (3) Mary Boone, who married Joel Naff, and had issue: Rev. B n Naff of Callaway; Cephas Naff; Rev. Will Naff of Roanoke; Mollie Naff;

Sarah Naff; Helen Naff, who married Benson M. Phelps of Roanoke; (4) Martha D. Boone; (5) James Boone, who died young; (6) Dewitt Boone, who died young; (7) Samuel M. Boone, who married a Miss Flora; (8) Charles Boone, who married Jane S. Ross, and had issue: Doshia and Cora; (9) Ellen Boone; (10) Sarah Boone.

Joseph Boone married Keziah Wray, and had issue: (1) Frances Boone, who married Lee Angle; (2) Drucilla Boone, who married Benjamin Layman; (3) Maudise (Mandin?) Boone, who married Mary Montgomery; (4) Robert; (5) Joe Ben; (6) Bettie; (7) Martha and (8) Lucy.

Stephen Boone married Mahaley Oyler, and had issue: Mary Jane Boone, who married Henry Plunkett; Elizabeth Boone, who married Anthony Plunkett; William Boone, who married Lydia Miller; Robert Boone, who married Arena Brubaker; Stephen Boone, who married, first, Amanda Naff, and second, _____ Bussey.

Benjamin Boone married Susan Oyler.

Levi Boone

Rev. Andrew Boone married Lucy Ann Fralin, and had issue: Mary, John, Stephen, Rachael.

Jacob Boone was born in Berks County, Pennsylvania, in 1749, and lived in Maryland before coming to Franklin County, where he died in 1814. It is stated that he served as a soldier in the Virginia Continental Establishment, and received 36 pounds, March 17, 1782. He was the founder of Boone Mill, and built a saw mill and grist mill near the present town which bears his name. In 1814, while turning a log at his mill, he fell and his leg was crushed, causing his death. His wife was Catherine, and his children were:
(1) Mary, who married Udwick Kesler, and lived at Boone Mill.
(2) Peter, who married Catherine (Herold) Willis, and, lived at Boone Mill.
(3) Elizabeth, (called Betsy), who never married.
(4) Abram, who left Franklin County about 1824.
(5) Jacob, who left Franklin County about 1824.
(6) John, who married Susan Fowler. He served in the War of 1812, and lived and died in Boone Mill.
(7) Catherine, who married John Jamison, a veteran of the War of 1812. Their home was in Boone Mill.
(8) Isaac, who married Clarisy Kinsey, and lived at Boone Mill.
(9) Susanna, who married, first, Daniel Noftsinger, and, second, Jacob Abshire, and lived at Boone Mill.
(10) Daniel, who married Mary Saylor, and moved to Berrien, Michigan.
(11) Nancy, who married Daniel Fisher and lived near Boone Mill.

Mary Boone, born December 12, 1772, married Udwich
Kesler on August 1, 1789, and had issue: (1) George Kesler,
born November 24, 1791, died February 5, 1854. He was single.
(2) Peter Kesler dropped dead. (3) Joseph Kesler died of typhoid fever. (4) Rachael Kesler married Jacob Boone, son of
John Boone, August 31, 1807. (5) Elizabeth Kesler married Solomon Fisher. (6) Catherine Kesler was married to Peter Hickman
in 1812, by Rev. Wilson Turner, and went to Berrien Springs,
Michigan. (7) Barbara Kesler, second wife of Jacob Boone, son
of John was, married December 17, 1832, by Rev. Moses Greer.
(8) Jacob Kesler was single. (9) John Kesler went to Michigan.
(10) Polly Kesler married Leonard Dangerfield.

Mary Boone Kesler died March 23, 1853, and her husband
died in 1854. Both are buried at Boone-Hardy graveyard, Boone
Mill.

Peter Boone, was married by Rev. Wilson Turner, June
27, 1807, to a widow, Catherine Herold Willis (Mrs. Charles),
and had issue: (1) Fleming Boone, who was married to Susan Kinsey, on February 24, 1829, by Rev. Edwin G. Cafamp. (2) Cornelius Boone, who went to North Dakota. (3) Jacob Boone, who married Mary Hammond, and went to Indiana. (4) Susan Boone, who
married Edward Campbell, and lived at Pocahontas, Virginia. (5)
Mary Boone, who married Benjamin Herold, her first cousin, and
lived in Pocahontas. (6) Isaac Boone, who married, on September 29, 1845, Mary L. Wade of Bedford. (7) Otey Boone, who went
to the State of Washington. By her first husband, Mrs. Boone had
a son named Charles Willis. He married Tenesia Boone, and removed
to Indiana.

Elizabeth Boone died unmarried.

Abram Boone, son of Jacob and Catherine Boone, left
Virginia in 1824, and settled in the Miami Valley near Dayton,
Ohio. He had a son Danial Boone, who lived in Troy, Ohio, and
a grandson Albert E. Boone, born in 1845, who lived in Zanes-
ville, Ohio.

Jacob Boone, son of Jacob and Catherine Boone, moved
to Augusta County, J. T. Landis of Detroit, Michigan, has the
orginial affidavit, dated February 2, 1832, executed by Jacob
Boone relating to the sale of two shares in the Franklin County
Grist and Saw Mill and the dower interest in the lands of Jacob
Boone to Isaac Boone. Daniel Boone was also a party to this sale,
and it appears that Jacob and Daniel sold their interest to their
brother Isaac.

John Boone, who was in the War of 1812, married Susan
Towler, daughter of Thomas and Mary Spangler Towler, and had issue:
(1.) Tom Boone, born 1812, died 1884. He was single, and subject
to epileptic "fits. (2) Elizabeth Boone born February 24, 1813,
married Cyrus Price. (3) John Boone married first, Susan Shave,

second, Judy Moore. (4) Jacob Boone, lived in Lynchburg. (5)
Mary Boone married Zachfield Wade and had issue: two daughters,
Susan and Kate; Susan married Dr. Terrell of Bedford, Kate mar-
married twice, and both husbands bore the name of Wade. (6) Kitty
Boone, died single. (7) Susan Boone, died single. (8) Harriet
Boone, married Peter Price. (9) Henry Boone, died single. (10)
Sarah Boone, married on April 6, 1848, David Shanks of Salem.

Catherine Boone married Januray 6, 1806, John Jamison,
who was in the War of 1812, and had issue: (1) Elizabeth Jamison
who married Goodman A. Wright; (2) Nancy Jamison who married
John M. Smith. (3) Samuel Jamison who married, first, Sallie Web-
ster and, second, Catherine Brubaker. (4) Mary Jamison, single.
(5) Isaac Jamison, single. (6) Catherine Jamison who married
Lewis Webster. (7) Barbara Jamison who married William A. B.
Wright. (8) Henry Jamison, who married Sallie Showalter. (9)
Joseph Jamison, single. (10) John Jamison, who married, first,
Elizabeth Akers, and second, Christian Hartsell, and third, Mary
Wood. (11) Jane Jamison, who married Richard Drewry. (12) Jacob
Jamison, who married Lavinia Fralin.

Isaac Boone, son of Jacob and Catherine Boone, born
December 20, 1786, died May 28, 1841, was married May 5, 1817 to
Clarrisy (Clore) Kinsey, daughter of Jacob and Elizabeth Hartsell
Kinsey. She was a sister to Susan Kinsey, who married her brother-
in-law Peter's son Fleming Boone. Isaac ran the mill which he
bought from Jacob and Daniel. He also ran a tavern, and lived in
the old mill house now located directly on the highway at Boone
Mill, Virginia. He had two children, Ferdinand Boone, who mar-
ried Eliza Austin, and William R. Boone who married a Miss _____
Motley.

Susanna Boone, was married April 15, 1807, to Daniel
Noftsinger, by whom she had a daughter, Elizabeth, who married
Wilson Turner, March 8, 1824. Noftsinger was killed by a runaway
team, and his widow married Jacob Abshire, on February 27, 1811,
by whom she had issue: (1) Alice Ann Abshire, who married Otey
Kinsey. (2) John Abshire, who married Sallie Ann Mitchell. (3)
Randolph Abshire, who married, first, Tolitha Angell; second, Polly
Isler; third, Cloe Kingery; and fourth, Tessie Wright.

Daniel Boone, son of Jacob and Catherine, was born
November 12, 1791, married Mary Sayler, and located in Berrien
Springs, Michigan. Their children were: (1) Henry, born December 17, 1821, died August 2, 1907, at Berrien Springs. (2) Preston, born 1823, died November 3, 1904, at Berrien Springs. (3)
John, born November 9, 1825, died August 31, 1904, at Berrien Springs.
(4) Fleming, born in Salem. (5) Jacob, born in Salem. (6) Abram,
born in Salem. (8) Samuel, born in Salem, (9) Mary C., born in
Salem, (10) Thomas M., born in Salem, (11) Eliza H., born in Salem.
He died September 4, 1872. A complete record of his family is
contained in the History of the Boone Family by Mrs. James R. Spaker

of Buffalo, New York.

Nancy Boone, married Daniel Fisher, and had issue:
Elizabeth Fisher.

Fleming Boone, son of Peter, and grandson of Jacob
Boone was married February 24, 1829, to Susan Kinsey and had
issue: (1) Beverly B. Boone, married, first, Lizie Luston;
second, Mittie Turner, and had two children, George and Lottie,
by the second marriage. (2) James Boone, died in infancy. (3)
Irvin Boone, died in infancy. (4) Ternesia Boone, married Charles
Willis, and went to Indiana. (5) Mark Boone, married Nancy Mary
Fowler, and had four children, Cub, Earl, Tiny and Jubal. (6)
Elizabeth Catherine Boone, married Andrew J. Brichey. (7) Aley
Anne Boone, married Jack Phelps, (8) Norman Boone, married Annie
Noble, (9) Mary Louisa Harriet Boone, married James Fishburn,
(10) Mildred Boone, burned to death in 1852. (11) Louis Tilman
Boone, died in childhood.

Isaac Boone, son of Peter and Catherine Herold Willis
Boone, grandson of Jacob Boone, was born 1816. He married Mary
Wade, daughter of Isaac Wade, of Bedford County, on September 29,
1845, and had issue: (1) Callie P., born July 17, 1846, died
November 10, 1878. She married W. H. Smith. (2) William, who
married, first, Miss Murray, and second, Miss Martin. (3) Kate,
who married Robert Aker. (4) Edward, single. (5) James F.,
single, (6) Seabary, single. (7) Tom, who married a Miss Wagoner,
(8) Walter, remained single, (9) Ernest I., who married Berta Sub-
lette, lives in Roanoke, and is a member of the firm Thurman and
Boone. (10) Charles, who married Tiney Boone, daughter of Mark
Boone, (11) Belle, who married John Neeley. She died in 1933.
(12) Allie, who married a man named Armstrong.

THE BOOTH FAMILY

Thomas Booth, Sr., was born ca. 1715. He patented
land in Amelia Co., Va., in 1735, and his will, dated Sept. 15,
1758, was probated in June 1766, in Amelia Co. He devised
338 acres and other property to his son John. He apparently belong to the Surry and Sussex branch of the Booth Family. In his
will, he mentions his children:

(1) Thomas Booth,m. Elizabeth, Nov. 4, 1772. He and
his wife conveyed to John Gilliam, Sr. 382 acres which had been
deeded to him by his father.
(2) George Booth,d. 1767. His will, dated Sept. 10,
1764, was probated July 23, 1767, in Amelia Co. m. Judith McEwen,
(d. subsequent to 1770) dau. of William McEwen. A deed dated
Jan. 16, 1746, from William McEwen conveyed George Booth and Judith,

his wife, 250 acres in Amelia Co. A deed from his father dated
April 21, 1749, gave him 250 acres in Amelia. Issue: William;
John; David; Nathaniel; George; Ann; and Elizabeth, who m. her
cousin, Peter Booth, son of John, Dec. 29, 1783.

    (3) William Booth.

    (4) Nathaniel Booth. On May 28, 1771 (D. B. 11, p. 272,
Amelia Co.), he conveyed to Archer Johnson 326 acres which had
been deeded him by his father on Apr. 21. 1749.

    (5) John Booth, b. ca. 1747, will probated in Franklin
Co. Dec. 7, 1807.

    (6) Joyce Booth.

    (7) Ann Booth.

       John Booth, in 1769, settled his accounts as Executor
of his father's estate (W. B. 2. p. 299, Amelia Co.) On Oct. 24,
1772 (D. B. 12, p. 46, Amelia Co.), John Booth of Amelia Co. conveyed to Thomas Griffin Peachy Tract No. 1, on which John Booth
now dwells, being part of 1554 acres granted to Thomas Booth, Sr.,
father of the said John. On Sept. 29, 1735, the said Thomas,
having conveyed to his sons, Thomas, William, George and Nathaniel,
1210 acres of the 1554 acres, devised the rest to John Booth, Jr.
Tract No. 2 was granted to William Starke by patent Sept. 8, 1736,
and he conveyed the same to John Booth, May 10, 1754. Tract No.
3 was part of the Simmons tract which the said John Booth lately
purchased of John Chappell.

       On Mar. 24, 1772, Joseph Calland and Mary, his wife, of
Cumberland Co., conveyed to John Booth of Amelia Co. 150 acres on
the south side of Staunton River in Bedford Co. On Mar. 13, and
14, 1772, John Booth patented 46 and 250 acres, respectively, on
Staunton River. Issue of John Booth were, as follows:

    (1) Agnes Clardy.

    (2) Richard Booth, d. 1832. He patented 362 acres in
Franklin Co., in 1787, and 79 acres in the same Co. in 1796.

    (3) Peter Booth (will dated Nov. 10, 1826, probated Jan.
1, 1827, in Franklin Co.) In 1797 he patented 266 acres in Franklin Co. He m. 1st Elizabeth Booth, his cousin, dau. of George
Booth (son of Thomas Booth, Sr.) Dec. 1783 (M. L. B. Bedford Co.,
George Booth security) m. 2nd Nacy Blades, ca. Aug. 23, 1808.
(Antenuptial agreement, dated Aug. 23, 1808, of record in Franklin Co.)

    (4) John Booth.

    (5) Stephen Booth, living in Tenn. at date of his father's
will.

    (6) Mary Cuttry.

    (7) Benjamin Booth.

    (8) Thomas Booth. Issue, as shown by will of his father:
Frances, James and Thomas. A Thomas Booth of Franklin Co., served
in the Revolution in 8th Va. Regiment and was placed on Pension
Roll Oct. 28, 1786. Members of the Booth family were the first
makers of felt hats in Franklin Co.

       Issue of Peter Booth's 1st. marriage:

13

(a) Benjamin; (b) Peter; (c) Judith, who m. a Mr.
Welch, prior to Sept. 3, 1827; (d) Nancy, who m. Jesse Bradley;
(e) Elizabeth, (b. Jan. 29, 1801, d. Mar. 31, 1860), who m. Benjamin Hancock, (b. June 16, 1782, d. Mar. 25, 1860) Oct. 20, 1817.

Issue of Peter Booth's 2nd. marriage:

(f) Abraham; (g) Christopher, who m. Mary L. Hancock,
dau. of Benjamin Hancock, who m. Elizabeth Booth; (h) John, under
21, in 1826; (i) William, under 21, in 1826; (j) Harrison under
21 in 1826; (k) Sally, under 15 in 1826; (l) Agnes, (b. 1821, d.
1893) m. William Thomas Hancock, son of Benjamin Hancock, who m.
Elizabeth Booth; and (m) Rhoda Ann, under 15, 1826.

THE BOWMAN FAMILY

John Bowman, progenitor of the Franklin County Bowmans,
is said to have been born in Lancaster County, Pennsylvania, a-
bout 1764. He may have been descended from Daniel or Jacob Bowman,
who arrived in Philadelphia October 2, 1729 on the ship
"Adventurer". John Bowman, with his brothers Jacob, Benjamin,
Peter, and, perhaps, also Joseph, settled in Rockingham County,
Virginia, about 1785 or earlier. John removed to Franklin County.
On October 6, 1788, he bought 230 acres on Griffith Creek from
Martin Ihoy for 30 Pounds. In 1789, he was deeded 100 acres in
the same locality by his friend Jacob Cradler, consideration "Love
and Good Will". Later in 1789, he purchased 116 acres on Little
Creek from Robert Mead, and in 1792, he bought another parcel of
230 acres from Robert Mead. He died in 1804, leaving to his wife,
Elizabeth, his home, plantation and 500 Pounds in money. His widow
was remarried June 29, 1811 to Chrisholm Holland Griffith.

Children of John and Elizabeth Bowman:

(1) Christian, m. Hanna Rinehart of Botetourt County;
    removed to Floyd County.
(2) John, m. February 11, 1813, Parizade Ferguson, dau.
    of John Ferguson.
(3) Peter, m. September 3, 1804, Mary Saunders.
(4) Susannah, m. January 7, 1805, Jacob Peters.
(5) Daniel, b. October 7, 1785; m. November 14, 1817,
    Catherine Naff, dau. of Jacob Naff; d. September
    23, 1833. Catherine b. September 10, 1795, d.
    April 17, 1878.
(6) Fanny, m. Dec. 26, 1808, John Barnhart.
(7) Eve, m. July 30, 1812, Daniel Barnhart.
(8) Elizabeth, m. Sept. 30, 1805, Samuel Montgomery.
(9) Benjamin, b. 1804; m. July 15, 1826, Sophia Hill
    Ferguson, dau. of John Ferguson; d. 1873.

The will of John Bowman, entered for probate in Franklin

County, September 4, 1871, names his wife Parizade and the following children:

    (1) Leroy H.
    (2) John F., m. Dec. 20, 1842, Elizabeth Boone
    (3) Martha, m. Jan. 21, 1839, John Sink
    (4) Joel I., m. Oct. 3, 1838, Irene Layman; d. before 1866.

    Peter Bowman left no will. However, since his widow, Mary Saunders, is listed alone in the Franklin County census of 1850, he died before that date. Their children listed in the 1850 census were:

    (1) Milinda, b. 1810
    (2) Elizabeth, b. 1811

    Daniel Bowman lived on the original John Bowman plantation, where he and his wife, Catherine Naff, and his son Daniel and his wife Hannah, are buried. The children of Daniel and Catherine Bowman were:

    (1) Elizabeth, m. March 15, 1838, Abraham Peters.
    (2) Jacob, b. Nov. 10, 1819; m. Aug. 8, 1839, Mary Flora; d. July 1876.
    (3) George, b. 1824, m. Elizabeth Syder.
    (4) William, b. Jan. 7, 1828; m. Feb. 16, 1854, Mary Graybill of Botetourt County and great grand daughter of John Graybill who removed from Pennsylvania to Virginia in 1780; d. Nov. 25, 1919.
    (5) John, m. Sally Flora.
    (6) Isaac, b. 1827, m., Dec. 3, 1849, Hannah Naff.
    (7) David, b. 1833, m. Catherine Naff.
    (8) Daniel, b. Jan. 21, 1837; m. March 7, 1865, Hanna Flora, b. 1837, d. Oct. 23, 1901, dau. of Isaac and Elizabeth Flora; he d. March 26, 1923.
    (9) Rebecca N., m. Sept. 19, 1849, John Kinzie.
    (10) Susannah, b. 1835, m. Orren Kenzie.

    Benjamin Bowman was reared at Wirtz, Franklin County. In 1857 he settled in Cape Girardeau County, Missouri, where he was a miller, teaching this trade to his son, Samuel Sterling, who in turn taught it to his nephew, William Chesley, son of Benjamin Leroy. In 1893, William Chesley Bowman helped to start a mill at Sikeston, Missouri, which has grown to a corporation worth about $1,000,000, known as The Scott County Milling Co. The children of Benjamin and Sophia Bowman were:

    (1) Lucy Ann, b. May 29, 1827, in Franklin County.
    (2) Elizabeth Mary, b. June 17, 1829, in Franklin County.
    (3) Charles Chisholm, b. Aug. 31, 1831, in Franklin County.
    (4) John Otea, b. Aug. 25, 1833, in Franklin County.

(5) William Edwin, b. Apr. 20, 1835, in Franklin County.
(6) Benjamin Leroy, b. Jan. 31, 1837, in Franklin County. A Baptist Minister; father of William Chesley Bowman and grandfather of Joe Bowman of Sikeston, Missouri.
(7) James Orin, b. Feb. 6, 1839, in Franklin County.
(8) Columbus Carroll, b. May 27, 1841, Franklin County.
(9) Samuel Sterling, b. Oct. 27, 1843, near Charleston, W. Va.
(10) Sophia Perizade, b. March 3, 1846, near Charleston, W. Va.
(11) Thomas Anderson, b. May 7, 1850, near Charleston, W. Va. Father of Thomas Dewitt Bowman, Consul General in Italy, stationed at Naples.

JOEL I. BOWMAN

The following children of Joel I. and Irene A. Bowman are mentioned as grandchildren in the will of John Bowman, entered for probate in Franklin County September 4, 1871. They are also listed in the 1850 census of Franklin County.

(1) John A. b. 1839.
(2) Palmyra I., b. 1840, m. _____ Peters.
(3) Frances P., b. 1842, m. _____ Barnhart
(4) David L., b. 1844
(5) Martha A., b. 1846, m. _____ Peters.
(6) Daniel A., b. 1848.

JACOB BOWMAN

Jacob Bowman of Franklin County died in 1876. His widow, Mary Flora, b. May 24, 1822, dau. of Jacob and Hannah (Brower) Flora, m. (2) Joseph Boone, son of Jacob Boone and Rachel (Kessler) Boone. She died Oct. 10, 1907. Jacob Bowman, his wife Mary and son Jonathan are buried in the George Bowman farm cemetery. The children of Jacob and Mary Bowman were:

(1) Daniel, b. 1840, m. Dec. 5, 1867, Hannah S. Peters, dau. of David and Nancy (Stover) Peters.
(2) Jonathan, b. June 26, 1842, d. July 30, 1869; unmarried; a school teacher.
(3) Martha, b. 1844, m. Jacob Flora.
(4) George, b. Nov. 20, 1847, d. July 4, 1919; m. Feb. 10, 1870, Emily Mildred Akers, b. Jan. 26, 1851, dau. of Nathaniel S. and Elizabeth (Boone) Akers. Their daughter Mary Elizabeth Bowman m. Thomas Hardin Bowman.
(5) Hannah, b. 1849, m. Daniel Naff.
(6) Catherine, m. Owen Flora.

(7) Elizabeth, m. Samuel Ikenberry.
(8) Samuel, m. Alie Angle; she was b. Sept. 3, 1860, d. Dec. 30, 1927.
(9) Ellen, m. James Wray, removed to Kansas.

GEORGE BOWMAN

He removed to Botetourt County, Virginia. The children of George and Elizabeth (Snyder) Bowman were:

(1) William, removed to California.
(2) David, m. _____ Layman
(3) Nancy, m. James Wicklam
(4) Price, m. _____ Obenchain; resided in Roanoke.
(5) Rosa, m. Charles Kinzie.
(6) Dorus, m. _____; resided in Trinity, Virginia.
(7) Betty, m. _____ Davis.

WILLIAM BOWMAN

He resided in Franklin County. The children of William and Mary (Graybill) Bowman were:

(1) Sarah C., b. Dec. 6, 1854; m. Joel Wray, and removed to Dayton, Ohio.
(2) James A., b. Aprl 19, 1856; M. _____ Flora.
(3) Martha Ann, b. March 11, 1858; m. Charles Saul, and removed to Ohio.
(4) Rufus O., b. Jan. 13, 1860; d. June 20, 1862.
(5) Jonas D., b. Nov. 13, 1861; m. Lucy _____.
(6) Thomas Hardin, b. March 2, 1864, m. Mary Elizabeth Bowman, dau. of George Bowman.
(7) Susan Emily, b. July 23, 1866; m. James Flora of Franklin County and Roanoke.
(8) Henry Ezra, b. Dec. 18, 1868; m. Emma Shelor, and removed to Roanoke.
(9) George William, b. Oct. 7, 1871; m. Evelyn Boone, and resided at Wirtz, Franklin County; d. July 28, 1936.
(10) Daniel Cary, b. June 7, 1874; m. Elizabeth Barnhart and resided at Boone's Mill, Franklin County; d. Sept. 9, 1933.

JOHN BOWMAN

The children of John and Sallie (Flora) Bowman of Franklin

County were:

(1) Susie, m. David Mountcastle.
(2) Frances, m. Austin Hylton (brotherof C. D. Hylton), and removed to California.
(3) Abraham, removed to Illinois, where he married.
(4) Catherine, m. Daniel Jackson; mother of Neely Jackson.
(5) Benjamin, b. Feb. 6, 1845; m. Julia Henry; resided at Bent Mountain, Floyd County, Virginia.
(6) Daniel
(7) Isaac, m. Nancy Peters
(8) Eva, m. Preston Peters
(9) Julie, m. Louis Brubaker.

ISAAC BOWMAN

Isaac Bowman m. Hannah Naff, and removed to Indiana. Their children were:

(1) Benjamin
(2) George
(3) Henry
(4) Charles
(5) John
(6) Jessie
(7) A daughter

DAVID BOWMAN

The children of David and Catherine (Naff) Bowman of Franklin County were:

(1) Susan, m. Stephen Peters
(2) Joel, m. _____ Pollard
(3) David, m. (1) Dec. 13, 1861 to Sarah Naff, dau. of Abraham and Hannah (Peters) Naff; (2) Mary Elizabeth Austin (called Molly).

DANIEL BOWMAN

The children of Daniel Bowman and Hanna (Flora) Bowman

(1) Hannah, m. Benjamin Naff
(2) J_____, m. Lydia Idenberry
(3) Mary, m. (1) Cephas Naff; m. (2) Thomas Webster.

(4) Sallie, m. Thomas Montgomery.
(5) Betty, m. Douglas Webster.
(6) Jacob, m. _____ Kinzie.
(7(Cleveland, m. Bessie Cummings.

REBECCA (BOWMAN) KINZIE

The children of John and Rebecca (Bowman) Kinzie of Franklin County were:

(1) Orren, m. Susan Ann Tench.
(2) Baxter, d. in his teens.
(3) John William, m. Lassie Teel.
(4) Samanthia George Ann Catherine, m. John Kinzie.
(5) Achilles, m. _____ Akers.
(6) Charles.
(7) Eva.
(8) Sue Elizabeth.

THOMAS HARDIN BOWMAN

Rev. George Bowman m. Emily Mildred Akers, dau. of Nathaniel S. Akers and Elizabeth Boone of Franklin County. Their daughter, Mary Elizabeth Bowman b. Oct. 22, 1875, m. Thomas Hardin Bowman Feb. 20, 1896. Their children were:

(1) Esther May, b. May 9, 1897; m. Terry W. Peters, resides in Roanoke.
(2) Florence Emily, b. Sept. 18, 1898, m. Earl Ray White; resides in Roanoke.
(3) George Ervin, b. Apr. 19, 1900; d. Sept. 29, 1900.
(4) Emmert Owen, b. July 11, 1901; m. Elizabeth Wargo; manager, J. J. Newberry Co. Stores, Inc. Malone, New York.
(5) Fred Edward, b. Aug. 4, 1903; m. Lillian Layman; resides in Roanoke.
(6) Ruth Ann, b. Dec. 25, 1904; m. Glenwood H. Lucas; resides in Roanoke.
(7) Charles Abraham, b. Nov. 11, 1907; m. Nora Evans; resides in Roanoke.
(8) Eva Catherine, b. Oct., 1910; m. Warren Creasy; resides in Roanoke.
(9) Carl Thomas, b. Aug. 28, 1913; m. Louise Bradley; resides in Roanoke.
(10) Joel Christ, b. June 10, 1916, m. Helen Strickler; resides in Roanoke.

ESTHER MAY (BOWMAN) PETERS

Children of Terry W. and Esther May (Bowman) Peters:

(1) Hazel Marie, b. April 2, 1919.
(2) Geraldine, b. June 17, 1922.

FLORENCE EMILY (BOWMAN) WHITE

Children of Earl R. and Florence Emily (Bowman) White:

(1) Thelma Ruth, b. April 15, 1919.
(2) Dorothy Aileene, b. May 11, 1921.

EMMERT OWEN BOWMAN

Child of Emmert Owen and Elizabeth (Wargo) Bowman:

(1) Virginia Elaine, b. May 14, 1939.

FRED EDWARD BOWMAN

Children of Fred Edward and Lillian (Layman)Bowman:

(1) Robert, b. March 28, 1931.
(2) Betty Ann, b. May 13, 1935.

RUTH ANN BOWMAN LUCAS

Child of Glenwood H. and Ruth Ann (Bowman) Lucas:

(1) Marlene, b. Sept. 27, 1932.

JOEL CHRIST BOWMAN

Child of Joel Christ and Helen (Strickler) Bowman:

(1) Martha Ellen

THE BRODIE FAMILY

William F. Brodie, m. Seney B. Mason, March 18, 1850, and had issue:

(1) John F. b. 1851.
(2) Louisa, b. k852.
(3) William H., b. 1854.
(4) Charles C., b. 1856.
(5) George W., b. 1858.
(6) Etta, b. 1860.
(7) Rose, b. 1866.

John F. Brodie, m. Elizabeth Williams in 1871, and had issue:

(1) Emmett J., b. 1872, m. Callie Burnett and had issue: Talmage, Wilbert, Cabell, Cassie, Daisy, Elizabeth, Bernard, Gladys, and Ray.
(2) William T., b. 1873, m. Margaret Bell. No issue.
(3) Charles B., b. 1875, m. Freda Byrd, and had issue: Forest; who m. Estelle Wilson; Ethlyn; Kathryn, who m. Ralph Catlett; Mildred; and Benjamin.
(4) John B., b. 1877 (twin), m. Bessie Philpott. No issue.
(5) George L., b. 1877 (twin), m. Betty Wingfield, and had issue: Clifford, who m. Geneva Owens on Sept. 2, 1933.
(6) Effie, b. 1874, d. 1879.
(7) Betty, b. 1881, d. 1906.
(8) Alpheus, b. 1884, m. Annie Williams, and had issue: a. Amon., b. Frances, c. Anne Zane.
(9) Samuel M., b. 1886, d. 1907.
(10) J. Everett, b. 1888, m. Mary Helen Byrd, daughter of Silas Wingfield and Susan (King) Byrd, and had issue: Virginia Louise, b. in Missoula, Montana, July 21, 1918; Stephen Duncan, b. in Roanoke, January 3, 1925; Lawrence Thomas, b. in Missoula, October 15, 1932; and Nancy Joe, b. in Missoula, August 29, 1934.

Louisa Brodie, m. Lewis Nunn, and had issue:

1. Seney b., m. Owen Thomasson, and had issue: Glendon, Jesse, Robert, Lee, Mary Lou, and Myrthe;
2. Minnie, m. Archer Thomasson, and had issue: Clifton, Brodie, and Lewis;
3. John, m. Martha Hurd, and had issue: Majessie, Lucy, Ethel, and Elinor.

William H. Brodie, m. Frances Mason, and had issue:

1. Daisy, b. 1877, m. John Turner of Fairfax County, and had issue: Reginald, Howard, and Velma.
2. Erie, b. 1880, m. William Campbell of Richmond, and had issue: Ruthven, Arthur, Raymond, Norman, Frances, Evelyn, Charles, James and Ruth.
3. Etta, b. 1884, unm. Home, Washington, D. C.
4. Marvin, b. 1894, m. _____. Home, Columbus, Ohio. Had issue: Katherine, and William Marvin.

Charles C. Brodie, m. Lucy Elizabeth Cook in June 1880, and had issue:

1. Frederick A., b. June 2, 1881, d. infant.
2. William C., b. September 10, 1884, unm.
3. Elizabeth M., b. March 17, 1886, m. William G. Lester, Oct. 25, 1910, and had issue: W. G. Jr., b. Oct. 23, 1911; Frederick, b. June 29, 1913; John K., b. Nov. 8, 1916; and Katherine, b. December 27, 1919.

4. Seney M., b. April 9; 1888, m. 1st. Samuel Woodall and had issue: Wendell, b. 1907, m. 2nd W. J. Cook on Sept.
1910, and had issue: Mary, b. Sept. 24, 1911, m. Clyde Clucas,
1932, and the Clucases had issue: Robert b. Aug. 30, 1933; and
Mary, d. May, 1934, at Greybull, Wyoming.

5. Charles C., b. Jan. 8, 1890, m. Hattie L. Davis,
and had issue: Mildred, b. 1918; Charles C., Jr., b. 1920, d.
1925; David C., b. 1924; William C., b. 1926; Ruth, b. 1929;
and Elizabeth, b. 1930.
6. Mamie Wingfield, b. April 2, 1892, m. B. G. Hurd,
June 1913, and had issue: Charles, b. 1914, d. 1917; and Benjamin Justus, b. August 1916.
7. Frederick A., b. June 2, 1894, m. Essie Martin
on Dec. 25, 1927, and had issue: Nina, b. Sept. 30, 1928; Jean,
b. Feb. 2, 1930. Essie Martin Brodie d. Feb. 1930.

George W. Brodie, m. Alice Craig in 1881, and had issue:

1. William Muncie, b. Oct. 6, 1882, m. Nannie Pitts
and had issue: Elsie, Elfie, Harold, and Alice. Home: Texas.
2. Lillian, b. June 1885, m. W. B. Frailin, and had
issue: Thelma, Howard, and Bailey. Home: Texas.
3. Carrie, b. Nov. 1888, m. H. C. Copenhaver, and
had issue: Alice, Gordon, and Wesley. Home: Richmond.
4. Annie, b. Feb. 2, 1891, m. Arthur C. Martin, and
had issue: Patrick, Margaret, Edith, Harold, Calvin, Edna Mae,
and Rebecca Anne. Home: Snow Creek.
5. George F., b. Aug. 24, 1893, m. Myrtle Belcher,
and had issue: George, and Robert,; Home: Snow Creek
6. Harold, b. May 4, 1896, d. in World War I.
7. Mildred, b. Nov. 1902, d. 1906.

Etta Brodie, m. Thomas Dillon. No issue.

Rose Brodie, m. Charles Craig, and had issue:

1. Roy C., b. March 1889, m. Ruth Armstrong, and
had issue: Richard, and Ernest Clay. Home: Wisconsin.
2. William Stafford, b. Jan. 1894, m. Mildred Craig,
and had issue: Marie. Home: Martinsville.
3. Jesse C., b. May 1896, killed by D. and W. Train,
ca. 1917.
4. Moody, b. Oct. 1902, m. Bertha Motley. Home:
Washington, D. C.

THE BROWN FAMILY

Frederick Brown, son of John Brown of Cumberland County,
lived in Brunswick and Lunenburg Counties. He was b. ca. 1745,
and, on Aug. 12, 1767, was living in Lunenburg County. That he

served in the Revolution is shown by a manuscript vol. in Virginia State Library, known as Auditors Accounts XVIII, 532. He moved from Cumberland to Halifax County ca. 1784. His mother's name was Ann, and he had brothers, John Jr., Davis, Joseph, and Benjamin. The next record of Frederick Brown is in Pittsylvania County, where he bought land in 1797. His wife's name, Milly, appears in a deed dated Aug. 23, 1784. Their children were: John, Tarleton, Reuben, Frederick, Lockey and James.

John Brown, son of Frederick and Milly Brown, lived in Franklin County, where he bought land on Aug. 3, 1808, from Skelton, Reuben and Susanna Brown. His will, made May 20, 1835, was probated June 5, 1838. In it he names his wife, Sally, his grand-daughter Phoebe Person, child of his daughter Phoebe; his sons, John, Reuben, Frederick and William; his daughters Polly Brooks, Nancy Gorman, Sally and Lucy. To Lucy, he forgives a debt of $200 contracted by her husband, George W. Dickinson. This will is of record in Will Book 4, 395, Franklin County. A Court order for the distribution of slaves among the heirs of John Brown is dated Oct. 1, 1849. The nine heirs were: W. A. Brown; Greville P. Jefferson; George W. Dickinson; Andrew S. Brooks; Sarah E. Gorman, and Mary Jane Gorman, children of Armistead M. Gorman and wife; Reuben S. Brown; W. A. Brown; and Frederick R. Brown.

The wife of John Brown was Sally Rives, daughter of Capt. Frederick Rives, who was b. ca. 1736, in Prince George County, d. ca. 1815, in Franklin County. He was the son of Joseph Rives, grandson of George, and great grandson of William. Capt. Frederick Rives served as a Justice of Henry Co. when that county included his home on Pigg River. He was one of the men appointed to select the site for the court house, and was a captain of Pittsylvania County militia in 1772. He married Mary Magdalene Steagall, daughter of John Steagall, on July 21, 1761, according to a marriage bond of record in Amelia Co. The will of John Steagall of Amelia, recorded in 1769, mentions his wife Winifred, and his daughter Lucy True.

Mary Magadalene Steagall Rives was a granddaughter of Thomas Bottom, of Amelia Co., who, in a deed dated Feb. 28, 1762, conveyed to "Mary Magadalene Rives of Brunswick Co. one negro woman slave named Anaky, and one negro girl named Doll, and a negro boy named Hampton, for and in consideration of the affection he hath for his granddaughter Mary Magdalene, wife of the said Frederick". His will dated May 10, 1765, names his daughter, Jane Vaughan, his granddaughters, Frances Worsham and Mary Hubbard, and his son, Thomas Bottom.

On April 13, 1812, Frederick Rives of Franklin Co., deeded 500 acres on Pigg River in Franklin Co., to his daughters Patsey Lumsden, Phebe Still, Sally Brown, Elizabeth Quarles, Lucy Cowden, and Mary Bottom; formerly, Patsey Rives, Phebe Rives, Sally Rives, Elizabeth Rives, Lucy Rives, and Mary Rives. It was recorded June 1, 1812. Frederick Rives died prior to Jan. 19, 1815.

The children of Frederick Rives and Mary Magdalene Rives were: 1. George; 2. Joseph, who m. Mary Frances Prunty, Feb. 15, 1804; 3. Alexander; 4. Burwell; 5. Patsey, who m. Charles Lumsden, May 16, 1787; 6. Phoebe, who m. Murphy Still, July 23, 1795; 7. Sarah, who m. John Brown; 8. Elizabeth, who m. James Quarles; 9. Lucy who m. James Cowden; and 10. Mary.

Sally Rives, daughter of Frederick and Mary Magdalene Rives, b. Dec. 5, 1773, m. John Brown of Franklin Co. July 8, 1793, and d. Mar. 20, 1849. John Brown, b. in 1765, d. May 19, 1838, buried at Dickinson's Store. His wife is buried there also.

The children of John and Sally Rives were: 1. Phoebe R. m, Doctor Person Oct. 3, 1814; 2. Lucy, m. George W. Dickinson, Sept. 2, 1816; 3. John Spotswood, m. Mary Ann Patterson, May 29, 1838; 4. Reuben Skelton; 5. Frederick Rives, m. first Jane Prunty, Oct. 2, 1838, second, Elizabeth Cheadle Brown, Dec. 23, 1852; 6. William Alexander, m. 1st. Sarah Preston, 2nd. Sue Lewis Finney; 7. Polly, m. Andrew S. Brooks; 8. Nancy W.,m. Armistead M. Gorman, on Feb. 27, 1826; 9. Sally H. m. Greenville P. Jefferson, Jan. 6, 1840.

Phoebe R. Brown, who m. Person, had issue: Phoebe Person, had issue: Phoebe Person.

John Spotswood Brown, m. Mary Ann Patterson, and had issue: 1, Anne Eliza, m. Tarleton Brown; 2. Norburn; 3. Virgil, m. Hattie Jefferson; 4. Taylor; 5. Wylie; 6. Filmore; 7. George W., 8. Alexander; 9. Mary Jane m. C..T. Poindexter; 10. Nannie; and 11. Sallie Euphemia.

Frederick Rives Brown, son of John and Sallie (Rives) Brown, b. July 1, 1813, in Franklin Co. and lived on Snow Creek until 1888 when he removed to Martinsville. He died Nov. 8, 1896. His will, made May, 20, 1895, was proved in Dec. 1896. His first wife was a sister of Betsy Prunty, the mother of Susan Lewis Finney, the second wife of Col. William Alexander Brown. His second wife was a daughter of Tarleton and Lucy (Moorman) Brown, and granddaughter of Tarleton Brown Sr. and his wife Nancy.

Frederick Rives Brown had issue by his marriage to Jane Prunty: 1. Eliza Jane, b. July 9, 1839, d. Jan. 9, 1851; 2. Nancy Washington, b. Mar. 29, 1844, d. May 16, 1863; and 3. John R.

John R. Brown m. Anne Eliza Vial, Oct. 26, 1882, an d had issue; 1. John Andrew, who m. Pattie Smith, and had issue: John Andrew Brown Jr., Corinne, Pattie and Moss; 2. Nannie Jane, who m. Dr. Charles P. Smith, and had issue: John and Charles P. Jr.; 3. Alice, who m. Edward Gaines; 4. Frederick R. who m. Etta Burge; 5. Willie; 6. Rosa, who d. in infancy; 7. May, who m. George M. Finley, and had issue: May, Ellen Catherine, Virginia; 8. Annie who m. Louis C. Claybrook; 9. Kate who m. C. E.

Van Pelt; 10. Lucy who m. S. Douglas English.

The children of Frederick Rives Brown by his marriage to Elizabeth Cheadle Brown were: 4. John William, b. Oct. 19, 1853, d. April 10, 1890; 5. Lucy Clark, b. May 6, 1855, m. Henry Clay Lester on Aug. 10, 1871, d. Mar. 28, 1920; 6. Tarleton Frederick, b. Sept. 16, 1861, d. in Martinsville, May 8, 1895.

Tarleton Frederick Brown m. Ann Eliza Brown, (b. Feb. 8, 1862, d. Feb. 18, 1901), daughter of John Spotswood Brown, and had issue: 1. Lizzie May, b. Jan. 15, 1884, d. Sept. 15, 1901; 2. Mattie T., b. Apr. 13, 1885, m. George M. Andes; 3. John Spotswood, b. June 14, 1886, d. Oct. 29, 1886; 4. Lucy Gaines, b. July 13, 1888', m. Dr. M. E. Hundley; 5. Willie James, b. Sept. 5, 1889, d. Sept. 11, 1899; 6. Rives Spotswood, b. May 3, 1894, m. Cornelia Gregory, May 20, 1916, and has one son, Rives Spotswood Jr.

William Alexander, son of John and Sally (Rives) Brown, m. 1st. Sarah Preston and, 2nd, Susan Lewis Finney, daughter of Amos and Betsy (Prunty) Wingfield Finney, granddaughter of Jesse and Nancy (Finney) Prunty, great granddaughter of Robert and Frances Prunty, and had issue:

1. Sallie E. Brown b. Jan. 13, 1862, d. May 11, 1862.

2. William Barnes Brown, b. Mar. 23, 1863, m. Loula Virginia Dudley, (b. Sept. 15, 1871, d. Apr. 18, 1907), daughter of Thomas and Lydia (Cundiff) Dudley, and had issue: Doris Dudley, who d. Jan. 1928. William Barnes Brown succeeded his father in the Virginia Legislature, and died Apr. 7, 1916.

3. Sallie E. Brown, b. Oct. 10, 1865, attended Gordonsville (Va.) Female Institute, m. Nov. 29, 1883, Gustave B. Dudley, son of James Henry and Julia Ann Elizabeth Dudley. They lived at Union Hall until they removed to Martinsville. She died, on July 18, 1919. G. B. Dudley died, on July 30, 1925. Their children were: Ruby Lewis, who m. J. E. Howard; Dr. W. Brown, who m. Marion McCrary Moir, and has 2 daughters, Sarah Elizabeth and Frances McCrary; Dr. Gustave B. Jr., who m. Priscilla Flint Humbert, and has 2 sons, Frank Humbert and Samuel Calvert; and Virginia Spotswood, who m. Samuel Stanhope Walker, and has 2 children, Ann Spotswood and Lee Dudley Walker.

4. Walter Spotswood Brown, b. June 18, 1868, attended Milligan College, owned Brown's Warehouse at Martinsville, m. Virginia Williams, a granddaughter of Senator R. E. Withers, and d. Nov. 10, 1907.

5. Lula Mary Brown, twin of Walter Spotswood, b. June 18, 1868, attended Gordonsville Female Institute, and Mary Baldwin College, m. George William Coan, son of John O. and Mary Jones Coan of Ridgeway, Secretary of Reynolds Tobacco Co., of Winston Salem, and had issue: George William Jr., and Mary Lewis. George William Coan Jr., m. Mary Wiggins and has 3 children: George William,

III, James, and Mary Spotswood. He has served as Mayor of Winston-Salem. Mary Lewis Coan m. Kenneth F. Mountcastle, and has
2 sons, Kenneth Jr., and George.

6. George F. Akers Brown, named for his father's friend,
Col. George F. Akers of Ky. was b. Jan. 3, 1872, attended Milligan College, has been mayor of Martinsville since 1917, served on
the town council 23 years before becoming mayor, manufactured
tobacco with his brother, Walter S. Brown, and his brother-in-
law, Gustave B. Dudley, and later conducted the mercantile business of Brown and Company.

G. F. A. Brown m. Minnie Mathews, and had issue: 1.
Catherine Craighead, who m. John Randolph of New York and has a
son, Akers Brown Randolph; 2. Sue Lewis, who m. Wayles R. Harrison of Danville, and has 3 children, Carolyn Brown, Wayles R. Jr.,
and Sue Lewis; 3. Mary Loula, who m. Charles W. Boothe Sr. and
has a daughter Mary Brown; 4. Lucy Akers, who m. J. Douglas Bassett Jr., of Bassett, and has 3 daughters, Minnie, Jane and Lucy;
5. Minnie, who m. Charles M. Hart Jr.

Mary Brown, nicknamed Polly, daughter of John and Sallie
Rives Brown, m. Andrew S. Brooks.

Nancy W. Brown m. Armistead M. Gorman on Feb. 27, 1826,
and has issue: Sarah E., and Mary Jane.

Sally H. Brown m. Grenville P. Jefferson, Jan. 6, 1840.

THE CAHILL FAMILY.

John Cahill, progenitor of the Franklin County family,
came from Ireland. He was born about 1760, and married Diana
Garner (born October 10, 1769) in 1789, and had issue: Nancy,
Peregrine, Thomas, John, Susannah, Mary, Nathaniel, Diana, Maria,
and Sallie. He died April 1, 1817.

John Cahill Jr. was born February 15, 1797, married, and
had issue: Thomas, Peregrine and Jack.

Susannah Cahill was born June 21, 1799, married George
K. Deshazo, in 1822, and died December 8, 1862.

Mary Cahill was born November 9, 1804, married James
Price, and had five children, including William of Roanoke and
Thomas P. of Natural Bridge.

Nancy Cahill married David Philpott.

Nathaniel Cahill was born in 1807, and died in 1826.

Maria Cahill was born November 25, 1811, and married Co -
lumbus King, December 13, 1829. She died June 28, 1833 and left

one son, John W. King.

Peregrine Cahill, born September 19, 1792, married
Ann Pyrtle and had issue: Mary, Sally, Lucinda, Diana, Maria,
Thomas, Perry, John Carr, Jesse and Obediah.

Thomas Cahill, born October 20, 1794, married Clemen-
tine Turner, and had issue: Nancy, Eliza, Jane, Thomas, Marshall,
John W., and Zachary Taylor.

Of the children of Perry Cahill:

Mary J., married Capt. Thomas G. King in 1830, and had
issue: Susan Ann, John Lewis, Thomas Jesse, Mary Jane, Anna,
George Perry, and Sally Lou.

Sally dau. of Peregrine, married James Turner; Lucinda
married Joseph Thomasson; Diana and Maria never married; Thomas
married Margaret Thomasson.

Zachary Taylor Cahill, who was born May 26, 1847, mar-
ried, first, Sallie Akers (no issue) and, second, Harriet Bous-
man, and had issue: Bessie W., John Taylor, Lorenze Dow, William
Price, and Gustavus B. John William Cahill, born about 1830, mar-
ried Betsy Ann Finney, and had issue: Victoria, who married
John Burgess; Lenora; Thomas; Jennie, who married Jesse King;
Alice, who married James Hodnett; and Zachariah, who married
Florence Williams.

Zachariah and Florence (Williams) Cahill had issue:
(1) Annie, who married William Frazier, and had issue:
    Ray and Deane.
(2) Maggie, who married Luther A. Wingfield, and had
    issue: Melton, Rives, twins named Maidie and Marie
    and triplets named Ina, Iris and Ivy.
(3) Esther, who married William Pinckey Wingfield had
    issue: Rudolph William, b. July 5, 1924; Lorena,
    b. Aug. 28, 1925, d. Nov. 8, 1931; Douglas b. Oct.
    18, 1926, d. May 28, 1928; and Robert Earl, b. Dec.
    5, 1928.
(4) Claudia, who married Roy Whitehead, and had issue:
    Alice, Hazel and Morris.
(5) Thomas, who married Ruby Jones, and had issue:
    Edith.
(6) Dillard.
(7) Harry.
(8) Jewel.

Benjamin Marshall Cahill, son of Thomas Cahill Sr., was
born about 1832, married Tamesia Young, and had issue:
(1) B. M. Cahill Jr., married Kate Lewis, and moved
    to Winston, North Carolina.

(2) Loula Cahill, married Joe L. Trogdon of North
   Carolina.
(3) Dora Cahill, married Hugh Binford of Madison,
   North Carolina.
(4) Lelia Cahill, married A. B. Poindexter.
(5) Tamèsia Cahill, married Walter Dunn.
(6) Dr. James Cahill, married Marie Chappell.
(7) Dr. William Cahill, married Ann Richardson.
(8) Beatrice Cahill, married Jesse Richardson of leaks-
   sville, North Carolina.
(9) Holt Cahill, married Lettie Carter of Stonesville,
   North Carolina.
(10) Edgar Cahill, married Fannie Flynn of North Carolina. He served in the 10th Virginia Cavalry,
   C. S. A.

THE CALLAWAY FAMILY

Thomas, William, Joseph, Francis, John, Richard, James,
and their two sisters were the children of Joseph Callaway of
Carolina County, Va., and he, in turn, was the son and only child
of Joseph Callaway Sr., also of Carolina Co.

Thomas Callaway, b. Oct. 12, 1700
William Callaway. In 1754 was appointed first County
Lieutenant of Bedford County, Va., and was a justice of the first
court of that county, serving until 1775. He was also a member
of the House of Burgesses. He died in 1777
Joseph Callaway III, who died of fever early in life
Francis Callaway, commissioned sheriff of Bedford Co.
John Callaway, lived and died in Bedford Co.
Richard Callaway, b. about 1717, killed by the Indians,
March 8, 1780
James Callaway d. intestate in Bedford. His children
included:
Flanders 1754-1828, married Jemima Boone
James Jr., 1756-1835
Micajah, 1758-1849
Chesley, 1759-1846, a pensioner of the Revolutionary
   War
Edmund, 1764- 1818

Quoting an old family Bible, we also have the following dates:
1. Thomas Callaway b. ca. 1712
2. William   "   b. 1714
3. Joseph   "   b. 1716
4. Francis   "   b. 1718
5. John   "   b. 1720
6. Richard   "   b. 1722
7. James   "   b. 1724

8. Elizabeth Callaway b. 1726
9. Mary Ann   "   b. 1728

THE CARPER FAMILY

Nicholas Carper (d. 1813), of Botetourt County, Virginia, was born in Maryland, and was still living in that state in 1777. In 1778 or soon thereafter he removed with his wife Elizabeth and children to Fincastle.

Their third child, Henry, was born in Maryland in 1775, and died in Franklin County, Virginia, June 27, 1853. He was sheriff of Franklin County in 1834-35. He married in Franklin County February 17, 1801, Nancy Greer, daughter of Moses Greer, who served as a captain in the American Revolution. Henry and Nancy (Greer) Carper had one son, and at least seven daughters:
1. Elizabeth S. Carper, m. January 24, 1824, Lawson Carter
2. Moses Greer Carper (1805-1858); clerk of county court, Franklin County, 1838-52; clerk of circuit and district court, 1848-58; m.(1) November 27, 1834, Catherine Tate; a daughter of Caleb Tate, clerk of the Franklin County Court; (2) in Henry County, Jane Elizabeth Jones (born December 11, 1809, died April 13, 1901), daughter of Gabriel Remi Jones and Mary (Bryant) Jones.
3. Mary Carper, b. 1808; m. Chattin T. Pollard, son of Chattin and Nancy (Greer) Pollard. (Their daughter, Julia A., married Wesley I. Thomason).
4. Louise Carper, m. Peter Price.
5. Harriet K. Carper, m. September 23, 1833, Col. Lewis B. Taylor.
6. Julia Ann Carper, m. October 19, 1838, George Persinger.
7. Evaline C. Carper, m. September 4, 1839, David Overfelt.
8. Alzira E. Carper, m. November 25, 1847 (1857?), Jeremiah Griggs (September 25, 1800-May 6, 1871), son of Jeremiah Michael and _____ (Minter) Griggs; was for many years clerk of Henry County court.

Jane Elizabeth Jones (Carper) was the daughter of Gabriel Remi Jones and Mary Bryant Jones. Gabriel Remi Jones (born July 12, 1785, died July 21, 1853) was the son of Benjamin Jones (born April 25, 1752, in Culpeper Co., died 1843, in Henry Co.). Benjamin Jones was the son of Joshua Jones, of Culpeper Co., who married Isabel Norman in 1751 (their children, in addition to Benjamin, were John, James and Thomas). Benjamin Jones married, September 7, 1776, in Prince William Co., Elizabeth de Remi (Devereaux Jarrett performed the ceremony), and they settled on Jones' Creek in Henry Co., near Martinsville.

Mary Bryant (Jones) (born October 10, 1784, died March, 1869) was the daughter of James Bryant Jr. (born Powhatan Co., January 1, 1758) and Jane Forsee (born Powhatan Co., August 29, 1740, died July, 1776).

Benjamin Jones, a physician, was active in politics, representing Henry Co. in the General Assembly. His wife, Elizabeth, lived to be over one hundred.

Issue of Moses Greer and Catherine (Tate) Carper:

1. Henry E. Carper, b. 1836; clerk of circuit and district court, Franklin County, 1858-62.
2. Nicholas Charles Carper, b. 1838; clerk of circuit and district court, Franklin County, 1862-65. Relinquished clerkship to enter Confederate Army, in which he eventually became a captain.

Issue of Moses Greer and Jane Elizabeth (Jones) Carper:

1. Robert Beverley Carper, b. 1844; at the close of the Civil War he settled in the West.
2. James Jones Carper, (1846-February 24, 1900); clerk of county court, Franklin County, 1871-1900; clerk of circuit and district court, 1897-1900; m. in Botetourt County, Virginia, December 20, 1871, Mary Edmundson Wilson (b. 1848, d. June 3, 1909), daughter of Maj. John Thomas Wilson and Mary E. Wilson, of Salem, Virginia. Issue:

(1) James Nicholas Carper, clerk of Franklin Co., until his death in 1902.
(2) Mary Jones Carper m. Charles B. Willis, of Roanoke.
(3) Emma Carper m. Dr. George W. Hooker, of Roanoke.
(4) Norwood Greer Carper (1883-1937); president of the Johnston-Carper Furniture Company, Roanoke; m. Margaret Helms.
(5) Thomas Wilson Carper b. Franklin Co. 1878. Clerk of court, Franklin Co.; m. Elizabeth Taliaferro Greer, December 9, 1913. Issue:

(a) Edith Taliaferro
(b) Mary Wilson
(c) Emily

3. Moses Greer Carper, Jr., b. 1850; m. Mary Turnbull.

THE CLAIBORNE FAMILY

The descendants of Nathaniel Herbert Claiborne in Franklin Co. are Mr. H. Dalton Dillard, Mrs. William Ruffin, Mrs. Albert Crosby Jr., T. W. Carper, N. G. Carper, Mrs. George Hooker and Mrs. Charles B. Willis. Anne and Sarah Saunders, and the children of Robert Lovelace are great nieces and nephews.

Nathaniel Charles Claiborne, son of Nathaniel Herbert Clairborne, was born at "Claybrook" on Blackwater. He represented Franklin County in the Virginia Legislature, and practiced law in Rocky Mount before removing to St. Louis where he became prominent in legal and civic circles.

Thomas B. Claiborne, son of Nathaniel Herbert Claiborne, was born at "Claybrook" in Franklin County, and, though grotesquely caricatured by the Virginia press, was a man of pleasing personality and sound judgment. He served for a time as Judge of the County Court of Franklin.

James R. Claiborne, son of Nathaniel H. Claiborne, practiced law in Rocky Mount, and served in the Confederate Army. He removed to St. Louis and represented that city in the Missouri Senate, also serving as Judge of the city's Criminal Correction Court.

Ferdinand Claiborne was a prominent tobacco manufacturer in Franklin County in 1844. His factory was located about one mile north of Rocky Mount. He was also engaged in the merchandise business in Rocky Mount at the same time.

William Augustine Bathurst Cole Claiborne married Sarah, daughter of Col. Lewis Turnbull of Franklin County, on October 22, 1828. It is said that Sarah Turnbull Claiborne's grandparents escaped from France during the Revolution in two large kettles slung across the back of a pack mule.

THE COOPER FAMILY

Among the earliest Coopers of record in Franklin County were three brothers, Charles, John and Thomas. According to the old marriage bonds, Charles married Jane Richardson on March 7, 1786; John married Sarah Hall in 1793; Thomas married Nancy Cornelius on August 25, 1797. They were sons of Thomas whose name appears in the first list of Tithables for Pittsylvania taken July 17, 1767, by Peter Copeland. This list was made the year Pittsylvania was formed from Halifax. This Cooper family was in Lunenburg County until 1752, when the formation of Halifax from Lunenburg left the family in the new county.

William Stirling Cooper, son of Charles and Jane (Richardson) Cooper, married, first, Susannah Andrews and had issue: four sons, William S. Jr., Gideon, George and Herbert. William Stirling Cooper, married, second, Ellie Willis, on December 6, 1819, and had issue: James, Benjamin, Sallie, Raney, William, Louisa and Charity.

William S. Jr., son of William Stirling and Susannah (Andrews) Cooper, married Nancy Martin on March 3, 1828.

George Cooper, son of William Stirling and Susannah (Andrews) Cooper, married Mary ("Polly") Wingfield on September 23, 1824, and had issue: (1) William, (2) Emaline, (3) Mary Ann, (4) Eliza, (5) Charles, (6) George, (7) Morgan, (8) Nannie.

I. William Cooper, son of George and Mary (Wingfield) Cooper, married Julia Gatewood Williamson. He was
killed in Pickett's charge at Gettysburg, and left no issue.
His Widow married John O. Bernard, and had issue: (1) Sallie
Elizabeth, (2) Fannie Sophia, (3) Mary Cassie, (4) Silas Williamson.

II. Emaline Cooper, daughter of George and Mary
(Wingfield) Cooper, married William Pinckard, October 16, 1848,
and had issue: (1) Walter Leake, (2) Charlotte Temple, (3) Emma
Augusta, (4) Mary Ann, ("Mollie"), (5) Lucinda Wise, (6) Nancy,
(7) John William, (8) Charles W., (9) Eliza, and (10) Minnie.

1- Walter Leake Pinckard married Lucy Neff, and removed
to Missouri.

2- Charlotte Temple Pinckard, unmarried.

3- Emma Augusta Pinckard married W. C. Stafford of Missouri,
and had issue: Rudolph and William. Rudolph died young, William married Claudia Morris of Kansas City.

4- Mary Ann Pinckard Married Peter Stockton, and had issue:
(1) Emma, (2) Gordon. They removed to Washington County.

5- Lucinda Wise Pinckard married William Otis ("Ote") Jamison in 1883 and had issue: (1) William; (2) Walter, who married Era Bondurant in 1925; (3) Mary; (4) Lucy, who married Elijah Ramsey in 1920; and two who died in infancy.

6- Nancy Pinckard married, first, Charles F. Pinckard in
1880, and, second, Frank Pinkard in 1883. She had issue by her
first husband, Lera Pinkard, and by her second husband Jesse,
Clara and Homer. She and her third husband, Henry Hayner, lived
in Missouri.

7- John William Pinckard married Nannie Taylor in 1890,
and removed to Pulaski County. They had issue: (1) Leonard,
(2) Claude, (3) Bertha, (4) Lizzie, (5) John Jr., (6) Lucy,
(7) Nancy, (8) Chloe, (9) Sadie and (10) Nellie.

8- Charles W. Pinckard died unmarried in 1901.

9- Eliza Pinckard was married on October 4, 1891, to George
T. Person, and had issue: (1) Billy, who died as an infant, (2)
Louise, (3) Kathleen, (4) John, (5) Emaline, (6) Minnie, (7)
George, (8) Doris and (9) William.

Louise Person married Dr. Walter H. Cobbs in 1920,
and had issue: Walter H. Jr., Billy, Cabell, Carrington and
John. They live in Rocky Mount.

Kathleen Pearson married Leon Hetrick in 1920, and
lives in Pittsburgh.

John Pearson married Maude Bright, in 1923, and
lives in Charlotte, North Carolina.

Emaline Person married, in 1930, Minor Skinnell.
They live in Rocky Mount.

Minnie Pearson married in 1925, Sam Emler, and had

issue: Louise, born 1927; and Doris, born 1931.

George Pearson Jr., married Agnes Austin in 1928. They live in Pittsburgh.

Doris and William, unmarried, live in Pittsburgh.

10- Minnie Pinckard married John Miller, in 1897, and removed to Bristol, Tennessee. They had issue: (1) Pauline, born 1900; Pauline married R. J. Bailey, of Narrows, and has a son R. J. Jr. Herbert married Martha Vandevanter of Bristol, and has a son Jack, and a daughter, Elizabeth.

III. Mary Ann Cooper married Greene Gravely, and had issue: (1) George C., (2) James M., (3) William E., (4) Mary, ("Mollie") L., (5) Lewis, and (6) Delia.

George C. Gravely, son of Greene and Mary Ann (Cooper) Gravely, married, first Julia Hunt, and had issue: (1) William Shawver who lives in West Virginia; (2) Julia; (3) Elizabeth; and (4) J. S. Jr. George Gravely married, second, Paulina Oakes, and had issue: (5) Herman, who married Lenora Craig, and had issue: Herman, Bessie and Annie; (6) Bessie, who married Edward Wood, and had issue: Elmer, Paul, and Helen; and (7) Annie, who married John Washburn and had issue: John, George, Paulina, Seward, Peggy, and Carey. George Gravely married, third, Cordie Bernard. No issue.

James M. Gravely, son of Greene and Mary Ann (Cooper) Gravely, married Pollie Belcher and had issue: Talmage, who died young, and Oscar.

William E. Gravely, son of Greene and Mary Ann (Cooper) Gravely, married Mary Parker, and had issue: Gervais, Elizabeth, Paul and David. He died at his home in Brodhead, Kentucky, several years ago.

Mary ("Mollie") L. Gravely, daughter of Greene and Mary Ann (Cooper) Gravely, married Beverly A. Davis.

Lewis Gravely, son of Greene and Mary Ann (Cooper) Gravely, married Algie Williams, and had issue: Burton, William, Lewis, John, Mildred, Garnet, Virginia and Pauline.

Delia Gravely, daughter of Greene and Mary Ann (Cooper) Gravely, married George O. Young,.and had issue: George, Walter, William, Charles, Annie, and Belle. Walter Young married Virginia Wiltsie, and had issue: Wiltsie and W. L. Jr. Annie Young married Rev. Melville O. Williams. They are missionaries in China, and have a son and a daughter, Ann and Melville Jr. Belle Young married Dr. Summerdahl of Roanoke, and had issue: Freddie and Patricia Lee.

IV. Eliza Cooper, daughter of George and Mary (Wingfield)

Cooper, married Calvin Martin, and had issue: (1) Edward Everett, (2) George Patrick, (3) John William, (4) Ella Reed, (5) Mary ("Mollie") Wingfield, (6) Emma Carver, (7) Annie Cordelia, (8) Sallie C., (9) Matilda and (10) Clara.

1- Edward Everett Martin, married Lily Montrief and and issue: (1) Luther, (2) Clinton, (3) Mastin and (4) Everett Jr. Luther Martin married Mary Davis and had issue: Leslie, Evelyn, Davis and Patrick. Clinton Martin married Lily Turner, daughter of Larkin Turner, in 1908, and had issue: Ruby, Frances, Georgia, Ed, Bill, Douglas, Winnie, Mildred, Lillie, James, and Lois. Mastin Martin married Belva Gregory, and had issue: Lelia, Janie, Maggie, William, and Bernard. Everett Martin Jr., married Pearl Davis, and had issue: Davis, Sallie, Ramon, Pearl, Gertrude, and Sam. Everett Sr., married, second, Ellen Doyle, and had issue: Reynolds, Lizzie, Mattie, Doris and John.

2- George Martin (IV) married Nannie Montrief, and had issue: Patrick, Margaret, Edith, Calvin, Harold, Edna, and Rebecca.

3- John W. Martin married Lutie Montrief, and had issue: 1. Buell, who married Bertha Walker, and had issue: Kathryn Walker; 2. William, who married Laura Eanes, and had issue: Kenneth, Deward, Verlie and William; 3. James; 4. Redmond; 5. John; 6. Blanche, who married Buford Gregory, in 1925, and had issue: Barbara, Bernice and John Stone; 7. Elizabeth, who married William Walker, in 1923, and had issue: Hazel, William, John, Billy, Lutie and James; and 8. Olga.

4- Ella Reed Martin married, first, Perry Trent, and had issue: Thomas Trent, who married Gertrude Overholt and had issue: Thomas Watson and the Twins, Pamela and Meredith. Ella Reed Martin, second, William Jasper Wingfield.

5- Mary ("Mollie") Wingfield Martin married Burwell Washburn, and had issue: John, Eliza Martin (Martie), George, Joseph, Calvin, William and Mary. John Washburn married Annie Gravely, and had issue: John Jr., Patrick, Paulina, Seward, Peggy Anne and Carey. Martie Washburn married George Walker, and had issue: Olita, Joseph, Polly, Annie Laurie, George W., Davis B., Winifred, Marjorie, and Burton. George Washburn died overseas during the World War. Joseph Washburn married Gladys Cooper. William Washburn is unmarried. Calvin Washburn married Lucille Hundley, daughter of Robert Hundley, and had issue: Calvin Jr., Mary Washburn married Rev. Clifford Ramsey, and had issue: Leon Clifford.

6- Emma Martin married Stephen Martin.

7- Annie Cordelia ("Delia") Martin, married Luther Martin.

8- Sallie C. Martin married Samuel L. Cook, and had

issue: William, John, Samuel, Benjamin, and Stephen.
9- Matilda Martin married William Martin, and had
issue: 1. Oliver, 2. Patrick, 3. Kathleen, 4. Rob Roy, and 5.
Eliza. Oliver Martin married Gladys Woody.
10- Clara Martin died young.

V. George W. Cooper, son of George and Mary (Wingfield)
Cooper, married Susan Sophia Williamson, and had issue: 1. Lawson Williamson, 2. George William, 3. Mary Cornelia, 4. Sue Elizabeth, 5. Nannie Lewis, and 6. Julia Gatewood.

Lawson Williamson Cooper married Bertha Anderson of
Buckingham County, in 1908, and had issue: 1. Leone Anderson,
2. Lawson Jr., 3. Helen, 4. Preston Stockton, 5. George Edward,
6. William, 7. James W., and 8. Carey Stegar.

George William Cooper died March 29, 1903.

Mary Cornelia Cooper unmarried, taught in Franklin
schools for many years.

Sue Elizabeth Cooper died, unmarried, October 17, 1933.

Nannie Lewis Cooper was married in 1930 to D.W. Ramsey
of Sydnorsville. No issue.

Julia Gatewood Cooper married Crispin C. Stone on December 24, 1921, and had issue: Mary Elizabeth, born October
27, 1922; James C., born May 14, 1924; and Nancy Page, born September 7, 1925.

VI. Charles Cooper, son of George and Mary (Wingfield)
Cooper, married Paulina Orvis, and had issue: 1. Calvin, and
2. Hattie. They lived in Fowler, Missouri,

VII. Morgan W. Cooper, son of George and Mary (Wingfield)
Cooper, married Haseltine Parker, daughter of Bluford and Mary
(Williams) Parker, and had issue: 1. George Bluford, 2. Mary
W., 3. Lou Emma, 4. Elizabeth, 5. Annie, 6. William, and 7. Charles,
8. Thomas.

George Bluford Cooper (October 21, 1869-June 10, 1919)
married Cassandra Bernard, daughter of John O. Bernard, on November 26, 1895, and had issue: (1) Landon J., born October 9,
1896, died in 1908; (2) Gladys, born February 28, 1899, married
Joseph B. Washburn on May 15, 1920, and had issue: Gordon Bluford, Edith Bernard, Joseph Bryan, Miriam and Janis; (3) Russell,
born March 20, 1901, died April 26, 1918; (4) Bernard W., born
October 7, 1903, married Ella Bowles, September 4, 1926, and had
issue a son named Russell Wayne, born November 18, 1933; (5) Kinsey, born November 4, 1905, lives, unmarried, with his widowed
mother at Boone Mill: (6) Mildred Frances, born September 24,
1908, married Paul Naff on July 26, 1930, and had issue: George
Bluford, born March 3, 1932, and Mary Sue, born February 9, 1933:
(7) Mary Cassie, born February 5, 1914, married Elmer Saul on
October 15, 1932, and had issue: Arthur Landon, born September

19, 1933.

Mary W. Cooper, married in 1890 to J. P. Walker, and
issue: (1) Felix, who married Ethel Dudley, and had issue:
Stuart and Dickey; (2) Rudolph, who married Thelma Mays, and
had issue: Ramon; (3) Bertha, who married Buell Martin, and
had a daughter named Kathryn Walker; and (4) Haseltine, unmarried.

Lou Emma Cooper died Young.

Elizabeth Cooper married Robert Hundley, on March 8,
1905, and had issue: (1) Hampton, who died young; (2) Robert
L. Jr.; (3) Hunbert; (4) Lucille, who married Calvin Washburn;
(5) Dorothy, who married Joel Smith; and (6) Elizabeth, unmarried.

Annie J. Cooper married Walter Haynes on December 19,
1909, and had issue: (1) Irvin, who married Louise Cooper, and
has a son Irvin; (2) Glynwood; (3) Melvin, who married Janie
Adkins, and had a son named Hulet; (4) Bluford; (5) Haseltine,
who married Gordon Byrd; and (6) Evelyn.

William Cooper married Pearl Hundley, and had issue:
(1) Christine, who married George Craig in 1932, and has one
child; (2) Andrew, who married Vera Perdue in 1930; (3) George,
(4) Othello, (5) Elizabeth.

Charles Cooper married Odessa Fralin, daughter of George
Fralin, and had issue: (1) Louise, who married Irvin Haynes,
and has one son, Irvin Jr.; (2) Raymond, who married Bessie Cotton; (3) Thelma, unmarried; and (4) Thomas who died young.

VIII. Nannie Cooper, daughter of George and Mary (Wingfield)
Cooper, married, in 1865, Christopher ("Kit") Law, and had
issue: (1) Pemberton, (2) Gustavus Milton, (3) Henry Sheffield,
(4) George Cooper, (5) Wingfield, (6) Annie, (7) Loula, (8) Olivia,
(9) Allie, (10) Lelia, (11) Virgie, and (12) Betty.

Pemberton Law (VIII) died young.

Gustavus Milton Law married Annie Cooper, and had issue:
(1) Robert, (2) Gustavus, Jr., who teaches in the Snow Creek
High School; (3) James, and (4) Nannie, who married Otho F. Hester.

Henry Sheffield Law (VIII) married Daisy Hutchinson ,
and had issue: (1) William (2) Louise. (3) Royal, (4) Katherine, (5) Lucy, and (6) William. Louise married a Mr. Reid.

George Cooper Law (VIII) married Willie May Campbell,
daughter of William Campbell, and had issue: (1) Wingfield,
(2) Cooper Price, (3) Newton, (4) Stella, (5) Virginia, (6) Page,

(7) Willie, and (8) Carlton.

Wingfield Law died in youth.

Annie Law married Clarence Cooper and died without issue.

Loula Law married Daniel Law and had issue: (1) Cuyler; (2) Christine, who married Dr. Nye, and removed to South America where she died young; (3) Ruth, who married a Mr. Mackay; (4) Lucy; and (5) John. The Daniel Law family removed to Ohio in 1930.

Olivia Law married Henry Hutchinson, and removed to West Virginia. They had a son Dr. William Hutchinson, who practices medicine in West Virginia.

Allie Law married, first, Michael ("Mike") Zeigler, and had issue: (1) Benjamin, (2) Cameron, and (3) Lelia. She married, second, S. A. Gravely, and had a son, S. A. Gravely, Jr. Cameron Zeigler married Everett Blackwell, and had issue, Marguerite and Betty. Lelia Zeigler married a Mr. Riggs, and had two sons. S. A. Gravely Jr., died young.

Lelia Law died young.

Virgie Law married Archibald Adams, and had issue: (1) Ruby, (2) Mildred, (3) Reva, and three sons who died in childhood. Ruby Adams married William Shearer, and had issue, William Jr., and John. Mildred Adams married Herbert Husk of Bluefield, West Virginia. Reva Adams married Hoge Strother of Roanoke.

IX. Herbert Cooper, brother of the George Cooper who married Mary ("Polly") Wingfield, married Sallie King, and had issue: (1) Stirling, (2) William Herbert, (3) George King, (4) Virginia, (5) Martha, (6) Ann Eliza, and (7) Julia.

Stirling Cooper (IX) married Ann Williamson, and removed to Missouri.

William Herbert Cooper (IX) married a Miss King, and had issue: (1) Benjamin Herbert, (2) George., (3) Jack, (4) Mary L(, (5) Julia F., and (6) Sallie. Benjamin Herbert Cooper married, first, a Miss Shelton, and had issue: (1) Nannie Ruth, (2) Katherine King, and (3) Benjamin Herbert Jr. He married, second, Lillian George, and had issue: a son, (4) George Philip. George M. Cooper married a Miss Williams, and had issue: (1) Clarence, (2) Frank, (3) Jack, (4) Sam, (5) Ruth, (6) Sallie, (7) Julia, (8) Mary, and (9) Margaret. Julia married George Mitchell.

George King Cooper, (IX) married Nannie Bernard, and had issue: (1) William, (2) Jesse, (3) Richard, (4) Sallie,

(5) Mollie, (6) Elizabeth, (7) Julia, and (8) Minnie. Sallie Cooper married John King. Mollie Cooper married a Mr. Matthews. Elizabeth Cooper married John Bousman. Julia Cooper married Bond Eames, and had one child, Mary Eames. Minnie Cooper died young.

Virginia Cooper, (IX) daughter of Herbert, married Edwin Tench, and had issue: (1) Isham, (2) Sallie, (3) Annie, and (4) Lucy.

Isham Tench married Sallie Campbell. Sallie Tench married Bond Eames, and had no issue. Annie Tench married Thomas Dudley, and had issue: (1) Todd, (2) William, (3) Graydon, (4) Essie, and (5) Lillian. Lucy Tench, unmarried.

Martha Cooper, daughter of Herbert, (IX) married a Mr. Eanes, and removed to Texas.

Ann Eliza Cooper, daughter of Herbert, (IX) married John King.

Julia Cooper, daughter of Herbert, (IX) married Isaiah White, and had issue: (1) George, who married Roselle Cooper; and (2) Pattie, who married Edward Hill, and had issue: Sallie, Robert and Isaiah.

William Stirling Cooper, son of Charles and Jane (Richardson) Cooper, married, second, Lucy Ellie Willis, and had issue: (1) James, (2) Benjamin, (3) William, (4) Louisa, (5) Sallie Raney, (6) Charity.

Dr. James Cooper married a Miss Frantz. Benjamin Cooper married Betty Parker, and had issue: (1) William, (2) Benjamin, (3) Stirling, (4) Abell, and (5) James. Sallie Raney Cooper, daughter of Stirling and Ellie (Willis) Cooper (IX), married Richard Williamson, and had issue: (1) Richard, (2) Susan, and (3) Nannie. Richard Williamson died young. Susan Williamson married Thomas O. Bernard, and had a son named William. Nannie Williamson married Benjamin Wade, and had issue: (1) Ethel, (2) John, and (3) Elizabeth. Ethel died in childhood. Elizabeth married a Dr. Hall.

Gideon Cooper, was married to America Law on April 5, 1824, and had issue: (1) Greene; (2) Tazewell; (3) Sparrell; (4) Giles; and (5) Harriet B., who married Pinckney Greene Wingfield on September 6, 1850; (6) Letitia Anne; (7) Virginia; (8) Ponetta; (9) "Van" Cooper, who married Lucy ("Stumpy") Parker, and (10) Jeanette.

Of Daniel Cooper little could be secured for this volume.

Augustua Cooper, brother of Daniel, married, and had issue: (1) Robert, (2) Thomas, (3) Johnson, and (4) Betty.

Robert married Nannie Pinckard, and had issue: (1) Clarence, (2) Thomas, (3) Samuel, (4) Harry, (5) Annie, (6) Minnie, (7) Pearl, (8) Nannie Helen, (9) Bessie, and (10) Irene.

Clarence married, first, Annie Law; second Lera Wood. He had issue by his second marriage; Thomas and Minnie.

Thomas removed to Montana, and had issue: Vesta Cooper.

Samuel had two children.

Harry died in early manhood.

Annie married Gustavus Law, and had issue: Robert, Gustavus, James, Nannie.

Minnie married James Webb, and had issue: Frank, Raymond, John, Jim Alex, Minnie Pinkard, and Mary Jane.

Pearl married Mason Bailey, and had issue: Frances and Kathleen.

Nannie Helm married James Kabler, and had issue: (1) Helen Virginia, and (2) James Junior.

Bessie married Grayson Bailey, and had issue: Grayson Bailey Jr.

Irene married Guy Bralley, and had issue: Frances Irene.

Thomas Cooper son of Augustus and brother of Robert, married Maggie Hutchinson, and had issue: (1) Thomas Jr., and (2) Addie Price, who married a Mr. Gordon.

Johnson Cooper, son of Augustus Cooper and brother of Robert and Thomas, died unmarried.

Betty Cooper, daughter of Augustus Cooper and sister of Johnson, married J. R. Gregory, and had issue: (1) Robert, (2) Walter, (3) Johnson, (4) Thomas Taylor, (5) Willie James, (6) Essie, (7) Lizzie, (8) Edith, and (9) Leware.

Robert Gregory died young.

Walter Gregory married Effie Hodges, and had issue: Helen Frost.

Johnson Gregory had one son.

Thomas Taylor Gregory married Mary Taylor, and had a daughter.

issue: Willie James Gregory married John Lavinder, and had Lucille and Paul.

Essie Gregory married Lewis Hunt.

Lizzie Gregory died young.

Edith Gregory married Walter Reynolds.

Leware Gregory married John Greer, and had issue: James Edwin Greer.

Creed Cooper, married Nannie Hodges, and had issue: (1) Beulah, (2) Ida, (3) William Brown, (4) Virgie, (5) Lizzie, (6) Nannie, (7) Myrtle, and (8) Alvie.

Beulah Cooper married J. B. Law.

Ida Cooper also married a Mr. Law.

Virgie Cooper married a Mr. Parcell, and had a son named Denver.

Lizzie Cooper married Benjamin Muse.

Nannie Cooper married Cleveland Slaten.

Myrtle Cooper married a Mr. Ferguson.

Alvie Cooper married Ira Culler.

Of Mordecai Cooper, the author has heard much, but has little authentic information to offer. It is said that one of his sons, Taylor, married Betty Miles.

THE CRAGHEAD FAMILY

John Craghead was born in 1804-5 in Franklin County, where he spent his entire life. He married Sarah (Sally) Powell. He died in 1859. His widow lived to be 102 years old. They had children as follows: Thomas Lodowick, John, Robert, Charles, Townley, Alexander, Virginia, Catherine, and Lily.

Virginia married Mr. _____ Mattocks; Emily married John Morgan; Catherine married Dr. Spencer James, and had issue: Dr. John James, of Pittsylvania.

Thomas Lodowick, born in 1819, married Lucinda Baker, granddaughter of Henry Koger and Mary King. Their children were: Sallie, Angeline, Pocahontas, and Loula. He lived on Staunton river in Franklin County. He had a large farm and many slaves. He was a great hunter, and enjoyed the game which was so plentiful in his day. He joined the Confederate Army, and was taken prisoner to Point Lookout, where he died in 1864. His daughter, Sallie, married John H. Mathews, in 1867. Loula married Sam Hill, and had issue: Sam, Robert, William, Lucy, Loula, Thomas, Lodowick, Catherine, and Overton.

Pocahontas Craghead married John Coleman, and had issue: James, Alf, Harrison, Loula, and Ethel.

Ruth Angeline was married in 1870 to Morgan A. Coleman of Henry County, and had issue: George, Robert, Thomas C., Bruce, Sallie, Ida and Alice.

George married, and had issue: Burwell, Clyde, Ruby, and Alvis. He died young.

Thomas C., married Azzie Davis in 1912.

Sallie married Joseph Bassett of Charlotte, North Caroline; Ida married T. C. Mathews, of Martinsville; Bruce married Essie Hodnett, of Reidsville, North Carolina; Morton married Lottie Hundley, of Pittsylvania; and Alice married G. C. Pratt, of Martinsville.

Mrs. Walter Craghead of Jetmore, Kansas, in her research work in Missouri, says that John, born in 1805 had a brother Charles, b. July 13, 1810, in Virginia who died Jan. 7, 1886 in Missouri, and he married Elvira Ann Saunders, in Virginia, and had issue: William, who remained in Bedford County; John; Sallie, who married a Mr. Holland; Fannie, who married Thomas H. Halley, and died in Virginia; Cornelia Anne, who married a Mr. Gooldy; and Charles P. Jr., who married a Miss Hatcher. Also John and Charles Sr., had a sister Nancy, who married her "double cousin", William Craghead, May 13, 1822, Franklin County, and went to Missouri to live.

In "Marriage Bonds of Franklin County, Virginia the following marriages are listed:

        Craghead, John & Elizabeth Hale, April 3, 1789
        Craghead, John & Jane Martin, Jan. 1, 1842
        Craghead, John & Julia Smith, dau. William, Dec.
            18, 1830
        Craghead, John B. & Sally Hale, dau. James T.,
            Oct. 28, 1823
        Craghead, Robert & Nancy Powell, Nov. 18, 1892
        Craghead, Timothy & Mary Agee, Dec. 6, 1802
        Craghead (Craighead), Townsend & Sarah Bernard,
            dau. Peter, Jan. 14, 1824
        Craghead, William & Susannah Maxey, March 4, 1828
        Craghead, William & Nancy Craghead, dau. John,
            May 13, 1822
        Craghead, William & Jean Dunn, dau. Thomas, Jan.
            13, 1800

THE DAVIS FAMILY

The will of Edward Davis, wife Mary Davis, probated in Charles County, Maryland, July 21, 1736, gives the children as follows: Richard, Edward, David, Henry, John, Peter, Ann, Elizabeth, Susannah, Mary Garden, William, James, Edward, the younger, Thomas, and Luke.

The will of the third son, David Davis, was probated May 23, 1770, in Charles County, Maryland,. This will shows that David Davis' wife was Ann Davis, and their children were Joseph Waters, David, Charles, Elizabeth, Ann Barker and Susan.

The history and genelogy of the descendants of Charles Davis, third son of David and Ann Davis, will be followed in this section. The following record was received from the original Charles County, Maryland records, in Trinity Parish:

"Charles Davis was the father of Peter, Benjamin, Thomas, Eleanor and Ann Davis. Their mother, second wife of Charles Davis, was Ann Dent.

"Charles Davis's first wife was Sarah Moreland, married May 11, 1762. Moses Davis, son of Charles Davis and Sarah Moreland, was born April 29, 1763. Sarah Davis was born September 26, 1764. Issac Davis was born April 9, 1766. Lydia Davis was born March 14, 1768. Joshua Davis was born April 28, 1770.

"Eleanor Davis, daughter of Charles Davis and Ann Dent, was born April 7, 1777. Benjamin Davis was born September 9, 1778. Thomas Blackburn Davis was born August 23, 1782.

"I hereby certify that the above is a true copy from the registry of Trinity Parish, Charles County, Maryland, given under my hand this 20th day of August, 1787."

"Teste: James Waters, Registrar."

"I certify also that I have agreeable a letter placed the age of Peter Davis, (son of Charles Davis and Ann Dent, his wife) on the above register born August 13, 1786.

"Teste: James Waters, Registrar."

Ann Dent, wife of Charles Davis was one of nine children of Hatch Dent and his wife Ann Dent of Charles County, Maryland. That Charles Davis, with his wife and children, went into Henry County, Virginia, is shown by a will which was probated July 27, 1807.

That Charles Davis served as a private in the Revolutionary War is shown by the records of the Adjutant General's office of the U. S. War Department. His pension commenced Sep-

tember 4, 1789, under the act of June 7, 1785 of the Virginia
agency pension. This record shows that Charles Davis' application was destroyed in 1814, and gives the date of his death
as February 1, 1807.

The incomplete history of Peter, Benjamin, and Thomas
Davis, three sons of Charles Davis and Ann Dent Davis, will be
given here.

Benjamin, son of Charles Davis and Ann Dent Davis,
married Nancy Hurd, daughter of William Hurd. Their ten children were:

> William Davis, married Lucy Craig
> Mary Davis, married Woodson Ramsay
> Betsey Anne Davis, married Tansy Ramsay
> Winnie Davis, married Thomas Ramsay
> Peggy Davis, married a Minteer
> Jane Davis, married John Nunn
> Charles Davis, died at the age of 21 years
> Nancy Blackburn Davis, died at the age of 16 years
> Benjamin Davis, married Eleanor Hicks and moved to
>   Georgia
> Jesse Hurd Davis, married Susan A. Koger

Jane Davis Nunn and John Nunn are the parents of William Riley Nunn, who married Mrs. J. M. Davis, widow of J. M.
Davis, in 1921. The children of William Riley Nunn by his former wife are:

> George Dann Nunn, married Hattie Ramsay--12 children
> Ruth Nunn, married Ernest Hurd--2 children
> Susie Nunn, married Tom Turner--5 children

The children of Jesse Hurd Davis and Susan A. Koger
are:

> John Benjamin Davis, married Betty Stovall
> Gillie Coleman Davis, married Haley W. Ramsay
> Pinckney G. Davis, married Lucy A. Jones
> Rufus F. Davis, unmarried
> E. J. Davis, married (1) Sally Davis, and (2) Minnie
>   H. Davis
> Lloyd T. Davis, married Emma Jamerson
> D. W. Davis, married Mary Shumate. They live in Hen-
>   ry County, Va.--3 children.
> Lulu E. Davis, married N. S. Goode
> Peter Davis, son of Charles Davis and Ann Dent Davis,
>   married May Hurd, daughter of William Hurd.
>   She lived to a ripe old age, and was affectionatley
>   called "Old Aunt Polly Davis". Their children
>   were:

Jonathan Davis, married (1) Turner, (2) Turner, and
(3) Smith
Laban J. Davis, married Letisha Pettigo
Thomas B. Davis, married Martha Coleman
Peter Perkins Davis, married (1) Emily Wade, and (2)
Mary F. Holland
William H. Davis, married Betsey A. Napier
Benjamin Dent Davis, married _____ Draper
Jane Hickey Davis, married Jesse Lavinder
Margaret C. Davis, married Jos. Jones
David Davis, married (1) Nancy G. McGhee, and (2)
White

The children of Peter Perkins Davis and Emily Wade
Davis are:

John P. Davis, married Mary Jane Mitchell, daughter
of John Mitchell and Elizabeth Napier Mitchell. Their children
are:

Emily W. Davis, married E. L. Kelly
J. Mitchell Davis, unmarried
Mary Elizabeth Davis, unmarried
Sarah Jane Davis, married Jos. W. Kelly--issue Mary
Davis & Emily Ball Davis
Charles Peter Davis, married Kate Decottes--issue Chas.
Peter Davis
Anne Ursula Davis, unmarried
Robert Davis, unmarried, died March 13, 1918.

The children of Peter Davis and Mary Holland Davis
are:

F. E. Davis, married Lillian Trent
Sallie E. Davis, married E. J. Davis
T. H. Davis, married Lillian Hurd
C. W. Davis, married (1) Ida Townes, and (2) Virginia
Grantham
Fletcher Davis, unmarried
Frank Payne Davis, married Ellie Walker--issue Frank,
Pond, and Sarah
Harry Holland Davis, married Lena Seward--issue Le-
wellyn and Everette H. Davis
Maud Wall Davis, married Sidney P. Childers--issue
Mary Anne, Sydney P. and Vincent
Jesse Guy Davis, married Audrey Dickerson
John Peter Davis, sheriff of Henry County, died, while
serving his third on February 17, 1898, aged 45.

John Mitchell Davis, son of John Davis, succeeded his
father at the age of 24.

D. S. Davis, son of Benjamin S. Davis and Anne Hunter

Davis, has been elected to the Office of Treasurer of Henry Co. for seven successive terms.

James P. Davis, son of Benjamin S. Davis and Anne Hunter Davis, moved to Kokomo, Indiana. He has represented his county in the Legislature and Senate. He was the nominee of his party for Congress in 1928.

E. L. Davis, son of Laban J. Davis and Letitia Pettigo Davis, lives in Martinsville

Everette J. Davis, son of Jesse H. Davis and Susan Koger Davis, also lives in Martinsville, and is engaged in the tobacco business.

Beverly A. Davis, son of David H. and Nancy G. Davis, lives in Rocky Mount. David H. Davis served as a Confederate soldier. He died in 1907, at the age of 76. Beverly A. Davis' first wife was Nettie Barrow, daughter of Benjamin Barrow. The one child of this marriage is Mrs. W. S. Morris. At his second marriage, Mr. Davis wedded the daughter of Mr. G. D. Gravely. Four children have been born to their marriage: Mamie, the daughter, is the wife of Owen Reynolds of Craig County. The sons David H., Beverly A. Jr., and Russell are all associated with their father in the law profession.

Thomas Blackburn Davis, son of Charles Davis, married Louvica King, daughter of Stephen King in 1805-issue as follows: Julia, Louania, Betsey, Mary, Lucinda, Sampson J., and Louis.

Julia Davis, married Charles Smith--eight children.

Louania Davis, married David Mavity, and moved to Indiana. They had a large family, and Dr. Mavity of Fowler, Indiana, is the son of this union. Betsey Davis married George Goode--issue: Julia B. Goode and Lizzie Goode. Julia married Jonas Goode. She has a large family. Lizzie Goode married James Stone. She, too, has a large family.

Mary Davis, married Jonathan Davis of Henry Co. Their one daughter, Louvica Davis, married William Hurd. She died in 1887.

Lucinda Davis, married Jos. Doss. Their daughter, Julia A. Doss, lived in Franklin.

Louis Davis, died when young.

Sampson J. Davis, born in Franklin County, November 28, 1812, married Basheba Turner, and died March 9, 1880. His wife was born October 18, 1810, and died September 21, 1885. Their children are:

Adeline Mildred Davis, born September 3, 1837, was married on November 4, 1869, to Samuel S. Good, and moved, first,

to West Virginia and later, to Lexington, Nebraska. There were
seven children (1) Sam Good, married in California; (2) Nannie
Good, married William McCarter, and now lives in California--
issue: Nora McCarter, married in California, and has two children; (3) James Good, married in California, and has one son and
one daughter; (4) Lulu Good, married William Decker, and now
lives in Berkley California. She has one son, Harold; (5) Lon
Good, married Emma Decker, Lexington, Nebraska. They have four
children: (6) William Good, married Phoenie Anthony, in Lexington, Nebraska. They have four sons; and (7) Elbert Good, married in California, and has a family. Samuel S. Good died June
19, 1893. Adeline Good died at Lexington, Nebraska, April 9,
1915.

Louvica Anne Davis was born September 3, 1839. She
married Thomas H. Nunn on November 3, 1870. Two children were
born: Ruth Ellen and John Sampson. Louvica Davis Nunn died
March 7, 1913. T. H. Nunn died July, 1920.

Elizabeth Sarah Davis was born July 2, 1841. She mar-
ried James A. Pyrthle, March 13, 1861. They had eight children.
In 1868, they moved to West Virginia; in 1875, they moved to
Flum Creek, now Lexington, Nebraska.

Solomon King Davis was born January 11, 1843. He volunteered in the services of the Confederacy. He became orderly
Sergeant, and was accidently killed in May 1864.

Lucinda Loutisha Davis was born August 25, 1844. She
never married. Died May 2, 1904.

Julia J. Davis was born March 8, 1846. Died in childhood.

George T. Davis was born October 25, 1847, and died
in childhood.

Benjamin Franklin Davis was born June 1, 1849. He
was married October 15, 1875, to Syrilda May of West Virginia.
Five children were born.

Nora Montery Davis married Dr. Leonard Harter--issue:
Helen, Doris and Stuart. Edgar Davis married Sevilla Passmore
--issue: three sons and one daughter. Edgar F. Davis died at
Long Beach, California, February 15, 1929. Willie Davis died
August 10, 1897.

Dr. Everett Davis married in Los Angeles, California.

The Benjamin Franklin Davis family lived at Lexington, Nebraska, for twenty-five years, then removed to Long Beach,
California. Syrilda Davis, wife of Benjamin Franklin Davis,
died May, 1906, in Long Beach, California. Benjamin Franklin

Davis married again in California.

James Marshall Davis was born December 1, 1851. He was married, January 20, 1878, to Letha Matilda Nunn. On November 7, 1879, a daughter was born, Bettie Davis; she died January 6, 1691. James Marshall Davis died December 18, 1917. Letha Matilda Nunn Davis married William R. Nunn March 19, 1920.

Ruth Matilda Davis, was born June 4, 1856. She was married, December 7, 1879, to George W. Goode. George W. Goode died in May, 1882. Two daughters were born: Julia and Georgia. Georgia Goode married George Hilton. She died in 1904. Julia. Goode married William M. Alexander, and now lives in Fieldale, Virginia. She has six children: Dorothy Matilda, Mary Ruth, Albert Richard, Martha Lyle and Louise.

Callie Ruth Hilton, daughter of Georgia Hilton, married Walter Adam. Mary Ruth Alexander married Dewey Cecil Gordon, August 4, 1923. Dorothy Matilda Alexander married John A. Bryant, November 15, 1919--issue: Dorothy Marie Bryant, Jacqueline Dale Bryant, and Doris Ruth Bryant.

THE DILLARD FAMILY

The Franklin County Dillards trace their lineage to 1660, when George Dillard, 26, from Wiltshire, England, appears in the militia enrollment at Jamestown.

James Stephen Dillard, son of George, was born in England in 1658, married a Miss Govans or a Miss Page (record not clear), and settled in James City County.

James Dillard, son of James Stephen, was born in 1698, and married Lucy Wise in 1724. Issue: Thomas, Nicholas, James, Stephen, John, William Terry, Mary and Sally.

James Dillard, Jr. born in 1727, settled in Amherst County where he and his wife lived, died and were buried.

Of the children of James Dillard Jr. (1727-1794), a son Capt. John Dillard, came to the Franklin area during the Revolutionary period, and bought land on Horsepasture Creek, now in Henry County. He was born in 1751, married Sarah, daughter of George Stovall of Pittsylvania, and had issue: James, George, Ruth, Pattie, Jane, Athey, Elizabeth, Mary Ann, Peter Hairston, and John (known as General John).

Robert Hairston, son of Peter Hairston, a Scotsman of Albemarle County, lived near Capt. John Dillard, and married Ruth Stovall, sister of John Dillard's wife. Captain Dillard gave his brother-in law's family name, and in this way that the name Hairston first came into the Dillard family.

James Dillard, eldest son of Captain John, was born in

1779, married Lucy Moorman in 1809, and died in 1859. He was the father of John Henry Dillard, a judge of the Supreme Court of North Carolina, who was born in 1819, and married Ann Isabelle, daughter of Gen. Joseph Martin. General Martin was the founder of Martinsville.

George Dillard, son of Captain John, married Elizabeth, daughter of William Hill, and settled in Missouri where he has numerous descendants.

Ruth Dillard, eldest daughter of Captain John, married John Spencer, son of Moses Spencer, who was a soldier in the Revolution.

John Dillard was born in 1783, and married Matilda Hughes, daughter of Col. Archelaeus Huges and Mary (Dalton) Dillard. Issue: Peter Francisco, John Lee, James Madison, and George Penn. Of the children of John Dillard: Dr. Peter Francisco Dillard married Elizabeth Hairston. Issue: Dr. Peter Francisco Jr., who became a physician, and settled in Mississippi soon after the Civil War; John Jr., who moved to West Virginia; Lula, who died unmarried. Dr. Peter Francisco, Sr., died early in life, and his widow married John Reamey and had other children. John Lee, second son of General John, married Isabella Jones, and died without issue. He was a Lieutenant Colonel in the Confederate Army. James Madison, third son of General John, died unmarried. Dr. George Penn Dillard, son of General John Dillard, married Miranda Brooks, and had issue: George; Matilda; Miranda; Wilthem; Sarah, who married Nicholas Hairston; Matilda, who married Shelton Penn; Mary; Jenny, who married William Watkins; and Ann, who married Dr. Richard Watkins.

Peter Hairston Dillard married Elizabeth, daughter of Maj. John Redd. She was born in 1792, and died in 1837. Her husband died 30 years later. Issue: John Redd, Overton Redd, Martha Ann, Sarah, Mary, Lucy, and George Penn.

Overton Redd Dillard married Sallie Martin; Martha Ann married Col. Hughes Dillard; Sarah married William P. Watt; Mary married Harrison Spencer; Lucy married Lewis Williamson of Charlotte, North Carolina; and George Penn married Nancy Penn.

Pattie Dillard married Capt. Peter Shelton, a soldier in the War of 1812.

Jane Athey Dillard married a man named Mays.

Elizabeth Dillard married, first, Peter Hairston and, second, Capt. John Dillard.

Mary Ann Dillard died unmarried.

Archelaeus Hughes Dillard settled in the Western part of Pittsylvania which later became Patrick County. He married Mary, a daughter of Samuel Dalton of Patrick County, and had issue:

Leander; Archelaeus; William; Jane; John; Samuel; Reuben; Nancy;
Madison Redd; Matilda, who married General John Dillard; and Sal
lie who, married Col. Joseph Martin. Joseph Martin had been a
"long hunter", and had lived in Albemarle County. About 1770
he bought land in Pittsylvania County on Leatherwood Creek on
which he made his home. He was active in Indian affairs along
the frontier, and acted as Indian Agent for Virginia for several
years. He married first, Sarah Lucas, and , second, Susannah
Graves, and had issue: Susannah, William, Elizabeth, Brice, Joseph, Jesse, Thomas, Lewis, and Alexander. He served in the Virginia Legislature for several years.

Archelaeus Hughes Dillard was born in 1817, and became
active in political life. He was defeated by Jubal A. Early in
a contest for a seat in the Virginia Convention of 1861. He was
a member of the Virginia Legislature in 1855-56, and a Presidential Elector in 1854. He died in 1901.

Archelaeus Hughes Dillard married his cousin Martha Ann
Dillard in 1840, and had issue:

(1) Elizabeth Redd, who married Daniel Arrington of
Franklin County.
(2) Matilda Hughes, who married Capt. William Chamber-
lain of Norfolk, and had issue: Mary, who married Ferguson Reed
of Norfolk; and William who married a Miss   Frank.
(3) Martha who married William J. Penn. of Botetourt.
(4) Lucy who married James Frank Wingfield, son of
Judge Gustavus A. Wingfield. She died October 2, 1934.
(5) John Lea, born 1847, who married Elizabeth Spencer of Henry County. He was a cadet in Virginia Military Institute during the War, and as such participated in the Battle
of New Market. He continued in the Confederate States Army until
the end of the war, after which he studied law in the University
of Virginia and became Judge of the Henry County Court, the youngest judge to occupy that bench. His son Harry died of small pox
in 1875.

(6) Peter Hairston Dillard was born in Henry County,
October 15, 1850, but in 1857 his parents, Archelaeus Hughes and
Martha Dillard (cousins), removed to Rocky Mount. His paternal
grandfather was Gen. John Dillard. His maternal Grandfather was
Col. Peter Dillard, a brother of Gen. John Dillard. Peter Hairston Dillard was educated under a private tutor and at the Unives-
ity of Virginia. He was admitted to the bar in 1871; for eighteen
years he was commonwealth's attorney of Franklin County; and in
1924, he was elevated to the bench as circuit judge. On November 6, 1872, he married Lydia Nash, daughter of Dr. Thomas Nash,
and had issue:
(a) Herbert Nash, attorney, who married Mary Celestia
Greer, daughter of Dr. Thomas Bailey and Celestia
(Taliaferro) Greer, and had issue: Mary Adela;
Elizabeth Nash, who married Hugh Ewing Jr., of
Richmond; Peter Hairston II, Attorney; Kate Greer,

who died an infant; Celestia Taliaferro; and Herbert Nash Jr., a graduate of Harvard. Herbert Nash Dillard died Oct. 13, 1935.

(b) H. Dalton, attorney, who married Ethel Covington Hale, and had issue: Lydia Hale, who married William C. Ruffin of North Carolina; and Josephine Claiborne, who married Albert G. Crosby Jr., of Roanoke.

(c) Percy Hunter, and attorney, unmarried.

(d) Carter Lee, Attorney, unmarried.

(e) Adele Nash, who married John Kent Shepherd of Winston-Salem, and had issue: Benjamin Dillard, and Adela Nash.

(f) Lucretia Frances, who married John Hairston Dangerfield of North Carolina and had issue: Adela Carter.

Judge Peter H. Dillard died Feb. 7, 1935.

(7) Hughes, who married Mattie Wilson of Chatham, and had issue: Ann Garland, who married W. W. Green of Bowling Green; Elizabeth Redd, who married Ross G. Travis, of Bowling Green; and John Wilson, who married Mary Taylor of Winston-Salem. Hughes Dillard was commonwealth's attorney for Pittsylvania for many years, and at the time of his death had been Judge of the Circuit Court for a long period. He was born in 1854 and died in ca. 1919.

(8) Mary, who died an infant.

Dr. John Redd Dillard, son of Peter Hairston Dillard, was born about 1830. He married, first, Margaret Brown, by whom he had the following children: Elizabeth, Martha Hughes, and Lucy Ashton. By his second marriage to Adele Lee, a kinswoman of Robert E. Lee, he had issue: George, Peter, John, Caroline, Annie, William, Robert, Charles, Adele, and Helen.

Of Dr. John R. Dillard's children by Margaret Brown: (1) Elizabeth Brown married first, Tyler Hairston; second, Charles Angle; and third, Lumsden Ayers; (2) Martha Hughes married first, Robert Jordan of Charlotte, and second, P. P. Watson; and (3) Lucy Ashton married Thomas S. Brown of Wytheville. Of Dr. Dillard's children by Adela Lee: (4) George Lee Dillard married Florence Echols of Bluefield, West Virginia; (5) Caroline married first, Charles Wilmot of Texas, and second, Walter H. Penn; (6) Annie married J. Murray Hooker, a member of Congress; (7) William married Nellie----------; (8) John married Nell Prince of Bluefield, West Virginia;(9) Robert never married; (10) Charles died unmarried; (11) Adela married William L. Pannill, of Reidsville, North Carolina; and (12) Helen married Thomas Morris.

Dr. John Redd Dillard was a graduate of Jefferson Medical College of Philadelphia, and practiced his profession at Spencer, Virginia.

John Lea Dillard, civil engineer, married Mary S. Taylor of North Carolina, and had issue; a daughter Elizabeth McCaw,
who married Richard Joshua Reynolds II, tobacconist of Winston-
Salem. They have a son, Richard Joshua Reynolds III.

THE DILLON FAMILY

Jesse Dillon, born 1749, in Galway County, Ireland,
married Mary Elizabeth Blankenship, and came to America about
1786, settling near Haleford. He died in 1833. His wife was
born in 1759, and died in 1842. Both are buried near Cross Roads,
and near the home of Thomas Holland and Dee Dillon. Jesse Dillon owned eleven hundred acres of land in the vicinity of Haleford and Cross Roads. At his death he owned eighteen slaves.
He willed his land equally to his five sons.

Jesse Dillon and his wife had issue: 1- Henry (Hal),
2- Asa, 3- Arthur, 4- Jesse Jr., 5- William, 6- Delilah, 7- Elizabeth, 8- Martha, and 9- Fanny.

Henry, born March 4, 1779, married Joanna Pasley October 5, 1810. He died August 21, 1875, and his wife died July
29, 1873.or 1883. Both are buried on the old (Hal) Dillon farm
near Haleford. There are no inscribed stones at their graves.

Henry Dillon and his wife had issue: 1- Jesse, II, born
October 24, 1802, died July 27, 1819, from swallowing a plum seed.
2- Sally, born October 29, 1804, died April 11, 1852. She married Peter B. Forbes. 3- Elizabeth, born February 5, 1807, died
May 15, 1850. She married Thomas J. Forbes June 29, 1825. 4-
Robert Pasley, born June 18, 1809, married Martha Dillon, a daughter of his uncle Asa Dillon, in 1831. Robert died October 27,
1910, and his wife died July 11, 1893. Both are buried on the
old Hal Dillon farm near Haleford. 5- Mary Dillon, born January
1, 1812, died August 10, 1898. She never married. She was buried
on the old home place near Haleford. 6- Joanna, born July 5, 1814,
died April 1903. She is buried at Dillon's Mill. 7- Henry Clay,
born May 19, 1818, died December 22, 1877. He married Lucy Ann
Akers, June 9, 1853. She was born October 12, 1831, and died
October 12, 1877. Both are buried in the Presbyterian Cemetary
in Lynchbur. 8- Jesse Dillon III born October 3, 1820, died September 8, 1896, and was buried at Dillon's Mill. 9- Julia Ann,
born May 8, 1823, died February 27, 1911. She married William
Aaron Powell December 6, 1842. He was born February 12, 1821,
and died July 26, 1882. Both are buried on the old Powell farm
near Scruggs. 10- Joanna, born August 20, 1829, died February 8,
1860. She married Andrew Teral Meador November 6, 1855. He
was born in 1835. Date of his death unknown.

Robert Pasley Dillon and his wife Martha had issue:
1- Nancy Jane, who married Henry Dillon, a son of Arthur Dillon;
2- Ransone, who died at the age of 2 years; 3- Fleming, who died

in infancy; 4- Harvey, who died in infancy; 5- Silas, who married Ailey Ann Powell; 6- Henry Clay, who married Sarah Jane Ferguson; 7- John Calvin, who married Sarah Elizabeth Plybon, 8- Julia Frances, who married Lilburn (Mountain) Pasley; 9- Martha Ann, who married Lee Boston Divers; and 10- Sally Elizabeth, who married William Singleton Scott.

Henry Clay Dillon had issue: 1- Samuel Henry, 2- Rufus Alburn, 3- Sarah Elizabeth, 4- a son not named, 5- William Patterson, 6- Robert Lee, 7- Jesse Emmet, 8- Carrie Belle, 9- Lucy Miona, 10- Luther Miner, and 11- Lillie Estelle.

Jesse Dillon III, and his wife Sarah Jane Webster had issue: 1- John Henry, 2- James Robert, 3- William Samuel, 4- Louisa Mary Jane, 5- Martha Ann, 6- Jesse Thomas, 7- Sarah Elizabeth, 8- Lucy Adalaide, 9- Julia Mildred, 10- Charles Lewis, 11- Deborah Ida, 12- Lavinia Paxton, 13- George Everett, 14- Fannie Leslie, 15- Lafayette Hampton, and 16- Bunyan Webster.

Julia Ann Dillon married William Aaron Powell, and had issue: 1-Sallie Mary, died unmarried; 2- Joanna Francis, married George William Perdue; 3- Henry Clay, never married; 4- William Anthony, married first, Julia Catherine Perdue, and second, Mary Louise St. Clair; 5- Julia Ann, married Bishop Ayers; 6- Martha Hayden, married Waddie Curen Belcher; 7- Jesse Booker, married Sophia Allen; 8- Mildred Katherine, married William Henry Fralin; and 9- Alice Patra, married first, John David Fralin, second, Jefferson David Fralin.

Asa Dillon, son of Jesse Dillon and Mary Elizabeth Blankenship, was born in 1762. On August 13, 1798 he was married to Elizabeth Greer. She was born in 1764, and died November 1860. Asa died in November 1860. Both are buried in the Lively Cemetery, near Lindside, West Virginia. There are no tombstones at their graves. Asa Dillon and his wife settled near Lindside, in Monroe County, West Virginia, about 1830. They had issue: 1- Snellings, 2- Quincy Perry; 3- Asa Jr.; 4- Temperance, 5- Betty Bxa Bandy, 6- Martha, 7- Greer, 8- Henderson, and 9- Jefferson.

Snelling never married. His grave is supposed to be near Cross Roads.

Quincy Perry, married first, Catherine McGhee, and second, Jennie Chambers.

Asa Jr., married Joanna Jane Saunders.

Temperance, married William Pasley.

Betty Brandy, married first, Samuel Sturgeon, and second Michael Gross.

Martha, married Robert Pasley Dillon, a son of Henry.

Greer, married Lucy Spradling.

Henderson, married first, Falishia Crawford, and second, Susanna Fisher.

Maiden name of Jefferson's wife unknown.

Arthur Dillon, son of Jesse Dillon and Mary Elizabeth Blankenship, born in 1777, died January 5, 1864, married Jane Ross. They are buried in an isolated burying ground.between the Tyree Dillon farm and the old Mark Perdue place. They had issue: 1- Henry, 2- Asa, 3- Alexander, 4- Nancy, 5- Susanna, and 6- Catherine.

Henry was born June 7, 1809. On December 7, 1864, he married Peggy Brown; and on October 4, 1855, he married Nancy Jane Dillon. The latter was born February 26, 1833, and died August 1, 1902. Henry died December 7, 1864.

Asa, son of Arthur Dillon, was born November 22, 1812. He married Mahala Hutts, December 15, 1836. She was born October 7, 1814, and died November 8, 1896. Asa died April 7, 1884. Both are buried near Cross Roads. It is said that Asa Dillon was a lover of whiskey and fisticuffs, and that he broke his arm in a fight, thus escaping service in the Confederate Army.

Alexander, died from burns, unmarried.

Nancy Dillon, married an Allen, and settled in Ohio.

Susannah (Soocy), married Ammon Oyler. Nothing known of her children.

Katherine, married Mark Perdue. The father of Mark was Meshach Perdue, who married Nellie Dillon, probably a sister of Jesse Dillon, the first. Mark Perdue was quite wealthy. He dealt in real estate and manufactured liquors.

Jesse Dillon, Jr., son of Jesse Dillon and Mary Elizabeth Blankenship, married Rebecca Plybon, January 18, 1808. The dates of their births and deaths, and the place of burial is unknown. They settled in Lawrence County, Ohio, about 1830. They had issue: 1- John, 2- Flemmon, 3- Margaret, 4- Sperrill, 5- Davis, 6- Stephen, 7- Rebecca, 8- Mary, 9- Jesse, 10- Dan, and 11- Delilah. Nothing is known of this family except that Stephen had a son named William Flemmon Dillon who married Pearl Armena Jacobs, and had two daughter, Pearl Oden and Rachel Dillon, now (1934) living. William Flemmon Dillon was president of the First National Bank of Shreveport, Louisiana, and operated the street car lines of that city. He also owned and operated a line of steam boats on the Red River and the Mississippi. He was drowned January 1-, 1918, while duck hunting on Cadda Lake, near Shreveport.

William Dillon, son of Jesse Dillon and Mary Elizabeth Blankenship, was born in 1786. He married Mary Plybon Starkey, widow of John Starkey, April 3, 1809. She died May 16, 1876. Her birthdate is unknown. Both are buried in the Tyree Dillon graveyard near Cross Roads. William Dillon and Mary Plybon Starkey Dillon had issue: 1- Lewis, 2- Rebecca, 3- Jacob, 4- Lydia,

5- Jesse Clay, 6- James Reed, 7- Moses, 8- Tyree, 9- Thomas, and 10- Silas. Lewis married Lucy Greer February 6, 1832. They had eighteen children. Rebecca married Josiah Bouseman. Nothing is known of them. Jacob married first, Naoma Greer, and second, Mary Jane Duncan. Jacob went to Barren County, Kentucky, in 1834. He only had one son that lived to maturity. This son married but died without issue, hence the name Dillon does not survive through this family.

Lydia, born April 9, 1817, married Stephen Sink. They raised a large family in both numbers and size. Two of their sons were giants.

Jesse Clay, born August 23, 1820. He married Gillie Frances Dudley January 8, 1850, and had eight children.

James Reed, born May 14, 1824, died January 15, 1911. He married Mary Jane Smith in 1849, and had nine children.

Tyree Thomas Dillon, born February 13, 1826, married Annie Elizabeth Divers, January 11, 1858, and had thirteen children.

Elizabeth, daughter of Jesse Dillon and Mary Elizabeth Blankenship, married William Pasley, May 12, 1812. They had two children: Robert, born June 21, 1812, and William Jr. Robert married first, Frances Hayden Pasley, and second, Mary Basham. After the death of Elizabeth Pasley, William Pasley lived with Temperance Dillon, daughter of Asa Dillon and Elizabeth Greer, in a common law marriage, and had several children by this union.

THE DUDLEY FAMILY

Gwin (Gwynn) Dudley came from Lunenburg to that area of Bedford now embraced in Franklin ca. 1779. McAllister (Section 157, p. 136) says Gwin Dudley served as sergeant in Capt. John Wilkerson's Company of Bedford Militia during the Revolution. He was given 111 acres in Franklin Co. for his services according to a land grant by Gov. Robert Brooks (Treasury warrant No. 14, 882, Dec. 2, 1782), the grant being delivered to Moses Greer Dec. 6, 1800. Dudley's first Franklin Co. home was above Kemp's Ford. The chimney of the old house is still standing (1935), and bears the inscription "G. D. 1795." A deed (Deed Book No. 5, p. 60) dated Mar. 8, 1805, shows that Gwin Dudley and his wife, Mary, deeded James Dudley 67 acres on Gill's Creek for 50 pounds. The land is described as "the place on which Thomas Dudley formerly lived". Deed Book No. 7, p. 496, dated Aug. 5, 1816, shows that Gwin Dudley conveyed to Levi Dudley 200 acres "for and in consideration of love for his son."

Gwin Dudley m. 1st. Mary E. Hale, dau. of Col. Hale, and, 2nd, Mary Pasley, dau. of Robert Pasley, on Aug. 17, 1797.

The children of Gwin and Mary E. (Hale) Dudley were: 1. Thomas; 2. James; 3. Stephen; 4. Levi; and 5. Elizabeth.

I. Thomas Dudley, son of Gwin and Mary (Hale) Dudley, m. Mancy Pasley, Jan. 16, 1800, (The Pasleys came to Franklin from Fluvanna Co. ca. 1800), and had issue: 1. Gillie F., 2. Ransome; 3. Gwin; 4. John; and 5. Sparrel. 1. Gillie F., m. Jesse C. Dillon 2. Ransome m. Julia Jones, and had issue: Tom, Ben, Nannie, Stella, Alex, Jennie, Martha, Joe, Lilburn, and Hattie. They moved to Missouri Mar. 28, 1868. 3. Gwin m. Nancy Eliza Smith, Jan. 21, 1833, and had issue: Lucy Mary, Thomas, Gillie Ann, Gwynn Tyler, and Nancy Eliza. Lucy Mary m. William Hunt, and went to Missouri ca. 1855. They had 2 sons; Alonza and James. Thomas m. Lucy Smith, while he was in the Confederate A my, and had issue: Eliza, Sallie, and Thomas Early. Gillie Ann m. William Bernard of Union Hall, and had issue: Gwynn Tyler, Cora Lee, William Frank, Andrew Thomas, Fannie, Belle Rivers, and Feranda Pink. Gwynn Tyler m. Ann Holland, Sept. 5, 1865, and went to Missouri in 1868. They had 3 daus.: Nannie Bet, who m. John W. Divers; Lucy Mary, who m. Gwynn Tyler Bernard; and Cora Lee who never married. Nancy Eliza m. Benjamin Board, and had issue: Willie, Henry, Gwynn Tyler, Lulie, Ama, Eudoxie, Nellie, Tom, Major and Claud. 4. John Dudley m. Jane Perdue July 6, 1840, and had issue: Fannie, who m. Richard Hamner; and Sparrel, who m. Frances Holland, and had Tom, John Peter, and Henry Dudley of Rocky Mount.

II. James Dudley, son of Gwin and Mary (Hale) Dudley, m. Katie Beasley, and had issue: 1. William m. Frances Dudley, Mar. 6, 1846; 2. Robert m. Nancy Dudley (a dau. of Levi), and had issue: Otey, Jim, and William; 3. Fannie, m. Benjamin Robinson; 4. James A., m. Mary F. Dudley, Oct. 6, 1845; and 5. Julia Ann, m. John R. Robertson, Oct. 18, 1858.

III. Stephen Dudley, son of Gwin and Mary (Hale) Dudley m. Pattie Kemp, dau. of Thomas and Esther Kemp, on Mar. 2, 1812. His will, dated Nov. 17, 1832, is of record in Will Book 3, p. 525. The inventory of his estate was taken November 17, 1832. Their children were: 1. Hopy A.; 2. Gillie S.; 3. Katherine M.; 4. Mary F.; 5. Harriet M.; 6. James Henry; 7. Silas J.; 8. Thomas W.;

1. Hopy A. m. Samuel A. Powell 7, 1833, and moved to Missouri. 2. Gillie S. m. Caleb Heptinstall, Oct. 10, 1839, moved to Bedford, and had issue: Silas, Julia, and Laura. 3. Katherine m. Isaac D. Brooks Oct. 1839, no issue. 4. Mary F. m. James A. Dudley, a cousin, Oct. 6, 1845, and had issue: Elvira, Ada, Julia, William, Mary, and James. 5. Harriet M. m. John Wm. Powell, removed to Wisconsin, thence to Montana. 6. James Henry m. 1st., Julia Ann Elizabeth Dudley, Oct. 31, 1848, and 2nd., Sue M. Goad. 7. Silas J. m. Ann Parke Smith, and had issue: (a) Pattie, who m. John Dickerson; (b) Oliver Witcher, who m. Lucy Estes, and had issue: Oliver Witcher Jr., who m. Marion Boatwright, and Estes, who m. Catherine James of Danville; (c) Henry; (d) Mollie, who m. Dr. Daniel D. Dickerson; (e) Victoria, who m. Shy Berger; and

(f) Hattie, who became the 2nd. wife of Dr. Dan Dickerson.

      IV. Levi Dudley, son of Gwin and Mary (Hale) Dudley, m. 1st., Polly Kemp, dau. of Thomas Kemp, on Mar. 27, 1802, and had issue: (1) Peyton; (2) Nancy; (3) Thomas; (4) Betty.

      (1) Peyton, m. Elizabeth Gilbert, and had issue: Thomas, Robert, Jimmy, Tee, Emma, and Olivia. Thomas d. young; Robert m. Emma Lovelace and had issue: Ella, Hattie, Pearl, Ollie and Otha; Jimmie m. Dink Dudley, dau. of Samuel and Lucinda Holland Dudley, and had issue: Eugie Della, Arthur, and Ila; Tee m. Sarah Pasley granddaughter of Solomon Pasley, and had issue: Clifford, Clarence, Claud, and Clarice; Emma m. Dr. Reuben Simcoe, and had issue: Vernie and Pearl; Olivia m. Henry Clay Dean Halley, and had issue: Ethel, Earl, Henry Clay Dean, Jr., Thomas Peyton, and a dau. who d. infant.

      (2) Nancy m. Robert Dudley, son of James and Katie Beasley Dudley, and had issue: Otey, James and William.

      (3) Thomas, m. 1st. Temperance Heptinstall, Aug. 7, 1826, and 2nd. Lydia A. Cundiff.

      (4) Betty, m. Samuel Pasley, and had one dau. Laura, who m. Charles Hamilton, and had two daus. Victoria and Lucy.

      Levi Dudley m. 2nd. Elizabeth Gilbert, Jan. 2, 1817, and had issue: (5) Ursula; (6) Samuel; (7) Stephen, and (8) Lucy.

      (5) Ursula m. Oliver Perry Divers, Sept. 2, 1839, and had issue: Peyton Dewitt, b. Nov. 8, 1841, m. Henriette Hudson, Dec. 19, 1867; Gillie Anne, b. Nov. 13, 1843, m. Henry Clay Chitwood; Thomas Jarvis Gilbert, b. Feb. 3, 1846; Samuel Lee, b. Sept. 9, 1840; Peter Tilmond, b. Apr. 7, 1847; William A., b. Aug.27, 1849; Elizabeth Mary, b. Oct. 9, 1851; and Oliver Perry, b. June 10, 1854.

      Peyton Dewitt Divers, m. Henrietta Hudson, Dec. 19, 1867, and had issue: Alice Lee, b. Dec. 12, 1868, m. Rev. James O. Shelburne; Oliver Perry, b. May 29, 1870; Charles P., b. May 2, 1872, m. Bessie Lockhart; Ursula Anne, b. Mar. 15, 1874, m. Samuel H. Simpson; Mary Frances, b. 1875, m. Robert L. McNeil; George Thomas, b. Aug. 8, 1881, m. Evelyn Martin; Sallie Holland, b. Dec. 5, 1885, m. Nathan B. Hutcherson; Emma Gilbert, b. Dec. 25, 1887, m. Cephas G. Shelburne; Henrietta Bernard, b. Aug. 1890, m. Wiley R. Davis; and Douglas Shelburne, b. Aug. 1892, m. Lucretia Flansburg.

      Gillie Anne Divers m. Henry Clay Chitwood, and had issue: Squire, Dr. E. T., Joseph H., Herbert, Oliver Perry, Jarvis, and Cora Elizabeth

      (6) Samuel Dudley m. Lucinda Holland, Jan. 19, 1846, went to Missouri, and had issue: Fannie, Mary, Sallie, Dink and Willie. Mary m. Peter Kemp, son of Dudley Kemp; Sallie m. a Hol-

land; Dink m. James Dudley, son of Peyton Dudley; and Willie d. at 21.

(7) Stephen Dudley, m. Charlotte Heptinstall, Feb. 3, 1834. Issue: Doc. Bob, George, Riley, Sarah, Amanda, Emily, Mary and Nettie.

(8) Lucy m. William Wright.

V. Elizabeth Dudley, probably a dau. of Gwin and Mary (Hale) Dudley, m. Stephen English, Jan. 3, 1791. John Hale signed the marriage bond with Stephen English. There are records of Gwin D. English probably a son of Elizabeth Dudley and Stephen English.

Thomas Dudley, son of Levi Dudley and Polly Kemp, was b. Sept. 3, 1804, and acquired considerable means by trading lands and horses. He was called "Trading Tom". He d. Jan. 7, 1883, and is buried near Old Glade Hill. His 1st. wife was Temperance Heptinstall, dau. of Caleb and Tege (Greer) Heptinstall. She was b. July 11, 1805, d. Nov. 30, 1857, and is buried at the Old Dudley place near Scruggs.

Caleb Heptinstall and Tege Greer were m. Nov. 7, 1796. he served in the Revolution. His record is in the Virginia State Library ("Revolutionary Soldiers Vol. 4., p. 213"). His will is recorded in Will Book 2, p. 621, Franklin Co. The will, made Oct. 30, 1824, was probated Dec. 6, 1824. In Will Book 3, p. 8, in the dower of Tege Heptinstall, recorded Mar. 7, 1825, she is called the widow of Caleb Heptinstall. Will Book 4, p. 171, Partition of Lands of Caleb Heptinstall, Oct. 1, 1832, names his children as follows: 1. Temperance, m. Thomas Dudley Aug. 7, 1826; 2. Ann m. Daniel Ferguson, Jan. 27, 1816; 3. Sophia m. John P. Ferguson, July 27, 1825; 4. Jenetta m. John G. Tate, May 21, 1827; 5. Julia Ann m. Jesse N. Tate Nov. 20, 1827, and had a son Caleb; 6. Charlotte m. Stephen Dudley, Feb. 3, 1834; 7. Thomas; 8. Rebecca; 9. Elizabeth, m. Banks Basham, May 5, 1810; and 10. William m. Permelia Phelps Dec. 7, 1819.

The children of Thomas Dudley and his 1st. wife, Temperance Heptinstall, were: 1. Mary Frances; 2. Tilmon P. L.; 3. William R; 4. Stephen O., b. Nov. 13, 1831, d. Dec. 19, 1831; 5. Julia Ann, b. Nov. 26, 1832; 6. Thomas O., b. July 4, 1836, d. Aprl 21, 1837; and 7 Amanda Angeline, b. Oct. 20, 1840.

1. Mary Frances Dudley m. Thomas W. Dudley, Dec. 17, 1840, and had issue: Tom, who d. at the age of 75; Peter, who m. Nelly Newbill; Mahlon, who d. at 16; Amanda; Mattie, who m. James Goode Saunders; Mary who m. Eff Poindexter; and Roxie who m. John Dudley, son of her uncle Bill.

2. Tilmon P. L. Dudley m. Mary E. Holland, Nov. 22, 1849, and had issue: Jim, m. a Miss Lynch; Bogie m. Sis Perdue; Davis, m. Millie Holland; Albert, m. Ida Holland; Laura, m. a

Miss McCall; Charlie, m. Gillie Ann Bennett; and Julia, m. Tom
Perdue.

3. William R. Dudley, (Bill) m. Fannie Kasey, and had
issue: 1. John, m. Roxy Dudley, his cousin, and their dau.
Mary Fannie m. Chapman W. Dudley; 2. James m. Betty Poindexter;
3. Lelia m. Alex Mattox; 4. Cora m. Lee Gills; 5. Jennie m. Ben
Sutherland; 6. Carrie m. Charlie Gills; 7. Blanche m. Tom English;
8. Harvey m. Susie Turner; and 9. Bogue d. at 18.

5. Julia Ann Elizabeth, b. Nov. 26, 1832 m. her cousin,
James Henry Dudley.

6. Amanda Angeline Dudley (Mandy) m. Cephas Poindexter,
and had issue: 1. Ella, who m. 1st, Silas Dudley, son of James
Henry and Julia Ann Elizabeth Dudley; 2. Emma, who m. Gillie Saunders; and 3. Forest.

Lydia M. Cundiff, 2nd wife of Thomas Dudley, was b. Jan.
20, 1844, and d. July 1, 1913. They had a son Walter, who d. at
5; and a dau. Loula Virginia (b. Sept. 15, 1871, d. Apr. 18, 1907)
who m. William B. Brown, son of Col. William A. Brown, and had
a dau. Doris Dudley who d. Jan. 1928. Julia Ann Elizabeth Dudley,
dau. of Thomas and Temperance (Heptinstall) Dudley was the 1st
wife of James Henry Dudley, son of Stephen and Pattie (Kemp)
Dudley. James Henry Dudley's father was a brother of Levi Dudley,
father of Thomas Dudley. Their mothers were sisters and daughters of Thomas Kemp.

Thomas Kemp served in the Revolution. His wife's name
was Esther as shown by a deed of Aug. 15, 1817, conveying 172
acres to James Dudley for $200.00. The first record of Thomas
Kemp in Franklin Co. is in connection with purchase of land there
in 1796. He d. there in 1831. Thomas Kemp, b. Nov. 14, 1761, m.
Esther, and had issue: 1. Polly, b. Dec. 1783, m. Levi Dudley,
Mar. 27, 1802; 2. Walter, b. Oct. 2, 1785, m. Catherine Hows-
man, Apr. 25, 1817; 3. Patty, b. July 31, 1787, m. Stephen Dudley,
Mar. 2, 1812; 4. John, b. July 18, 1789; 5. Jane C. b. Mar. 31,
1791; 6. Susannah, b. Nov. 21, 1792; 7. William b. Nov. 24, 1794,
m. Ardra English, Aug. 2, 1819; 8. Nancy, b. Oct. 12, 1796; 9.
Lucy b. Sept. 13, 1789; 10. Robert b. Oct. 12, 1800, m. Mary Holland, Nov. 17, 1823; 11. James b. Jan. 4, 1803, m. Nancy English,
June 5, 1820; 12. Joannah (?) b. Feb. 4, 1805; 13. Sarah W. b.
Feb. 25, 1811, m. Peter H. Holland, Feb. 1834. Thomas Kemp d.
prior to 1831, as the Administrators Account of his estate bears
that date in Will Book 4, p. 245.

James Henry Dudley, son of Stephen and Pattie (Kemp)
Dudley, b. May 1, 1828, lived near Scruggs, and later at Union
Hall. He was a merchant, Post Mater, Justice of the Peace, and
Confederate Soldier. He m. 1st. Julia Ann Elizabeth, dau. of
Thomas and Temperance (Heptinstall) Dudley, (b. Nov. 26, 1832,
d. Nov. 10, 1875) on Oct. 31, 1848. Henry F. English signed the
marriage bond with him. James Henry Dudley Sr., d. at Union Hall,

Dec. 12, 1905. His will, written Oct. 4, 1901, and probated Jan.
1, 1906, is in Will Book 25, p. 73. Gustave B. Dudley and A. M.
Dudley were executors of the will. The children of James Henry
Dudley and his 1st. wife, Julia Ann Elizabeth Dudley, were: 1.
Octavia Ann, b. 1850, d. 1861; 2. Eldridge M; 3. Stephen William;
4. Silas T.; 5. James Henry Jr.; 6. Gustave Beauregard; 7. Albert
McLeod; 8. Julius Kemper; 9. Emmitt Edgar; and 10. Willie Octavius.

    2. Eldridge M. Dudley, b. Apr. 26, 1852, d. Apr. 8,
1925. He was a merchant at Union Hall, removed to Bachelor Mo.
in 1884, thence to Auxvasse, where he operated a store and a mill,
and dealt in real estate. He m. Clara Angle (who d. Sept. 24,
1932), and had issue: Belle, who m. Walter Young, and lives at
Fulton Mo.; Joe H. who m. Elizabeth Murry, lives in Oklahoma City,
has 2 daus: Martha Lake and Joe Ann; Frank R., who m. Nancy____?.
has 3 children: Jane, Frank and John, and is pastor of Central
Presbyterian Church, Oklahoma City; Julia, who m. Tate McCue, has
2 daus: Marjorie and Frances, lives at Rector, Ark; Kate, who
m. Sam Boles, and lives at Glasgow, Mont.; Charles, who m. Emma
Tate Yates, has a dau. Jean Angle, and lives at Kansas City, Mo.;
and Doris Dean, who m. John Suggett, has 1 dau., Beth June, and
lives at Enid, Okla.

    3. Stephen William Dudley, b. May 17, 1855, d. July
7, 1861.

    4. Silas T. Dudley, (b. Mar. 5, 1857, d. June 5, 1892)
m. Ella Poindexter, and had issue: 1. Edgar; 2. Lena, who m. Frank
Hutcherson; 3. Gertrude, who m. Oscar Hutcherson; and 4. May, who
m. John Holland.

    5. James Henry Dudley Jr., (b. Jan. 13, 1859, d. Jan.
24, 1889(was a merchant at Glade Hill, m. Nannie Street, and
had issue: 1. Vernor; 2. Dr. Morton L., who m. Mary Dickinson,
and has 2 sons; Morton Jr., and Sherwood; 3. Dr. Harry G., who
m. Mabel Perkins, and has 4 children: Gordon, James, Ann and
Lois; and 4. Roy, who m. Grace Endicott, and lives in Missouri.

    6. Gustave B. Dudley (b. June 1, 1861, d. July 30, 1925)
m. Sallie L. Brown (b. Oct. 10, 1865, d. July 18, 1919), dau. of
Col. William A. and Susan (Finney) Brown, and had issue: 1. Ruby
Lewis, b. Nov. 23, 1884, attended the Classical Female Seminary
at Martinsville, and Woman's College in Richmond, m. J. E. Howard
of Caswell Co., N. C., Dec. 20, 1906; 2. Dr. William Brown, b.
Jan. 24, 1887, educated in Lynchburg College, Washington and Lee
University, and Medical College of Va.,m. Marian McCrary Moir of
Winston-Salem, Nov. 29, 1916, has 2 daus: Sarah Elizabeth, b.
Feb. 21, 1919, and Frances McCrary, b. Oct. 14, 1922; 3. Dr. Gu-
stave B. Jr., b. Nov. 14, 1892, educated in Washington and Lee
University, and Medical College of Va. m. Priscilla Humbert of
Clifton Forge, Dec. 6, 1922, and has 2 sons: Frank Humbert, b.
Aug. 25, 1923, and Samuel Calvert, b. Mar. 4, 1935; 4. Virginia
Spotswood, b. Oct. 15, 1897, educated in Bethany College, taught
in high schools of Beaver, Pa., Welch, W. Va., and Martinsville,

m. Samuel Stanhope Walker of Greenville, S. C., June 10, 1920, and has 2 children: Ann Spotswood, b. Apr. 25, 1925, and Lee Dudley, b. July 20, 1930. S. S. Walker came to Martinsville when his father, R. L. Walker, organized the Martinsville Cotton Mill in 1910. He was graduated from North Carolina State College at Raleigh (Textile engineering), and is now president of the Va. Underwear Company.

7. Albert McLeod Dudley, b. Dec. 23, 1862, d. Sept. 5, 1925, removed to Martinsville, and engaged in the tobacco, ice and coal business, m. Ada Hancock and had issue: 1. Albert H., m. Lillie Gaines; 2. Harvey, m. Laura Bartlett; 3. Corrie H., m. Virginia Sparks; and 5. Mabel, m. Charles W. Holt, and has a dau., Mabel Hancock Holt.

8. Julius K. Dudley of Danville, b. Dec. 26, 1864, only child of James Henry and Julia Ann Dudley now living, m. 1st. Ella Bernard, and had issue: 1. Ella, who m. Leon R. Drake of S. C. and has a son, Leon Jr.; 2. Bernard; and 3. Grady who d. young. He m. 2nd, Florence Parker, and had issue: 4. Emmitt Irvine, d. infant; 5. Carolyn d. infant; 6. Frances, d. infant; 7. Guy Rucker, who m. Ruth Boyles, and has issue: Guy, Joe, and Jane; 8. Wallace Lee; 9. James Nicholas; and 10. Elizabeth, who m. John J. Dratt of Caroline County.

9. Emmitt Edgar Dudley, b. Apr. 20, 1867, d. Mar. 14, 1934, m. Viola Love and had: Haddon, Emmitt, Lucille, Ernest, Gladys, Gerald, Howard, and Clara Belle.

10. Willie Octavus Dudley, b. Jan. 7, 1870, d. Jan. 4, 1892, while at college in Poughkeepsie, N. Y.

The 2nd. wife of James Henry Dudley, Sue M. Goad, b. Sept. 23, 1848, d. Nov. 17, 1922, had a son Chapman Walter Dudley, who m. a cousin, Mary Fannie Dudley, and had 2 children: Belle, who m. Ben Sutherland, and Lucille, who m. Jake English. Lucille d. in 1933.

THE EARLY FAMILY

The old Christ Church Register of Middlesex County gives the names of Thomas and Elizabeth Early; the name of their son Jeremiah, born 1705; his marriage in 1728 to Elizabeth Buford (born 1709); the birth of their son John in 1729; and death of his mother in 1716. Thomas Early was lost at sea, and little is known of him.

Elizabeth Buford was the daughter of Thomas and Elizabeth Buford of Lancaster County. The families of Early and Buford were friends, and when Jeremiah Early was orphaned at eleven years of age, Thomas Buford (later his father-in-law), became his guardian.

The nine branches that sprung from the marriage of Jeremiah Early and his wife, Elizabeth Buford, in their order, are as follows:

(1) John Early, of Orange, born 1729, married Theodocia White; died 1773.

(2) Jeremiah Early, of Bedford County, later Franklin County, born 1730; married first, Sarah Anderson, born 1732, died 1770; second, Mary Stith, born 1773.

(3) Sarah Early married William Kirtley, and moved to Boone County, Kentucky.

(4) Joshua Early, of Bedford, later Franklin County, born 1738, married Mary Leftwich. This Joshua Early was the famous Methodist Bishop, John Early, and of Capt. Joshua Early, Jr., who was killed in the War of 1812.

(5) Joseph Early, of Madison, County, Virginia, died 1784; married Jane _____; in 1776 was a First Lieutenant in the Revolutionary Army; and in 1783 was elected a member of the Virginia Legislature.

(6) Jacob Early, of Wilkes County, later Clarke County, Georgia, married (?) Elizabeth Robertson in Bedford County.

(7) Anne Early married Joseph Rogers, and moved from Madison County to Bryant's Station, Kentucky, in 1782.

(8) Hannah Early married Capt. John Scott, and moved in 1782 to Scott County, Kentucky, near Frankfort.

(9) Joel Early married Lucy Smith, of Culpeper County, and in 1792 moved to a large tract of land on the Oconee River in Georgia. He was the father of Gov. Peter Early of Georgia, and was a Lieutenant in the Revolutionary War. He was a delegate to the Virginia Convention of 1778. Early County, Georgia, was named in honor of Governor Peter Early.

Col. Jeremiah Early, of Bedford, later Franklin County, was the second son of Jeremiah Early and of his wife Elizabeth Buford. He was the Lieutenant in the French and Indian War; Captain of the Bedford militia in 1758; Colonel of militia in 1778; sheriff: and a justice of the peace of Bedford County from 1759 to 1779, when he died being then forty-nine years old. He was the proprietor of the Washington Iron Mines, which later became the property of his sons John and Jubal Early, of Franklin County. Col. Jeremiah Early had a family of eleven sons and daughters; the eldest, Jacobus, was a Captain of the county militia in 1781; his fourth son, John, was a delegate to the Virginia Convention of 1778. He made a visit to Georgia with the intention of purchasing property there but was taken ill, and died soon after his return to his home in Franklin County, leaving a widow and two very young sons, Joab and Henry, who were placed under the guardianship of Col. Samuel Hairston.

THE FERGUSON FAMILY

The first person of the name in Franklin County was Alexander Ferguson (1740-1817), who m. Mary, dau. of Capt. Thos. Parker. His name first appears on a return dated Fort Pitt March

17, 1778. It last appears on a muster roll dated Fort Pitt April
5, 1778. Bedford County records show he was living there April
22, 1782. When Franklin was formed, his home was cut off in the
new county. He supplied beef for soldiers of the Revolution.

Alexander Ferguson had sisters, Elizabeth, Margaret and
Mildred. He mentions nine children in his will.

Alexander Ferguson Jr., b. 1765, m. Nancy Wood, lived
at Lynchburg, and had a son, Thomas (1789-1870), who m. 1822,
Elizabeth Catherine Beaumont (1798-1833), dau. of Mathew Beau-
mont (1749-1803), son of Joseph of Yorkshire, Eng., and a dau.
Mary, who m. Anthony Simmons. An Old Bible at Redwood names
other children of Alexander Ferguson, Jr., as follows: Daniel,
James, Thaddeus and Stephen. Census records (1820) show Thomas
Ferguson had wife and 4 children. Stephen Ferguson m. Rhoda
Greer, had a dau. Elizabeth Greer, who m. Peter Louis Holland.
Their dau. Rhoda Ann, m. Guinn Dudley. Their dau. Ada Lucy Mary
Dudley, m. Tyler Bernard, and lived in Gannaway Co., Mo. Their
dau. Dula Bernard, m. Clayton Hook, editor of the Auxvasse (Mo.)
Review. Eldridge Marcellus Dudley m. Clarinda Emmaline Angle,
who was named for hergrandmother, Nancy Emmaline Lee, (m. Buford
Wills) dau. of Francis Ludwell Lee, who m. Sallie Moorman of
Bedford in 1804.

Eldridge Dudley was the son of James Henry Dudley and
Julia Mary Elizabeth Dudley, dau. of Thomas Dudley and Mary Hep-
tenstall. James Henry Dudley was a son of Guinn Dudley.

Elizabeth Parker Ferguson (b. 1768-1838), m. William
Smith (1752-1845), a soldier in the Revolution. They had 12
children: (1) Thomas, b. 1786; (2) William H., b. 1788; (3) Mary,
b. 1790, m. Kemwill Clement Gilbert; (4) Samuel, b. 1793, m. Julia Holland, dau. of Peter and Elizabeth Greer Ferguson (5) Frances, b. 1795; (6) Elizabeth, b. 1797, m. S. Poindexter; (7) Martha, D. , m. Thomas Holland, had dau. Julia, who m. James Alexander Ferguson of Culpeper Co., and had children: (a) Thomas;
(b) Femeretta, m. Lorenzo Gibson Waters (parents of Icland Waters
of Callaway Co., Mo.); (c) Oscar; (d) Ann, m. a Mr. Atkinson;
and (e) Bruce Ferguson; (8) Stephen Smith, b. 1802; (9) Susan,
b. 1806, m. Col. Field Allen Hancock of Jackson, Co., Ala.; (10)
Julia, b. 1808, m. John Craighead, settled in Callaway Co. Mo.;
(11) Sarah Parker Smith, b. 1811. m. her cousin, Wright Smith,
son of Henry Smith and Frances Burk, who came to Warren Co. Mo.,
in 1837; and (12) Nancy Smith, m. a Mr. Holland.

Kemwill Clement Gilbert, son of Michael Gilbert of Franklin Co., m. Mary Smith, ca. 1790. Their dau. Angeline, m. James
McCall of Callaway Co., Mo. Robert H. McCall m. Elizabeth Gilbert. They were parents of Dr. Greene Day McCall of Fulton, Mo.
Frances M. McCall m. Thomas Gilbert of Callaway Co., Mo.

Henry Heth, Captain of Independent Virginia troops in

the Revolution, m. a Miss Gilbert in Buckingham Co. in 1783. They were the parents of Sally Jane Heth (or Heath), who m. Edmund Smart, son of a Revolutionary soldier of Lynchburg.

Eli V. Ferguson, b. 1780, m. but had no issue at census of 1820. He represented Franklin Co. in the legislature 1881-2.

Daniel Ferguson, twin of Eli, b. 1780, m. 1806, Jemima Saunders. Eli and Daniel Ferguson are named in Alexander Ferguson's will of 1817, of record at Rocky Mount.

Stephen Ferguson, m. Margaret Turner, dau. of Micajah Turner, had 6 children.

Mary Ferguson, m. a Mr. Beard, had several children, and removed to Ky. The Shrewsbury, Beard and Dowell families are among her descendants.

Susannah Ferguson, m. a Mr. Short.

Martha Ferguson, m. a Mr. Donahue, and one of this family m. Keziah Saunders.

Daniel Ferguson, m. Jemima Saunders in 1806. She d. 1837. They had 10 children, 7 born in Franklin Co., and 3 in Montgomery Co. Mo., where they settled prior to 1824. Many of their descendants live in Missouri, some in Texas (near Arlington and Dallas), and others in Louisiana. A son, Dougald, d. young. Other sons, John, Joseph, Martyn (or Morton), and daughters, married into the Phelps, Clare, Coleman, Nunnelly, Punmill and Dodd families.

Jane Smith Ferguson, b. March 11, 1824, Montgomery Co. Mo., m. Feb. 23, 1842 David Jackson Ferguson, b. Jan. 16, 1824, in Nelson Co. He was the son of James B. and Rachael (Matthews) Ferguson, a descendant of Colonial Governor Matthews, and was related to the Henry, Claiborne, Jackson, Lewis and Merriwether families.

William B. and David Ferguson, brothers, and Robert Bolling Ferguson, a son of Maj. James Boswell and Sallie (Gay) Ferguson, of Goochland Co., settled in St. Louis, Mo., ca. 1840. Robert Bolling, d. in St. Louis. David removed to Central, Mo., ca. 1842, and m. Jane Smith Ferguson. William B. lived near St. Louis for several years, and was the founder of Ferguson, Mo., to which he gave 10 acres. He m. Louise Watson Ferguson, sister of David Jackson Ferguson.

Rachael, m. Morton Ferguson, brother of Jane Smith Ferguson of Montgomery Co., Mo.

Jane Smith Ferguson was named for her Uncle William Smith, who m. Frances, dau. of Samuel Burke of Hanover Co. Frances Burke's sister, Elizabeth, m. Dr. William Cabell, a physician of Henrico County.

James, m. Susan Bowen, had 8 children, two of whom were named for Robert E. Lee. One died young, and another became a Baptist minister. One son bore the name Milton.

David, m. Margaret (Peggy) Punmill. Their youngest dau. Alice, m. R. L. Morgan, has 5 children, and lives in Shreveport, La.

The old Ferguson home in Goochland Co., was called "Fairfield". The family intermarried with the Burwells and the Marshalls. James Ferguson, who m. Judith Eldridge, was probably a brother of John Ferguson, who m. Anne Green, though some claim he was a brother of John B. Ferguson, who m. Mildred Marshall Wright. He had a brother, Abraham, who m. Nancy Smith, and moved to Fayette Co. Ky.

David Jackson Ferguson was a Baptist minister. His son, James Taylor Ferguson, was a minister of the Disciples Church. Bible records, show David and Jane (Smith) Ferguson had 14 children: Elizabeth, Evelyn, Amanda, Nancy Ellen, James Taylor, John William, Joseph Morton, Rachael Jane, Sally Ann, Leonard David, Segiùs Frances, infant (unnamed), Mary Rebecca, and Henry Clay.

Rev. James T. Ferguson, m. 1st, Margaret, dau. of Marmaduke and Elizabeth Scott Dallas, of Pittsylvania Co. in 1868, (no descendants), and, 2nd, Betty Laughlin, 1886. Of the 2nd marriage there were 4 sons: Arthur Duke, Austin Victor, James Taylor and Guy V.

Arthur Duke Ferguson, physician of Fulton, Mo., recieved his degree of MD in 1906, and has served as the president of the Callaway Co. Medical Association. He was m. in 1901 to Adah Redden, dau. of James Walker and Sarah (Hays) Redden of Callaway Co. She was educated at William Woods College, is a member of the State Genealogical Commission, has compiled and published two volumes of county historical records. Their dau. Margaret Adele, m. J. R. Henderson, of Jackson, M., has two children, John Robert and Carolyn Margaret, publishes "The Bard", a poetry magazine, and writes poems and short stories.

Austin Victor Ferguson, m. Brooxie Hunt, and had issue: Frances (who m. E. Snodgrass), Otho G., Mary Margaret, and Darrell.

James Taylor Ferguson III is a Kansas City physician. He frequently supplies Disciple pulpits there. He m. Carrie McCaskey of Columbia, Mo. She was the first National President of the Federated Council of Church Women, and represented the Council at Oslo, Norway, in 1936. They have 2 sons: J. Harry of the United

Press, New York City, and J. T. III, who won his M.D. degree
in 1936. The former m. Frances Meredith Marriner of North
Carolina, has a dau. Julie.

Rev. Guy V. Ferguson, is a minister of the Disciples
of Christ. He m. Mary Turpin, in 1903. She died leaving 2
daughters: Mrs. Thomas Fry of California, and Mrs. Stephen
Sumner Bagley of St. Paul, Minn.

Many citizens of Missouri are descendants of Franklin
County families. Among them the Gilberts, Bells, McCalls, Dud-
leys, Smiths, Lees, Randolphs, Walkers, Heaths, Marshalls, Gib-
sons, Byrds, Harveys, Carringtons, Browns, McAfees, Pasleys,
Poindexters, Bryants, Greers, Eldridges, Burwells, Beauchamps,
Stevens, Bakers, Diggs, Harts, Smiths, Carltons, Moores, Samuels,
Browns, Overtons, McIntires, Andrews, Dixons, Moormans, Lynchs,
Smarts, Leftwichs, Hopkins, Whartons, Watsons, Bedfords, Mackeys,
Harrisons, Carters, Saunders, Coles and Hunters.

Mr. Ovid Bell, author of local histories and a publisher,
is from the Bell and Gilbert families. Dr. E. B. Craighead, one-
time President of Tulane University, was descended from the Smith
and Craighead families.

THE FINNEY FAMILY

John, Peter and Zack Finney, brothers, with their sister,
Nancy, came from Amelia County, by way of Pittsylvania County, and
settled in Franklin County about 1790.

John Finney was born September 17, 1774, and married
Elizabeth Prunty (called "Polly" in the marriage bond) January
18, 1802. There were nine children of this union: John, Thomas,
Franklin, Robert, Joshua, William, Nancy, Betsy, and Polly.
At the death of Elizabeth, John Finney married Susannah Mitchell
(November 17, 1824). They had two children: Marshall and Jane.
John Finney died June 18th, 1844, and was buried near Mt. Bethel
Church.

Zack Finney, born ca. 1776, married Sarah Jane Brown
on December 7th, 1821. They had eight children: Jackson, Sanford, Zack Jr., George, Betsy Ann, Dolly, Jane and Caroline.

Jackson (full name William Andrew Jackson Finney) married a Miss Muse. He represented Pittsylvania County in the
Virginia Legislature in 1874-75.

Sanford Finney married Mary Swanson, daughter of Francis and Frances Chattin (Muse) Swanson, of the family which later
produced Senator Claude A. Swanson.

In Pittsylvania County Will Book 2, on page 468, is recorded the will of Mrs. Frances Chattin Muse Swanson, devising property to her daughter, Mary A. S. Finney, and her grandson, Frances W. C. Finney, and appointing Sanford R. Finney executor. In Franklin County Deed Book 30, page 374, is recorded a deed from Dudley S. Muse, his wife, to "F. W. C. Finney, S. R. Finney and Mary A. Finney, children of Sanford R. Finney, deceased, being the land heired by children aforesaid from the estate of Zachariah Finney."

Zack Finney, Jr., died unmarried.

George Finney married a Miss Frith.

Betsy Ann Finney married her cousin, John Finney.

Dolly Finney married John Smith.

Jane Finney married John Ward.

Caroline Finney married Bolin Brown.

Peter Finney, one of the four who came to Franklin from Amelia, was born ca. 1778, and married Ann Walker ca. 1818. They had three children: Wesley L., Louisa Walker and Charles C.

Wesley L. Finney married his cousin, Martha C. Finney, on October 30th, 1846.

Louisa Walker Finney married Charles C. Lee on October 13th, 1835, and had a son, William Peter Francis Lee, who inherited the brick house which Charles C. Lee built on his large plantation in the upper Snow Creek Valley. W. P. F. Lee generally known as Captain Lee, married Nannie Susan Barrow, and had six children: Charles B., Robert R., Lula Watkins, Annie Page, William Ludwell, and Nannie Susan. The two sons first named became prominent physicians.

Ann Finney, daughter of Peter, was the first wife of Robert Prunty. They were married May 17, 1845. She died about 1850, leaving a son Robert.

Nancy Finney, who came with her three brothers from Amelia to Franklin County, was born ca. 1780, and married Jesse Prunty on March 18th 1802. They had seven children: John, Thomas, Robert, Elizabeth, Jane, Jesse and Frances.

John Finney, son of John and Elizabeth (Prunty) Finney, was born in 1803, and married Frances, daughter of John and Mary (Love) King. They had six children: Mary, Sally Ann, James L., John, Jacob and Babe. Mary married Frank Fralin. Sally Ann married William T. DeShazo, and died on January 4, 1922, aged 87 years. James L., married Susan Napier. John was killed at the Battle of Seven Points. Of Jacob and Babe, no information. John and Frances (King) Finney lived on Snow Creek, where he manufactured tobacco for many years. He died in 1883.

Of Thomas Finney, son of John and Elizabeth (Prunty) Finney, no data.

Franklin Finney, son of John and Elizabeth (Prunty) Finney, was born ca. 1808, married, and settled, presumably, in the area now embraced by Estill and Madison Counties in Kentucky.

Robert Finney, son of John and Elizabeth (Prunty) Finney, married Mary Morris, and settled in Kentucky near his brother Franklin.

Joshua Finney, son of John and Elizabeth (Prunty) Finney, was born June 15, 1812, and married Carolina Staples. They had two children: Mollie and George. George was a prominent business man in Danville, Va., and died in Florida ca. 1880. Joshua Finney's home was in the western part of Henry County, where he died April 20, 1856.

William Finney, son of John and Elizabeth (Prunty) Finney, married Ruth, daughter of Jacob Clark of Patrick County, and settled near Ridgway, later removing to Martinsville, where he died in 1890. Their children were Molly, Annie and Carrie. The last named married Charles J. Angle of Greensboro, N. C.

Nancy Finney, daughter of John and Elizabeth (Prunty) Finney, married John Bondurant on November 4th, 1828.

Of Betsy Finney, daughter of John and Elizabeth (Prunty) Finney, no information.

Polly Finney, daughter of John and Elizabeth (Prunty) Finney, married George Napier.

Marshall Finney, son of John Finney by his second marriage to Susannah Mitchell, married Mary East, and had three children, Annie, Callie and John J. Annie married William D. Hill; Callie married Polk Mills; and John J. married Mattie Philpott. Marshall Finney died April 17th, 1864, and is buried near Mt. Bethel.

Jane Finney, daughter of John Finney and his second wife, Susannah Mitchell, married Mr. Thomas, and lived near Mt. Bethel.

Other members of the Finney family whose marriage bonds are in the Clerk's office of Franklin County, but who do not appear in the foregoing genealogy, are: Nancy Finney and Alexander Dunn, February 10th, 1824; Riley Finney and Ellender Slone March 27, 1793; John Finney and Ruth Smith, Sept. 2, 1805; Lewis Finney and Elizabeth Stuart, Feb. 5, 1808; Amos Finney and Elizabeth Wingfield, Jan. 6, 1834.

Members of the Finney family were near the present Frank-

lin County area before the first county had been formed from
Amelia. Thomas Finney was a witness for John Stuart in a land
transaction in 1738. In 1746 he conveyed to William Harris,
overseer of "Finnywood", several pieces of land. It is thought
that the four members of the Finney family who came to Franklin
about 1790 were grandchildren of Thomas Finney of "Finnywood."

THE FISHBURN FAMILY

Note: The following was taken from a letter from
Junius Blair Fishburn to Junius Parker Fishburn, dated Feb.
2, 1926.

Until I found an old book in an old secretary that was
willed to me by my uncle, John Robert Fishburn, at his death, which
happened in Texas July 20, 1886, while visiting there, none of us
knew anything about our great-great-grandfather, but from the information in this book as well as a letter written on Dec. 26, 1830,
by your great-great- great-grandfather, John Fishburn, we would
have known very little about the early Fishburns in this country.

First, I will start with John Fishburn, with the information written in his own handwriting in Dec. 1830, when living
in Allen Co., Ky. This information gives the date of his birth,
that of his wife, as well as his 9 children and 55 grandchildren,
44 of whom were living at that time (1830). This information is
written on 4 sheets of paper, still well preserved, with memoran-
dums on it, as well as a certificate in the little book in which
I found it, each of which verifies the other.

John Fishburn was b. Feb. 6, 1762. Susanna Kitterman,
his wife, was b. Mar. 2, 1760, and d. Nov. 27, 1826. He does not
state where either were born, but he was supposed to have been
born in Lancaster Co., Penn. as that was all the information we
had from my grandfather. They were m. Mar. 12, 1782, and the
record does not say where. He lists the following as his children:
1. Peter b. Jan. 9, 1783
2. Jacob b. Mar. 25, 1785 (your great great grandfather)
3. Frederick b. Nov. 19, 1786
4. Mary Anna . b. July 2, 1788
5. Christina b. Feb. 22, 1790
6. Christopher b. Feb. 12, 1792
7. Elizabeth b. Jan. 19, 1794
8. Barbara b. Dec. 19, 1795
9. Mary Magdalene b. June 10, 1798 (d. June 11, 1798)

The following is a list of the grand children of John
and Susanna Fishburn, I am copying it just as he had it.

Child	Grandchild
1. Peter	Susanna b. July 4, 1806, d. Oct. 1821
2. Peter	John b. Dec. 19, 1807
3. Frederick	Elizabeth b. Mar. 21, 1808

```
 4. Peter        Mary Ann b. Oct. 11, 1809
 5. Frederick    Susanna b. May 11, 1810, d. Aug. 22, 1829
 6. Peter        Jacob b. Nov. 5, 1810
 7. Jacob        Samuel b. Jan. 25, 1811
 8. Anna         Henry Huffman, b. Dec. 29, 1811
 9. Peter        George Harger, b. Sept. 5, 1812
10. Jacob        Elizabeth b. July 2, 1813
11. Frederick    Mary Ann b. July 2, 1813
12. Christopher  Smith b. July 22, 1813, d. Feb. 10, 1818
13. Peter        Nancy Hail b. Apr. 14, 1813
14. Anna         Peter b. Apr. 15, 1814, d. May 12, 1814
15. Christina    Susanna Kittaman b. Feb. 8, 1815
16. Christopher  Anna b. Apr. 27, 1815
17. Anna         Jemima b. Oct. 10, 1815
18. Frederick    Christina b. May 30, 1816
19. Peter        Elizabeth b. July 1, 1816
20. Christopher  Elizabeth b. May 23, 1817
21. Christina    John b. June 23, 1817, d. Sept. 23, 1820
22. Anna         Susanna b. Aug. 18, 1817
23. Peter        Channey Harrison b. Mar. 1, 1818
24. Elizabeth    Lavena b. Feb. 15, 1818
25. Barbara      Susanna b. Jan. 12, 1819
26. Christopher  Patsy b. June 18, 1819
27. Frederick    John b. July 1, 1819
28. Anna         Elizah b. Sept. 6, 1819
29. Peter        Henry Kittaman b. Feb. 18, 1820, d. Mar. 6, 1820
30. Elizabeth    Smith b. Feb. 18, 1820 d. Oct. 1822
31. Barbara      George b. May 1, 1820
32. Jacob        Susanna b. Sept. 30, 1820
33. Anna         Martha b. Dec. 13, 1821
34. Barbara      John b. Jan. 11, 1822
35. Christopher  Wesley b. Jan. 29, 1822
36. Christina    had a son b. Dec. 17, 1821, d. Dec. 17, 1821
37. Elizabeth    Christopher b. Sept. 6, 1822, d. Sept. 19, 1822
38. Christina    Nathan b. Jan. 27, 1822
39. Barbara      Joseph b. Dec. 22, 1823
40. Christopher  Susanna b. Mar. 7, 1824
41. Frederick    Barbara b. Mar. 21, 1824
42. Anna         John Fishburn b. June 12, 1824, d. June 11, 1826
43. Christina    Sealy b. Oct. 4, 1824
44. Jacob        Sarah b. May 14, 1825, d. May 15, 1825
45. Barbara      Milley b. Dec. 30, 1825
46. Christopher  Wilson b. Mar. 15, 1826
47. Anna         David Boman b. July 6, 1826
48. Jacob        Mary Ann, b. Aug. 11, 1826
49. Frederick    David Bhealer b. Sept. 4, 1826
50. Barbara      Mary Ann b. Mar. 22, 1828
51. Anna         Elizabeth b. May.14, 128
52. Christopher  Bluford b. July 12, 1828
53. Frederick    Jacob b. Feb. 22, 1829
54. Jacob        Peter b. Jan. 5, 1829
55. Barbara      Elizabeth b. Apr. 20, 1830
56. Anna         Jacob. b. Aug. 18, 1830
```

While I am not sure it looks like John Fishburn might

have been the son of John Phillip Fishburn, Sr., who was born
in 1722, and came to America in 1749, and died in 1795. Or it
is possible he belonged to one of the children of Phillip, Jr.,
who was married twice, and had 18 children, who scattered all
over this country.

Jacob Fishburn, (sometimes called John Jacob Jr.),
son of the above John, (who was sometimes called John, Sr.), was
b. Mar. 25, 1785, and d. Oct. 1, 1844 in Franklin Co., Va. He
lived in Franklin Co., and married Ann Wagner. I have under-
stood that they had the following children:
1. Betsy, who m. a Dent. She has a dau. Betty now living
in Detroit.

2. Samuel, who m. Frances Tinsley, Mar. 28, 1832. (Your
great-grandfather). Frances Tinsley was b. Dec. 24, 1811.

3. Susan, who m. a Graham of Floyd Co.

4. Mary, who m. a Stephenson of Floyd Co., and had 1 child-
Rosa Birchfield, who m. a Whitescarver (now living in Salem and
Roanoke). One of the Whitescarver girls married a Mr. Ray Dou-
that, at present living at 1214 Hamilton Terrace, Roanoke.

5. Peter, (the youngest) who m. and went to Tennessee to
live, and there are several children and grandchildren now living
near Knoxville, Tenn.

Samuel Fishburn, your great-grandfather, who m. Frances
Tinsley Mar. 28, 1832, lived in Franklin Co., and died in Big
Lick, Va., Feb. 12, 1879. Frances, his wife, d. in Roanoke, Aug.
14, 1900. They had the following children:
1. Jacob W. b. Feb. 4, 1833, d. Feb. 12, 1883, in Texas.

2. Reuben Harvey b. Feb. 27, 1835, d. Apr. 26, 1914, in
Roanoke.

3. Ferdinand Blair, b. Aug. 20, 1836, d. in Camp Chase, O.,
during the War where he was a prisoner.

4. Benjamin Bailey b. Aug. 12, 1838, d. Nov. 15, 1857

5. James Addison (your grandfather) b. Mar. 18, 1840, at
Sydnorsville, Franklin Co., d. in Roanoke, Jan. 3, 1921, at 714
Campbell Ave.

6. Elizabeth Jane b. Jan. 10, 1842, now living on Tenth
St. as Mrs. J. A. Woody.

7. Peter Hopkins b. Jan. 1, 1844, d. at Floyd Courthouse Jan.
26, 1884. (Meth. Minister)

8. Susan Emeline b. Feb. 14, 1846, d. July 7, 1909, in Roanoke.

9. Amarilla Ann b. Mar. 4, 1848, d. Sept. 11, 1918, in Franklin Co.

10. Tipton Lewis Tinsley b. Nov. 20, 1849, d. in Roanoke April 11, 1921.

11. John Robert b. Oct. 31, 1851, d. July 20, 1886, near Mexia, Texas.

12. Junius Lee (after whom I was named) b. Dec.14, 1853, d. near Sydorsville Aug. 20, 1858.

Your grandfather, James Addison Fishburn, was b. Mar. 18, 1840, m. Mary Louise Harriett Boone, of Boones Mill, Va., Sept. 13, 1864. She was b. June 3, 1845, at Boones's Mill, Franklin Co., and d. Roanoke Sept. 1, 1922, the dau. of Fleming Boone and Susan Kinsey Boone. The following are their children:
1. Junius Blair b. Sept. 27, 1865 about 1 mile west of Boones Mill at the old Boone home. Married Theresa Grace Parker, in Cleveland Tenn., Sept. 5, 1895, now living at 726 Thirteenth St., Roanoke. She was b. July 10, 1874, in Cleveland, Tenn., the dau. of John Henegar Parker, a banker, and Mary Kezia (Smith) Parker.

2. Minnie Tinsley b. July 4, 1867, 1 mile south of Perryville, Ky., on the east side of the creek on a hill at the covered bridge, at the old James Tinsley home, where our father and mother were living at the time. Married Edward L. Stone in Roanoke, Va. Apr. 10, 1890.

3. Emma Elizabeth b. Apr. 10, 1869, Mitchelsburg, Ky., at the old Fishburn home on the hill just west of the station. Married J. Harry Girvin in Roanoke, Apr. 16, 1901.

4. Susan Frances b. Dec. 9, 1870, at same place. Married Rev. W. J. Prout.

5. Mary Louise b. Dec. 8, 1872, at same place.

6. Ernest Boone b. Oct. 4, 1874 at same place. Married Anne Davant in Roanoke.

7. Charles Robert b. Jan. 7, 1877 at Rolling Fork, Ky. about 4 miles south of Mitchellsburg. Married Judith Marshall in Roanoke.

8. Walter Deering b. May 30, 1880 in Danville, Ky. south side of Main St., west of Fourth, m. Lillian Rhodes Snapp.

9. Harry Proctor b. May 4, 1882 in Big Lick, Va. on Water St. near tobacco factory, married Frances Butterfield in Moscow, Idaho.

The following are the children of Junius Blair Fishburn:

Junius Parker Fishburn b. Sept. 30, 1895 at 727 Thirteenth St., Southwest, now the Shull home. Married Katherine Rhodes

Nelson Jan. 14, 1926, at 2nd. Pres. Ch. in Roanoke.

      Mary Evelyn Fishburn b. Mar. 6, 1898 at 777 Thirteenth St., S. W. Roanoke, next door to birth place of Junius Parker. Married George Scott Shackelford, Jr., of Orange Va., Feb. 26, 1927, at 726 13th St., S. W., Roanoke.

      Ernest Louise Fishburn b. Aug. 10, 1900, same place.

      This brings a direct line from John Fishburn, 1762, down to your marriage last month. One of the old Fishburn Bibles was burned in a fire of one of the dwellings before the War, and the Boone Bible was burned in a fire about 1865, and not only the Bible was lost but also one of the children, Mildred, the dau. of Fleming Boone, and a sister of your grandmother Fishburn. She was about 12 years old.

      The Goode connection of the Fishburns you can find in the Virginia Cousins, starting with Amarilla Goode, mother of Frances Tinsley. Frances Tinsley was the wife of Samuel Fishburn, your great-grandfather.

      You will find the Tinsley connection in a copy of the Tinsley Genealogy, as we were connected with all the Franklin Co. Tinsleys. Your great-grandmother was a dau. of Willis Tinsley and a sister of Ben Tinsley, James Tinsley, Tipton Tinsley of Baltimore and others.

      There are quite a lot of relatives in the way of Goodes and Tinsleys in Ky. and Texas. Your grandfather, J. A. Fishburn, lived in Texas before the Civil War. After his marriage in 1864, he moved, in Jan. 1867, to Perryville, Ky., and lived at Perryville, Mitchellsburg, Ky., Rolling Fork, Ky., and Danville, Ky., until Dec. 1, 1880, when he moved back to Roanoke. He fought in the Civil War, as did all his brothers, on the southern side. You will also find that about 7 of the older boys fought in the Rev. War, as well as the War of 1812, and in the Mexican War of 1848. Most all of them were Democrats, and most of the older ones were raised Presbyterians. The first ones built Lutheran Churches at what is now Hershey, Penn. and a number of them are buried there. There are also two of the old stone residences standing yet.

      From Penn. the family came down the Valley of Va. and settled in Augusta Co. and Franklin Co. All of those who have "e" on their names added it about 1830 to 1850.

      Jacob Willis Fishburn was the first one to go to Texas prior to the Civil War. He was the oldest son of Samuel Fishburn. The family of Peter Fishburn that moved to Tenn. still lives out in that part of the country.

      As to your own father, I was Cashier, Pres., and Chairman of the Board of the National Exchange Bank for 37 years, and am now Chairman of the Executive Committee, and connected with a

number of other business enterprises of Roanoke, I am a member
of Greene Memorial Methodist Church. We have lived in Roanoke
since 1880, when it was Big Lick. We moved into our present
home on Oct. 8, 1908, 726 Thirteenth St., S. W. Roanoke.

THE GLASS FAMILY

Dudley Glass, Sr., (will dated Nov. 17, 1824, pro. in
Halifax Co., Oct. 22, 1827) m. 1st, Frances Priddy (Prideaux);
2nd, Sally _____. He served in Capt. Milner's Co., in the
Revolution. (See Halifax Co. Records, 1774-1777, and William
and Mary Quarterly of Jan. 1927, p. 60). In his will he names
wife, Sally and:

(1) Son, John Glass, who m. Maitland Simmons

(2) Dau. Frances Glass, who m. Thomas Lipscomb Ragland, of Halifax

(3) Dau. Molly Farmer

(4) Son, George Glass, and his four children: John S., Patsy Walner, Frankie Walner and Dudley.

(5) Dau. Judith Irby, and her children: John, Frankie, Polly, Patsy, Dudley, Betsy, William, Harrison and Sally Irby, who m. Thomas Martin

(6) Son, Dudley Glass, and

Annie Sparks, relationship not stated.

John Glass who m. Maitland Simmons, dau. of Thomas Simmons of Halifax Co., ca. 1800; moved from Halifax to Franklin, Dec. 13, 1815. John Brown and Sally, his wife, of Franklin Co., conveyed John Glass of Halifax Co., 400 acres on Island Creek, a branch of Pigg River, Apr. 1, 1816. He d. Oct. 19, 1840, in Franklin, on the homestead later bought by John Brown.

Issue:

(I) Dudley Glass, b. 1801, d. unm.

(II) Patience Glass, b. 1803, m. Jacob G. Machenheimer, brother of Gabriel, who, with his brother, came from Baltimore, Md., and settled in Franklin. Issue:

(A) Martha Patience Machenheimer, m. Robert Burrell Rives, b. in Franklin Co., and in Richmond in 1904. He was a Confederate soldier, and after the war went to Colorado. He lived there till 1902, and returned to Va. He is buried in Riverview Cemetery, Richmond. Issue:

(1) Jacob Joseph Rives, (b. Dec. 16, 1856, d. Nov. 24, 1920) m. Annie Page Collins, g.g.g. dau. of Patrick Henry. His widow lives in Lynchburg. Issue:

    a. Rosalie Henry, b. Aug. 24, 1899, at Halifax Courthouse.

    b. Martha, b. Jan. 11, 1901, d. in infancy.

    c. Page Lewis, b. Jan. 13, 1902, at Halifax Courthouse, m. David Hugh Oglesby, Mar. 12, 1921. Issue: David Hugh, b. Jan. 21, 1922; and Page Lewis, b. Sept. 29, 1925.

    d. Frances Josephine, b. Nov. 6, 1905 at Martinsville, m. William Robert Phelps, Dec. 26, 1923. Issue: William Robert, Jr., b. Nov. 30, 1922.

    e. William Burwell, b. Feb. 10, 1909, at Richmond.

    f. Elizabeth Lovelace, b. Dec. 31, 1911, at Halifax Courthouse.

(2) Frances Patience Rives, d. 1929, buried in Richmond, m. Alfred Sidney Herndon, (d. Apr. 17, 1907) of Pittsylvania. Issue:

    a. Mary Rives Herndon, b. Nov. 26, 1888, m. Morton Edward Sewall, Aug. 17. 1918. Issue: Morton Edward, b. Dec. 20, 1919; and Mary Belt; b. Aug. 15, 1924. Home: 526 London Ave., Baltimore, Md.

    b. Lewis Sidney Herndon, M.D., b. June 22, 1889, m. Eunice Stewart of Charlotte N. C., Mar. 22, 1917; educated in Medical College of Va.; served in World War; wounded at Soissons and in the Argonne; decorated; now practicing medicine at 33 Johnson Ave., Newark, N. J.

    c. Nancy Herndon, m. Dr. Thomas A. Lamb, of Richmond, in 1913. Issue: Rives Maupin Lamb, educated in Hampden-Sydney College. Home: Alexandria.

    d. Martha Herndon, m. Raymond H. Lee, at Richmond. Among issue: Frances Herndon Lee.

    e. Josephine Rives Herndon, m. Thomas Lee Newton, June 26, 1928, in Richmond. Home: West Point.

(3) Josephine Machenheimer Rives, m. John Thomas Haynes of Franklin Co. Issue:

    a. Winston Rives Haynes, educated V. M. I. University of Richmond, Medical College of Va., and

and George Washington University.
Practicing medicine at Silver Springs,
Md.

    b. Walter Machenheimer Haynes.

    (4) Lilly Machenheimer, d. in infancy.

(B) Susannah Machenheimer, m. Abram Booth Hancock,
2nd wife. No issue.

(C) Joseph Glass Machenheimer, d. unm. in Civil
War; buried in Hollywood Cemetery, Richmond.

(D) Nannie Machenheimer, d. unm.

(III) Amelia Glass, m. Coleman Bennett.

(IV) Judith Glass, b. Sept. 2, 1815, d. Franklin
Co., in 1839, m. William Swanson Muse, (b. Dec. 24, 1808).

(V) Frances Elizabeth Glass, b. 1807, d. Aug. 1897,
m. 1st, Moses Walkler, Apr. 20, 1830; m. 2nd, Ashford Keen (d.
Nov. 15, 1876). Issue by 1st marriage:

(A) Martha Elizabeth Walker, b. Sept. 8, 1832,
d. June 28, 1881, m. Col. Abram Booth Hancock,
Nov. 3, 1847, in Rockingham Co., N. C.

Issue by 2nd Marriage:

(B) Catherine Keen, m. William Machenheimer, son
of Gabriel Machenheimer.

(C) Julia A. Keen, m. Thomas Richard Hancock,
son of William Thomas Hancock.

(D) Sally Keen, d. unm.

(E) David Keen, m. a Miss Fuller of Danville.

(F) Charles Keen, m. and lived in the state of
Washington.

(VI) Martha Ann Glass, b. 1809, d. June 24, 1895.
In her 76th year she m. a Rev. Gray of Botetourt Co.

THE GOODE FAMILY

David Goode I, was born in Germantown, Pa., ca. 1740,
and died in 1819. He m. Elizabeth Waltz in Germantown. They
removed to Maryland, thence to Franklin County, in 1790, settling on

Chestnut Creek, near the present site of Providence Church, on the "Old Carolina Road". They were of German descent. Elizabeth Waltz Goode never learned to speak English. Most of the Goodes of the Valley of Virginia, and of Franklin, Craig, Patrick and Henry Counties are of Pennsylvania Dutch origin. The Goodes of Eastern Virginia are largely of English descent.

Jacob, Fountain and David G. Goode of (Waidsboro) Franklin Co. William P., George W. and Thomas H., were descendants of David Goode I. All of these, except Jacob, were the sons of David Goode II, while Jacob was the son of David Goode I.

David Goode I, made his will on May 23, 1812 (D. B. II, p. 276) and it was proven in a court held for Franklin Co., Aug. 3, 1819. He could have been a son of one of the Guth brothers who migrated from Germany to Pennsylvania in 1763, as it was only 27 years after this date that he was living in Franklin.

The tax records of Franklin Co. show David Goode and George Goode as land owners in 1792-1793. Valentine and Jacob Goode, sons of David Goode I, were land owners in 1794, and David Goode Jr., was a land owner in 1798.

The early Goodes were long-lived people. Several grandchildren of David Goode I, lived into the twentieth century. His son, David Goode II, b. 1776, died in 1862. Sally (Goode) Young, daughter of David II, b. ca. 1810, lived to be over 100 years old. Jacob, son of David I, was b. 1792, d. 1887. Jacob's son, David, b. 1819, d. 1910. Issue of David I, and Elizabeth Waltz Goode:

(1) George, b. ca. 1772, m. (1st) Ellen Davis, and (2nd) Sallie Williams.

(2) Elizabeth, b. 1774, m. (1st) _____ Peters, and (2nd) Ben Ray.

(3) David II, b. 1776, d. Nov. 8, 1862, m. (1st) Sallie Ramsey, (2nd) Malinda Miles, (3rd) Ruth Feazell, and (4th) Jane Tate.

(4) Valentine, b. 1777

(5) John, b. 1780, m. Jane Standley, d. in War of 1812.

(6) Samuel, b. 1782, m. Nancy Craig of Henry County.

(7) Catherine, b. 1785, m. _____ McCall.

(8) Nancy, b. 1787, m. Daniel Ramsey.

(9) Sally, b. 1790, m. John Adams.

(10) Jacob, b. 1792, m. (1st) Alice Mullins, and (2nd) Katherine Oxley.

(11) Mary Ann, b. 1794, m. Sam Altic.

(12) Jane, b. 1796, m. Abram Williams.

David Goode II, lived.near the present site of old Providence Church, and gave the land on which the church was built in 1833. Issue of David Goode II, by 1st marriage:

(1) Sally, m, Lewis Young.

By 2nd marriage:

(1) George Woodard, b. ca. 1825, d. in Mercer Co., W. Va., 1901 (twin) m. Julia Mason. Was member of Co. B., 57th Va. Regiment.

(2) Thomas Harvey, (twin) b. ca. 1825, m. Letitia King.

(3) David Gardner III.

By 3rd marriage:

(1) Martha, m. Maxey.

By 4th marriage:

(1) Henry Fountain Goode, b. 1833, m. (1st) Pattie Hankins, and (2nd) Emma Coleman.

(2) Jemima Goode, b. ca. 1840, m. Edward Harrison, and lived near Providence Church.

(3) Sue Goode, b. Jan. 10, 1842, d. Jan. 20, 1925, m. Rev. Gilbert Mason, b. 1830, d. 1910.

(4) William Patrick Goode, b. Nov. 22, 1844, m. Lindsey Oxley, living in 1934 in Confedrate Soldiers Home in Richmond.

(5) Lockey Goode, b. 1846, d. July 27, 1933, m. Richard Dillard of Franklin Co.

(6) Mary Goode, b. 1848, m. Ferdinand Stanley.

George Woodard Goode and Julia Mason had issue:

(1) Lewis, b. 1858, living at Athens, W. Va., had 9 children.

(2) Joseph, b. 1860, moved to Tenn. Had 5 children.

(3) Jennie, b. ca. 1862, m. E. M. Kanode. Had 9 children, lives at 411 Stanley Ave., Roanoke.

(4) Nannie, b. 1865, deceased.

(5) Mary, dec'd.

(6) Ida, b. 1867, dec'd. Had 5 children.

(7) George W. Jr., b. 1869. Lives at Gardner, W. Va.
Has 4 children.

(8) Tuemore, dec'd. Had 7 children.

(9) Minnie, never married.

(10) Adam.

(11) Bertie.

Thomas Harvey Goode and Letitia King, and their children, John Lewis, and Charles H., moved to Iowa.

David Gardner Goode III, b. in Franklin County, July 18, 1827, d. Mar. 5, 1900, m. Mary Frances Turner, b. Feb. 26, 1833, daughter of Meshach and Nancy (Martin) Turner of Franklin Co. He was a Confederate soldier. Issue of David Gardner Goode III, and Mary Frances Goode:

(1) Peter Leftwich, b. Feb. 5, 1853, d. 1924, m. Emma Woolwine.

(2) Fanny, b. 1855, m. Thomas McGhee of Franklin Co.

(3) William Gardner, b. Apr. 4, 1857, d. March 6, 1930. He m. Callie Bettie Williams (1859-1933) dau. of Wiley P. Williams of Franklin Co.

(4) Benjamin Meshach, b. Mar. 19, 1859, d. Jan. 6, 1922, m. Fannie Mildred Ross, b. Dec. 12, 1865, the dau. of Capt. Abram Burnett and Catherine (James) Ross of Henry Co.

(5) Joseph..Hamrick, b. Apr. 17, 1861, m. Martha Jane Eggleston of Henry Co. Lives at Bassett.

(6) David Henry IV, b. Apr. 29, 1863.

(7) Nannie Bettie, b. Dec. 14, 1865, d. 1934, m. Wiley P. Woody.

(8) Norman Soloman, b. May 7, 1868, m. Lula Davis. Lives in Henry Co.

(9) Florence, b. May 3, 1873, m. Ernest L. Scott of Franklin Co. Moved to Roanoke.

(10) Louisa, b. 1875, (dec'd) m. Pleasant Mason. No children.

Issue of Peter Leftwich and Emma (Woolwine) Goode:

(1) Mary, dec'd, m. _____ Tully had one child.

(2) Fred, dec'd.

(3) Emory, m. _____ Jones. They live in Fayette Co., West Va., and have several children.

(4) Grace, m. L. E. Huffman, Agent for Aetna Life Insurance Co., and lives at Charleston, W. Va. L. E. Huffman Jr. is a graduate of W. & L. University.

(5) William, lives in Washington D. C.

(6) Neva, m. _____ Jones.

(7) Effie.

Issue of Fanny Goode and Thomas D. McGhee:

(1) Minnie, m. Milton Goode, of Lanahan.

(2) Walter

(3) Wilmer, m. Miss Kirks, and has several children.

Issue of William Gardner Goode and Callie Bettie Williams:

(1) Olea, b. 1880, d. 1910, m. Guy Philpott.

(2) Pearl, b. 1881, dec'd. M. _____ Taylor, and had a son, Truman Taylor, who lives at Fieldale.

(3) William D., b. 1883, m. Blanche Wade, lives in Roanoke, has 3 children: William David Jr., Hilda and Frances.

(4) Lera, b. 1885, m. Will Ross of Patrick Co.

(5) Odessa, dec'd.

(6) Roy, dec'd.

(7) Selma, m. _____ Bryant, has 4 daughters: Mae, Edith, Lourine and Erma.

(8) Wharton, m. _____ Seay lives at Louisa, Ky. Children: Joy, Gay and A. W. Jr.

(9) Marvin, World War I Veteran, m. and lives in Pennsylvania.

(10) Gladys, m. Elijah Mullins, lives a Lanahan.

(11) Emory H., m. Virginia Self of Martinsville, has one child, Emory H. Jr.

Ross:

Issue of Benjamin Meshach Goode, and Fannie Mildred

(1) Benjamin Clifford, b. July 21, 1892, m. Mary Rebecca Williamson, daughter of Richard Silas and Maggie (Prunty) Williamson of Martinsville, on Nov. 24, 1932. They have one daughter, Mary Williamson Goode.

(2) Mabel Clare, b. Sept. 21, 1894, a public school teacher.

(3) Abram Maury, b. Apr. 21, 1897, m. Grace Eleanor Ramsey of Sydorsville, has a daughter, Margaret Eleanor Goode. He is postmaster and merchant at Henry.

(4) Virgil Hamlin, b. July 31, 1902.

(5) Frances Catherine, b. July 31, 1904, school teacher in Henry Co.

(6) Beatrice Augusta, b. Dec. 1907, was graduated from State Teachers College, Farmville, and is teacher in Fayette Co. West Va.

ton:

Issue of Joseph Hamrick Goode and Martha Jane Eggleston-

(1) Alzie, dec'd.

(2) Virgie, of Washington D. C.

(3) John Letcher, dec'd. m. Lucy Davis of Martinsville. Had 2 children: Ray and Dulce.

(4) Esther, dec'd. m. Clifford Shaw, an attorney of New Haven, Conn. Issue: 3 children.

(5) Dora, dec'd.

(6) Joseph, m. Miss _____ Crute of Farmville, lives at Alexandria. Mr. Goode has a government position, and Mrs. Goode teaches.

(7) Glenwood, m. Harry Lee Daughtery, of Bassett, has a son, Harry Lee, Jr.

David Henry Goode IV, m. Rosa Nutter, moved family to Oklahoma Territory in 1885, then to Olathe, Colo., where he now lives. He is a merchant and farmer. Children: Charley, Frank, and David, all business men of Orange, Cal.; and Esther and Thomas of Olathe, Colo.

Bassett:

Issue of Nannie Bettie Goode and Wiley P. Woody of

(1) Benjamin P., m. Lucy Stovall of Martinsville.

(2) Annie, m. Herbert Stone of Henry Co., has several children.

(3) Ernest, m. Miss Jarrett of Henry Co., (4) Mitchell, (5) Claude, (6) Russell, (7) Charlie, (8) Lula, m. Eggleston, (9) Pearl, (10) Mary, (11) Harold, and (12) Earl Woody.

Issue of Norman Solomon Goode and Lula Davis:

(1) Holmes Irving, in business in Bristol

(2) Lula Irene, m. Mr. Bowen, railway agent of Roxoboro, N. C.

(3) David Hurd, m. Catherine Jones of Martinsville, has 1 daughter, Ann Goode

(4) Hampton Gray, pharmacist

(5) Norman S. Jr., m. Mary Winn of Martinsville

(6) Mary Sue, m. Robert Via, of Franklin Co. Principal of Henry High School

(7) Harold D., m. Margaret Bruce French of Lumberton, N. C.

(8) Virginia Dare, student at Harrisonburg Teachers College

(9) Mildred, student in Martinsville High School.

Issue of Florence Goode and Ernest L. Scott:

(1) Charles D., (2) Garrett, (3) Ben Turner, (4) Eva, (5) Frances, and (6) Elizabeth

Issue of Henry Fountain Goode, Confederate soldier, by 1st m:

(1) Berta, m. Wash Ingram of Ferrum, and has serval children.

Issue by 2nd m.

(1) Milton, m. (1st) Maude McGhee, and m. (2nd) Minnie McGhee. Issue: Stafford and Sterling (twins). Issue, 2nd. m: Kyle Goode of Roanoke.

(2) Ryland, m. Maggie Ramsey, daughter of Thomas A. and Eliza (Pace) Ramsey. Issue: Grace, m. O. L.

Slayton of Draper N. C.; Clare, m. Harry G. Lea,
Rocky Mount; Frank, successor to his father in
the motor business at Rocky Mount; and Billy,
student at Rocky Mount.

Issue of Sue Goode and Rev. Gilbert Mason:

(1) Martha J. Mason, b. Oct. 29, 1857, m. J. W. Mc-
Ghee of Franklin Co., had issue: William H. Patrick, Rainey, India and Inez.

(2) W. H. Mason b. Dec. 12, 1859, m. Alice Jarrett, and
had issue: George, Walter, Bell, Raymond, Lucy and
Horace.

(3) Frances Mason, b. June 22, 1862, m. C. B. Pinkard,
and had issue: Ed, Susie, Mattie, Clyde, Forrest,
Noel, Bessie, Eva, Carrie, and Kenna.

(4) Pleasant B. Mason, b. Mar. 8, 1864, m. (1st) Lula
Coleman, and had issue: Myrtle, Taylor and Wil-
liam; m. (2nd) Louisa Goode. No issue; m. (3rd)
Virginia Pinkard, issue: Robert,

(5) Silas A. Mason, b. Aug. 8, 1868, m. Laura Mason,
had issue: Augusta.

(6) Dr. Elijah L. Mason, M.D., b. Feb. 23, 1871, m.
Viola Hines, lives in Washington D. C., has one
son, Jack.

(7) Lindsay P. Mason, b. July 2, 1874, d. July. 17, 1898.

(8) Nerva E. Mason, b. Feb. 19, 1877, m. Ollie Young,
had issue: Nora, Kennis, Harold, Edna, Wilda, Ola,
and Angie.

(9) Ezra Mason, b. July 16, 1881, m. Selma Moore, had
issue: Jewell and Jack. Home: Roanoke.

Issue of William Patrick Goode, and Lindsey Oxley:

(1) Madison David, of Griffithsville, West Va. Is a
merchant, farmer and teacher, and has represented
his district in the West Va. General Assembly.

(2) Virginia Tate, m. Carl Williams.

(3) Ella Franklin, m. Albert Henderson.

(4) Henry Franklin, Huntington, West Va.

(5) Florence, m. L. J. Ashworth.

(6) George Harvey

(7) Mary, m. E. H. Holstein.

(8) Martha Tate, m. Edward Harrison.

Issue of Lockey Goode, and Richard Dillard:

(1) Titus; (2) Annie, m. Chas. Angle; (3) Oliver;
and (4) Newton.

Issue of Mary Goode: George and Charlie Stanley.

Samuel Goode, son of David Goode I, lived near the
present town of Bassett, and had issue:

(1) Thomas, m. _____ Hill; (2) David, m. _____ Adams;
(3) George, m. _____ Edwards; (4) Samuel, m. Adeline
Davis; (5) Sally, m. Alfred Oxley; (6) Elizabeth, m.
Matt Edwards; and (7) Kate, m. Lewis Bowles. All 7
moved to Lincoln Co. W. Va.

Issue of George Goode, son of David Goode I, by 1st m.:

(1) Julia Ann, m. Jonas Goode, son of Jacob and Alice
(Mullins) Goode.

(2) Elizabeth, m. (1st) _____ Stover; m. (2nd) James
Stone.

(3) Lucinda, m. Emuel Yancey Gardner, and moved to
Carroll Co.

(4) Frances, m. William Turner, son of Mechach and
Nancy (Martin) Turner.

(5) Puss, m. James Gardner, lived in Carroll Co.

(6) Matilda, m. _____ Hall, moved to Carroll Co.

Deed Book XI, pp. 119, 175 and 243, records the names
of 3 daughters of Samuel Goode, Jr., as having sold their shares
in the estate of their father to Abraham Goode, son of David
Goode I and a brother to Samuel Goode, Sr. Children of Samuel
Goode Jr. are:

(1) Elizabeth, m. Peter Klingenpeel; (2) Catherine,
m. George Crider; and (3) Sarah, m. Samuel Kesler.

Elizabeth, daughter of David Goode II, was a widow in
1812 as she was mentioned as Elizabeth Peters in her father's
will of 1812. David Goode II, in his will, dated Mar. 4, 1851,
(D. B. VII, p. 288) refers to Elizabeth Ray's children.

Jacob Goode, son of David Goode and Elizabeth (Waltz)
Goode, was born in Franklin Co., m. Alice Mullins, and had issue:

(1) William, b. ca. 1816, m. (1st) Oxley; and (2nd)

Katie Oxley

(2) David, b. Feb. 7, 1819, d. Mar. 10, 1910, m. Nancy Thomas

(3) Mary, b. 1821, never married

(4) Sally, b. 1824, m. James Thomas, son of Nathaniel Thomas. Moved to Wyoming Co., W. Va.

(5) Ollie, b. 1826, m. Peyton Pearson of near Providence Church.

(6) Alice, b. 1827, m. William Whitlow

(7) Jacob, II, b. m. Mary McMillon

(8) Elizabeth, b. 1831, m. Alexander Moore

(9) Jonas, b. 1833, m. Julia Ann Goode, daughter of George Goode Sr., his first cousin

(10) Jane, b. 1835, never married

(11) Juda, b. ca. 1836, m. Ed Massey

William Goode, son of Jacob and Alice (Mullins) Goode, had issue:

(1) Lucy, m. (1st) _____ Thornton; and (2nd) ____ Byrd.

(2) Sarah, m. Thos. Thornton

(3) Thomas, m. (1st) _____ Oxley (no children); and (2nd) _____ Smith

(4) Marshall, m. (1st) Oxley; and (2nd) _____.

This family moved to Griffithsville, W. Va.

David Goode, son of Jacob and Alice (Mullins) Goode, b. in Franklin Co. He and his wife, Nancy Thomas (1821-1891), daughter of Nathaniel Thomas of Franklin Co., moved to Wyoming Co., W. Va. in 1855, where Pineville is now located. Issue:

(1) Letitia, b. 1842, d. 1926, m. Harvey Green. Children: Shadrach, David, Nancy T., Alice Joshua and Pierce.

(2) Anne, b. 1844, d. 1929, m. Greenbury Buchanan. A Union soldier. Children: William F., Isabel, Thomas W., Virginia and Cathie.

(3) Lemuel, b. Sept. 17, 1846, d. Feb. 15, 1919, m. Tabitha Ramey (1850-1898)

(4) Frances, b. 1848, d. 1925, m. James R. Cook, a Confederate soldier.

(5) Silas, b. Feb. 28, 1850, m. Nancy Short. Children: Robert, J. Ken., Everett, J. E., Gusta, Lake, Booker, Hannibal and Herbert. Home Pineville, West Va.

(6) Milton, b. 1851, d. 1932, m. Eliza Phillips, had issue: Wiley, David, Flora, Nancy and Biddie.

(7) Virginia, b. 1853, d. 1915, m. Elihu Green. Children: Juda, Ira, Charles, Epp, Mont, and Virgie.

(8) Levi (1855-1929), m. Sarah Mitchell. Children: Alex, James, David, Nancy, Ellen, George W., and Frances. George W. is principal of Hewitt High School.

(9) Fount (1859-1913), m. Mary Vandivort. Children: William Curtis, Lawrence, Roscoe, Joseph C., Clayton and Pearle.

Issue of Lemuel Goode and Tabitha Ramey:

(1) Rev. G. Pendleton Goode, b. Dec. 26, 1868, m. (1st) Lizzie Cook, daughter of Senator W. H. H. Cook; (2nd) Cornelia Vandivort; and (3rd) Ada Brooks. He was ordained to the Baptist ministry in 1900, taught school for 40 years in Wyoming Co., W. Va., was elected Secretary of the Wyoming Historical Society in 1925, and has written many articles on Wyoming County history and genealogy.

(2) George W. Goode (1870-1917), member of Wyoming Co. Court (1908-14), m. Sena Halsey, and had eleven children.

(3) Frank (1872) m. (1st) Elsie Cannaday; and (2nd) Martha Snuffer. Had 6 children.

(4) Mary F. (1874-) m. F. L. Halsey, had 13 children.

(5) Odey J. (1876) m. Rhoda Miller, lives in Roanoke, has 8 children.

(6) T. Jeff (1878-) Wyoming Co. official, m. Nannie Halsey, has 8 children.

(7) C. Phil (1882-) m. Nan Tilley, has one son.

(8) Juda E., (1884-) m. Abe McKenney, Pax, W. Va. has 8 children.

(9) Grover C. (1887-) m. Ida. Lemon, has 4 children.
Home: Maben, W. Va.

(10) Ida M. (1890-) Willie E. Clay, has 7 children.

(11) Roscoe C. (1893-), Sanesville, W. Va. m. Jesse
Lee Clay, has 4 children.

Issue of Sally Goode, and James Thomas:

(1) John; (2) Jeff; (3) Jake; (4) Emily, m. B. P. Cook;
(5) Lizzie, m. Floyd Cook; and (6) Sarah m. Fernan-
dez Cook.

Issue of Ollie Goode, and Peyton Pearson:

(1) Emeline Pearson, m. Morgan Ramsey, son of Joseph
Ramsey, and had issue: (a) Ida Ramsey, m. John Cover-
stone, lives in Roanoke; and Lucinda Ramsey, m. Cole
Dyer, lives near Henry.

Issue of Alexander and Elizabeth (Goode) Moore:

(1) Mordecai, (2) Peter, who m. Bettie McGhee, daughter of John McGhee of Franklin Co.

Issue of Jonas Goode,(of Co. "B" 57th Va. Regiment,
C. S. A.) and Julian Ann Goode:

(1) Marshall, and (2) Thomas.

THE GREER FAMILY

I. William Greer and Mary Anne Finch of English ex-
traction, were married in Ireland and came to America about 1735,
and settled in Anne Arundel County, Maryland. They had eight
sons and one daughter. The four oldest sons were born in Ireland, and the other children were born in Maryland. The names
of these sons and daughters are as follows:

1. William, born in Ireland, remained neutral during the Revolution.

2. James, born in Ireland, remained neutral during the Revolution.

3. Shadrack, born in Ireland, served in the British
Army during the Revolution.

4. John, born in Ireland, remainded neutral during
the Revolution. John Franklin Greer said, "upon information
through Helen Orr English, wife of William E. English of Indianapolis, Indiana, I believe this John Greer was one of the first
settlers of Tennessee."

5. Aquilla, born in Maryland, was a Revolutionary soldier.

6. Benjamin F., probably born in Maryland, and probably American soldier.during the Revolution.

7. Walter, probably both in Maryland, and probably American soldier during the Revolution.

8. Moses Greer, Sr., born in Maryland, June 2, 1744, married Nancy Bailey, daughter of Thomas Bailey of Prince George County, and settled in Franklin County; was representative of Franklin County in the Virginia legislature for several terms; was surveyor and farmer; died in Franklin County, May 10, 1834. This Moses Greer is designated Moses Greer Sr., by the Greer family and is the progenitor of the Franklin County family. He was one of the first three Justices of the County Court, and in 1832 he was presiding justice. He served as a Captain in the War of the Revolution.

9. Rebecca, married a Divers. Their daughter, Nancy Divers, was the second wife of Samuel Wood Greer, and mother of Joseph Hampton Greer. After the death of Samuel Wood Greer, in Monroe County, Missouri, December 1, 1851, Nancy returned to Virginia, and married George W. Kelly, a Primitive Baptist preacher. Samuel Wood Greer was a son of Moses Greer Sr.

John Hampton Greer states: "at the outbreak of the Revolutionary War, William Greer and his four oldest sons, having taken the oath of allegiance to the King of England, remained neutral. All sons of Moses Greer Sr., who were born or who became of age in the United States went into the Revolutionary Army of America. Shadrack, one of the eldest sons, went into the British Army and was afterwards disowned by his younger brothers."

II. Moses Greer, Sr., and Nancy Bailey's children were:

1. William Greer, married Miss Shelton, and settled in Davidson County, Kentucky. Their son.Moses married a Mrs. Charlton. Her maiden name was Catherine Pollard. She was a daughter of Chattin D. Pollard who married Molly Greer.

2. Moses Greer, Jr., married Susannah Wood and settled in Franklin County. He was grandfather of Joseph Hampton Greer and great grandfather of John Franklin Greer. He was a Primitive Baptist minister, and baptized Thomas Bailey Greer, Chattin D. Pollard and Theoderick F. Webb.

3. Walter Greer, settled in Franklin County. He married Katherine Harkrider.

4. John Greer, settled in Bledsoe County, Tennessee, at Grassy Cove. Their son, John, married Sara Jane Pollard.

5. Thomas Bailey Greer, married Ursula Webb. A Primitive Baptist preacher, he represented Franklin County in the General Assembly, as did his father, and his son Moses Theoderick Greer. Thomas Bailey Greer died in Missouri about the time of the Civil War. His widow, Ursula, was living in Franklin County shortly after the Civil War.

6. Betsy Greer, married James Callaway and settled in Franklin County, and had issue: Watt, who married _____ Hale; Thomas; Nancy, who married Theoderick Webb; and Miranda, who married James Leftwich. Betsy Greer is buried in Paris, Monroe County, Missouri.

7. Nancy Greer, married Henry Carper and settled in Franklin County. Moses Carper, son of Henry and Nancy (Greer) Carper, married, first, a Miss Tate and had issue: (1) Henry, who died unmarried, and (2) Nicholas, who married, first, Sallie Turnbull, and second, Jane Jones, and had issue: (a) Beverly, who died unmarried; and (b) James Jones Carper, who married Mary Wilson, and had issue: (i) James N., who died unmarried; (ii) Mary Jones, who married C. B. Willis; (iv) Norwood, who married Margaret Helms; and (v) Moses Greer Carper, who married Lillie Turnbull.

8. Molly Greer, married Chattin D. Pollard, September 13, 1790, and settled in Franklin County. She was the maternal grandmother of Joseph Hampton Greer and Samuel Wood Greer.

9. Sarah Greer, married Samuel Thompson, November 20, 1797.

10. Nelly Greer, married William Shelton, settled in Davidson County, Tennessee.

11. Catherine (Kitty) Greer, married William Leftwich, a Primitive Baptist preacher. They lived in Franklin County and died without issue.

III. Moses Greer, Jr. born May 12, 1768 was married to Susannah Wood, who born November 29, 1776. He died September 30, 1848. His wife died November 29, 1857. He was born, lived and died in Franklin Co. He and his wife were buried at the old homestead near Gogginsville. Their children were:

1. Samuel Wood Greer, born August 7, 1797, married May 28, 1823, to Frances Doggett Pollard, born December 22, 1794, daughter of Chattin Doggett Pollard and Molly Greer (See II-8). Frances Doggett Pollard Greer died in Monroe County, Missouri, October 31, 1844. Samuel W. Greer and his family left Franklin County September 11, 1838, in company with Webbs, Pollards and others numbering nearly a hundred, including several slaves. They drove over the Alleghany Mountains, through Tennesse and Kentucky, crossed the Ohio River at Parker's Ferry into Gallatin County, Illinois, and crossed the Mississippi River at Alton. They reached Monroe County, Missouri, on the thirty-first day of October, 1838, making the whole trip in wagons. Samuel Wood

Greer lived in Monroe County, Missouri, until hisdeath, on December 4, 1881. He made several visits to Virginia and on one of them married his second wife, Nancy Divers, November 4, 1850. She was a daughter of Aquilla Divers, who was a son of Rebecca Greer Divers, (See I-9). After the death of Samuel Wood Greer, on December 4, 1881, his widow returned to Franklin County and married a Primitive Baptist Preacher named George W. Kelly. Samuel Wood Greer and his first wife, Frances Doggett Greer, are buried in the Willis burying ground on the old Lee Willis farm, about seven miles southwest of Paris, Monroe County, Missouri.

2. Witherston Shelton Greer, married Mary Kyle, November 26, 1820, and settled in Bledsoe County, Tennessee, in 1838. He kept a post office called Grassy Cove in Bledsoe County.

3. Charlotte Greer married Daniel Warner of Virginia, April 23, 1831.

4. Nancy Greer married Daniel Noble of Virginia, September 9, 1823.

5. Sarah Greer married William Wright, October 1, 1823.

6. Catherine (Kitty) Greer married Robert J. Webb, August 23, 1834, and moved to Missouri about 1839. In the fall of 1845 they returned to Franklin County, where they died soon after the Civil War.

7. Moses Carper Greer, who married, first, Nancy Childress, January 7, 1845, and second, Nancy Wood, a widow, daughter of Stepehn Wood, he being a brother of Susannah Wood Greer. After her death, he married a widow in Indiana. He and his second wife had a son named Moses, and three or four other children.

8. Thomas Stepehen Greer married Catherine Tate, and settled in Franklin County. They were the parents of Col. George H. T. Greer.

9. William Walter Greer, married a Miss Sink.

IV. Samuel Wood Greer and Frances Doggett Pollard (See III-1) had issue:

1. Joseph Hampton Greer, born in Franklin County, April 5, 1824. He moved to Monroe County, Missouri, with his father, where he was married to Nancy Read Kelley on October 1, 1848. One child, William Thomas, was born to this union. Nancy died February 1, 1149. She was born November 1, 1828. After her death Joseph Hampton Greer was married on November 7, 1852 to Agnes (Read) Barnes, widow of Benjamin F. Barnes. She was the daughter of Samuel Read and Nancy Baldwin Read and was born November 28, 1822. She died March 9, 1899. She was a cousin of

the first wife. Joseph Hampton Greer and wife Agnes (Read) Greer
are buried in the New Hope Cemetery in Audrian County, about ten
miles west of Mexico, Missouri.

2. ·Susan Catherine Greer, married George Anthony
Maddox and had issue: Jesse Maddox.

3. Mary Elizabeth Greer, died single.

4. Searafine Eleanor Greer married her cousin Tazewell Wright, son of William and Sarah Greer Wright (see III-5)
and moved to California in 1852. They had issue: Emma, Cornelia and Theodosia. She died January 31, 1868, and is buried
on Hilton (or Milton) Creek, about sixteen miles from Boise,
Idaho.

5. Moses Greer, died single in California, and is
buried in San Luis Obispo.

6. Frances Greer, married, first, Charles Warren,
and second, _____. She died without issue and is buried
in Lewis County, Missouri.

V. Joseph Hampton Greer married, first Nancy Read
Kelley (see IV-1) and had issue: William Thomas Greer of Paris,
Monroe County, Missouri. He was born November 1, 1847, and was
married November 5, 1868, to Ruth Elizabeth Trussell, and had
issue: Ada, who married David C. Pool; Ardena, who married Frank
C. Coates; and Kirkland, who married Kitty Moss. Ada had one
child, Lloyd; Ardena had one child, Pauline; and Kirkland had one
child. Joseph Hampton Greer married, second, a widow, Agnes
Barnes, whose maiden name was Read (see IV-1). She had four
children by her first husband, Benjamin F. Barnes, whose names
were:

1. Nancy Ann Barnes, born January 8, 1843, married
James F. Brinker, January 20, 1859, and died in 1912.

2. James Samuel Barnes, born May 7, 1845, married
Laura Brockman, March 15, 1867, died D cember 11, 1910.

3. Darwin Read Barnes, born January 20, 1847, married Julia Burton, November 4, 1868.

4. William Cartmill Barnes, born June 6, 1848, married Ella Hopkins, March 3, 1875, and was living in Victoria,
Texas in 1914.

Joseph Hampton Greer and Agnes Read Barnes Greer had
four children:

1. Benjamin Wood Greer, born August 7, 1858; married Minnie Baldwin, August 23, 1882; died June 13, 1912, leaving
three children: Harry Marcus, Lynn Wood, and Archie Dean.

2. Hiram Smith Greer, born May 1, 1855, married
Florence Reed, May 15, 1883, now (1914) living in White Hall,
Illinois. They had two children, Hiram Franklin and Annie Ruth.

3. Joseph Pendleton Greer, born March 30, 1857; married Leta Settle, June 23, 1894, and had issue: William Wood-
ford Greer, born ca. 1894, now living in Monroe County, Missouri
(1914). Joseph Pendleton Greer died August 23, 1911.

4. John Franklin Greer, born January 7, 1860, married November 9, 1884, to Ida May Baldwin (born May 3, 1864),
and had issue: Margaret Agnes, born September 9, 1886, died
July 21, 1889; Jessie May, born May 16, 1889; Nellie, born April
2, 1893; Frances, born August 28, 1898; Mamie born September
1, 1900; and Hugh Hampton, born July 18, 1908.

Witherston Shelton Greer and his wife, Mary Kyle (III-
2), had issue: William, Thomas, Moses, Samuel, Henry Clay, Witherston S., and probably others.

Charlotte Greer (see III-3) and husband, Daniel Warner,
had issue: Susan, Emily and George. George was in Vernon, Texas,
about 1890. Emily was living near Dallas, Texas, in 1876, with
her third husband, a Mr. Starr. Her second husband, (named Fuqua)
was drowned in the Trinity River. Susan married a Mr. Denton.
She was widowed and living in Sulphur Springs, Texas, in 1876.

Nancy Greer and husband, Daniel Noble (III-4), had
issue: Mary Ann, William B., Moses G., John D., Emily, Eliza
and Susan. Mary Ann married Joel Harper, who died January 22,
1892. She was living in 1896 with her daughter, Mary Ann Noble,
(born November 24, 1824, died March 13, 1912) who married a Mr.
Pasley in Fulton, Missouri, Mary Ann Harper's son, John, was
living at Georgetown, Texas, with his uncle, Moses Noble, in 1876.
Moses Greer married Cornelia Wood, of Rocky Mount. He moved to
California about 1865, and from California to Texas. He was
living at Georgetown, Texas, in 1901 and had two sons: Alfred
Early, of Temple, Texas; and R. Wood Noble, a surgeon in Kings
Daughters Hospital in Temple, Texas.

Emily Noble married Robert Lavinder of Franklin County.
They both died in Montgomery County, Missouri. They had issue:
Moses, Joseph, John, Headley, Emma, Susan, and two other sons,
and two other daughters. The unnamed four were the youngest
children. Susan married Isham Boone of Franklin County. They
moved to Montgomery County, Missouri, where she died prior to
1900. They had several children, among them a daughter named
Marietta.

William B. Greer died in young manhood, unmarried.

John D. Greer, married Eliza Wood, sister to his brother, Moses Greer's wife. Eliza died November 28, 1900, at the
age of 68, leaving two grandchildren named Annabelle and Tate.
He died in Lynchburg, shortly before 1910.

Sarah Greer and husband, William Wright (III-5) had issue: Tazewell G., Susan Ann and Moses Theoderick. Tazewell Wright married his cousin Serafina Eleanor Greer, a sister of Joseph Hampton Greer (IV-4). The three daughters of Tazewell and Serafina Wright were in California in 1889. Susan Ann married Thomas F. Taylor and moved to Alabama or Mississippi about 1850. Moses Theoderick Wright married and lived in Franklin at the old homestead.

Catherine Greer and husband, Robert J. Webb (III-6) had issue: Susan, Ann, Moses and Jacob. Jacob Webb was a physician and served as surgeon in the Confederate Army. He married Henrietta Taylor. No issue. Moses Webb died while serving in the Confederate Army. Susan and Ann were living on the old homestead, both single, in 1890.

Walter Greer and Katherine Harkrider (II-3), had issue: Catherine, Sarah, Mariah and John. John married Nancy Overfelt, a sister of Berry Overfelt. Sarah married Berry Overfelt.

Thomas Bailey Greer and wife, Ursula Webb (II-5), had issue: Ursula Jane, William Armistead Burwell, Moses Theoderick, Thomas Bailey, John Henry, Walter Callaway and Catherine Bailey Greer, who married Zachary T. Wade. William Armistead Burwell Greer, physician, was living in New Cambria, Missouri, in 1877. He married Laura Mason and had issue: Thomas, Louisa, Emma.

Ursula Jane, daughter of Thomas Bailey Greer, married Walker Wright, of Montroe County, Missouri, and had issue: James L., Thomas S., Robert, and probably others. James L. was County Clerk of Monroe County, Missouri, for sixteen years.

Walter Callaway Greer married Elizabeth Craig, at Macon City, Missouri. He had several children, and served with the Union Army in the War between the States.

Theoderick Greer borther of Ursula, married, first, Nancy Callaway, and had issue: Elizabeth, who married John R. Martin; Emily, who married Dr. Quincy Bowyer; Tazewell Armistead, who married Addie Darnell; Henry Callaway, who married Sallie Pinkard, and moved to Colorado; Mary Catherine, who married John H. Carter; Theoderick Fitzgerald, who married Mary Ann Scott; Byrd Landgon, who married Pattie Pinkard; Serena, who died unmarried; James Thomas, who married widow Julia Franklin Wade Patterson; Ramsey, who married, first, Mary Adkins, and second, Julia Patterson Wade, widow of Henry Wade.

Ramsey Greer and Julia Patterson Wade, his second wife, had issue: Nannie Cicily, who married Street Greer; and Julia Franklin, who married Mr. Holland of Durango, Colorado; and Beauregard.

Nancy Webb, sister of Theoderick Greer, married Dr. Beard and lived in Missouri. They had among other children, a blind son who walked from Missouri to Franklin County.

Creed Greer, brother of Theoderick, married Mahala Booth, and had issue: Mary, who married Dr. Norborne Noell; Maria, who married Dr. J. H. Greer (and had one son named Street); John C., who married, first, Sally Noell, and, second, Mary Cassell, daughter of Nick Cassell; Benjamin Booth, who married Docie Darnell; Theoderick, who married in West Virginia a lady whose name is unknown to the writer; and Thomas, who married a Miss Duncan of Bedford County.

Among the early settlers of Virginia was Giles Carter. Theoderick, son of Giles Carter, had a daughter who married John Webb, of Amherst Co. Cuthbert Webb, son of John, had a son Theoderick, who married Sarah (or Sallie) Huff. Their daughter Ursula married Thomas Bailey Greer. In 1838, Ursula and Thomas Bailey Greer joined the caravan of covered wagons to Monroe County, Missouri. There he lived, died and was buried. The following children of Thomas Bailey Greer: Thomas Bailey, John Henry, Moses Theoderick, Walter Callaway, and Catherine Bailey returned with their mother to Rocky Mount where they lived in a house on Main Street, later owned by the heirs of Mrs. Maria Turnbull. Thomas Bailey, John Henry, and Moses Theoderick Greer became physicians and practiced in different sections of Franklin.

Dr. Thomas Bailey Greer served on Virginia's first Board of Medical Examiners. He was associated with Dr. Hunter McGuire in modernizing surgery. He married, first, Celestia Taliaferro, daughter of Dr. Richard M. and Polly (Hale) Taliaferro; and, second, Kate Claiborne, widow of Colonel Frederick of South Carolina.

John Henry Greer attended school at Patrick Court House. His room mate was J. E. B. Stuart, who became famous as a Confederate General. When quite young, John Henry Greer ran away from home, went to New York, met some noted actors and played minor parts with Edwin and John Wilkes Booth who were his remote relatives. There also he met Henriette Sontag, the great singer, for whom a post office in Franklin County was named. Ole Bull, also playing in New York at the time, was attracted by the Virginia lad and became his life long friend. John Henry Greer served as assistant surgeon in the 37th Battalion Virginia Cavalry. When off duty, he would lighten the hours of the soldiers by playing his banjo and relating his New York experiences. He was married, first, to his cousin Maria Webb, and, second, to Elizabeth Mosby Wade. Thomas Street Greer was his son by the first marriage. His home on Chestnut Creek was noted for its hospitality.

Moses Theoderick Greer married Louisa Thompson and practiced medicine near Callaway.

Catherine (Kitty) was sent to Hollins Female Institute where she remained during the war. There is a legend that once when the 37th Battalion Virginia Cavalry passed Hollins with bands playing and colors flying, Kitty Greer led a bevy of girls in dancing on the campus. After the war she married Zachary Taylor Wade and had issue: five daughters and one son.

In a family Bible owned by Mrs. Florence Wade Becker of Bluefield, West Virginia, is found the following: I, Henry Wade, son of Henry, was born in Hanover County, Virginia, 1740. I was married to Lucy Turner of said county, August 30, 1761. My son, Luke, was married to Martha Stanley, of Halifax County, November 10, 1775. My son, Andrew, was married to Sarah Petty, of Halifax County, December 2, 1790. He was married to his second wife, Elizabeth Kimball, of Anson County, North Carolina, November 24, 1795. My daughter Pollie was married to Thomas Stokes, of Lunenburg, February 22, 1797. My son, Zachfield, was married to Polly Johnston, of Campbell County, August 15, 1799. My daughter, Oreander, was married to Richard Jones, of Halifax, October 15, 1806. My son, Henry, was married to Pollie Stone, of Halifax, March 27, 1806. He was married to his second wife, Polly Waln, January 23, 1810. My daughter, Sarah was married to Matthew Hobson, of Halifax, December 24, 1811. My son, John Wade, was married to Elizabeth Hobson, of Halifax, December 24, 1812."

The father of Henry Wade who owned this Bible, was born in New Kent County, in 1690, and married Judith Via. He had three sisters, Maragaret, Mary and Sarah, and one brother, Anthony. He was the son of James Wade of New Kent. The mother of Elizabeth Hobson was Elizabeth Mosby, a descendent of Batholomew Truehart, who came from England with his son Daniel, and settled near Meadow Bridge, in Hanover County. Daniel Truehart married Mary Garland. His daughter Susannah, married Gen. Wade Mosby, Jr., a son of Littlebury Mosby and his wife Elizabeth Netherlands.

John Wade and Elizabeth Hobson had issue:

1. Henry, who married Julia Patterson, daughter of Andrew Patterson and Pollie Pinckard. Their children were: (a) Andrew, who served in Company G, 57th Virginia Regiment; (b) John Henry (married Nannie DeHaven), served in Company K, 10th Virginia Cavalry; (c) Zachary Taylor, who married Catherine Bailey Greer; and (d) Elizabeth Mosby, who became the second wife of Dr. John Henry Greer.

2. John Wade was sheriff of Franklin. He married, first, Palmyra Ashinghurst, whose mother was a daughter of Robert Hill; and, second, her sister, Adelia Ashinghurst.

3. Zachfield Wade, married Louisa Ashinghurst, and lived at the old Ashinghurst home, probably the oldest house in Franklin County. He served in the 57th Virginia Regiment, C. S. A.

4. Benjamin Wade, married first, Mary L. Taylor; second, Ann Hurt. He served as Colonel in the 57th Virginia Regiment and was killed at Gettysburg while leading a charge.

5. Mosby, married a daughter of John Patterson, and died without issue:

6. Sarah, married James Patterson and had issue: (a) John, who married Cecily Poindexter; (b) Tazewell, who married Nannie Arrington; (c) Addison, who married, first, Miranda Finney, and second Lily Hutchingson; and (e) Charles, who married Helen Pinckard.

7. Drusilla, married Jackson Whitehead, and had issue: (a) John, who married a Miss Graves; (b) Joseph, who married in Colorado; (c) Victoria, who married John Glenn; and (d) Elizabeth, who married Peter Booth.

8. Emily, who married Peter Booth.

9. Lucy Ann, married William Patterson who was Captain of Company G. 57th Virginia Regiment.

10. Julia, married first, James Patterson, second, Thomas Webb, by whom she had a son, T. F. Webb, who married Celestia Greer.

11. Juliana, married Frank Patterson. Julia and Juliana Wade were twins.

Celestia ("Essie") Wade, daughter of Zachary Taylor Wade and Catherine Bailey Greer, married, first, Benjamin Waldo Butler of Edgefield, South Carolina, a descendant of Captain Behethland who was associated with the London Company in 1607 in its Virginia explorations. They had one daughter, Laura Behethland, who married Thomas Pinckney Moore, of Charlotte, North Carolina. Mrs. Butler married, second, Cabell Smith, a descendant of Pocahontas, and had issue: Mary Cabell Smith.

On April 27, 1931, the D. A. R. appointed Celestia Wade Butler Smith as Organizing Regent of the Capt. Moses Greer Chapter, Daughters of the American Revolution, to be located at Rocky Mount. The name was to honor Capt. Moses Greer, who served with General Washington. The prospective members of the chapter (all descendants of Captain Greer) were as follows: Martha Conway Greer, Sarah Greer, Gladys Greer, Alice Greer Davis (Mrs Lemon), Page Nelson Price, Alice Waddey Peters, Marion Greer, Catherine Skinnell, Winifred Cabell Skinnell Davis (Mrs. Russell), Bessie Moseley, Mary Cabell Smith, Mary Adele Dillard, Celestia Dillard, Elizabeth Epperson, Catherine Wade Moore, Harriet Baxter Moore, Celestia Wade Butler Smith (Mrs. Cabell), Emma Carper Hooker (Mrs. George), Elizabeth Edmondson (Mrs. Andrew Lewis), Bessie Greer Moseley (Mrs. Herman), Mary Adela Dillard (Mrs. Herbert), Laura Behethland Moore (Mrs. Thomas Pinckey), Mary Jones Carper Willis (Mrs. Charles B.), Lucy Price Greer (Mrs. George Cabell), Mary Claiborne Willis Brown (Mrs. Henry D.), Edith Greer Carper (Mrs. T. W.), Flora Greer Parrish (Mrs. Beverly), Lydia Greer Dripps (Mrs. William), Kitty Greer Ramsey (Mrs. Harold), Butler Epperson Bowles (Mrs. Frank), Josephine

Wade Epperson (Mrs. Joseph), Eva Wade Greer (Mrs. Norborne Taliaferro), Emma Wade Skinnell (Mrs. William Erskine), Maude Wade
Snider, Corrie Horne White (Mrs. Walter), Mary Moseley Montogmery
(Mrs. James N.), Annie Greer Brodie (Mrs. J. M.), Celestia Greer
Webb (Mrs. T. F.), Wren Horne Baldwin (Mrs. Ernest). The organization of the chapter has not been completed at this writing.
(1935).

THE HANCOCK FAMILY

I.

(1) John Hancock, b. ca. 1730, probably in New Kent Co.,
d. in Patrick Co., Nov., 1802; moved to Albemarle (Now Fluvanna)
Co.; late in life he moved to that part of Henry Co. from which
Patrick Co. was taken. He m. Elizabeth Maddox, dau. of John
and Elizabeth Maddox, Oct. 16, 1755.

On Aug. 1, 1777, John Hancock, of Fluvanna Co., deeded his son Benjamin 182 acres on Cunningham Creek, and his son
Lewis 87 acres adjoining the lines of Thomas Jefferson, John
Haden and Henry Haislip. (D.B. 1, pp. 18 and 19). On Jan.
27, 1799, John Hancock and Elizabeth his wife, of Patrick Co.,
in consideration of $260.00, deeded land to Jacob Ma o, of Flu-
vanna Co. (D.B. 3, p. 505), and on Sept. 13, 1802 (D.B. 4, p.
182), they deeded him 147 acres in consideration of $100.00.

John Hancock left a will dated Nov. 10, 1802, pro.
in Patrick Co., Dec. Court, 1802, in which he devised his son
Lewis Hancock "the land whereon I lived in Fluvanna Co.," and
the balance of his estate he devised to his wife for life or
widowhood, and then to be divided among his children, viz:

II.

(1) Benjamin Hancock, b. ca. 1756, d. at Lebanon, Wilson Co., Tenn., 1817. On Dec. 25, 1800, Benjamin Hancock and
Nancy, his wife, of Patrick Co., deeded property in Fluvanna
Co., to Poindexter Noell. A Benjamin Hancock was appointed Ensign by Fluvanna Co. Court, April 2, 1779.

(2) Lewis Hancock, (See below).

(3) William Hancock, b. 1759.

(4) Major Hancock, b. 1760. Probably m. a Miss Fuson.
A Major Hancock was sowrn into office as an Ensign by the Goochland Co. Court, May 17, 1780. Under date of Nov. 7, 1818 (D.B.
5, p. 194, Patrick Co.), Major Hancock, of Wayne Co., Ky., gave
William Hancock, of Patrick Co., a power of Attorney "to sell
a tract of land whereon I formerly resided in Patrick Co."

(5) Nancy Hancock, b. 1764, m. Jesse Corn, Feb. 21,
1780 (M.L.B. Fluvanna Co.). He d. prior to Sept. 27, 1810,

as on that date (D. B. 3, p. 347, Patrick Co.), Wm. Hancock gave bond "to pay the orphans of Jesse Corn, dec'd. all such estate or estates as now or shall hereafter appear to belong to said estate." Under date of Oct. 3, 1818, (D. B. 5, 195, Patrick Co.). Nancy Corn, Admrx., John A. Corn, Richard Sharp, Wm. Corn, Jesse Corn, James Sharp, Samuel Corn, Joel Chitwood, William Chitwood and Dicy Corn, by her guardian, Wm Hancock, heirs and distributees of Jesse Corn, dec'd, conveyed 174 acres on the North side of Sycamore Creek to Richard Barbour. (See also D. B. 5, p. 388, Patrick Co., for conveyances from the same parties to John Hancock).

(6) Rhodie Hancock, b. 1766, m. Samuel Lane, Oct. 28, 1784. (Marriage of record in Minute Book 1, p. 7, Fluvanna Co.) Samuel Lane, b. 1760, was son of Jacob and Mary (Bradshaw) Lane.

(7) Elizabeth Maddox Hancock, b. 1768, m. Wm. James Mayo (b. Aug. 21, 1769, d. Aug. 1, 1849) son of Jacob Mayo, April 11, 1790 (marriage license of record in Henry Co.). (See will of Jacob Mayo dated Oct. 15, 1809, pro. Fluvanna Co. Dec. 28, 1812).

(8) Judith Hancock, b. 1770, m. Valentine Mayo, son of Jacob Mayo, prior to 1802.

(9) Susannah Hancock, b. 1772, unm. in 1802.

(10) Mary Hancock, b. 1774, m. James Morrison, prior to 1802. John Hancock, in his will, mentions his dau. Mary Morrison's two eldest children, Allen and Jeney.

(2) Lewis Hancock (John) b. in Albemarle Co., in that part which is now Fluvanna Co. ca. 1757, and d. intestate near Union Hall, 1828, at the old home-place, more recently known as the John Zeigler Homestead. (see inventory and appraisement of his estate dated Mar. 14, 1828, of record in Franklin Co.) He married Celia (Duncan) Oglesby, widow of Shadrack Oglesby and dau. of George and Ann Duncan, Dec. 29, 1778, in Fluvanna Co. Shadrack Oglesby left will, dated Oct. 18, 1777, pro. May 7, 1778, in Fluvanna Co. in which he mentions wife Celia Oglesby and "My two children, Nancy and Elizabeth." He appointed George Duncan and William Oglesby, Sr., Exrs. and guardians of his children. George Duncan left will, dated July 1, 1778, pro. Nov. 6, 1783, of record in Fluvanna Co., mentioning wife Ann, sons John, Fleming Willis, George, Tandy Patterson and Field Allen, and daus. Celia Hancock, Nancy and Mollie Fleming Duncan. On July 19, 1806, Lewis Hancock registered seven salves, of record in Franklin C., willed by Shadrack Oglesby to his wife, Celia, who later m. Lewis Hancock. On Oct. 6, 1785 (D.B. 2, p. 107, Fluvanna Co.), Lewis Hancock and Celia his wife conveyed to Adam Blair 87 acres and on June 2, 1800, (D.B. 4, p. 46, Fluvanna Co.), Lewis Hancock, Stephen Haynes and Peyton Young, of Franklin Co. conveyed 100 acres of land in Fluvanna Co. to Richard Perkins of Fluvanna.

George Duncan moved from Scotland to Albemarle Co.,
ca. 1750. He was b. 1730, and d. 1783, and was a Captain of
the Fluvanna Militia, being sworn in Sept. 4, 1777. His wife
was Ann Hall (d. prior to 1783), dau. of Richard and Ann Hall
of Albemarle Co.

Issue of Lewis and Celia (Duncan Oglesby) Hancock:

III.

(1) John Allen Hancock, b. ca. 1780, m. Sarah Ryan,
dau. of William Ryan, one of the early sheriffs of Franklin Co.
He moved to Tennessee prior to 1811, and to Alabama prior to
Nov. 2, 1801. William Ryan m. Sarah Swanson, dau. of William
Swanson. By a deed of gift dated Feb. 5, 1811, of record in
Franklin County, Sarah Ryan "for love and affection which I
bear my daughter, Sarah Hancock, of Smith County, Tennessee,
do give unto my said daughter one certain negro girl named Jenny,
devised to me by my father, William Swanson, of Oglethorpe County,
Georgia." Among their children were:

(a) John Hancock, of Austin, Texas, born of
Virginia parents, in Jackson County, Ala. Oct. 29, 1824; settled
in Texas in 1847, practiced law until Aug. 1851; elected judge
and served until 1855; member of the State Legislature 1860-1;
he refused to take the oath of allegiance to the Confederate
States, and was expelled; elected a member of the State Constitutional Convention of 1866; elected a Representative to the
42nd, 43rd and 44th Congresses, and re-elected to the 48th Congress as a Democrat. Died at Austin, Texas, July 19, 1893.
He had one son, John, living in Austin in 1890.

(b) William Ryan Hancock, who was killed in
the Mexican War.

(2) Benjamin Hancock, b. June 16, 1782, d. Mar. 25,
1860, m. 1st, Frances Holland; 2nd, Elizabeth Booth. (See III-
2).

(3) Field Allen Hancock, b. 1793, d. 1876, m. Susan
Smith, dau. of William Smith, of Mar. 4, 1816 in Franklin County.
(See will of William Smith, W. B. 6, p. 376, Franklin Co., dated
Mar. 5, 1842; pro. Aug. 7, 1848, wherein he mentions wife Eliz-
abeth and children, Samuel Smith, dec'd Frances Booth, Thomas
Smith, Susannah Hancock, Stephen F. Smith, Martha Holland,
Elizabeth Poindexter, Nancy Holland, William H. Smith, Sarah
P. Poindexter and Julia Craghead). Field Allen Hancock, moved
to Alabama prior to 1825, where they lived as neighbors. He
was a member of the Ala. Legislature for several terms. He left
several children, who moved to Texas and other Western States.

(4) Lucinda Hancock, m. Charles Powell, April 30, 1809,
in Franklin Co. He was adm'r of the estate of Lewis Hancock.
His report dated Sept. 19, 1829, is of record in Franklin Co.

(5) Frances Hancock, m. Peter D. Holland, son of Capt.
Peter M. Holland, Jan. 26, 1807. The will of Capt. Peter M.
Holland, dated Nov. 28, 1827; pro. April 4, 1839, of record in
Franklin Co., mentions children: John Meadow Holland, (b. 1778,
d. 1845), Peter D. Holland, Thomas S. Holland, Fannie Hancock
(wife of Benjamin Hancock) Millie McCall, Lydia Nemo, Nancy Smith,
Mary Smith and Jane Smith.

The Holland Family of Franklin Co. claims descent from
Michael Holland, originally of Hanover Co., later of Goochland,
Albemarle and Fluvanna Cos. He purchased 400 acres of land Aug.
17, 1730, from Samuel Burk in Goochland Co. (D. B. 1, p. 211)
through his son, Peter Holland of Caroline Co. in 1748, and who
purchased 600 acres in that part of Goochland Co. which is now
Cumberland Co. from William Allen of Albemarle Co., May 17, 1748.
(D. B. 5, p. 419, Gooch. Co.).

(6) Sophia Hancock, m. William Powell, Jan. 3. 1805.
She d. prior to 1828. They had three children: Thomas L.,
Samuel A. and William H.   The partition of land and slaves made
in obedience to a decretal order of the Franklin County Court
on June 11, 1828, shows William Powell was guardian of the above
named children at date of the settlement of the estate of Lewis
Hancock.

III. (2) Benjamin Hancock (Lewis, John), b. June 16,
1782, d. Mar. 25, 1860; m. 1st, Frances Holland, dau. of Capt.
Peter M. Holland, of Glade Hill, Jan. 6, 1806. Her brother,
John Meadow Holland, was member of the Virginia Legislature from
Franklin Co., and a Major in the War of 1812. .Benj. Hancock m.
2nd, Elizabeth Booth (b. Jan. 29, 1801, d. Mar. 31, 1860), dau.
of Col. Peter Booth, Oct. 30, 1817. Benjamin Hancock lived near
Union Hall. At his death he gave the home place to his son,
Charles Robert, who in turn devised it to his dau. Victoria,
who m. James Zeigler. His will, dated Oct. 8, 1859, pro. May
7, 1860, is recorded in Franklin Co.

Issue of Benjamin and Frances (Holland) Hancock:

IV.

(1) Raleigh Allen Hancock (living in Missouri in
1859) was the only child of Benjamin Hancock's first marriage
living at date of his father's will (1859)

(2) Phoebe H. Hancock, m. Robert Smith, April 20, 1826.
Capt. John Henry Smith, a son of this marriage, was killed while
leading his company in a charge at Gettysburg.

(3) Mary L. Hancock, m. Christopher Booth, son of
Col. Peter and Nancy (Blades) Booth, Sept. 3, 1832.

(4) William Thomas Hancock, (b. 1814, d. 1857) m.

Agnes Booth (b. 1821, d. 1893) dau. of Col. Peter and Nancy (Blades) Booth Jan. 23, 1838. (See IV-4)

Issue of Benjamin and Elizabeth (Booth) Hancock:

(5) John Silas Hancock, b. Jan. 21, 1818, d. June 30, 1906, m. Julia Ann Morgan (b. Jan. 23, 1833, d. Mar. 12, 1867), dau. of Capt. Samuel Morgan, Nov. 20, 1851. (See IV-5).

(6) Peter Lewis Hancock, m. Mary Annie English, Nov. 13, 1843. (See IV-6).

(7) Frances Jane Hancock, (b. Dec. 21, 1858) m. Ferdinand Price. (See IV-7)

(8) Abram Booth Hancock, b. Oct. 29, 1825, d. Dec. 1, 1903, m. 1st, Martha Elizabeth Walker, 2nd, Susannah L. Machenheimer, Sept. 26, 1883 (d. July 23, 1902). No issue by 2nd marriage. (See IV-8).

(9) Elizabeth Ann Hancock, (b. Dec. 11, 1829, d. Jan. 22, 1897) m. Tazewell Price. (See IV-9)

(10) Charles Robert Hancock, (b. Dec. 22, 1831) m. Sally E. Stone. (See IV-10)

(11) Christopher Harrison Hancock, m. Victoria Street, dau. of Wm. A. and Nancy Street, Jan. 22, 1857, in Franklin Co. (See IV-11)

(12) Nancy Katherine Hancock, m. John A. Street, son of Wm. A. and Mary Street, had one son, Charles Street, who died an infant.

(13) Julia A. Maria Hancock, m. John Randolph Zeigler, June 20, 1860, (See IV-13)

IV.

(4) William Thomas Hancock (Benjamin and Fannie Holland Hancock, Lewis, John), b. in 1814, d. 1857. On Jan. 23, 1838 he m. Agnes Booth (b. 1821, d. 1893) sister of his stepmother, dau. of Col. Peter and Nancy (Blades) Booth of Franklin Co. She was half sister of Elizabeth Booth, second wife of Benjamin Hancock who was her husband's father. Issue:

V.

(1) John Harrison Hancock, b. Jan, 1839, d. June 15, 1892, m. 1st, Cleopatra Mitchell, Dec. 7, 1865; m. 2nd, Fannie S. Hatcher, Nov. 30, 1869. (See V-I).

(2) Anne Hancock, d. 1904, m. James Matthew Hutchinson.

(3) Benjamin Peter Hancock. (See V-3).

(4) William Lewis Hancock, m. Virginia T. Simms, of Patrick Co. He was a Confederate soldier and Sheriff of Franklin Co.

(5) Fannie Hancock, m. John T. Morgan.

(6) Thomas Richard Hancock, b. 1848, m. Julia Annie Keen (b. 1852), dau. of Ashford and Frances (Glass Walker) Keen, Dec. 1, 1869, in Franklin Co. Issue: Ula, David Keen, William Ashford, Thomas Richard, Annie, Benjamin H., Eoline, Frank, Charles and Florence.

(7) James Ferdinand Hancock, (b. 1848, d. ca. 1887) m. Mary E. Zeigler, Feb. 23, 1871.

(8) Charles Hancock, m. Della Payne.

(9) Cleopatra Hancock, b. 1856 (living in 1928) m. George Taylor Hutchinson, Feb. 15, 1872.

(10) Abram P. Hancock, m. Mildred Turner Hopkins (b. Jan. 9, 1862, d. Dec. 10, 1899) Oct. 20, 1882. Issue: Hattie; W. Lawson, d. unm. Jan. 9, 1903; and Pierce Edward.

V.

(1) John Harrison Hancock (William T. Benjamin, Lewis, John), (b. Jan. 1839, d. June 15, 1892) m. 1st, Cleopatra Mitchell (b. July 7, 1838, d. Sept. 12, 1867). dau. Washington C. and Elizabeth (Bradley) Mitchell, Dec. 7, 1865, in Franklin Co.; m. 2nd, Frances Saphronia Hatcher, of Haleford, dau. of Maj. John Hatcher of Franklin, Nov. 30, 1869.

Issue of John H. and Cleopatra (Mitchell) Hancock:

(1) Ada Nye Hancock, (b. Sept. 10, 1866) m. Albert McLeod Dudley (b. Dec. 23, 1862, d. Sept. 5, 1925) Nov. 27, 1884, at Haleford. Issue:

(a) Albert Henry Dudley, b. Sept. 23, 1885, m. Mrs. Lillie Gaines Phillipa (b. Sept. 22, 1890), dau. of Maxwell C. and Lula Roane Gaines, June 8, 1921, Richmond. Issue:

1. Albert Henry Jr., b. Mar. 12, 1922;

2. Louis Roane, b. May 27, 1925;

3. Infant, b. July, 1928, d. July 1928.

(b) Harvey Mitchell Dudley, b. Jan. 24, 1887, m. Laura E. Bartlett, Dec. 25, 1911, Philadelphia.

(c) Carrie Hatcher Dudley, Bennettsville, S. C.
July 7, 1891, m. Zach A. Drake (b. Sept. 1, 1879), Sept. 15,
1915, at Martinsville. Issue: William Benjamin Drake, b. Jan.
29, 1924.

(d) Harrison Hancock Dudley, b. Feb. 21, 1893;
educated in Martinsville High School, Richmond College and Randolph-Macon College, Ashland; served in World War I; dealer in
lumber.

(e) Mabel Elizabeth Dudley, b. July 16, 1898, m.
Charles Wood Holt, Nov. 9, 1921, Martinsville. Issue:

1. Mabel Hancock Holt, b. Dec. 13, 1923.

Issue of John H. and Frances Sophronia (Hatcher) Hancock.

(2) Harrison Hatcher Hancock, b. Feb. 1, 1871, m.
Julia Harvey Duncan, Aug. 16, 1906, Haleford. Issue:

(a) Frances Starke, b. May 19, 1907;

(b) Lee Duncan, b. Dec. 17, 1910;

(c) Sallie Holland, b. Jan. 14, 1913;

(d) John Harrison, b. July 31, 1916.

(3) Mattie Lelia Hancock, b. July 24, 1876, d. unm.
in 1928.

V. (3)

Benjamin Peter Hancock (William T., Benjamin, Lewis,
John) b. in Franklin Co., June 19, 1842, d. Feb. 19, 1925, at
Washington, D. C.; m. Sarah Frances Hutchinson (b. Mar. 19, 1838),
dau. of John C. and Lucy (Meredith) Hutchinson, of Franklin Co.,
Mar. 21, 1865. He served in the Confederate Army; was wounded
three times; continued in the service until the close of the
war; and then settled at Hale's Ford.

Issue of Benjamin Peter and Sarah (Hutchinson) Hancock:

VI.

(1) John William Hancock, Roanoke, b. June 17, 1870, m.
Mary Carr Leffler, April 30, 1898.

(2) Lucy Mabel Hancock, Washington, D. C., b. June 11,
1873, m. Robert Marshall Lynn (b. Jan. 12, 1871, in Cumberland Co)

son of James Shirley and Helen (Daniel) Lynn, Nov. 12, 1901. Mr. Lynn has been a Washington correspondent for the Richmond News-Leader since 1922. Issue:

(a) Marshall Hancock Lynn, member of the Washington, D. C. Bar, b. Feb. 1, 1902, m. Nora Agnew Greenlees, of Washington D. C., Nov. 13, 1927. Issue: Mary Elizabeth Lynn, b. Feb. 3, 1928; and Charles Craggin Lynn, b. Jan. 5, 1934.

(3) Benjamin Hugh Hancock of Bluefield, W. Va., b. Jan. 6, 1876, m. Florence Coleman Haynes, dau. of William D. Haynes, of Franklin Co., May 26, 1903. She was b. Sept. 17, 1876. Issue:

(a) Benjamin Haynes Hancock, b. May 24, 1904, educated in Hampden-Sydney College and University of Virginia.

(b) Frances Meredith Hancock, b. Nov. 13, 1907, educated in Hollins College, and Salem College at Winston-Salem.

(c) Hugh Hancock, b. Mar. 26, 1910, d. April 27, 1911.

(d) William Thomas Hancock, b. Sept. 11, 1911; educated in Davidson College.

(e) Hugh Coleman Hancock, b. Jan. 24, 1917.

(4) Annie Hancock, b. April 2, 1879, d. April 26, 1887.

VI (1)

John William Hancock (Benjamin Peter, William T., Benjamin, Lewis, John), born at Hale's Ford, Franklin Co. June 17, 1870, m. Mary Carr (b. May 17, 1874), dau. of Philip and Olive (Parrish) Leffler, descendant of John Carr, of Loudoun Co., who served as an Ensign in the Revolution, and had issue:

VII.

(1) Mary Alice Hancock, Washington D. C. b. Mar. 14, 1901, educated in Wellesley College, m. Branch Spalding of Roanoke, July 27, 1925. Issue: Branch Hancock Spalding, b. Aug. 10, 1934.

(2) John William Hancock, Jr., b. Aug. 7, 1904, educated in V. P. I. and Wharton School of Pa., m. Hester Elizabeth Brinser, April 15, 1933, in New York City and lives there.

(3) Karl Bulow Hancock, b. Nov. 23, 1906; educated in public schools of Roanoke, Episcopal High School of Alexandria, University of Virginia, Harvard Graduate School of Business Administration, now engaged in banking at Roanoke.

(4) Elizabeth Dee Hancock, b. Oct. 3, 1912, educated in Hollins College, graduated June 1934.

(5) Benjamin Philip Hancock, b. July 12, 1908, d. June 29, 1909.

IV (5)

John Silas Hancock (Benjamin & Elizabeth Booth Hancock, Lewis, John), (b. Jan. 21, 1818, d. June 30, 1906) m. Julia Ann Morgan (b. Jan. 23, 1833, d. Mar. 12, 1867), dau. of Capt. Samuel Morgan, Nov. 20, 1851. Issue:

(1) James Abram Hancock, b. Nov. 1, 1852, d. Jan. 9, 1856.

(2) Eliza Jane Hancock, Roanoke, b. July 8, 1854, m. Augustus Thrash Sowder (b. Oct. 9, 1854) Oct. 13, 1875, at Copper Hill, Floyd Co. Issue:

(a) Clifton Hampton, b. Aug. 2, 1876, m. Sallie McCampbell, Nov. 16, 1904, Cave Spring, Roanoke Co.

(b) John William, b. April 14, 1880, m. Clara E. Gray, Sept. 18, 1912, Floyd Co.

(c) Maude Hancock, b. Oct. 31, 1881, m. G. M. Aldridge, Dec. 10, 1902, Floyd Co.

(d) Eugene Augustus, b. Aug. 5, 1883; m. 1st, Ora Curtus Poff, Dec. 28, 1904, Floyd Co.; m. 2nd, Iva Cannady, Nov. 26, 1925.

(e) Mamie, b. Oct. 31, 1885, m. Carl D. Beckner, Sept. 22, 1910, Roanoke.

(f) Kate C., b. July 17, 1887, m. Charles P. Aldridge, Dec. 25, 1907, Floyd Co.

(g) Samuel Morgan, (b. Dec. 18, 1889) m. Blanche Arthur, Huntington, W. Va., July 11, 1913.

(h) Eliza Jane, (b. Nov. 3, 1891) m. Lamar B. Lester, Sept. 14, 1918, Salem.

(3) Samuel Benjamin Hancock, Copper Hill, Floyd Co.,
b. May 21, 1857, m. Lula Jane McCampbell (b. Aug. 15, 1875, d.
Jan. 8, 1911) dau. of William Henry McCampbell, at Cave Spring,
Roanoke Co. Issue: Julia May, b. May 5, 1893; Lela Celeste,
b. Aug. 27, 1894; John McCampbell, b. May 26, 1896, m. Anna Oren
Garland, at Roanoke, Feb. 27, 1922; Laura Jane, b. Feb. 9, 1899;
Samuel Benjamin, b. June 9, 1901; Hugh Morgan, b. July 28, 1903;
Gladys Thelma, b. Feb. 19, 1906; William Henry, b. Nov. 19, 1908;
and Lula Ree Hancock, b. Jan. 7, 1911.

(4) Peter Morgan Hancock, of Ferrum, b. July 11, 1860,
d. July 19, 1929, m. Harriet Nora Sowder, April 12, 1888. Issue:
Mrs. S. E. Mason, Mrs. J. A. Luke, and one son, W. B. Hancock.

IV (6)

Peter Lewis Hancock (Benjamin, Lewis, John) (b. 1820,
d. Sept. 11, 1865) m. Mary Annie English (b. 1823, d. July 15,
1860), dau. of Johnson and Parmenas English, Nov. 13, 1843.
He represented Franklin Co. in the Virginia Legislature. Issue:

(1) John Callahill Hancock, b. Aug. 25, 1844, at Hales-
ford, d. Aug. 1891, m. 1st, Angie A. Saunders, dau. of George
G. and Martha J. Saunders, May 18, 1870, in Bedford Co., m.
2nd, Sallie Goodman Dodd (b. Oct. 5, 1848) Charlottesville, Dec.
20, 1883.

Issue of John Callahill Hancock by 1st marriage:

(a) Martha Lena Hancock, m. Judge Clifton Alexander Woodrum of Roanoke, in 1905. Judge Woodrum was Commonwealth's Attorney of Roanoke City, 1917-19; Judge of the Cor-
poration Court, 1919-1922; and has represented the Sixth District in Congress since 1923.

Issue:

(1) Clifton Alexander Woodrum, Jr., educated
in Washington and Lee University, now
practicing law in Roanoke.

(2) Martha Ann Hancock.

(b) Mary Effie Hancock, Roanoke, b. July, 1872,
m. W. L. Tinsley, June 6, 1905. Issue.

(1) John Hancock Tinsley, b. Sept. 1907.

(2) Willis Louis Tinsley, b. 1910, d. 1911.

Issue of John Callahill Hancock 2nd marriage:

(c) Harry Polkinhorn Hancock, Roanoke, b. at Hale's Ford, June 6, 1885, m. Brownie Hill, of Franklin, Tenn., Dec. 20, 1916.

Issue:

1. Virginia Rose Hancock, b. Mar. 17, 1918.

2. Harry Polkinhorn Hancock, Jr., b. Mar. 14, 1926.

(2) Sarah Hancock, b. 1846, m. J. Harvie Meador, Sept. 12, 1866. Among issue is a daughter, Mrs. A. U. Smith, 4916 Abbott Avenue, Dallas, Texas.

(3) Alice M. Hancock, b. 1856, m. Thomas. W. Crozier, dentist, of Monroe, W. Va., Dec. 2, 1880.

(4) Frances Katherine Hancock, m. Daniel A. Meador, Sept. 11, 1872. Among her issue is Mrs. Eli L. Sanger, 1011 S. Ervay Street, Dallas, Texas.

(5) William Tazewell Hancock, (b. Dec. 24, 1849, d. Dec. 24, 1849, d. Dec. 18, 1918) m. Mary Elizabeth Fletcher (b. Nov. 10, 1857, d. Oct. 18, 1925), dau. of John Lawrence and Nancy Lee (Harris) Fletcher, at Dallas, Texas, March 11, 1880. Issue:

(a) Lillian Carrie Hancock, b. Jan. 31, 1881, at Dallas, Texas, m. Dr. Elof T. Hedlund, of New Orleans, now Postmaster at Portland, Oregon. Issue: William Hancock Hedlund, b. Sept. 24, 1910; graduate of University of Oregon.

(b) Nellie Fletcher Hancock, Knoxville, Tenn., b. Sept. 18, 1882, at Dallas Texas, m. Charles David Dillender, Jan. 30, 1902, at Mineral Wells, Texas. Issue:

1. Richard David Dillender, b. July 11, 1903, at Dallas, Texas, m. Jennie Rebecca Caldwell, June 1, 1926, at Knoxville, Tenn. Issue:

a. Richard David Dillender, Jr., b. Sept. 19, 1927.

b. Samuel Caldwell Dillender, b. Sept. 25, 1931.

2. Dorothy Cecile Dillender, b. at Mineral Wells, Texas, July 18, 1904, m. George Aiken Caldwell (b. Aug. 26, 1897) Aug. 23, 1923. Home: Knoxville, Tenn.

(c) Victor Herman Hancock, Johnson City, Tenn.,

b. Oct. 9, 1884, Dallas, Texas, m. Pearl Lyle at Johnson City, Tenn., Dec. 6, 1918.

Issue:
(1. Martha Lyle Hancock, b. Oct. 6, 1919;

(2. William Eugene Hancock, b. June 26, 1924.

(d) John Oscar Hancock, b. Nov. 12, 1886, Dallas, Texas, d. June 22, 1898.

(e) William Albert Hancock, b. Feb. 27, 1889, Dallas, Texas, d. March 14, 1908, at Johnson City, Tenn.

(f) Lambert E. Hancock, Glendale, Arizona, b. Feb. 15, 1891, Dallas, Texas, m. Catherine Hamilton Thomas, of Bristol, June 15, 1915. Issue; Lambert E. Hancock, Jr. b. May 21, 1917, at Paris, Tenn; now at San Dimas, California.

(g) Ruby Elizabeth Hancock, Knoxville, Tenn., b. Aug. 22, 1896, Dallas, Texas, m. Daniel Evans Beasley of Paris, Tenn. (b. Feb. 9, 1894, d. Sept. 17, 1932), Nov. 22, 1916.

Issue:

(1. James Robert Beasley, b. Feb. 13, 1919, at Paris, Tenn.

(2. Daniel Evans Beasley, 35d, b. July 15, 1922, Paris, Tenn.

IV (7)

Frances Jane Hancock (Benjamin & Elizabeth Booth Hancock, Lewis, John), m. Ferdinand Price, Sept. 6, 1847. Issue;

(1) Katherine Warfield Price, (b. Jan. 5, 1854, d. Oct. 30, 1921) m. John Addison Moorman, M.D., (b. Dec. 19, 1843, d. July 16, 1912), May 18, 1875, in Franklin Co. Issue:

(a) Mary Maupin, b. Feb. 17, 1876, m. William M. Thompson, M.D., July 2, 1903, at Hale's Ford.

(b) Terrell, b. Oct. 21, 1877, d. June 6, 1879.

(c) Janie Hancock, b. June 27, 1879, d. Feb. 13, 1922, m. Lucius D. Morgan, M.D., Sept. 6, 1906, at Hale's Ford.

(d) Warren Lodowick, b. April 7, 1881; m. Burah Fay LeFew (b. June 10, 1895), dau. of Rev. C. B. LeFew, Oct. 18, 1916, at Salem. Issue:
(1. Mary Fay Moorman, b. Oct. 6, 1917, d. July

25, 1918.

(2. Warren Lodowick Moorman, Jr., b. July 25, 1919.

(e) John Hope Moorman M. D., b. May 6, 1883; educated in Randolph-Macon Academy and Medical College of Virginia; m. Lelia E. Heischman (b. Feb. 12, 1890), dau. of Jacob Heischman, April 19, 1914, at Conicville. Issue:

1. John Hope Moorman, Jr., b. Aug. 1, 1915.

2. Wilbur Chapman Moorman, b. May 6, 1919.

(f) Lily Chapman Moorman, b. April 2, 1885, d. Nov. 30, 1886.

(g) Carleton Moorman, M. D., b. Jan. 3, 1887, m. Nov. 16, 1927, Mary Katherine Smith, dau. of Dr. J. P. Smith, of Martinsville.

(h) Willie B. Moorman, b. Mar. 9, 1888, m. Lucius D. Morgan, M. D., Sept. 4, 1924, Norfolk.

(i) Grace C. Moorman, b. Nov. 15, 1890.

(j) Chapman S. Moorman, M. D., b. Dec. 27, 1892.

(k) Kathleen Moorman, b. Dec. 22, 1894, Portsmouth.

(2) Elizabeth Mary Price, b. July 29, 1848, d. April 18, 1919, m. William Watson St. Clair (b. Dec. 13, 1839, d. Jan. 20, 1899), Sept. 28, 1876, at Dillon's Mills. Issue:

(a) Walter St. Clair, b. June 4, 1877, m. Mrs. Margaret Barnes, nee Scott, at Rocky Mount, Aug. 12, 1912. He was educated in Roanoke College, represented Franklin Co. in the Legislature, and for many years was Ass't Cashier of the First National Bank of Rocky Mount. Issue:

1. Walter Price, b. May 14, 1913.

2. Margaret, b. Mar. 28, 1915.

(b) Marvin St. Clair, Bonestead, So. Dakota, b. Sept. 27, 1879, m. Emma Wood, at Bonestead. No issue.

(c) Abiah Kate St. Clair, b. Jan. 21, 1882, m. Stephen Ashby MacDonald, Sept. 11, 1912, at Rocky-Mount. Issue: Virginia St. Clair MacDonald, b. June 28, 1918.

(d) Virginia St. Clair (twin of Abiah Kate) b. Jan. 21, 1882, d. Nov., 1884.

(3) Sarah Virginia Allie Price, b. 1850, d. May 4, 1887, m. 1st, Capt. Abner Lee Dobyns in 1872, had one son, Abner Lee Dobyns, Jr., m. 2nd, George Madison Helms May 7, 1879, and had issue: (a) Olivia Helms, b. Dec. 20, 1880; Alumna of Hollins College, and Woman's College; m. F. L. Crutchfield, son of the famous Justice John Jeter Crutchfield; business man and civic leader of Richmond. Issue:

> George Helms Crutchfield, b. Oct. 13, 1904; educated in Augusta Military Academy, William and Mary College, University of Richmond, University of Virginia, spent one year of research work in Paris, now practicing law in Richmond; m. Marjorie V. Weile, Sept. 19, 1925, in N. Y. City. Issue: Frances Helms Crutchfield, b. Feb. 13, 1927; and Majorie Livingston Crutchfield, b. Mar. 7, 1929.

(b) George Cabell Helms, b. Jan. 10, 1882, d. Oct. 2, 1883.

(c) Allie Price Helms, b. Nov. 19, 1884, d. Mar. 25, 1892.

(4) Thomas Marshall Price, b. Sept. 1855, d. May, 1898, m. Elizabeth Burroughs, of Moneta, Feb. 10, 1878.

(5) Charles Benjamin Price, b. Jan. 5, 1858, d. Feb. 19, 1922, m. Celia Buford, of Oxford, Miss., in 1884.

IV (8)

Col. Abram Booth Hancock (Benjamin, Lewis, John), b. Oct. 29, 1825, d. Dec. 1, 1903; m. 1st, Martha Elizabeth Walker (b. Sept. 8, 1832, d. June 28, 1881), Nov. 3, 1847, dau. of Moses and Frances Elizabeth Glass Walker; m. 2nd, Susannah L. Machenheimer (d. July 23, 1902) Sept. 26, 1883, and had issue by 1st, marriage only:

(1) William Benjamin Hancock, b. Dec. 11, 1849, d. 1917, m. Eleanor Robertson, of Bedford County. Issue:

(a) Bessie Hancock, m. George Howard Guerrant of Danville. Issue: Eleanor Hancock.

(b) Daisy Hancock, m. Eugene Withers, of Danville. Issue: Margaret and _____ Withers. Eugene Withers served in the Virginia Senate, and the Constitutional Convention of 1901-02. He died in 1924.

(2) John Moses Talbert Hancock, b. Sept. 13, 1852, d. 1919, m. Mary Stone, dau. of Rev. T. J. Stone. No issue.

(3) Frances Elizabeth Hancock, b. in Franklin, Feb. 22, 1854, d. Jan. 10, 1922, at Wellsville, Mo., m. John Peter McCall, (b. in Franklin, Aug. 12, 1843, d. Mar. 21, 1918, at Wellsville, Mo.). Feb. 6, 1878, at Glade Hill, and moved to Wellsville, Mo. Parents of John Peter McCall moved from Franklin to Mo., prior to 1840, but he was born while his mother was visiting in Franklin. In 1861 he enlisted in St. Clair Co., Mo. Cavalry, and served in Mo. Ark., Miss. Tenn., and Ga. He was paroled at Jackson, Miss., May 13, 1865, and returned to his Mo. home July 7, 1865. Issue: (a) Martha Laura, b. Feb. 18, 1880, while her mother was visiting her parents in Franklin; d. Dec. 26, 1898, while student in Howard Payne College (now Central College) at Fayette Mo.; (b) John W. S., of Ft. Worth, Tex., b. Mar. 5, 1885, at Wellsville, Mo., Educ. Central College, served in World War I, Co. I, 357th Inf., 90th Div.; (c) Marie Ellen, of Farmington, Mo., b. Wellsville, Mo. Mar. 13, 1887, educ. Central Coll., Kirksville, Mo., Normal, and S. T. C., Warrenburg, Mo. m. Lester Keithley Rosser, (b. July 2, 1886, in Ralls Co., Mo.) Nov. 28, 1915, at Hannibal, Mo., (d) Wm. Abram of Farmington,Mo., b. at Wellsville, Mo., Aug. 18, 1889; and (e) George Talbot of Farmington, Mo. b. at Wellsville, Mo., Sept. 18, 1893, m. Iva James Brewer, Aug. 16, 1919, at Farmington, Mo. Served overseas in World War I, wounded Sept. 28, 1918, discharged Apr. 2, 1919.

(4) Laura Alice Hancock, b. Mar. 17, 1856, d. Sept. 8, 1880, m. Henry M. Turner, of Callaway, D_ec. 19, 1877. Issue:

(a) C. Emmett Turner, b. Jan. 16, 1879, m. Minnie R., dau. of Dr. R. M. Lemon, July 16, 1903. Issue: Virginia Hancock Turner, b. Nov. 19, 1911.

(b) Laura Turner of Philadelphia, Pa., m. Chas. J. MacGuffin, in Franklin Co. Issue: Harold Turner MacGuffin, b. Aug. 9, 1905.

(5) Mary Ella Hancock, b. Mar. 11, 1858, d. May 4, 1890, m. William Leftwich Turner Hopkins, Dec. 26, 1882.

(6) Charles Henry Hancock, Spanish-American War Veteran, b. Oct. 22, 1859, d. unm. at Rocky Mount, Mar. 21, 1915.

(7) Abram Oscar Hancock, b. Feb. 19, 1862, m. 1st, Isabella F. Baldwin, of N. Y., Nov. 8, 1888; m. 2nd, Mary Sue Whitmore (b. May 20, 1880), dau. of A. A. Whitmore, Methodist Minister of Chatham, Oct. 11, 1905. Issue:

(a) Abram Oscar, Jr., b. June 19, 1906, m. Elizabeth Gardner, Roanoke, June 9, 1928.

(b) Elizabeth Christian, b. June 15, 1907.

(c) George Walker, b. July 18, 1909.

(d) Marjorie S., b. July 28, 1911, Nov. 1, 1914.

(e) Emma Jane, b. Sept. 22, 1913.

(f) Virginius Lee, b. Mar. 28, 1916.

(g) John, b. June 25, 1919.

(h) Benjamin Arthur, b. Mar. 22, 1923.

(8) David Nathaniel Leonidas Hancock, b. Feb. 10, 1864, d. unm. Oct. 23, 1901. He was for many years clerk of the County Criminal Court of Orlando, Florida, and is buried in Orlando.

(9) Jubal Early Hancock, b. Oct. 6, 1866, unm.

(10) Daughter, unnamed, b. Oct. 10, 1868, d. same day.

(11) Walter Scott Hancock, (see V-11).

(12) George Walker Hancock, b. May 6, 1871, d. 1905, m. Mary Louise Keith (d. Sept. 8, 1896), of Timmonsville, S. C., Feb. 9, 1893. Issue:

(a) John Walker, b. Dec. 13, 1893, d. July 13, 1894.

(b) Katherine Louise, o. Mar. 21, 1896, m. Churchhill Boyce Carter.

(13) Mary Hancock, b. March, 1873, d. July, 1873.

V (11).

Walter Scott Hancock (Abram, Benjamin, Lewis, John), b. Nov. 19, 1869, m. Anna Spencer, dau. of Dr. Horatio Nelson Spencer, at St. Louis, Mo., Nov. 21, 1899

Issue:

(1) Walker Kirtland Hancock, sculptor; b. at St. Louis, Mo., June 28, 1901; studied art in Pennsylvania Academy of Fine Arts and at the American Academy in Rome; has exhibited in New York, Philadelphia, St. Louis, San Francisco, Rome and Florence; now director of sculpture at the Pennsylvania Academy of Fine Arts.

(2) Anne Spencer Hancock, b. Sept. 2, 1902; m. Alfred R. Watt, of Evanston, Ill., Sept. 2, 1925; lives at 733 Hinman Ave., Evanston, Ill.

(3) Laura Marshall Hancock, b. July 6, 1904. Instructor of Art as applied to Child Life in St. Louis Community School; m. John Gardner Flint, of St. Louis, Mo., June 16, 1930.

(4) Elizabeth Dwight Hancock, b. May 11, 1906, missionary at Nogoya, Japan.

(5) Deane Spencer Hancock, b. Sept. 28, 1907; educated in Washington University, St. Louis.

IV (9).

Elizabeth Ann Hancock (Benjamin and Elizabeth Booth Hancock, Lewis, John), Dec. 11, 1829, d. Jan. 22, 1897, m. Tazewell Price (b. Feb. 7, 1819, d. Dec. 27, 1897), Feb. 27, 1847. Issue:

(1) Elizabeth V. Price, b. 1848, d. May 6, 18__, m. Peter Kefauver of Copper Hill, Floyd Co.

(2) Ella H. Price, of Radford, b. 1850, m. Noah Hockman, who d. at Salem.

(3) Charles W. Price, b. Feb. 1852, m. Minnie E. Burroughs, Hale's Ford, Nov. 21, 1882.

(4) Benjamin Shores Price, b. May 26, 1854, living at Orlando, Fla., 1928; educated at V. P. I.; m. Lucy C. Camper (b. Dec. 13, 1865) May 7, 1889, at Bent Mountain. Issue:

(a) Mary A., b. Feb. 22, 1890, m. Rayman G. Higgins, Orlando, Fla., 1923.

(b) William Camper, b. Oct. 29, 1891; soldier in World War I; Captain Co. "K", Fla. National Guards; m. Mary Brown, Orlando, Fla., 1924.

(c) Louise E., b. April 14, 1893, Orlando, Fla.; Secretary to Postmaster.

(d) Albert B., b. June 29, 1895; soldier in World War I; m. Jane Chapman, Orlando, Fla.

(e) Robert E., m. Madeline E. Allen, Orlando, Fla., 1923.

(f) Herman C., b. May 3, 1904; educated in State University of Florida.

(5) Julia K. Price, b. 1856, living 1928; educated at Hollins College; m. J. W. Turner of Roanoke, who died in 1909.

(6) C. A. Price, b. 1860, d. Feb. 1888, at Pulaski; m. Oscar Laughton, Salem.

(7) Betty Lee Price, b. 1863, d. Aug. 12, 1927, at

Axton.

(8) Camie T. Price, b. 1870, Axton, m. Walter R. West, Bent Mountain, Mar. 1887.

IV (10)

(10) Charles Robert Hancock (Benjamin and Elizabeth Booth Hancock, Lewis, John), b. Dec. 22, 1831, d. Feb. 25, 1901, m. Sallie Edmund Stone (b. Jan. 20, 1840, d. Oct. 28, 1920), dau. of Edmund and Nancy Chapman (Dickinson) Stone, Feb. 10, 1858. Issue:

(1) Nannie Kate Hancock, b. Feb. 12, 1861, d. May 17, 1881, unm.

(2) Sallie Roberta Hancock, Christiansburg, b. July 20, 1863, m. Benjamin Rupert Powell (b. May 14, 1863), Nov. 15, 1888, at Union Hall. Issue:

(a) Annie Gertrude, Harlan, Ky., b. Nov. 11, 1889, educated in Blackstone College and Randolph-Macon College, Lynchburg, m. Mebane E. Shelton at Lynchburg.

(b) Mary Ruth, b. Mar. 1, 1893, educated in Randolph-Macon Inst., Danville, and in Harrisonburg Normal.

(c) Benjamin Rupert Jr., b. Mar. 19, 1895, attended Massey's Business College, Richmond.

(d) William Robert, b. April 10, 1897, d. May 12, 1901.

(e) Emmett Hancock, b. Oct. 17, 1903.

(f) Louis Bertrand, b. Jan. 6, 1906, educated in V. M. I., Lexington.

(3) William Early Hancock, M. D., Union Hall, b. April 18, 1866, d. Sept. 21, 1907, educated in Louisville Medical College.

(4) Mary Victoria Hancock, Penhook, b. Nov. 17, 1868, m. James B. Zeigler, Sr., Dec. 16, 1909.

(5) Bettie Chapman Hancock, b. Aug. 31, 1871, d. Nov. 14, 1892, m. Charles Q. Edwards, Nov. 14, 1891, in Franklin Co. Issue: Chapman Hancock Edwards, Altavista, b. Nov. 2, 1892, educated in Lynchburg College.

(6) Lillian Alice Hancock, Moneta, b. May 5, 1875, m. J. W. W. Turner (b. Aug. 7, 1866) Oct. 7, 1903, in Franklin Co. Issue:

(a) Robert Early, b. Sept. 3, 1904, attended Ferrum Training School.

(b) Mary Frances, b. May 6, 1906, educated in East Radford State Teacher's College.

(c) Annie Hancock, b. Oct. 27, 1907, educated in State Teachers College, East Radford.

(d) Edmund Stone, b. Oct. 10, 1909, attended Ferrum Training School.

(e) Dorothy Belle, b. May 23, 1913.

(f) Edith, b. Nov. 20, 1914, d. Nov. 24, 1914.

(7) Belle Williams Hancock, (b. Sept. 7, 1877) m. William S. Frazier (b. April 17, 1871) Mar. 26, 1897, in Franklin Co. Issue:

(a) Sallie Kathleen, b. April 26, 1903, educated in Virginia Intermont College, and Boston (Mass) Conservatory.

(b) William Stone, b. May 31, 1905, educated in V. M. I.

(c) Early Hancock, b. May 14, 1908.

(d) Herbert Anselm, b. May 21, 1910.

(e) Carleton Page, b. Mar. 29, 1913.

(8) Ethel Dickinson Hancock, Altavista, (b. Jan. 30, 1880) educated Harrisonburg State Teacher's College, and University of Virginia.

(9) Annie Sue Hancock, b. Aug. 17, 1882, d. Oct. 24, 1888.

(10) Julia Page Hancock, Altavista, b. April 18, 1885, attended S. T. C. at Farmville, m. F. S. Davis, June 19, 1912.

IV (11)

Christopher Harrison Hancock (Benjamin and Elizabeth Booth Hancock, Lewis, John), b. Nov. 26, 1834, in Franklin Co., d. May 12, 1893; m. Victoria Street (b. July 11, 1839, d. Mar. 12, 1897), dau. of Wm. A. and Nancy Street, Jan. 22, 1857. William Street represented Franklin Co., in the General Assembly 1844-47. Issue:

(1) William A. Hancock, Bluefield, W. Va., b. Nov. 19, 1858, m. Florence Cooke, dau. of James Anthony Cooke, of Franklin Co., Feb. 17, 1886. Issue:

(a) Percy Cooke, b. Nov. 29, 1886, m. Ethel Loraine
Hillman, of St. Paul, Oct. 23, 1912. Issue: James Anthony, b.
July 20, 1913; and Rolfe Louise, b. April 15, 1915.

(b) Viola Victoria, m. William Martin Blalock,
Dec. 16, 1925.

(2) John B. Hancock, b. Aug. 5, 1860, m. Lucy A. Poindexter (b. Feb. 12, 1862) Dec. 12, 1883, at Union Hall. Issue:

(a) William Letcher, Cape Charles, b. Oct. 1, 1884.

(b) Grace, b. Jan. 21, 1887, m. R. B. Harris, Roanoke.

(c) Moss, b. June 30, 1889, d. Sept. 10, 1910.

(d) Katie E., b. Nov. 26, 1894, m. F. L. Johnson,
Roanoke.

(e) Roy B., b. Sept. 3, 1897, m. Gladys Bryant,
Oct. 5, 1923, Roanoke.

(f) John C., b. July 3, 1900, m. Doris Thorpe,
May 5, 1926, at New Brunswick, N. J.

(g) Louise P., Roanoke, b. Nov. 21, 1902.

(3) Charles Street Hancock, b. Mar. 20, 1863, d. Dec.
11, 1923, m. Mattie Semones (b. May 28, 1874), dau. of B. S.
and Sarah Semones, Jan. 5, 1896. Issue:

(a) Guy C., b. Dec. 22, 1897, m. Stella Rhodes,
Oct. 15, 1921, at Roanoke. Issue: Guy C., Jr., b. July 9,
1928.

(4) Nancy Elizabeth Hancock, b. Aug. 27, 1867, m.
John W. Hammersly (b. June 27, 1871), July 2, 1895. Issue:

(a) Annie Ray b. April 14, 1896, m. William Butler,
Dec. 19, 1923, Salem.

(b) Russell, m. Lorina Thelma Etter, Sept. 27, 1927,
Salem. Issue: Lorina Thelma, b. July 9, 1928.

(5) Julia Kate Hancock, b. Feb. 16, 1869, m. John
W. Johnson (b. Sept. 19, 1871, d. Aug. 14, 1928) Oct. 11, 1906,
at Roanoke. No issue.

(6) Walter Roland Hancock, b. Mar. 30, 1872, m. Annie
Melville Gwaltney (b. Feb. 19, 1880), dau. of James W. and Susan
(Haley) Gwaltney, Feb. 10, 1898, at Winston-Salem, N. C. Issue:

(a) Louise Virginia, b. May 1, 1900; educated a t
Hollins College; m. Louis A. Voigt, Jr., Oct. 5, 1920, at Roanoke.

(b) Walter Roland, Jr., b. July 6, 1904; educated University of Virginia.

(c) Kenneth Linwood, b. Jan. 14, 1906, d. May 30, 1907.

(d) Everett Sherwood, b. May 11, 1911; educated Roanoke College and University of Virginia.

(7) Robert P. Hancock, b. Aug. 7, 1873.

(8) Lonnie W. Hancock, b. June 19, 1879.

(9) Daisy Claire Hancock, b. Oct. 21, 1881, d. Feb. 19, 1920, m. Guy Lucas Shertz (b. June 24, 1879) Dec. 31, 1901, at Roanoke. Issue:

(a) Elizabeth Victoria, Ridgeville, N. C., b. April 1, 1903, m. Eugene Foster, April 13, 1924, at Roanoke, and has dau. Betty Gene, b. July 29, 1927

(b) Charles Wallace, b. April 12, educated in V. P. I.

(c) Guy Louis, b. Nov. 15, 1909.

(d) Alvin Linwood, b. Nov. 21, 1911.

(e) John Albert, b. April 12, 1913.

(f) Louise, b. Nov. 8, 1916.

IV (14).

Julia A. Maria Hancock (Benjamin and Elizabeth Booth Hancock, Lewis, John), m. John Randolph Zeigler, June 20, 1860, and had issue:

(1) Michael Zeigler, m. Allie Law., dau. of W. D. Law. Among issue:

(a) Cameron, m. Everett Blackwell

(b) Benjamin

(2) Alpha Zeigler, m. and had issue: seven children.

(3) Morse Zeigler, b. Nov. 14, 1884, m. Samuel H. Sheppard (b. Oct. 5, 1875) Nov. 21, 1907, in Franklin Co. Home: Alexandria. Issue:

(a) Mary, b. Aug. 19, 1911.

(b) Hannah, b. Aug. 27, 1914.

(c) Samuel H. b. Sept. 19, 1916.

(d) Marvin, b. May 20, 1919.

(e) Morse, b. July 24, 1921.

(4) Katherine Elizabeth Zeigler, b. Nov. 10, 1866.
m. Dr. James Philemon Smith (b. Aug. 24, 1861, d. June 5, 1925)
Dec. 19, 1891. Issue:

(a) Hubert Zeigler, b. April 16, 1894, m. Leone
Eggleston, Apr. 8, 1925, at Spray, N. C. He was educated in
Randolph-Macon College, Ashland.

(b) Mary Katherine, b. April 14, 1896; educated
in Randolph-Macon Woman's College Lynchburg; m. Dr. Carleton
Moorman, Nov. 16, 1927, at Martinsville.

(c) James Randolph, dentist, b. July 27, 1901;

(5) Mary Zeigler, unm.

THE (THOMAS) HANCOCK FAMILY

(not related to the foregoing family)

I.

(1) Thomas Hancock, b. ca. 1734, d. in Franklin Co.
in 1803, m. Mary Shoemaker in Goochland Co., Mar. 25, 1758, she
died in Franklin Co., in 1812. Under date of April 20, 1763
(D. B. 8, p. 328, Goochland Co.) Thomas Hancock of Goochland
Co., conveyed Darby Ferlines of Chesterfield Co. 125 acres in
Goochland Co. located on the branches of Gennetto Creek. On
Oct. 10, 1779, Thomas Hancock was granted 90 acres in that
part of Henry Co. which later became Franklin Co. This land
was located on Beard's Creek, 15 miles southwest of Rocky Mount.
When the oath of allegiance was being administered in all of
the Virginia Counties during the Revolutionary War, Thomas Hancock of Henry Co. was among the list which took the oath on Oct.
31, 1777. He left a will of record in Franklin Co., (W. B. 1, p.
33), dated July 25, 1803, probated Dec. 5, 1803, in which he
names his wife, Mary Hancock; daughters, Nancy and Obedience;
sons, Benjamin and Stephen. He devised to his wife his real
estate for her life, and after her death, the lower half of
his tract of land was to go to his son, Benjamin Hancock, and
the upper half to his son, Stephen Hancock. Their mother died
in 1812, as the tax records show that Benjamin and Stephen Hancock came into possession of the land in 1813. It is likely
that he was related to Lewis Hancock of Franklin Co., as he named
Benjamin Hancock, Jr., a son of Lewis Hancock, and William Hancock, executors of his estate. Benjamin Hancock, born in 1782,
son of Lewis, was called "Junior" to distinguish him from Benjamin Hancock, the son of Thomas Hancock, who was born in 1760.
The tax records show that Benjamin Hancock, son of Lewis Hancock,

was called "Junior" till the time of his death in 1860.

Issue and dates of births as shown by the St. James Northam Parish of Goochland Co., by Rev. William Douglass.

II.

(1) Ann (Nancy) Hancock, b. Nov. 26, 1758, baptized Feb. 11, 1759, in Goochland Co. She is mentioned in her father's will, but it is not known whether or not she ever married or when she died.

(2) Benjamin Hancock, designated as "Senior" in the Franklin Co. tax records, b. Nov. 13, 1760, in Goochland Co., d. 1850 in Franklin Co. There was apparently no administration of his estate, and his land, on Beards Creek was carried on the tax records as "Benjamin Hancock, deceased" as late as 1863.

(3) John Hancock, twin of Benjamin, b. Nov. 13, 1760, baptised Jan. 6, 1763, in Goochland County. He probably died prior to 1803, as he is not mentioned in the Will of his father.

(4) Mary Hancock, b. June 3, baptised Jan. 6, 1763, in Goochland County. She probably died prior to 1803, as she is not mentioned in her father's Will of that date.

(5) Obedience Hancock, b. May 14, 1764, baptised Sept. 2, 1764, in Goochland Co. She was bequeathed certain property by her father, but there is no futher record of her.

(6) Stephen Hancock, b. June 6, 1766, baptised Sept. 7, 1766, in Goochland Co., d. 1825 in Franklin Co. His father devised him the upper half of his platation on Beard's Creek. In 1863 his land was still being carried on the tax records under the designation, "Stephen Hancock, deceased."

Jacob Hancock was assessed a property tax for the years 1826 and 1827.

THE HARPER FAMILY

Claiborne, son of John and Nancy Harper, was born in Amelia County, December 23, 1774. He married Mary Cabaniss, November 7, 1799. She was born August 15, 1776. The Harpers are of English, and the Cabaniss family is of French Hugenot descent.

Claiborne Harper was a soldier in the War of 1812. served in Capt. S. Thomas' Company, Virginia Militia, from July 31, 1813, then was transferred to Captain Neblett's Company, and served until October 1, 1813, when on account of bad health, he furnished Nath Walker as his substitute and was honorably discharged. He returned to his home in Nottoway County, and died February 7, 1814.

A deed dated February 2, 1835, and other records, show that his widow and children sold his Nottoway County land to Benjamin Ward, whose land completely surrounded it, for seventy dollars, and removed to a farm in Franklin County, settling near Taylor's Store. On February 7, 1827, William T. Harper, oldest son of Claiborne and Mary Harper, bought from John McCrery 160 acres of land on Gill's Creek for the sum of $850.00 (in 1934 this land was owned and occupied by Gracie Layman.)

Mary Cabaniss Harper spent the remaining years of her life in the home of her son Joel. In 1853 she applied for a pension of Bounty Land but the petition was denied. She died on January 10, 1870, at the age of 94, and is buried in the graveyard on the place. There are no markers to her grave. Claiborne Harper is buried in Nottoway County in an unknown grave.

Claiborne and Mary (Cabaniss) Harper had issue: 1. William Trenton, 2. Lucy, 3. Edmund, 4. Jesse, 6. James Claiborne, 7. Joel and 8. Robert Matthew.

William Trenton was born in Nottoway County, June 17, 1801. He was employed in St. Louis, Missouri, where he died, unmarried, August 4, 1832.

Lucy was born in Nottoway County, September 14, 1802, She died unmarried on November 17, 1835, and is buried on the Joel Harper place.

Edmund was born in Nottoway County, February 21, 1804, and died unmarried on October 1820.

Mary was born April 30, 1807. She married John Paine Collier, August 15, 1822. Mr. Collier was born in England, December 10, 1790. His father, with two brothers, came to America together. The father sailed for England rather than fight against his country. He was presumably lost at sea as he was never heard from again. John Collier went to Kentucky before his marriage, enlisted under Andrew Jackson, and served in the battle of New Orleans. One of his brothers became over heated in a wheat field and died. The other brother married and has many descendants. John Collier was a mason by trade and also a farmer. His oldest child was born in Virginia. The family were living in William County, Tennessee, in 1831-39. They afterwards settled in Graves County, Kentucky. Mary Harper Collier never revisited in Virginia after her marriage. John Paine Collier died February 15, 1885. His widow spent her last years in the home of her son, Joel Robert Collier. She died in 1886. Both are buried near Boaz Station, Graves County, Kentucky. There are no stones with inscriptions at their graves.

John Paine Collier and Mary Harper had issue: 1. Charles Claiborne, 2. William Paine, 3. Sally Ann Elizabeth, 4. Mary Jane, 5. Louisa Clark, 6. John James, 7. Nancy L., 8. Martha H., 9. Marcus Lafayett, 10. Harriet Angeline, 11. Joel Robert and 12. Pemelia Margaret. Charles married Nancy Ann Stokes. William Paine Married, first, Frances Ann Balance; second, Catherine Hayes; and third, Frances Elliott. Sally Ann married James Meadows. Mary Jane married William Balance. Louisa Clark married John Thomas Buckingham. John James married Margaret Buckingham. Mancy L., and Martha died unmarried. Marcus Lafayette never married. He served in Company B. 6th, Illinois Cavalry, during the Civil War and died in Camp, May 27, 1863. Harriet Angeline married, first, George Franklin Bolen, and second, Samuel Bales. Joel Robert married Nancy Jane Whitis. Permelia Margaret married George Byerley.

Jesse, son of Claiborne Harper, was born in Nottoway County, August 23, 1808. He was employed in St. Louis, Missouri, where he died October 28, 1831.

James Claiborne, sixth child of Claiborne Harper, was born in Nottoway County, January 11, 1810. He married Mary Showalter, November 24, 1842. She was born January 25, 1827, and died June 8, 1862. James died June 26, 1897. They are buried at Franklin near the lower Church at Cross Roads. There are no markers at their graves. After his marriage, James Harper settled on a farm near Cross Roads. James was too old for active service in the Civil War. He served as drill master at home. He was employed in St. Louis when his two brothers died. He built Taylor's Store, the house of Jesse Clay Dillon at Cross Roads, and the Jack Starkey and Tyree Dillon houses. He and his son Stephen built many of the old bank barns of Franklin County.

James Claiborne and Mary Harper had issue: 1. Nancy Mary, married Robert Irvin Bush; 2. Maria Catherine, married Samuel Moore; 3. Mildred Victoria, married Thaddeus Reed Dillon; 4. Charles Henry, never married; 5. Joseph Peter, married Ellen Virginia English; 6. James Robert, never married; 7. Stepehn Claiborne, never married; 8. Rhoda Elizabeth, married first, John William Lumsden, and, second, Fayette W. Harvey; 9. Sarah Lucy, married William Demorest Southall; 10. Jabez William, married Maggie Magdaline Pasley; and 11. Johnson Beauregard, married Sallie C. Bradley.

Joel, seventh child of Claiborne and Mary Harper, was born in Nottoway County, October 4, 1811. He married Mary Noble, June 11, 1844. She was born November 23, 1824, and died March 13, 1912. She spent the last years of her life in the home of her daughter Kate in Fulton, Missouri, and is buried there. Joel Harper died January 22, 1892, and is buried near Taylor's Store. Mary Ann Noble was a daughter of Daniel and Nancy (Greer) Noble. The father of Nancy was a son of Moses Jr. and Susannah (Wood) Greer. Joel and Mary (Noble) Harper had issue: 1. William Trenton, who married Lucy Mary Cook; 2. Nannie Noble, who married Zachariah Taylor Dillon, and settled in Missouri; 3. Sarah Cornelia, who married Jacob Dillon; 4. John Robert, died unmarried in Georgetown, Texas; 5. Lucy Ann, never married; 6. Daniel Noble, married Sallie A. Lumsden; 7. James Moses, married Pattie Willie Chambers; 8. Joel Thomas, married, first, Mary Ann Bowen, and, second, Sallie Frances Vermillion; 9. Emma, died at 16, unmarried; 10. Fannie Miller, married John M. Young; 11. Claiborne Owen, married, first, Lee Marion Pasley, and second, James Gooldy.

Robert Matthew, youngest child of Claiborne and Mary Harper, was born in Nottoway County, June 22, 1813. He married first, Lydia Hill, and second, Mary Ann Betz. He married Lydia Hill March 4, 1838. She was born March 14, 1820, and died March 4, 1851, and is buried in old Liberty Cemetery near Black Rock Church. Mary Ann Betz was born December 4, 1829, and died September 8, 1924. She is buried in Payson, Utah. Robert Harper died August 23, 1893, and is buried at Payson, Utah. Robert and his second wife were members of the Mormon Church, as are most of his descendants. They went to Utah in 1883, settling at Payson. His sons, John Claiborne and Edmund, were of the Council of Seventy. Robert Matthew Harper and his first wife had issue: 1. Charles Claiborne, who never married; 2. Mary Louise, who died at the age of fourteen; 3. John Claiborne, who married, first, Ruth Ann Hill, second, Mary Price Davis, third, Fanny Combs. The last named was living in Juarez, Mexico, in 1932; 4. Martha Elizabeth Harper, who died at the age of six years.

Robert Matthew Harper and Mary Ann Betz had issue: 1. Edmund Henry, who married Estella Victoria Dixon; 2. Robert Fulton, who died at the age of seven years; 3. Mary Fanny, who married William Keen Henry; 4. James Thomas, who married Almira Boyle; 5. Silas Benjamin, who married Sarah Amanda Shurtiluff; 6. Kenton Lee, who married, first, Maria Combs, and, second, Laura Ellen Taylor; 7. Beverly Davis, who married Mary Kasiah Boyle; 8. William Tell, who married, first, Evaline Ladel Wightman, and, second, Ellen Elizabeth Butler; 9. Walter Payton, who married Sarah Meleta Openshaw, and 10. Charles B. Harper, who died in infancy.

THE HILL FAMILY

The following information concerning the Hill Family of Franklin County was contained in a letter from Arthur Bernard, of Rocky Mount, to the author of this volume, under date of October 20, 1934.

My grandfather's mother was a daughter of Robert Hill, and my knowledge of that family is derived from tradition, and not from written records. Robert Hill came to this section from Dublin, Ireland, sometime prior to 1740, and secured possession of a large tract of land in the wilderness, where he built his home spent the remainder of his life. His wife, Velie Linus, was a member of an old Roman family that went from Italy to the British Isles shortly after the Roman conquest.

An effort has been made to identify her family with that of an early Bishop of the Christian Church, but, as far as I am now informed, there are no authentic records to establish that connection. Robert Hill died in 1778, not a very old man, and his wife survived him by several years. Three of his sons suffered violent deaths, two being killed by Indians, and a third by a colt which he was riding. The other two sons, Swinfield and Thomas, reached years of maturity and figured in various enterprises and functions of the pioneer community. Swinfield Hill commanded a company in the Revolutionary War and was a member of the first county court on its organization in 1784. He also served in other capacities of a public nature during most of his life.

I do not know who he married, nor the year of his death, and practically nothing of his children. The wife of Thomas Hill was Aliana Standifer, a family name that disappeared from the county in the early 1800's. I have sometimes seen the name in news items from Texas, but do not know if there is any relationship between the families of the two sections. Of the daughters of Robert Hill, three were married by gentlemen who moved to Tennessee - Wade, Barton, and Armstrong, - and as a consequence have no place in Franklin genealogy. A son of one of them - David Barton - became a close personal and political friend of Andrew Jackson; and served in Congress from Tennessee and, if I am not mistaken, as United States Senator from Missouri. Walter Bernard and Col. William Jones married the other two daughters of Robert Hill, and their descendants, with some exceptions, continued to reside in Virginia. One of the sons of Thomas Hill was killed by a panther, and the other son, and the daughters, with their husbands, moved to Tennessee. Walter Bernard, who married a daughter of Robert Hill, was a native of Frederick County, Maryland, and came to this section as a soldier in the Revolutionary War, in which struggle he attained the rank of Major, and at its close devoted his attention to the manufacture of iron and to other enterprises of the community. He died in 1841, in his 82nd. year. One of his sons, Linus, was killed in the War of 1812, and another of his sons, Zadok, commanded a company that went from this county to Norfolk to aid in protecting that city from British warships. Zadok Bernard's wife was Mary Kitchin, a daughter of Caleb Kitchin of Buckingham County, and his wife, Mary Arrington, of Amherst County. Zadok Bernard served for some time on the county court, composed at that period of Justices appointed by the Governor of the State. He died in 1871, in the 81st year of his age. Zadok's son, Thomas Hill Bernard, succeeded his father on the county court, was captain of militia prior to and in the early months of the Civil War. He was appointed by the Confederate authorities on a committee to collect for and distribute supplies to the families of soldiers in active service. At the close of the war he cooperated with Major DeKnight, a Federal officer, in establishing some form of order in the chaotic conditions prevailing at that time.

On the reorganization of the State government, in 1869, he was appointed county superintendent of schools, and in that capacity established the public school system in this county. He served eight years as judge of the county court, and afterwards as a member of the Electoral Board of the county, which closed his connection with government affairs. In conjuction with Perry Harrison, he aided in establishing a tobacco market in Rocky Mount after the completion of the Franklin and Pittsylvania railroad. He died in 1905, at 80 years of age. His wife was Sarah Eudalia, a daughter of Moses and Nannie Featherstone Eudalia of Charlotte County. She survived her husband twelve years, dying in 1917 in her 86th year. Some traditions existed among the older citizens of the county which if supported by actual facts would command a place in any history of this section. One of these concerns a supposed visit of John Brown to this county in 1858, at which time he posed as a doctor professing to treat Negro men for hernia and unmentionable diseases. During these private ministrations, he would sound his "patients" on their attitude toward measures of violence to secure liberation. To such of them as he judged would be sufficiently prudent, he would outline a method of cooperation in the scheme shortly to be launched for their emancipation. The plan which he seemed to have nursed in his own mind, was that these secret consultations would lay the groundwork for a bloody uprising among the slaves and aid in his campaign for devastation and destruction through the south. I am 75 years of age and write a very imperfect hand. I hope you can read it.

In the old Tan Yard grave yard at Rocky Mount are the following tombstones with legible inscriptions:

1. Robert Hill, 10 Aug. 1778

2. In remembrance- Violet Hill, Aug. 1803 (1808?)

3. In remembrance of Thomas Hill, dec'd. 1827

4. Linus Hill- dec'd __01

5. In Memory of Lucy Hill

6. In Memory of Ruth Bernard who departed this life 18th March 1841, aged 83 years, 18 days. (She was a daughter of Robert Hill)

7. In Memory- Walter Bernard, who departed this life 5 Feb. 1841, aged 82 years, 11 months, and 5 days.

THE HOOK FAMILY

Henry Hook was a manufacturer of Glasgow Scotland. His known issue are: 1. Thomas; 2. Charles, living in Jamaica some years after 1779; 3. Duncan, died in 1799, in Jamaica; 4. John, born 1745-46, at Glasgow Scotland, died 1808, at Hale's Ford, Franklin County, Va.; 5. Archibald, went to India; 6. Lionel; 7. Robert; and 8. a daughter who married Captain Fraser, and went to India.

In some letters, Major Campbell, "our Highland Kinsman" is mentioned.

John Hook, 4th son came to Virginia in 1758 (12-13 years old), in the employ of William and James Donald, Scotch merchants and shipowners, of Greenock, Scotland.

John Hook, lived, first, at Blandford, then after his marriage to Elizabeth Smith, daughter of Col. John Smith of Goochland, about 1772, he settled at New London, Bedford County, Virginia, where he kept a store until 1784, when he moved to Hale's Ford, Franklin County, Virginia. He was a merchant until his death in 1808.

He was constantly in law suits. Among some of the cases was that of Ross and Hook that began in 1785, and did not end until 1850, long after both of parties were dead. Patrick Henry was his lawyer in several cases, and in a letter to him, Hook says: "If you will only manage this case for me with the same energy and ability as you did against me when you defeated the ends of justice in Venable's case, we shall be sure to win."

John Hook also employed Edmund Randolph and Philip Norborne Nicholas as counsel at times.

John Hook and wife, Elizabeth, had two sons, and four daughters. 1. Henry, born 1775, died 1811, not married; 2. John Jr., died 1807, Nashville, Tennessee, not married, he had just begun to practice medicine; 3. Elizabeth, who married Christopher Clark, Joplin descendants in Richmond, Virginia; 4. Charlotte, who married Dr. Samuel Griffin, descendants live in Bedford, Roanoke and Campbell Counties, Virginia; 5. Margaret, who married Thomas West, and their daughters, Louisa, married Hobson; ⠒ and 6. Catherine, who married Bowker Preston, descendants are the Misses Holland, and the Nowlins of Campbell County, Virginia, and the Christians of Lynchburg, Virginia, also Capt. Thomas Bowker Holland of Co. D. 2nd, Va. Cavalry, and Lieutenant Thomas B. Davis of Lynchburg, who were both killed in the Civil War. Miss Holland's father also served from Manasses to Appomattox as did some of the Griffins.

THE HOPKINS FAMILY

I

(1) William Hopkins, b. ca. 1685, d. in St. Peter's Parish, New Kent, Dec. 16, 1755. His wife, Frances, surname unknown, d. Dec. 10, 1755. Due to destruction of the records of New Kent, James City and surrounding counties, by the Federal Army, it is impossible to name his parents. It is believed that he was a grandson of John Hopkins, who came from England with Henry Soane, in 1656, and settled in New Kent.

William and Frances Hopkins had 8 children, among whom was:

II

(1) Francis Hopkins, b. Feb. 27, 1737, d. 1804,

II (1)

Francis Hopkins (William) left a will, of record in Bedford Co., dated Feb. 21, 1803, pro. June 25, 1804. He m. Jane Cox, in Cumberland Co., Nov. 25, 1760. She d. in Bedford Co., ca. 1815. She was living in 1811, according to a suit of Hopkins vs. Carter (Orders 1809-11), and was dead Jan. 1, 1816, according to agreement, of Jan. 1, 1816, of her four children, dividing the slaves bequeathed her by her husband, Francis Hopkins. (D. B. "N", p. 452). Francis Hopkins gave bond in Cumberland Co., on Nov. 25, 1760, to marry Jane Cox. John Holman was his surety.

On Feb. 1, 1762, James Bagby of Cumberland Co., conveyed to Francis Hopkins of Cumberland, 600 acres in Amelia Co. The deed was witnessed by William and John Cox, and John Bagby. (D. B. 7, p. 666, Amelia Co.) In Aug. 1763, Francis Hopins and Jane, his wife, of Amelia Co., conveyed William Ware and Joel Meadoe 150 and 225 acres, respectively, (D. B. 8, pp. 189. Amelia Co.) In April 1773, and Oct. 1773, they conveyed 10 acres to John Green, and 215 acres to William Ware. (D. B. 12, pp. 54 and 138, Amelia Co.)

Francis Hopkins removed to Bedford C. from Amelia Co. ca. 1771. Bedford Co. records show that William Trigg, on Jan. 22, 1771, conveyed to Francis Hopkins of Amelia Co., 400 acres located on the South side of Otter River.

His wife, Jane Cox, dau. of Frederick and Elizabeth Cox, who left will dated May 4, 1754, pro. Jan. 27, 1755 in Cumberland Co. (W. B. 1, p. 90). She was a granddaughter of Bartholomew and Rebecca Cox (b. ca. 1665, in Henrico Co., d. 1730), who left will of record in Goochland Co., (in W. B. 1, p. 262, dated Jan. 14, 1730), and she was a great granddaughter of John Cox, the emigrant, b. ca. 1612, d. in 1696, left will dated Feb. 19, 1691, pro. Feb. 1, 1696, (Book V, p. 678, Henrico Co.)

Issue of Francis and Jane (Cox) Hopkins:

III

(1) John Hopkins,

(2) Price Hopkins, b. 1777, d. July 1845, m. 1st, Elizabeth Turner (b. July 10, 1781, d. July 11, 1810) dau. of Rev. James Turner, Oct. 13, 1801; and m. 2nd, Frances G. Claytor (d. 1860), dau. of Samuel Claytor, Dec. 31, 1812. He served in War of 1812. 12 children survived him.

(3) William Hopkins, b. ca. 1770, d. 1820, m. Elizabeth Clarke, of Powhatan Co., dau. of William Clarke Sr., Apr. 21, 1795. He served in War of 1812, and represented Bedford Co. in the General Assembly. He d. 1820, 7 children survived him.

(4) Martha (or Patsy) Hopkins, b. ca. 1766, m. John Walden, Apr. 6, 1786, Four children survived her.

III (1)

John Hopkins (Francis, William) b. Oct. 6, 1775, in Bedford Co. and d. there Mar. 19, 1821. The division of his estate is of record in Bedford Co. as of Dec. 26, 1825. He left numerous slaves and several plantations. He m. Mary (Polly) Turner, dau. of Rev. James Turner, of Bedford, Revolutionary soldier and a Presbyterian minister, Sept. 2, 1800. She was b. Aug. 25, 1779, and d. Jan. 10, 1848. (See her will pro. Jan. 24, 1848, W. B. "M", p. 540.)

Mary Turner's mother was Sarah Leftwich, (b. Jan. 20, 1762, d. Nov. 27, 1834) sister of Col. William Leftwich, and dau. of Augustine Leftwich, (b. ca. 1712 in New Kent Co. d. in Bedford Co. 1795); and granddaughter of Thomas Leftwich, (b. ca. 1660, in New Kent Co. d. 1730 in Caroline Co.) and great granddaughter of Ralph Leftwich, (b. ca. 1628, in England, d. in New Kent Co. ca. 1780), who patented 300 acres, in 1658, on the Piankatank River in New Kent.

John Hopkins gave bond in Bedford Co. Sept. 1, 1800, to marry Mary (Polly) Turner, dau. of James Turner. Frazier Otey was his surety. Issue of John and Mary (Turner) Hopkins:

IV

(1) Sally Leftwich Hopkins, (b. Nov. 20, 1801) m. James S. McAllister, attorney, Apr. 17, 1820, in Bedford Co. He d. July 11, 1824. Issue:

(a) Mary Bell, (b) Nancy J. T., and (c) John.

(2) James Turner Hopkins, (b. Mar. 6, 1803, d. May 12, 1836) m. Mary (Polly) Early, Dec. 15, 1824. Soon after her husband's death in 1836, she moved to Mercer Co. now West Va., where she died.

(3) Francis Hopkins, (b. Jan. 21, 1805) m. Emeline Cooke, dau. of Maj. William and Sarah Maxwell (Otey) Cooke (sister of Bishop Otey) Oct. 21, 1835. They moved to Arkansas. Maj. William Cooke was a son of Benjamin Cooke, son of John Cooke, son of Benjamin Cooke, son of Thomas Cooke, son of Mordecai Cooke, of Gloucester Co. Mordecai Cooke's dau. Mary (d. Jan. 21, 1723) m. Thomas Booth, of Gloucester Co.

(4) Jesse Turner Hopkins, b. Dec. 13, 1807, d. Sept. 5, 1877, m. Mildred E. Hewitt, May 17, 1826.

(5) Elizabeth Ann Hopkins, b. May 24, 1810, m. William J. A. Quarles, Jan. 29, 1828. They moved to Tenn.

(6) John Calvin Hopkins, b. Aug. 21, 1812, d. July 20, 1889, m. 1st, Maria M. Barnes, Sept. 22, 1829; 2nd, Louisa B. Gillespie, June 20, 1844; and 3rd, Elizabeth Ann Tabler, July 1, 1847. He moved to Tazewell Co. He had 10 children, one of whom, Francis Alexander, represented a Kentucky District in Congress.

(7) Dr. William Leftwich Turner Hopkins, b. Dec. 14, 1814, d. Aug. 5, 1873, m. Julia Ann Muse, Dec. 26, 1850.

(8) Harriet Hopkins, b. Jan. 11, 1817, d. Oct. 25, 1819.

(9) Mary Jane Hopkins, b. Jan. 31, 1819, d. June 20, 1890, m. Rev. William Henry Matthews, Presbyterian minister of Powhatan Co., Feb. 22, 1848.

(10) Harriet Burr Hopkins, b. Feb. 12, 1821, d. 1893, m. Robert G. Bell, Dec. 1, 1841. Issue: (a) Sarah Turner, m. John Wilson; (b) Mary; (c) Robert G., Jr., Confederate soldier, unm. killed Apr. 26, 1865; and (d) Kirkwood, of Montvale, b. Feb. 3, 1855, m. Maggie A. Baldwin, May 7, 1890. The foregoing births and deaths are recorded in the Bible of John Hopkins.

IV (7)

Dr. William Leftwich Turner Hopkins (John, Francis, William) b. Dec. 14, 1814, d. Aug. 5, 1873 was graduated from University of Pa., in 1838, located in Franklin Co. and practiced medicine 35 years. He m. Julia Ann Muse (b. Jan. 21, 1824, d. Feb. 22, 1916) Dec. 26, 1850, dau. of Henry Lawson Muse, veteran of War of 1812, and a member of the Va. Legislature. Issue:

V

(1) William Henry Hopkins, b. Aug. 13, 1852, d. Sept. 24, 1857.

(2) Mary Elizabeth Hopkins, b. Aug. 28, 1854, d. Sept. 21, 1913, m. Henry Clay Price, of Franklin Co. (d. Sept. 29, 1919) Mar. 29, 1877. Issue:

    (a) William Henry Price, b. July 14, 1878, at Dillons Mill; m. Elizabeth E. Deyerle, of Oklahoma, Sept. 28, 1904. He was educated in V. P. I., and he farms in Franklin Co. Issue: 1. Clay Deyerle, b. June 27, 1905; 2. Elizabeth, b. Feb. 15, 1910; 3. John William, b. Jan. 9, 1919; 4. Peter La Shores; and 5. Pauline, d. in infancy.

    (b) Annie Lee Price, b. Sept. 19, 1881, at Dillon's Mill, m. Graham Melville Ker, b. Oct. 21, 1879, in Mexico City, Feb. 6, 1907. She was educated at Oxford Academy, Floyd Court House; Roanoke City High School; and University of Mexico. Her husband's grandfather and Alexander Graham Bell were brothers. Issue: (1) Anita Melville Ker, b. May 28, 1908, in Mexico City; attended school in Berkeley, Calif. 1918-19; P. S. School No. 9, New York City, 1920-21, where she won the gold metal for scholarship; won competitive scholarship in Horace Mann High School, N. Y. C., 1921; student at Stuart Hall, Staunton, 1921-25, George Washington University, 1925; Wellesley 1926-30; and (2) James Alexander Ker, b. Mar. 19, 1911, d. 1914.

    (c) Minnie Estelle Price, b. Jan. 19, 1886, educated in State Norman, Farmville, and in Univ. of Va.

    (d) Mildred Turner Price, b. Apr. 6, 1888, Dillon's Mill; educated in State Normal, Farmville.

(3) Julia Sarah Hopkins, b. Jan. 3, 1857, d. June 22, 1863.

(4) Harriet Burr Hopkins, b. Dec. 31, 1858, d. Oct. 30, 1875.

(5) William Leftwich Turner Hopkins, b. Sept. 30, 1860 (living in 1935), m., 1st, Mary Ella Hancock, Dec. 26, 1882; 2nd, Mary Ann Rebecca Smith, June 4, 1895; and 3rd, Sallie Kathleen Stone, Sept. 9, 1916.

(6) Mildred Turner Hopkins, b. Jan. 9, 1862, d. Dec. 10, 1899, m. Abram P. Hancock, Oct. 20, 1882. Issue: (a) Hattie; (b) W. Lawson, d. Jan. 9, 1903; and (c) Pierce Edward.

(7) Ann Henry Hopkins, b. Dec. 26, 1863, d. Apr. 25, 1865.

V (5)

William Leftwich Turner Hopkins (Dr. Wm. L. T. H., John, Francis, William), had issue by 1st marriage:

VI

(1) William Benjamin Hopkins, M. D., of Tampa, Fla., m. Mary Conrad Nicholson, of Littleton, N. C. and had issue: William Benjamin Jr., (b. Mar. 25, 1924) and Elizabeth Johnson, (b. May 10, 1926).

(2) Oscar Leonidas Hopkins.

(3) Abram Hancock Hopkins, Judge at Rocky Mount.

(4) Col. Walter Lee Hopkins. Lawyer of Richmond, Va.

William Leftwich Turner Hopkins issue by 2nd marriage:

(5) Clack Dickinson Hopkins, M. D.

(6) Mary Alma Hopkins, educated in Blackstone College, Jackson College of Boston, Mass; taught in Southern College, Petersburg, was Dean for one year. On June 4, 1926, she m. David Bidwell Sabine, chemical engineer, of New York City.

(7) Anne Elizabeth Hopkins, b. in Franklin Co., educated in Blackstone College, Martha Washington College at Abingdon, Skidmore College, at Saratoga, N. Y., Emory and Henry College; and teaches at Boone's Mill.

(8) Lawson Muse Hopkins, Civil Engineer, b. in Franklin Co., educated in public schools, Roanoke College and V. M. I. at Lexington. He is now in the Engineering Department of the Illinois Central Railroad Co., at Des Moines, Iowa. He m. Edna Hodel, Sept. 20, 1930, at Peoria Ill.

THE (CHARLES) HOPKINS FAMILY

(not related to the foregoing family)

I.

(1) Charles Hopkins, b. ca. 1770, d. in Franklin Co. in 1850, m. Mary, surname unknown, ca. 1790. The first record of him is his name on the tax list of Franklin in 1793. He was probably a brother of Richard Hopkins, who settled in Patrick Co. in 1792, a year before Charles Hopkins settled in Franklin. On Feb. 1, 1800, Thomas Carter of Franklin conveyed to Charles Hopkins 330 acres on Lynville Creek, 20 miles northeast of Rocky Mount. (D.B. 4, p. 73) In 1813, Charles Hopkins bought 74

acres on Indian River, 18 miles northeast of Rocky Mount, and, in 1821, he deeded this land to Rebecca Williams. In 1825, Charles Hopkins and William, his son, owned, jointly, 200 acres, 20 miles northeast of Rocky Mount. He left a will (Franklin W. B. 7, p. 200) dated Jan. 12, 1847, pro. June 3, 1850, bequeathing all of his land and personal property to his sons, William, George W., and Henry G. "for the maintenance of myself and wife, Mary Hopkins, according to our wish and desire during our natural lifetime." Issue:

II.

(1) Massealey (Masselah) Hopkins, m. Jabez Dowdy, Nov. 9, 1810, in Franklin Co.

(2) Mary Hopkins, m. Isaac Wysong, July 27, 1811, in Franklin Co.

(3) Isaac Hopkins, b. ca. 1791, m. Rhoda Nimmo, Feb. 7, 1825. Inv. and appraisement of his estate made Nov. 19, 1837, (W. B. 4, p. 484) by Thomas Wright, John Board, and Reed Payne. Charles Hopkins bequeathed property to Rhoda Hopkins, widow of Isaac Hopkins, and to his son, Reuben Hopkins. George W. Hopkins was Adm. of Isaac Hopkin's estate. Issue: Reuben Hopkins, m. Sarah Praether, Mar. 17, 1853. They had at least one son, William J. Hopkins.

(4) John S. Hopkins, b. ca. 1792, m. Mary Dowdy, (b. 1799 in Bedford Co., d. Feb. 4, 1879, in Franklin Co., at the home of William Dowdy) dau. of Ezekiel and Mary Dowdy Jan. 1, 1816, in Franklin Co. He appears on the tax list from 1813 to 1821.

(5) Otey Hopkins, b. ca. 1799, first appears on the tax list in 1818, does not appear after 1828; m. Ann Simmons, Jan. 6, 1825, in Franklin Co.

(6) Jonathan Hopkins, b. ca. 1800, m. 1st. Mary Simmons, Apr. 14, 1821, in Franklin Co.

(7) William Hopkins, b. ca. 1804, m. Hannah Wilson and removed to Botetourt Co. Among issue: a. Theodore, m. Frances Angle, had a dau., Mary E. Hopkins who m. John W. Kesler, Dec. 16, 1879.

(8) George W. Hopkins, b. ca. 1811, m. Elizabeth Dowdy, Dec. 22, 1828, in Franklin Co. Among issue:

    a. Elender, of Botetourt, m. Daniel Gist, June 11, 1857

    b. George W., b. 1849, d. June 29, 1853

    c. Elizabeth, m. John E. Bowman, June 15, 1860

    d. Daniel A., m. Josephine Booth, dau. of John

H. and Nancy G. Booth

    e. Martha J., m. George Montgomery in 1863.

         (9) Henry G. Hopkins, b. ca. 1808, m. Elizabeth Sence,
Jan. 5, 1828, in Franklin Co. Among Issue:

    a. Bennett H., m. Catherine Mason in 1857. W.
        B. 14, p. 130, Sept. 16, 1864, shows Henry G.
        Hopkins Admr. of his estate.

    b. James A., m. Lucy A. Creasy, May 21, 1861

    c. Elizabeth, m. Daniel D. Mason, Aug. 18, 1857

    d. Catherine, m. John Creasy, Nov. 5, 1857

    e. Henry W., m. Maria F. Ham, Dec. 12, 1867; Maria
        F. Hopkins (widow) m. Francis G. Short, Apr.
        20, 1871.

II (6)

        Jonathan Hopkins, (Charles), b. ca. 1800, in Franklin
Co. d. in Kanawha Co., West Va., subsequent to 1870; m. 1st,
Mary Simmons, Apr. 14, 1821, in Franklin Co., and 2nd, Tempie
Philips in Franklin or Floyd. Jonathan Hopkins appears on the
tax list in Franklin Co., 1832-1838, on the Floyd Co., tax list
1838-41, and on the Mercer Co., (now West Va) list 1842-58.
The names of his children were supplied by Franklin Worth Hop-
kins, oldest child of his 2nd m., now (1935) living in Corbin,
Ky.

    Jonathan and Mary (Simmons) Hopkins had issue:

III.

        (1) Rheubin Hopkins, b. May 12, 1824, in Franklin
Co., moved to Mercer Co., W. Va., with his father in 1842, m.
Nancy Farley, dau. of Gideon and Dinah (Cook) Farley, May 12,
1848. Issue:

    a. Lewis Madison, b. Mar. 16, 1849, in Mercer Co,
        West Va.; living 1935; m. Mary Elizabeth Kea-
        ton, Oct. 17, 1872.

    b. William R., b. Oct. 20, 1850, m. Marinda Caw-
        ley, in 1879. Home: Lenore, W. Va.

    c. Martha, b. Aug. 1854, m. Floyd Phillips, in
        1876. Both deceased.

    d. Henry, b. 1854, m. Caroline Bragg.

    e. Mary A., b. 6, 1855, m. William M. Pennington,
        May 30, 1877. Both dec'd.

f. George W., b. June 29, 1857, m. 1st, Lilla Belle Belcher, m. 2nd, Mandy Phillips.

g. Lena, b. 1860, m. Robert A. Rogers.

h. Breckenridge, b. Sept. 16, 1864, m. Rachel Barton.

i. Judah, b. Feb. 2, 1870, m. David Farley.

j. Robert L., b. May 2, 1870, m. Mary Massie.

(2) Samuel Hopkins, (d. near Pipestem, Mercer Co., W. Va.) m. 1860, Rachel Farley, dau. of Gideon and Dinah (Cook) Farley, and sister of Nancy Farley, who m. Rheubin Hopkins.

(3) Simeon D. Hopkins, (d. near Pipestem, W. Va.) m. Sarah Eugene Newly, (b. 1834) dau. of John G. Newly, of Lee Co., in 1859, near Pipestem. Among issue:

a. John Henry, b. near Pipestem, moved to Corbin Ky., where he now (1935) lives; and

b. Josie.

(4) Charlie Hopkins, m. has a dau. Mary Sylvania, who lives at Rockhold, Ky.

(5) Celia Hopkins, b. in Franklin Co., m. John Horn in Mercer Co., West Va.

(6) Jack Hopkins, d. young in Whiteley Co., Ky.

(7) Martha Hopkins.

(8) Mary (Polly) d. in Columbus, Ohio, m. William Johnson.
(9) Rachel Hopkins, d. in Whiteley Co., Ky., m. Mr. Bennett.

(10) John Hopkins, lived in Mercer Co., W. Va., m. Sarah Kruger, dau., of John Kruger; d. 1863, in Tenn.

Jonathan and Temple (Philips) Hopkins had issue:

(11) Franklin Worth Hopkins, Corbin Ky., b. July 24, 1854, in Mercer Co. W. Va., living 1935, m. Sarah A. Cook (b. 1827, d. Jan. 13, 1925) dau. of Cornelius and Anna (Pettry) Cook, in 1866, in Mercer Co., West Va. No issue.

(12) George Hopkins, Logan, Ohio, b. near Pipestem, W. Va., m. Manda Pettry, dau. of John Pettry.

(13) Preston Hopkins.

(14) Shelby Hopkins.

(15) Albert D. Hopkins, Bownement, W. Va. b. Sept.
28, 1870.

(16) Susan Virginia Hopkins, b. near Pipestem, W. Va.

THE JAMES FAMILY

Samuel James, father of James Spencer James, died young.
His will in Orange County, dated Dec. 14, 1754, was probated
Feb. 27, 1755. He bequeathed his estate to his wife, Mildred,
during her lifetime or widowhood, and directed that in case she
died or re-married his brother, Thomas James, should be executor and divide his estate among his children. His children
are not named in the will. Mildred James qualified as executrix
of her husband, with William Taliaferro her security, in the
sum of one hundred pounds. (Will Bk. 2, p. 200).

At a court held for Orange County Sept. 23, 1754, on
the motion of Mildred James, her tithables were ordered to be
added to the lists (Orange Co. Order Bk. 1754-1763).

Mildred James, together with Col. George Taylor, E-
rasmus Taylor, Sarah Slaughter and Betty Slaughter, stood as
sureties at the christening of Nicholas Taliaferro, born 30th
October, 1757, son of William and Mary (Battaile) Taliaferro
of "Newington" on Mountain Run, Orange County, and grandson
of John and Mary (Catlett) Taliaferro. (Wm. & Mary Quarterly
Vol. 1 p. 147).

In 1785, William Bell, in the State Enumerations,
listed Mildred James as the head of a family, with three white
souls, 1 dwelling, and two other buildings. (Heads of Families,
Va., 1790). She appears on the Orange County personal property
returns for 1783, charged with one tithable, three houses, six
cattle, her slave being reported exempt. Mrs. James petition-
ed the General Assembly for the arrears due on the pension of
her late son, Catlett, soldier of the Revolutionary War. An
act passed on December 15, 1791, directed same to be paid.
(Hening, Vol. 13, p. 322). Her will dated Oct. 28, 1802, was
probated April 25, 1803. Jos. Atkins, her son-in-law, was
executor, with Spencer Atkins his security. She mentions her
daughter, Betty Smith, son James, granddaughter Milly James,
and leaves her land to Milly Atkins "her equal part with her
brothers." Her sons Catlett and Stephen had died during her
lifetime. She does not mention John, who is thought also to
have died during her lifetime. (Orange Co. Will Bk. 4 p. 74).

Catlett James was evidently the eldest son of Samuel
and Mildred James, and does not seem to have married. He served in the First Virginia Regiment, during the Revolutionary War,

and appears on the pay roll of Capt. Richard Taylor's Company, for May and June, 1777 (W. D. 18-1) and on the rolls of Captain Callohill Minnis' Company in May and June 1779. (W. D. 285-1). March 5, 1784, he drew pay as a soldier of Infantry (W 4, p. 234). In 1782, he appears on the Orange County personal property returns, charged with one free male and three cattle. He also owned a small tract of land, which passed, upon his death, to his mother. Catlett James died May 22, 1788, as shown by the petition to the Virginia Legislature, when his mother, Mildred James, asked that the arrears due him as a pensioner be paid her. (Orange Petitions #2532, Oct. 31, 1791).

Stephen James, son of Samuel and Mildred, was born in 1748, and died in 1782. He served in the Revolution, and on August 5, 1783, his pay as Corporal of Infantry, was paid to Thos. Asselin. (War 4, p. 232). He married Polly Pickett, daughter of John Pickett, of Culpeper County. The will of John Pickett bears date July 9, 1803. probated Sept. 17, 1803, in which he mentions his wife, Hannah, and children, John, William, Caty Hume, Elizabeth Settle, Polly James, Sally, Judith, Nancy, Hannah and Lucy. (Slaughter's Notes of Culpeper, part II, p. 53). He is evidently the John Pickett who received pay for services in the Revolutionary Army, Oct. 5, 1783. (War, 4. p. 306).

James Spencer James, son of Samuel and Mildred James, was born 1750, and died 1834. He gave bond in Orange County, August 21, 1780, for his marriage with Frances Davis, Philemon Davis being his security. (Orange Co. Marriage Bonds; also Va. Mag. Vol 26, p. 195). The marriage ceremony was performed Aug. 22, by the Rev. William Douglas (Douglas Register, p. 28). Spencer James is listed on the Orange County personal property returns for 1782, and is charged with his own head tax, five slaves (Palace, Jeffrey, Sharp, Billy and Charles), seven horses and four cattle. In 1783, he appears in the Henry County tax records as paying on himself, two slaves (Sam and Anthony), 1 horse and 1 covering horse.

In 1784, he had brought from Orange County three of the slaves he owned there and, for that year, is charged his own head tax, one slave over 16 years of age and two slaves under 16 years of age (Sharp, Billy and Charles), six horses, eight cattle and one covering horse. He purchased 400 acres in Henry County and received a grant of 100 acres adjoining it, but in Franklin County. When Franklin County was formed, he was in that area and appears on the Franklin County personal property returns for 1786 as "James Spencer James," being charged with one white tithe, two slaves under 16 years of age, seven horses, eight cattle and one stud horse. He married, secondly Frances (Fannie) Baker (1752-1814). In the will of his mother, Mildred James, probated in Orange County in 1803, he is designed as "son James", and she also mentions a granddaughter Milly James, probably his daughter.

James Spencer James had issue: (1) Catlett James, b.

March 3, 1786, d. July 3, 1863, m. Elizabeth Thompson, b. August 26, 1805, d. July 5, 1863; (2) Phebe Bird James, who m. Chesley Ashley of Smythe County; (3) Elizabeth James, who m. William James of Smythe County; (4) Braxton, d. unm.; (5) Fannie James, who m. Ezekiel James of Smythe County; (6) James D. James, who m. Miss Foster and moved to Georgia; (7) Catherine Emeline James, who m. Samuel W. Thompson, and, (8) Mildred Baker James, who m. Bartholomew Baker.

Betty, daughter of Samuel and Mildred James, is mentioned in her mother's will, but her husband's name is not available.

Mildred James, daughter of Samuel and Mildred, married in 1775, Joseph Atkins, (Va. Mag. Vol. 26, p. 192-Orange Co. M. Bonds). He was Joseph Atkins, Jr., born May 27, 1755, son of Joseph Atkins and Sarah Brokman, his wife, one of 13 children whose names appear in the Douglas Register. Sarah Atkins, daughter of Joseph and Mildred, was born Feb. 29, 1779, baptized August 5th, 1784; Jonathan was born April 25, 1782, baptized 1784; Parham was born July 29, 1789 and baptized August 21, 1790, Davis was born April 3, 1790, and baptized August 21, 1790. (Douglas Register, p. 153). Their daughter, Mildred Atkins, is not entered in aforesaid register, but is mentioned in the will of her grandmother, Mildred James, and was bequeathed an equal share with her brothers, and sisters in the grandmother's land.

John James, was probably the youngest son of Samuel and Mildred James, as apprentices were usually bound when about 14 years of age. The Orange County records show that in 1765, Mildred James, Widow, bound her son John to Hezekiah Brown, joiner, "to learn the art, trade and mistery of a Joiner and Carpenter." There were several John James's who served in the Revolutionary War, but it is difficult ot identify them. This John was supporter of the American cause as is evidenced by his signature to a petition presented to the House of Delegates of Virginia, December 5, 1777, by citizens of Orange County, "praying that the cultivation of tobacco may be restrained, and greater opportunity thereby given for the raising and manufacturing of articles necessary for the Army and the prosecution of the war." This is the last record of John James. His name does not appear on the 1782 tax returns, nor is he mintioned in the will of his mother, Mildred. He probaby died during her lifetime. Unless he was the John James to whom land was granted in Henry County, no descendants of Samuel James of Orange lived in Franklin save through the issue of James Spencer James.

Catlett James, b. May 3, 1786, d. July 3, 1863, was the eldest child of James Spencer James. He lived at the old James homestead and he was one of the administrators of his father's estate. B. Clifford Goode has an old ledger owned by James Spencer James, which lists items in the sale of the personal property of James Spencer James, who died in 1834.

Catlett James m. Elizabeth Thompson Dec. 21, 1826.

(Pitts. Co. Mar. B.). Pyrant Thompson was the signer of the Certificate. Elizabeth (Thompson) James, b. Aug. 26, 1805, d. July 5, 1863, was the daughter of Dr. Jennings and Elizabeth Thompson of Pittsylvania. Dr. Jennings Thompson was a soldier in the Virginia Militia during the Revolution. He was placed on the Pension Roll March 4, 1831.

Issue of Catlett and Elizabeth (Thompson) James:

(1) Pyrant Thompson James M. D. b. Jan. 5, 1828, m. Emily Ruth Woods, daughter of Col. Sam Woods of Franklin County. They and their children, Perry, Robert and Samuel Catlett, moved from Franklin County to Kansas City, Mo. Dr. Pyrant T. James died Dec. 29, 1890 and is buried at Whitehall, Mo.

(2) Fanny Davis James, b. Nov. 10, 1829, m. Thomas D. Childress of Montgomery County.

Issue:

(a) Catlett Childress, moved to Nebraska

(b) James S. Childress, m. Miss Smith

(c) Waddy Pyrant ("Vence") Childress, m. Miss Johnson, daughter of Dr. Johnson of Franklin County. Their children were: William, Edd, Johnson, Sidney, Hugh, Mary, and Anne Childress, all of whom are now living except William, who died in Roanoke.

(d) James S. Childress. Issue: Mamie, m. Dr. Rangeley; Stella; Jennie; Jas. S.; and Floyd.

(3) Elizabeth James, b. Oct. 7, 1831, d. Jan. 12, 1862, never married.

(4) Mary Anne James, b. Apr. 18, 1834, m. Capt. James Turner of Franklin County.

(5) Col. Waddy Thompson James, b. Aug. 12, 1836, d. May 14, 1926, m. Mary Jane Warren of Franklin County.

(6) Catherine James, b. Jan. 4, 1839, m. Capt. Abram Burnett Ross of Henry County.

(7) Phebe James, b. Aug. 7, 1843, m. Floyd Wall of Montgomery County. Issue: W. Frank, Waddy Thompson, Guy, Floyd, Alice, Elizabeth, Eliza Ellen, Fannie, Emma Jane, and Marie Louise.

(8) Mildred James, b. Aug. 7, 1843, m. James Wall, nephew of Floyd Wall. (They moved to Missouri).

Mary Anne James, b. Apr. 18, 1834, d. Aug. 26, 1856, daughter of Catlett and Elizabeth (Thompson) James, married Capt. James M. Turner, (died Oct. 2, 1872) a Confederate soldier

from Franklin County, on Nov. 24, 1853, and had issue: Bettie
M. Turner and George Catlett Turner. Bettie M. Turner, b. Sept.
19, 1854, m. John L. Philpott of Henry County on Sept. 14, 1876.
Issue: (1) George J. deceased; (2) James J., rural carrier
of Bassett; (3) B. Cabell, stockholder and director of furniture factory of Lexington, N. C.; and (4) Bettie Mae.

Stephen James (b. 1748, d. 1782) son of Samuel and
Mildred James (probably second son) married Polly Pickett (1753-
1840) of Culpeper Co. They moved to Smythe County.

Issue of Stephen and Polly (Pickett) James:

(1) Mary, m. John Horsley of Smythe County.

(2) Adam, 1772-1835, m. Phebe Baker (1774-1840)

(3) William, (1802-1862), m. Elizabeth Booker James,
(1803-67), his first cousin, daughter of James Spencer James,
Smythe County.

(4) John, m. Clara Taylor. Moved to Washington County.

(5) Jesse, m. Houston. They moved to Cass County, Mo.

(6) Ezekiel, m. Fanny James, his first cousin, daughter
of Spencer James, Smythe County.

(7) Sallie, m. Samuel Kincannon of Smythe County.

(8) Janet.

A reunion of the descendants of Samuel and Mildred
James is held at Smythe County. annually.

THE JAMISON FAMILY

The founder of the Franklin County family was James
Jamison. He was born in Glasgow, about 1650, the son of Alexander Jamison. From Scotland he removed to County Galway, Ireland, and about 1700, with his two sons, he came to America and
settled on the Susquehanna River in Southern Pennsylvania. His
son, John, born in 1680, in Ireland, came to America with his
father and his brother Robert, and spent the greater part of his
life as an Indian fighter and planter in York County, Pennsylvania,
and in Orange and Augusta Counties in Virginia. He was Captain
of the Augusta County Militia. He was the father of Thomas Jamison who was born November 7, 1732, who served in the campaign
which ended in Braddock's defeat.

Thomas Jamison and his brother Alexander served in
the Albemarle Company of Militia for the protection of the
frontier against the Indians. In 1756, Thomas married Jane Dickey of Loudon County. They were the parents of four children:

Samuel, John, Martha and William. They removed to Georgia, but on the death of his wife in 1763, he, with his children, return- ed Albemarle County to the home of his brother Alexander near Charlottesville. He removed thence to what is now Franklin County, near Shady Grove and Snow Creek, where he owned a plantation of about two hundred acres. Here he was married to Hannah Tag- gart, and to his second union ten children were born: Mary, Jane, Nancy, Katherine, Helen, Margaret, Alexander, Thomas, Hannah, and Rhoda.

In Franklin Deed Book 2, page 54, there is of record a deed to a farm from Thomas and Hannah Jamison to John Reed dated September 7, 1789, in consideration of one hundred pounds. This farm was adjacent to the lands of John Jamison, Senior, and John Jamison, Junior, both of whom, with William Stokes and Joshua Dillingham, witnessed the deed of sale.

Thomas Jamison was a good horseman and covered hund- reds of miles in Virginia. He was also fleet of foot. He be- came a prominent figure in the border wars, and was commissioned Captain in 1761. He served in the Revolutionary War, in the Virginia Infantry. He and his son John, in 1776, "were among the most respectabel families who subscribed to the oath of Al- legiance to the Commonwealth of Virginia, renouncing allegiance to King George III, early in the history of the determined re- sistance of the American Colonists to British oppresion." He and his sons, Samuel and John, participated in the Battle of Guilford Courthouse. He was enrolled, April 24, 1776, in White's Company, Sixth Regiment, and, on September 8, 1778, we find his name recorded on the roll of Capt. John Summer's Company, First Battalion, commanded by Co. Thomas Clark. Thomas Jamison and his brother Alexander were signers of the Albermarle Declaration of Independence.

Thomas Jamison was a personal friend of Thomas Jef- ferson and also of Patrick Calhoun, the grandfather of John C. Calhoun, who settled in Augusta County, in 1740, and removed to South Carolina. Mr. and Mrs. Thomas Jamison died in 1830 and are buried at Hebron Baptist Churchyard, Jefferson County, Indiana. The eldest son of Thomas and Jane (Dickey) Jamison was Samuel Jamison who served under Washington in the Revolution. The younger son was John, a soldier of distinction in the Con- tinental Army, who received a Captain's Commission.

There is of record in the North Carolina Archives, Book 22, pages 705-709-10, a petition dated June 1784, signed by John and Samuel Jamison among others, to "separate eastern North Carolina from the Western side of the mountains, forming the State of Franklin".

After the Revolution, Capt. John Jamison (1758-1842), and his wife Elizabeth lived on a farm next to that of his father, on Snow Creek, in Franklin County.

Capt. John Jamison and his wife decided to go west and so settled in Madison County, Kentucky, where he had been

granted land. Two of their sons remained in Franklin County
or soon returned for they were married there in 1806. It was
not unusual for them to ride to and from Kentucky. Samuel, the
older, married Winnie Byrd of Franklin County. To this union
eleven children were born: Louis, William, Thomas, Samuel, John,
Marshal, Wiley, Sallie, Elizabeth, Rhoda, and Jane. Their home
was near his father's at Shady Grove, Franklin County. He owned a large farm and many slaves. Several of their sons served
in the Confederate Army. He died a few years before the Civil
War, and his wife died during the war.

John Jamison, the other brother, was born September
3, 1783. He was married by Reverend Wilson Turner, on January
6, 1806, to Catherine Boone, daughter of Jacob and Catherine
Boone. They lived about four miles south of Boone's Mill in
Franklin County. Boone's Mill was then a station on the stage
coach line between Big Lick (now Roanoke) and Rocky Mount.
They were parents of eleven children: Elizabeth, Nancy, Samuel, Mary, Issac, Katheine, Barbara, Henry, John, Jane, and Jacob. John Jamison was a person of quiet habits, liberal in his
views, tolerant of the opinions of others, careful in the exer-
cise of his judgment, and hence, a safe counselor. He was a
good farmer and stock raiser and fond of horses. He took pride
in his vocation to the benefit of his neighbors. He was slender,
about six feet tall, blue eyes, fair complexion and wore a short
beard. He and his wife were devoted members and builders of
the Old Brick Dunkard Church. They would not own slaves. He
was drafted in the war of 1812 and though of the Dunkard faith,
went to Lynchburg for service. He did not serve however, for
peace was made about that time. He died October 5, 1864, and
his widow died August 29, 1866. They are buried at the Jamison
burial ground on top of the hill near their old homestead.

John Jamison, Junior, his father's namesake and fourth
son, was born at the Jamison homestead four miles south of Boone's
Mill on July 4, 1824. He was married on August 2, 1844 to Elizabeth Akers, the daughter of William and Lavinia (Capper) Akers.
She was born July 2, 1824, and died January 14, 1859, and was
buried at the Jamison burial ground. They established their
home about one mile north of Dillon's Mill and were the parents
of seven children: Martha Jane, Sarah Elizabeth, John Williams,
Lucy Ann, Hannah Katherine, Sue Lavinia, and Samuel Henry. The
mother of these children died when she was in the prime of woman-
hood and when her youngest son was less than a year old. She
was gentlewoman and traced her ancestry through her maternal
grandmother to Col. John Jamison, who was graduated from William
and Mary College, and became a leading spirit among the famous
Culpeper Minutemen. He was Clerk of the Court of Culpeper County
for thirty-eight years and a member of the Society of the Cin-
cinnati. He was also a member of the Masonic Lodge at Alexandria
with George Washington. His uncle David Jamison married Mildred
Smith, a daughter of Edmund and Agnes Smith and a kinswoman of
George Washington. This David Jamison was graduated from Prince-
ton in 1753, was Lieutenant Governor of Virginia in 1780-1781,
a merchant of Yorktown, and well-known throughout the state of

Virginia. He was a member of the Privy Council in 1777, and
a trustee of William and Mary College. He was a member of State
Senate of Virginia from 1776 to 1884.

John Jamison, son of John Jamison and Catherine Boone,
married the second time, January 29, 1861, to Christina C. Hartsell (a first cousin of his first wife) by Rev. Isaac Naff, a
Dunkard minister. She was born September 22, 1822, and died
May 1, 1881.. They had two children: Thomas and Josephine.
At the outbreak of the Civil War, John Jamison Jr., enrolled
in Company "G", Thirty-seventh Battalion, Virginia Calvary, and
served throughout the war, principally in Virginia. During the
latter part of the war he was assigned to duty in assembly pro-
visions for the Montgomery White Hospital, Montgomery County,
Virginia. His second wife died in the spring of 1881. He was
then married to Mary Wood, September 11, 1887, by Rev. Benjamin
Wray, a Dunkard minister. She was the daughter of Stephen and
Nancy (Cabiness) Wood, and was born near Taylor's Store, Franklin County, June 20, 1838, and died July 18, 1925. She is buried near Boone's Mill in Franklin County. Mr. Jamison died August 23, 1900, and is buried at the Jamison family burial ground.
He was a member of Bethleham Dunkard Church.

John William Jamison, the eldest son of John and Elizabeth (Akers) Jamison, was born near Dillon's Mill in Franklin
County, on January 22, 1849. As soon as he was old enough, he
was sent to a private school at Blackwater Meeting House and
later to Mansfield's Academy. He was a large boy for his age
and at twelve could do much work on the farm. The care of a
large family devolved upon him at the outbreak of the war and
with the help he was able to hire occasionally, he managed the
plantation while his father was serving in the Confederate Army.
Toward the close of the war he did considerable hauling of pro-
visions to Big Lick (now Roanoke) for the army. He was registered for army service the day he became sixteen and was assigned
to the service of Subsistence and Transportation. On April 4,
1878, John William Jamison was married to Sarah Elizabeth Webster, eldest daughter of John R. Webster and Catherine (Peters)
Webster, by Rev. Danial Bowman, a Dunkard minister. They "set
up housekeeping" on the farm where he was born about one mile
North of Dillon's Mill. It had previously belonged to his grandfather, William Akers. Here their two sons, John Ernest and
Edgar Forest Jamison were born. On June 3, 1891, John R. Webster died and that fall his widow came to live with her daughter and here she made her home until her death on June 12, 1897.

Mr. and Mrs. John William Jamison had the misfortune
to lose their home by fire on September 28, 1897. Temporary
housekeeping was set up in an outbuilding until timber was haul-
ed, sawed and a new house built. Mr. and Mrs. Jamison removed
to Roanoke in 1920, and transferred church membership from Piedmont Presbyterian Church, Calloway, to the First Presbyterian
Church of Roanoke. Their sons had previously removed to Roanoke
to engage in mercantile business.

THE LAPRADE FAMILY

The Laprade family is of French Huguenot ancestry. The first member of the family to settle in Franklin County was William Laprade. His father came to Pittsylvania from Chesterfield County. His grandfather came from France.

William Laprade gave bond to marry Harriet Boatright on December 22, 1834. They had issue: (1) Margaret Emma, (2) Mary Ann, (3) William T., (4) Martha Jane, (5) Jerusha, (6) Elizabeth, (7) Nancy, (8) Julia F. (9) John Samuel, and (10) George W.

(1) Margaret Emma, died unmarried in 1896.

(2) Mary Ann, married Maston Williams. No issue.

(3) William T., married Lucy Palmer and had issue: Mary V., Henry Lee, William, Robert, Lucy, John, Samuel and Charles.

(4) Martha Jane, married William Davidson and had issue: John W. C., Moses A., Mary F., Benjamin L., Samuel D., Nancy J., Ida E., and T. J.

(5) Jerusha, married William Henry Hatchett and had issue: Henry B., and Permelia W.

(6) Elizabeth, married George D. Amos and had issue: Pernella J., Eliza Boatright, Isabel, Winston, Julia and Josephine E.

(7) Nancy, married Logan Hatchett and had issue: Paxton Hill, and Logan Adolphus.

(8) Julia F., died unmarried in 1933.

(9) John Samuel, married Elizabeth Palmer and had issue: Roberta A., Callie E., Julia W., Dolly A., and Nannie E.

(10) George W., (October, 1855-September 14, 1923), married Mary Elizabeth, daughter of Thomas and Mary (Preston) Muse, on December 27, 1882, and had issue: (1) William Thomas, (2) Henry Watterson, (3) Mary, (4) Nannie E., (5) Essie, (6) George Swanson, (7) Eugene Preston, (8) James Robert, (9) R. Page, (10) Lloyd Stone, These married and had issue as follows:

(1) William Thomas, married Nancy Hamilton Calfel and had issue: Nancy Elizabeth.

(2) Henry Watterson, married Myrtle Snow Bennett and had issue: John H., Elizabeth, and Bennett Watterson.

(3) Mary, married David W. Davidson and had issue:

Edith E., Hazel May., Eloise Muse, George, David Carson, Francis, Mary Bell, Beatrice, Mattie, Raymond and Charles. Home: Roanoke.

(4) Nannie E., died unmarried in 1932.

(5) Essie, married Onley Board of Glade Hill and had issue: Gwendolyn, George Williams, Onley Smythe, Henry Cobbs, Edgar Wilson, Thomas B., and Essie Bell.

(6) George Swanson, married Vernie Thomas and died in 1923, leaving a son bearing his full name.

(7) Eugene Preston, married Lucile Lavinder and had issue: Robert Hooker, and Richard.

(8) James Robert, married Addie Gregory and had issue: James, Garnett, and Elizabeth.

(9) R. Page, married Lillie Lovell and had issue: Edith, Page Louis, and William Henry.

(10) Lloyd Stone, unmarried (1934).

Marriage Bonds.

Andrew Laprade and Sally Sink, November 11, 1816.

Benjamin Laprade and Nancy Horsely, December 29, 1823.

William Laprade and Harriet W. Boatright, December 22, 1834.

Benjamin Laprade and Mary Altick, August 7, 1848.

William W. Laprade and Catherine Sink, January 7, 1850.

James Laprade and Rosina M. Ramsey, October 23, 1849.

THE LAVINDER FAMILY

The Lavinders of Virginia are descended from Richard Lavinder of England and not from his brother who settled in South Carolina. Thomas, grandson of Richard Lavinder, settled in the Franklin area a few years before the formation of the county, and was connected with the Washington Iron Foundry. His brother, John, settled in the same area and operated a large plantation. He owned many slaves and, it is said, built a chapel and often preached to them. There is a tradition in the family that after his sermon he distributed to each slave a drink of brandy--a method which probably insured a congregation.

John Lavinder of Franklin County married Mary Depity

and had issue: Thornton, William, James, Joseph, Chilton, John, Mary, Frances, Nancy, Emily, and Jesse.

Jesse Lavinder, son of John, born 1791, married Jane Hickey Davis, in 1814, and had issue: Mary Letitia, John Peter, Samuel Henry, Emma Jane, Margaret Alzier, and Jesse Benjamin.

Mary Letitia married William Hurd and settled in Missouri where she has numerous descendants.

John Peter married, first, Mary Louisa Jones, and, second, Anna Fleming. He was a member of the 42nd Regiment, Confederate Army, and served throughout the war under Capt. Joseph Hereford of Leatherwood. He was with Jackson at Chancellorsville and the reins of "Old Sorrel" were tossed to him when Jackson was brought in mortally wounded.

Samuel Henry Lavinder married Martha Woodson Hill, daughter of Rev. W. W. Hill of Henry County, and had issue: Mary Catherine, and Jane Hickey (Kickey). He died in Florida 1876, and his widow married Charles Atley Hamilton.

Emma Jane Lavinder married Frank M. Wells, March 14, 1867 and had issue: Harry, who married Cora Fleming; and Jane Hickey, who married Anthony Hundley.

Margaret Alzire Lavinder married Joseph C. Ford in 1870, and had issue: Anna, Joseph, Jesse, Jane Hickey, and Mary Sherman.

Jesse Benjamin Lavinder, born September 22, 1842, was married to Alice Peters, daughter of Dr. Henry D. Peters of Leatherwood, and had issue: Henry George, Mary Peters, and Alice Greyson, Jesse Ben Lavinder also served in the 42nd Virginia Regiment under Captain Hereford of Leatherwood.

Henry George Lavinder was educated at the University of Virginia and practiced law with his uncle, Herbert Peters, in Bristol. He married Katherine Haynes, daughter of Judge H. H. Haynes of Bristol, and had issue: Laura Alice, and Katherine.

Mary Peters Lavinder married Richard B. Semple.

Alice Greyson Lavinder married David H. Pannill and had issue: Alice Christina, William Banks and Mary Lavinder.

Benjamin F. Lavinder, born _____, married Jenny Beheler and died in 1922. He was buried in the Wingfield burying ground on a farm belonging to the author of this volume. He had issue: Mary, who married William Harrison; Robert who married Edna Hooper; J. Byron, who married Elsie Frances Wingfield, a sister of the author of this volume; Duncan, whose marriage ceremony being performed December 20, 1922, by the author of this volume; and Kenneth, who married Gertrude Abbott.

At a reunion of the Lavinder family held in 1935, at the home of H. M. Lavinder, the following members of the family were present: Mr. and Mrs. Robert Lavinder and children, Homer and Ellen, of Rocky Mount; C. V. Lavinder and daughter, Virginia of Roanoke; Mr. and Mrs. C. W. Turman and son, Glenn, of Rocky Mount; Mrs. F. D. Bussey of Rocky Mount; Mrs. N. E. Wilkes of Bassett; Mr. and Mrs. D. L. Kendrick and son, D. L. Jr., of Bassett; Mr. and Mrs. T. F. Lavinder of Martinsville; Mrs. J. L. Lavinder and children, Wilburn and Nelda, of Roanoke. Others not of the immediate family present were: Mrs. V. A. Ames of Port Norfolk; Mrs. Ollie Guilliams of Roanoke; Miss Belva Holley of Rocky Mount; Miss Mary Hodges of Rocky Mount; Mr. and Mrs. Dennis Johnson of Rocky Rocky Mount; Miss Kate Brim of Rocky Mount; Charles Parcell of Rocky Mount; and Mr. and Mrs. Alfred Luke and daughter of Edith, of Roanoke.

THE LEE FAMILY

Franklin County has two Lee families. The Rocky Mount family, of which the late Judge John P. Lee was a conspicous member, and whose son, Carter C. Lee, now serves as County Attorney, claims descent from Charles Carter Lee, a brother of the celebrated Southern Chieftain. The other Lee family traces descent to Charles C. Lee, son of Francis Ludwell and Sally (Moorman) Lee and grandson of Richard Lee of Kentucky.

Charles C. Lee acquired a thousand acres of the most fertile land on Snow Creek on which he erected a brick structure of Colonial style which remains to this day the best house on Snow Creek. He owned this farm many years before he moved to it, probably as early as 1840. He had an overseer to manage it and he spent a portion of his time on Snow Creek and the rest in Ellyson, Montgomery County, known at that time as Big Springs. He owned the Big Springs property.

Charles C. Lee married Louisa Walker Finney On Oct. 13, 1835, and had issue: William Peter Frances Lee. W. P. Lee married Nannie Susan Barrow, daughter of Benjamin F. and Susan (Watkins) Barrow and had issue: Charles B., Robert R., Lula Watkins, Annie Page, William Ludwell, and Nannie Susan.

Charles B. Lee became a physician. He married Dora Workman and had issue: Charles B. Lee Jr. Dr. Lee practiced medicine for many years at Glen Jean, West Virginia. He died December 3, 1925, and was buried in Spring Hill Cemetery, Charleston. His wife died in 1927.

Robert Richard Lee became a physician and located in Martinsville where he practiced over forty years. He married Annie Mathews and had issue: Robert Richard Jr.

Lula Watkins Lee married Rawley W. Younger and had issue:

William L., who married Adela Cain of St. Mathews, South Carolina, and had issue: (1) William Lee Jr.; (2) John Robert, who married Catherine Preston, daughter of Dr. J. W. Preston of Franklin County and had issue: John Preston; (3) Charles Carter, and (4) Lee Barrow.

Annie Page Lee married William Callohill Turner and had issue: Nancy Lee Turner. Annie Lee Turner died at her home near Hollins College November 30, 1930. Eleven months later the daughter died from injuries in an auto accident. William Callohill Turner died April 7, 1934.

Judge William Ludwell Lee married Ann Hawkins and had issue: William L. Jr., and John Lee. Judge Lee now (1935) practices law at Fayetteville, West Virginia.

Nannie Susan Lee married George Jackson Penn of Floyd County, and now (1935) resides in Roanoke.

Captain W. P. F. Lee was educated at Trinity College, now Duke University, North Carolina. He left Trinity in his senior year to serve in the Confederate Army, becoming Captain of Company "B", 4th Virginia Infantry, Johnson's Division, Stonewall Brigade.

Captain Lee was an active Freemason being a member of two Lodges Snow Creek at Snow Creek and Piedmont at Martinsville. He held the office of District Deputy Grand Master. He lived almost his three score years and ten at his Snow Creek home, spending a few of his last years in Martinsville, where he died February 25, 1911. His widow died in Roanoke March 1913. Both are buried in Martinsville.

John Penn Lee, came to Franklin nearly a half century after the settlement of the Snow Creek family. He was married to Isabella Gilman Walker of Lynchburg on Dec. 2, 1896, and had issue: Catherine, who married Judge A. H. Hopkins; Carter C., who married Henrietta Shelburne; Richard, who married Dorothy Shelton; Dabney, who married Doris Bennett; and Dr. Henry who is (1934) unmarried.

THE MCNIEL FAMILY *

* Robert O. McNiel who prepared this genealogy, states that the form of spelling used by the persons named herein has been retained.

Jacob McNeal, Sr., pioneer ancestor of the McNiels of Franklin (b. Jacob Ireson, but assumed the name of his mother's 2nd husband), was born June 1759 near, Harper's Ferry. The Christian name of his father is not known. His mother was Mary, dau. of William (b. 1723, d. 1822) and Molly (Daton) Hughes. Welsh emigrants who settled in the Capon Valley section of Frederick Co. Mary Hughes Ireson, widow, m. ca. 1768, Thomas McNeel

(b. ca. 1747, d. 1809), one of several sons of a Scottish emigrant settler in Frederick Co. Thomas McNeel brought his wife
and step-son Jacob to Swago Creek in Greenbrier Co., later Bath
Co., now Pocahontas Co., W. Va., between 1768 and 1870, and
settled on a 300 acre homestead. There he operated a powder
mill.

Thomas and Mary (Hughes Ireson) McNeel had issue:
Jonathan (b. Nov. 29, 1770, d. Jan. 23, 1831) m. Jan. 23, 1792,
to Phoebe Moore (b. Feb. 13, 1774, d. 1867), and spent his life
on his father's farm and operated his mill and powder business;
Mary (b. Dec. 25, 1771, d. 1858), m. Nov. 16, 1785, to William
Ewing (b. 1756, d. 1822), and in 1810 moved to Gallia Co., Ohio;
Gabriel (b. Nov. 3, 1776, d. July 23, 1848), m. 1798 to Rebecca
Stephenson (b. Sept. 29, 1777, d. Dec. 14, 1833), and moved to
Jackson Co., Ohio, where he served as surgeon, civil engineer,
chemist, farmer and preacher; Naomi, m. (1) Mr. Smith, and (2)
Oliver Thomas; Absalom, m. 1804 to Comfort Smith and removed
to Ohio; and Enoch, m. Jane Moore and moved to Ohio.

In 1776, Jacob McNeal served as spy and ranger for
3 months in Capt. John Cook's Company on the Virginia frontier
in the Greenbrier country. In Mar. 1777, he enlisted as a guard
at Ft. Randolph where Point Pleasant is now located. In July
he joined Capt. John Henderson's Company, and served for several
months.

Conflict existed between the Shawnees and the whites
for years. In 1774, General Lewis defeated the Shawnee Chief
Cornstalk and made peace with the tribe, but within three years
the tribe was again hostile. Cornstalk, wiser for his defeat
and respecting the treaty, spoke for peace. When his counsel
was ignored, he informed the garrison at Ft. Randolph. Capt.
Matthew Arbucke, detained him and his two companions as hostages.
Cornstalk's son, Ellinipsico, hallooed from the river bank, and
was brought across to the fort and also detained. In the mean-
time two men from the fort crossed the river to hunt wild tur-
keys. One of them was killed from ambush and when his body was
brought to the fort his comrades overpowered the guard, of whom
Jacob McNeal was one, and killed the Indians. McNeal said that
Cornstalk begged them to kill him and to spare his son, but he
plead in vain. In his pension claim of Sept. 3, 1832, Jacob
McNeal stated that he tried to prevent the murder of the Indians.

He ended his military service in Nov. 1777, and bought
147 acres on Buckeye Mountain in what is now Pocahontas County,
W. Va. He lived on the frontier for the remainder of the Revolutionary War and was out frequently against the Indians.

Jacob McNeal m. Annie Stevens, c. 1783, and in 1790
settled in Franklin Co., on the south side of Blackwater. Two
land patents are extent conveying to him 362 acres. One for
312 acres is dated Aug. 19, 1794, and the other for 50 acres
bears date of Sept. 12, 1796. These 362 acres are acres are
between Wirtz and Rocky Mount.

Annie Stevens McNeal d. ca. 1800, was probably the

146

first person buried in the family cemetery on Blackwater.

Jacob and Annie (Stevens) McNeal had issue: (1) John (2) William, (3) Daniel, (4) Jacob Jr., (5) Elizabeth, (6) Rebecca, (7) Naomi, (8) Annie, and (9) Susannah.

(1) John ("Little John") McNiel (b. 1784, d. Dec. 1851) m. Aug. 5, 1805 Rebecca Griffith (b. 1784, d. 1854) dau. of Jonathan Griffith of Franklin Co. John McNiel returned to his father's 147 acre farm in 1808, later bought the land, and lived on it until his death. He enlisted in Bath Co., in May 1813, in the Sixth Regiment, Virginia Militia, under Capt. Griffin Lampkin, and served in the defense of Norfolk. John and Rebecca McNiel had issue: Jacob (b. 1822, d. 1842). "Little John" McNiel's discharge, dated Jan. 10, 1814, said he was "a brave and correct soldier." He was granted land for his military service.

(2) William McNiel also went to Pocahontas and lived on a part of his father's farm. He m. Esther (Hetty) Kinnison, died early, and his family removed to Pike Co., Ohio. Two of their children were Andrew and Brumwell.

(3) Daniel McNiel (b. 1791 in Franklin, d. Aug. 29, 1861, on Kimberlin Creek in Bland Co.) m. Jan. 1, 1821, Elizabeth Kennett (b. 1790, d. ca. 1840 in Floyd), dau. of Peter Kennett and Milly Blankenship. Peter Kennett and Milly Blankenship m. Oct. 26, 1789, in Bedford and moved to Franklin, and later to Floyd. Milly Blankenship was a dau. of William and Elizabeth Blankenship of Bedford. Daniel McNiel was a teacher. His home in Franklin was on 60 acre tract bought from his father. In 1830, he sold his land to Nathaniel H. Claiborne, and moved to Floyd Co. Daniel and Elizabeth (Kennett) McNiel had issue: William Kennett (b. Dec. 21, 1821, d. Feb. 3, 1888), m. (1) Nancy McNiel (2) Lucinda Helvey; Jacob (b. June 19, 1825, d. Aug. 17, 1908) m. Sept. 2, 1852, Delilah Kirby; Peter (b. May 7, 1827, d. Nov. 1, 1914) m. (1) Catherine Wade Ruckmand (b. May 22, 1831, d. Nov. 23, 1870) on June 23, 1853, and (2) Mrs. Ruth Hefner Selvy (b. ca. 1835, d. Aug. 1903) on Feb. 27, 1873; Lavinia m. John Fanning; Naomi, m. (1) Anderson Evans, and (2) Isaiah Bruce; Emillar m. William Hoback; Rebecca d. young; Daniel Osborne (b. Jan. 21, 1831, d. Mar. 30, 1915, at Mechanicsburg) m. May 19, 1859, to Sarah Ellen Wohlford (b. Feb. 9, 1844 at Wytheville, d. Aug. 24, 1909 at Mechanicsburg); and Elizabeth Ann (b. May 2, 1833, d. Mar. 14, 1908) m. Feb. 19, 1853 to Joseph Hoback (b. Aug. 10, 1832, d. Mar. 29, 1907). All the sons of Daniel McNiel served in the CSA.

(4) Jacob McNiel, Jr., (b. July 4, 1797, d. 1872) youngest son of Jacob McNeal, Sr., went to Pocahontas Co., lived with his brothers, m. Elizabeth Auldridge. He brought his family to Franklin ca. 1829, and settled on a 54 acre tract which, on Aug. 25, 1842, he sold to Joseph Altick, and moved to Floyd. Jacob Jr., and Elizabeth Auldridge McNiel had issue: James Ireson (b. May 31, 1822, d. Mar. 9, 1904) m. Lydia Smith;

William Burrell (b. Oct. 31, 1823, d. 1905) m. (1) Ellen Martin, and (2) Rebecca Sink; Mary; Elizabeth; Samuel Auldridge (b. Sept. 18, 1843, d. Jan. 31, 1915) m. Dec. 23, 1868, Sarah Elizabeth Poff (b. May 9, 1850, d. Dec. 18, 1898); Charles, who d. infant; Henry m. (1) Jane Manning, (2) Fannie Webb, and (3) Mary Smith; and Nancy m. William Kennett McNiel.

(5) Elizabeth McNiel went to Pocahontas Co., m. Charles Kinnison, and moved to Ohio.

(6) Rebecca McNiel (b. Nov. 25, 1789, d. Jan. 3, 1859) m. Sept. 3, 1811, her cousin John ("Big John") McNiel (b. Apr. 20, 1793, d. Nov. 10, 1861), lived in Pocahontas Co., and had issue: Phoebe (b. May 10, 1812, d. June 21, 1869); Elizabeth (b. Apr. 25, 1814, d. July 18, 1886) m. Daniel Kellison; Susannah (b. Nov. 30, 1815, d. Mar. 21, 1854); Ann (b. Aug. 15, 1817, d. Dec. 4, 1905) m. James Moore; Naomi (b. June 31, 1819, d. July 6, 1891) m. John Dilley; Rachel (b. Apr. 3, 1821, d. Nov. 24, 1887) m. French Thomas; Wesley (b. May 3, 1823, d. July 31, 1849) m. Hallie Sadler; Washington (b. Mar. 14, 1825, d. Feb. 19, 1854) m. Eveline Waugh; Jane (b. June 6, 1827, d. Feb. 19, 1895) m. William Kinnison; Margaret (b. Nov. 26, 1829, d. Dec. 27, 1900) m. David Leggett; and John W. (b. May 1, 1832, d. Dec. 26, 1885) m. Oct. 20, 1863, Cynthia Miller of Bland Co.

(7) Naomi McNiel, a spinster, disappeared and was never heard of again. Legal documents of the period refer to her as "dead or missing."

(8) Annie McNiel m. Charles Miller Sr., lived in Giles Co., had issue: John, m. Martha Bird; Abraham or Abram (b. Apr. 20, 1824, d. Apr. 15, 1897) m. (1) Rachel Hearn, and (2) Elsie Muncy; Charles K. m. Amanda Young; Jacob m. Jane Bruce; Lucinda m. William Suiter; and Alexander m. Jane Hamilton.

(9) Susannah McNiel m. Joseph Pauley, lived in Giles Co., had issue among whom were Susannah, who m. James Bogle; and Eliza who became the 2nd wife of John Fanning on March 3, 1859.

Jacob McNeal, Sr., m. Margaret (Peggy) Cool Mar. 2, 1812, and had issue: (1) Jonathan Hughes (2) Hannah, (3) Caroline, (4) Oriney, (5) Mary.

(1) Jonathan Hughes McNiel (b. Apr. 17, 1813, d. Nov. 19, 1888) m. Catherine Perdue (d. May 30, 1879) and had issue: (a) George, (killed in CSA near Petersburg); (b) John Edward, (b. Jan. 19, 1839, d. Apr. 30, 1919) m. Margaret Perdue; (c) Giles Henry (b. 1843, d. 1923) m. Elizabeth Brown (b. Mar. 20, 1849, d. Aug. 24, 1926) on Mar. 21, 1870; (d) Thomas J. (b. Dec. 16, 1845, d. July 31, 1913) m. Susan A. Hudson (b. Feb. 18, 1849, d. Feb. 21, 1923) Nov. 18, 1868; and (e) Jonathan P. (b. May 16, 1847, d. June 3, 1903) m. Sally Hudson. These sons of Jonathan H. McNiel lived on the Franklin Co. homestead. Two of the sons

sold land in 1891, for the right of way over which the N & W Ry now operates. All of the sons served in the CSA. Four children unnamed died in infancy.

(2) Hannah McNiel m. John Crowell. It is thought they lived in Pocahontas Co., before moving west.

(3) Caroline McNiel m. Lewis Hodges and lived in Franklin. She spent her last years in the home of her nephew, Giles H. McNiel. Of known issue: Lewis and Jane.

(4) Oriney McNiel m. Riley Pugh Sept. 10, 1833, probably settled in Pocahantas Co., before moving west.

(5) Mary McNiel was drowned when young in Blackwater.

Jacob McNeal Sr., d. in 1841 and was buried in the ancestral graveyard. The Inventory of Appraisement, dated April 20, 1841, was signed by N. H. Claiborne, Sials Perdue and R. Purdue, appointed by the Court. Jacob McNiel Jr., was Administrator. Some of the descendants of Jacob McNeal, Sr., still live on the old Franklin County homestead.

THE MARSHALL FAMILY

The will of Thomas Marshall is of record in Westmoreland County, dated May 21, 1704. His son William married Elizabeth Markham, and their son Thomas was the father of John and Samuel Marshall. The former became Chief Justice of the United States Supreme Court.

Samuel Marshall married Cassandra Alfriend and settled on the headwaters of Leatherwood Creek. Issue: (1) Dennis, (2) Lewis, (3) John, (4) Ben, (5) Susan, (6) Sally and (7) Nancy. They spent the remainder of their lives here and were buried nearby on the Wesley Griggs place west of Dyer's Store.

(1) Dennis Marshall was born in 1768, and died in 1843. He married Frances Harper and had issue: Samuel, Benjamin, Alfriend, Lewis, Dennis, Polly, Sally, Frances, Cassandra, Nancy, and Patsy.

(2) Lewis moved to Kentucky.

(3) John operated a store and a tobacco factory at Shady Grove in Franklin. He had as partner his brother.Ben.

(4) Ben married Sallie Dugger, and died without issue.

(5) Susan married William Barrow.

(6) Sally married Elisha Arnold, and had issue: Samuel, John, James, Elisha, Franklin, Nancy, Cynthia, and Lucy.

Samuel Marshall, oldest son of Dennis Sr., manufactured tobacco in Franklin. He died of cholera in Baltimore about 1834.

Lewis Marshall, youngest son of Dennis Sr., married Mary Ann Nance, and moved to Missouri. Their children were: Hugh, Samuel, Nancy, Giles, and Benn. He lived near Hannibal.

Benjamin Alfriend Marshall, born November 13, 1800, was educated by his father Dennis, Sr., and married Nancy Nance, a daughter of Reuben Nance for whom Nance Mountain was named. Reuben Nance was twice married and had twenty-two children, all born between 1765 and 1809.

Benjamin and Nancy Marshall had issue: Mary B. b. 1822; Reuben D. b. 1823; Nancy M., b. 1825; Frances M., b. October 22, 1827; Peyton S.; Sarah L.; Benjamin A.; Martha J., Susan B.; Edmond S.; Julia E.; Abigail M.; Cassandra A.; Melissa L.; William H.; and Eliza L., b. April 17, 1846.

Frances married William David Stultz. He died at Bear Creek, Cedar County, Missouri, October 31, 1833. His wife died March 31, 1865. Both are buried there.

Polly Marshall married Dubartis Dempsey, and had issue: Mary, Hamala, and Ann Eliza.

Sallie Marshall married Charles M. Wingfield. Issue: Francis, Mary, Ann, Jane, Julia, Sally, Louisa, Walter, and William.

Frances Marshall married John Gravely and had issue: Judy, Marshall, Jabe, Harriet, Sally, and John W.

Elizabeth Cassandra Marshall married William Clark in 1826 and had issue: Ann, Cassandra, Nat, Howell, Mary and John. After his death the family removed to Texas.

Patsy Marshall married Benjamin Connoway, and removed to Missouri. Issue: Dennis, Francis, Sally and Martha.

THE MARTIN FAMILY

This branch of the Martin family came from Alsace-Lorraine and first settled in America at Amsterdam, in Botetourt County.

James Albert Martin, (born April 22, 1851) and Sarah Electra Payne (born August 1, 1849) were married at Newport in Giles County, May 16, 1872. They settled at Callaway and had issue: (1) Loulie, (2) Mamie, (3) Walter, (4) Frances, (5) Samuel, (6) Carrie, (7) Lelia, (8) Anne, (9) Josephine, and (10) Alma.

(1) Loulie married R. A. Barnhart, merchant and farmer at Callaway.

(2) Mamie married William L. Thornton of Winston-Salem and had issue: Winfred Lewis, Clare, Loulie, Mary, James, Alice, William, and Samuel. Winfred Lewis Thornton was born at Ferrum in 1896, attended the public schools of Winston-Salem and took a course from the University of Chicago in traffic management. He is the author of numerous briefs for the Carolina Shippers Association, Incorporated, argued before the Interstate Commerce Commission. He married Mildred Cone and has two daughters, Mildred and Lamotte.

(3) Walter Martin died in 1884.

(4) Frances Martin died in 1882.

(5) Samuel married Frances Sheahan of New York City, and has a daughter named Dorothy.

(6) Carrie married Dr. L. G. Pedigo of Roanoke and Salem.

(7) Lelia married J. L. Carter of Madison, Missouri. He was principal of the High school in Martinsville when the author's younger sisters were graduated therefrom and later was principal of Ferrum Training School.

(8) Anne is a nurse in Lewis Gale Hospital of Roanoke, and assistant to Dr. W. R. Whitman.

(9) Josphine died about 1890.

(10) Alma married Beverly V. Michel, formerly chief petty officer on the U. S. S. Maui, and now pay clerk of the Norfolk and Western Railway. They have one child, Beverly V. Michel, Jr.

THE MITCHELL FAMILY

In the early records of Franklin and surrounding counties, the name of this family is spelled Michel, Michell and Mitchell. Louis Michel made a journey to the area, now in Franklin, in 1702. Two of the first settlers in this area, if not the very first, were Aaron Pinston and Peter Mitchell. Pinston lived on Tewshominy (now Aaron's Creek), and, according to William Byrd was the highest inhabitant up on the south side of Dan River. Byrd says he lived there as though safe from danger, and observes that he and his stock would be safe if the bears, wolves and panthers were as harmless as the Indians. When Byrd made his second journey to this area, he stopped at the forks of the Dan and Staunton Rivers. A few miles beyond the forks was the house of Peter Mitchell, who is referred to as being "the highest inhabitant up."

Charles Mitchell is included in a Pittsylvania County list of Tithables taken by Peter Capeland July, 17, 1767. James Mitchell is listed as a Tithable of Pittsylvania by Archibald Gordon in 1767. There was also a James Mitchell who signed the petition in 1837 for a dirt turnpike to be built from Danville by Rocky Mount and Big Lick (now Roanoke) to Fincastle. Rev. James Mitchell was Minister in 1796 to the old Wet Sleeve Presbyterian Chruch near Callands, Pittsylvania. This church was established largely through the efforts of Samuel Calland soon after the Revolution and was the first Presbyterian Church in Pittsylvania. Rev. Mitchell rode horseback from his home in Bedford County, sixty miles away to serve the Wet Sleeve congregation. William Mitchell is named in Maude Carter Clement's History of Pittsylvania as a subscriber to the Wet Sleeve Church in 1784. It is also stated that "Mitchell's home was at Callands, where he had built a substantial brick residence." Charles Clay (1672-1760), the great-grandfather of the celebrated Henry Clay, married Mary Mitchell. His grandson, Matthew, represented Pittsylvania County in the Virginia Legislature from 1790 to 1794.

The Mitchell family, for the propose of this history, will not be carried farther back than Archibald Mitchell from whose sons, Elisha and William J., descended the persons whose appears in this genealogy.

Elisha Mitchell married Eleanor Gregory on April 26, 1832, and had issue: William Lindsay, and Mary Anne.

William Lindsay Mitchell was married in 1857 to Sarah Bondurant, daughter of Robert and Ruth (Meredith) Bondurant, and had issue: (1) Albert, (2) Emma, and (3) William Lindsay.

(1) Albert Mitchell, born September 13, 1858, married Maria S. Mason on November 11, 1880, and had issue: Sadie, Mary, Bess, Bett, William, Thomas, Samuel, and David. He sold his farm to Tazewell T. Wingfield, father of the author of this volume, in 1893, and removed to West Virginia.

(2) Emma Mitchell, born in 1860, died 1873.

(3) William Lindsay Mitchell, born in 1862, married Susie McGhee, on Nov. 26, 1884, and had issue: (a) Lawson, (b) Roy, (c) Emma, (d) Clyde, (e) Robert, (f) Ola, and (g) William.

(a) Lawson Mitchell married Bessie, daughter of Joseph Bennett on November 28, 1912, and had issue: Virginia, Ina, Talmage, Lois, Russell, Edith, Glen, Howard, and Andrew.

(b) Roy Mitchell was killed in World War I, on September 28, 1918.

(c) Emma Mitchell married German Hylton, on July

4, 1917, and had issue: Helen, William Mitchell, Dorothy Evelyn, and Robert Cabell.

(d) Clyde Mitchell married Estelle Stultz on November 27, 1913, and had issue: Elizabeth, Wayne, Catherine, Ralph, and Linville.

(e) Robert Mitchell married Belle Draper on November 26, 1922 and had issue: Robert, Mildred, and James.

(f) Ola Mitchell, unmarried as of 1935.

(g) William Mitchell, unmarried as of 1935.

William J. Mitchell, son of Archibald named in the opening paragraph of this chapter, was born in 1797, married Mary (Polly) Bondurant, daughter of Jacob Bondurant on October 12, 1819, and had issue: (1) Benjamin Franklin, (2) Thomas Bondurant, (3) William J., (4) Eliza, (5) Sarah and (6) Edwin.

(1) Benjamin Franklin, was born in 1829. He was married to Nannie Abingdon and had issue: Betty and Virginia, who died young; Richard, who married a Miss Shumate; Annie, who married Tazewell Cannaday; Alice, who was the first wife of Tazewell Tarleton Wingfield, father of the author of this volume; and Ella, who married Edward Craig and had five children, one of whom, Benjamin Giles, married Lucy Wingfield, a sister of the author of this volume.

(2) Thomas Bondurant Mitchell was born in 1829. He saw service in the 10th Virginia Cavalry, C. S. A., and was at Appomattox at the Surrender. He married Katherine Price of Ridgeway, and had issue: William, Lula, Anna, Belva, and Edwin. He lived and died at Shady Grove. The author of this volume is now the owner of his former estate.

(3) William J. Mitchell married Mary Price, daughter of Maj. John Price, of Ridgeway, and had issue: William Lindsay, Albert Fletcher, Robert, Mollie, Laura, and Kittie.

(4) Eliza Mitchell married James W. Trent and had issue: William, Charles, and Mollie. They removed from Franklin to Strawberry Plains, Tennessee.

(5) Sarah Mitchell married Robert Trent, a brother of her sister Eliza's husband, and had issue: two daughters whose names are unknown to this writer. They lived at Strawberry Plains, Tennessee.

(6) Edwin died unmarried.

William D. Mitchell, son of Thomas Bondurant, married, first, Anna Jones, and second, Jennie McKiver. He had issue by his first marriage: William J., and Bessie.

Anna Mitchell, daughter of Thomas Bondurant, married James P. Garrett of Ridgeway and had issue: Alma, Kate, Paul, Annie, Peter, Rachael, William, and Ruth.

Belva Mitchell, daughter of Thomas Bondurant, married Jefferson Sparrow and had issue: Kathleen and Rose. Rose died unmarried. Kathleen married Alex Mahood.

William Mitchell, son of William J. Mitchell and Mary Price, married first, Lucy Trotter and had issue: Joseph T., Edward R., and Elizabeth. He married, second, Annie Haygood, and had issue: Mary Frances, Sally Ann, Wade, and George.

Joseph T. Mitchell, son of William Mitchell and Lucy Trotter, married Frances Stovall and had issue: William, Jubal, Edward, Trotter, Joseph, Landis, and Nannie. The last named was the first school teacher of the author of this volume. She married George D. Craig of Patrick County. Joseph married Loula Lester Hurd, and Landis married Mary Garrett of Ridgeway.

Edward R. Mitchell, son of William and Lucy Trotter Mitchell married Martha Schoolfield. No issue.

Elizabeth, daughter of William and Lucy Trotter Mitchell, married John W. Morris and died without issue.

Mary Frances, daughter of William and Annie Haygood Mitchell, married Jack Dillon and had issue: Joseph, who married a Miss Blackwell.

Sally Ann, daughter of William and Annie Haygood Mitchell, died unmarried.

Wade, son of William and Annie Haygood Mitchell, died unmarried.

George, son of William and Annie Haygood Mitchell, married Florence Stovall and had issue: Harry, Annie, Elizabeth, Dora, James, Hughes, and Wade. Harry married Maud Cahill; James married Brooksie Frye; Hughes married a Miss Overton; and Wade married a Miss Bouldin.

THE MONTGOMERY FAMILY

Most of the Montgomerys of Franklin County are descendants of Samuel Montgomery II who lived about four miles south of Boone's Mill at the old Montgomery home where Thomas Franklin Montgomery, a great grand son, now resides.

His father Samuel Montgomery (of Scotch-Irish descent) married a Miss Wood of England and came to America at the close of the 18th century. He settled in Rockingham County, North Carolina.

Samuel Montgomery I had five sons: John I, Andrew, Samuel, Robert and James. Robert went to Southwest Virginia, Tennessee, and later to Illinois. Another son went to Albama. The other two remained in North Carolina.

Samuel married a Miss Bowman. Issue: John II, Andrew, James, Samuel, Delila, Annie and Elizabeth. He married second a widow Gossett (nee Elizabeth Ikenberry). Issue: Joel, Eli, Hannah, Sarah (Sallie), and Lydia.

John II, son of Samuel, married Rebecca Naff. Issue: Abraham Stover, Jacob, John III, William, Cyrus, Samuel, Elizabeth, Martha, and Mary.

Abraham S., son of John II , married Amanda Victoria Kinsey of Taylor's Store. Issue: (1) John Robert, (2) William, (3) Charles, (4) Walter Newton, (5) Arba Jenas, (6) Emma, (7) Ella, (8) Rinda (9) Lecta, (10) Rebecca, (11) Sallie, (12) Alice, and (13) Durah.

(1) John Robert married Virginia Willis of Ferrum. Issue: Carmi, Delmer, Coy, Clyde (dau.), Josie Arnold and Mattie. Home: Bowls, W. Va.

(2) William died young

(3) Charles died young

(4) Walter, married Ethel Compton. Issue: Ethel May. He married second, Edith Naff. Issue: Mary Louise.

(5) Arba married Ida Peters. Issue: Alfred, Howard, Eva, and Mildred.

(6) Emma never married.

(7) Ella married Walter A. Bernard. Issue: Willis, Fred, Mirl, and Ada. Home, Dayton, Ohio.

(8) Rinda married W. S. Boone of Boone's Mill. Issue: Elise (Elsie), Emma, and Kathryn. Elsie married Earnest Mattox, Leesville. Kathryn married Herman Hurst, Pulaski.

(9) Lecta married W. T. Blakenship of Wirtz. Issue: Exie, who married Marvin Childress. Home, Columbus, Ohio.

(10) Rebecca married Sylvester McConnell Maiden, son of John Maiden of Washington County. No issue.

(11) Sallie married Gus D. Boone of Boone's Mill. Issue: John Paul, Peyton Stover, Cecil Edward, and Mary Elizabeth. She married second, F. M. Bryan. Mary Elizabeth married William Chapman. Issue: William Jr., and Jean. Home, Philadelphia, Pa.

(12) Alice married Edward Cooper of Rocky Mount. Issue: Elizabeth Montgomery.

(13) Durah married Thomas Reece Moore. Issue: Thomas Reece Moore, Jr.

Jacob, son of John II, issue unknown.

John III, son of John II, had issue: Robert, Lizzie, and Maggie. Home: Kansas.

William, son of John II, married Mary Roberts. Issue: (1) John Franklin and (2) James William. He married second Emma McGhee. Issue: (3) Clyde Ruffner, (4) Lloyd Munsey, (5) Maude Anne, (6) Georgie Garnette, and (7) Etta Pearl.

(1) John Franklin, married Florence Porter. Issue: Frond M., Dulcie, Elsie, Juanita, James and Zella. Home: Huntington, W. Va.

(2) James William married Esther McDonald. Issue: Thelma.

(3) Clyde Ruffner married Florence Millander. No issue: Home, Columbus, Ohio.

(4) Lloyd Munsey married Juanita Gray. Home, Lexington, Ky.

(5) Maude Anne married R. B. Fugate. Issue: Fern, Sallie, Stella and Mary. Home: East Stone Gap, Va.

(6) Georgie Garnette died young.

(7) Etta Pearl married C. N. Lawson. Issue: Thomas, who lives at Kenova, W. Va.

Cyrus, son of John III, married Mary Sigmon. Issue: Walter C., Peter, Charles, John, Samuel, Samantha and Lucy.

Samuel, son of John II, married Delia Pinkard. Issue: Laura, Edith, Mamie, and Ethel.

Elizabeth, daughter of John II, married Luke Heckman. Issue: James, John VI, Orren, Rufus, Cephas, Rebecca, Martha, Sallie, Emma, Ida, and Glenna.

Martha, daughter of John II, married David Hale. Issue: William, John, Mollie, Maggie and Flora.

Mary, daughter of John II, married James Ferguson. Issue: Robert, Bessie, Mattie, Ella, Mary Sue, and Blanche.

Andrew, son of Samuel, married Sallie Peters. Issue: (1) Henry, (2) Michael, (3) Owen, (4) Riley, (5) David, (6) Mary, (7) Sarah, (8) Susan, and (9) Catherine.

(1) Henry, issue unknown.

(2) Michael, married a Miss Turner. Issue: (a) Joel, (b) Henry, (c) Riley and (d) Ida. He married, second, Lizzie Peters. Issue: (e) Ella. He married, third, Hattie Bashore. Home, Missouri.

> (a) Joel married Elizabeth Reece. Issue: Oscar, Myrtle, Aurelia, Florence, Nellie, and Hazel.
>
> (b) Henry married Emma Reece. Issue: Mabel, and Bessie.
>
> (c) Riley married a Miss Heck. Issue unknown.
>
> (d) Ida married Henry Reece. Issue: John, Fred, Frank, Elmer, Clarence, and Jennie.
>
> (e) Ella married Elmer Flora. Issue: Riley, Harvey, Henry and Harley.

(3) Owen married first, Catherine Flora; second, Lydia Denlinger, issue: (a) Albert, (b) Mary Elizabeth, and (c) Bertha; and, third, Ellen King. Home: Dayton, Ohio.

> (a) Albert, married Leona Ulrey of Ohio. Issue: Russell, Robert, David, Albert Jr., and Grace.
>
> (b) Mary Elizabeth married James Harman. Issue unknown.
>
> (c) Bertha, married Charlie Floth. Issue: Adam and Ethel.

(4) Riley married Rebecca Lesh. Issue: Nellie, Zora, Opal, Cletis, and Ruth. Home: Indiana.

(5) David, son of Andrew, married Parthenia Montgomery, daughter of Joel, son of Samuel. Issue: (a) John VII, (b) Charles, (c) Walter, (d) Joel, (e) Amos, (f) Mary, and (g) Sallie.

> (a) John VII, married Cora Kingery. Issue: Roy, Clyde, Cabell, Joseph, Daniel, Annie, Ruth, Bertha, Esther, Lois, and Rachel.
>
> (b) Charles married Leah Brubaker. No issue.
>
> (c) Walter married Bessie Kennett. Issue: Curtis, Malcomb, and Dallis.
>
> (d) Joel married Annie Jamison. Issue: Christian, Levi, Jacob, Howard and Frances.

(e) Amos married Effie Flora. Issue: Kenneth, Howard and Cletus.

(f) Mary married Charles Peters. Issue: Raymond, Elsie Mae, Hazel, Lucile and Mary Jane.

(g) Sallie married Orren Bower. Issue: Lester, Orville, and David.

James, son of Samuel, married Susan Naff. Issue: George, Isaac, Peter, Robert, Elizabeth, Fanny, Jane, Irena, and Cynthia.

Samuel, son of Samuel, went to Southwest Virginia, and later to Illinois. No further information.

Joel, son of Samuel, married Sallie Brooks of Staffordsville. Issue: Charles, Cephas, Benjamin, Lee, Mollie, Julia, Agnes, and Parthenia.

Charles, son of Joel, married Elizabeth Flora. Issue: (1) Thomas Frahklin, (2) George W., (3) Cephas A., (4) John Dexter, (5) Riley Benjamin, (6) Virginia Lee, (7) Rosa Belle, (8) Lura Amanda, (9) Zaida Ellen, and (10) Sallie Elizabeth.

(1) Thomas Franklin married Sallie Bowman, daughter of Daniel Bowman II. Issue: Quincy, Jesse, Daniel, Vinnie, Elsie, Ava, and Bernice.
Quincy married Goldie SMith Hawkins of Roanoke. Vinnie married Clyde S. Givens of Newport. Issue: Clyde Straley, Jr. Elsie married John Cline Layman of Troutdale. Issue: John William. Ava marries Elmer D. Naff, Boone's Mill. Jessie, Daniel and Bernice not married.

(2) George W. died young.

(3) Cephas A. married Ellie Gibson of Winnsboro, Texas. Issue: Gibson, Mary Jean and Elizabeth.

(4) John Dexter married Annie Kate Givens of West Virginia. Issue: Anita.

(5) Riley Benjamin married Lucy Katherine Walker of Middlesex County. Issue: Riley, Hunter and Ann.

(6) Virginia Lee married Charles O. Flora of Boone's Mill. Adopted a daughter named Ruth, who married Wilson Alshire.

(7) Rosa Belle married Berkley T. Flora, Boone's Mill. Issue: Quentin, Albert, Newton, Ora, Elizabeth and Eloise. Quentin married Helen Crumpacker of Bonsack; Albert married Mildred Flora of Wirtz; and Ora married Parker Flora of Boone's Mill.

(8) Lura Amanda married Walter Laprade of Boone's Mill. Issue: Norman, Ralph, Galen, Virginia, Mabel, Hattie, Doris, and Katherine.

(9) Zaida Ellen married D. Cleveland Bowman, Boone's Mill. Issue: Herman, and Grace.

(10) Sallie Elizabeth married Lewis Laprade of Boone's Mill. Issue: Wilford, and Wallace.

Cephas, son of Joel, married Miss Frank Teel. Issue: (1) William, (2) Charles, (3) Lawrence, (4) Effie, (5) Edna, (6) Nora, (7) Clara, and (8) Livie.

(1) William married Mary McKillip of Wenatchee, Washington. Issue: Jack and Virginia. Home: Wenatchee.

(2) Charles, married Betty Martin. Issue: Howard, and Ethel.

(3) Lawrence married Mary Craft of Botetourt County. No issue.

(4) Effie married Cornelius Flora of Boone's Mill. Issue: Buren, Cecil, Wilford, and Lois.

(5) Edna never married.

(6) Nora married Thomas Naff of Boone's Mill. Issue: Russell, Ralph, Theo, Berlen, Don, Thelman, Mabel, and Katherine.

(7) Clara married Doc Flora of Boone's Mill. Issue: Billy, Fred, Beatrice, and Christian.

(8) Livie married A. W. Lynch of Roanoke. Issue: Wesley, Franklie, Gene, and Wyvaughn.

Benjamin, son of Joel, married Rosa Lee Peters of Boone's Mill. Issue: (1) Clarence, (2) Creed, (3) Billy, (4) Raymond, (5) Etta, and (6) Blanche.

(1) Clarence married Dora Mason of Ferrum. Issue: Ann.

(2) Creed married Edna Mason of Ferrum. Issue: Janice, and Mary Jean.

(3) Billy, not married.

(4) Raymond, not married.

(5) Etta married W. B. Hancock of Ferrum. Issue: Benjamin, Jack and Elaine.

(6) Blanche married John R. Young of Ferrum.

Lee, son of Joel, married Lelia Saul. Issue: (1) Edgar, (2) Harry, (3) Nellie, (4) Maggie Lee, and (5) Melva.

(1) Edgar married Grace Terry. Issue: Frank, Rachel, and Cathryn.

(2) Harry married Lenora Bowman. Issue: James, Harry, Ina, and Erma.

(3) Nellie married Parker Peters of Wirtz. Issue: Lee Thomas.

(4) Maggie Lee not married.

(5) Melva not married.

Mollie, daughter of Joel, married M. D. Boone, of Wirtz. Issue: William, Curtis, Thomas, Price, John, Dexter, Robert, Cline, Harry, Macy, India, and Bessie.

Julia, daughter of Joel, married, first, Abraham I. Flora of Wirtz. Issue: Ernest, Charlie, Norman, Corrie, and Sallie. She married, second, Franklin P. Flora. Issue: Zora.

Agnes, daughter of Joel, married George Jamison of Boone's Mill. Issue: Walter, Dexter, and Nettie.

Parthenia, daughter of Joel, married David A. Montgomery of Wirtz, son of Andrew.

Of the other son and daughters of Samuel Montgomery:

Eli died young.

Delila, Annie, and Elizabeth never married.

Hannah married Jacob Naff, and had issue: Lydia, Susan, Mary and Manga.

Sarah married Rufus Brooks, and had issue: James, and Frank.

Lydia married Peter Keslar, and had issue: Bettie, Sarah, and Martha.

THE MOTLEY - MARTIN FAMILY

Orson Martin of "Breckenridge", names eight children in his will, bearing date of April 1858, with the codicil dated July 21, 1859, both being of record in the Clerk's office of Henry County, Va.

The children named are:

Robt. H., who may have m. a dau. of George Dickinson
Chas. F.
James L.
Wm. O., who m. Mary K. Riddle, Nov. 3, 1842
Samuel H., who m. _____ Dickinson, dau. of George
Joseph T.
Jane, who m. John M. Barding May 7, 1838
Mary Grant

Charles F. Martin, son of Orson, married (May 9, 1846) Sarah Lawrence, dau. of Henry Lawrence and had issue:

Joseph, m. Valentine Martin's daughter
Samuel Henry (Bugg) m. Sallie Stultz
Nannie Sallie, b. Mar. 20, 1850, m. J. F. Motley,
who was born June 30, 1850

Charles F., m. second, Elizabeth (Betty) Cox, and had issue:

Mary, who m. Wm. Thos. Wright, a son of Louis and
and Cassie Wright
Wm. Tyler, who m. Sallie Burch and settled in Char-
lotte Co. Va.
Alice, who m. Louis (Lewis) Wright, bro. of Wm.
James Moore, who m. _____ Pugh, and settled in
Charlotte Co.
George, killed in horse race, never married
Rufus, died infant

Nannie Sallie Martin, b. Mar. 20, 1850, d. Apr. 22, 1913, dau. of Chas. F., m. John Fontaine Motley, (b. June 30, d. May 1, 1897) and had issue:

Sallie Gravely, b. Aug. 6, 1869-70, d. May 4, 1929,
m. B. F. Amos, Dec. 20, 1891
Henry George, b. July 9, 1871, m. first, Leanna
Reynolds; and, second, Lou Arrington
Mary Susan, b. May 20, 1873, m. Tazewell Tarleton
Wingfield, Jan. 21, 1892
Martha Frances, b. May 29, 1875, d. Dec. 4, 1922, m.
first, William F. Mills, and second, J. J. Oakes.
John Lafayette, b. July 25, 1877, m. Nannie Kate
Reynolds.

Nannie, b. May 29, (Aug. 28, 1881), m. John H. Black-
well, and had son Louis J., and dau. Edna. John
H. d. May 27, 1948
Sallie Lou Motley, b. Mar. 15, 1885.

Henry G. Motley, b. July 9, 1871, d. Nov. 27, 1938,
m. first, Leanna Reynolds, on June 23, 1898, and had issue:

> John H. Motley, b. June 8, 1899, who m. Daisie
> Campbell, and had many children
> Richard W. Motley, b. Sept. 9, 1900, who m.
> Myrtle Gregory, and had 3 children
> Charles Lewis, b. Jan. 22, 1902, d. Sept. 4,
> 1908

Lenna, d. Feb. 11, 1904. Henry G. Motley, m. second,
Lou Arrington on Dec. 26, 1906, and had issue:

> Mildred L. Motley, b. Oct. 24, 1907, who m.
> Walter Woody Dec. 22, 1934-no children
> Nannie E. Motley, b. July 16, 1910, m. Wil-
> lard C. Bennett, Oct. 18, 1934. No child-
> ren.
> Paul E. Motley, b. Oct. 22, 1914, who m. Vir-
> gie Edwards, Jan. 9, 1932, and had many
> children.
> Lucy M. Motley, m. Claiborne Haynes. She
> was b. Sept. 19, 1917, and m. Jan. 9, 1932
> Silas Arthur Motley, b. June 20, 1924

Family of John Lafayette, b. July 25, 1877, and Kate
Reynolds Motley:

children:
Nannie Pernelle, m. Samuel Wm. Gilbert, and had 8

> Berniece Evelyn, m.Jack Young
> Frances Pernelle
> Samuel W. Jr.
> Charles Marvin
> Jean Elaine, b. Dec. 28, 1932, d. Dec. 14, 1934.
> Judith Anne
> Mary Etta
> Vivian Carol

Farrie Louise, m. George William Motley, and had George
Jr.
Willie Kate, m. Earl Leslie Bolick, and had Robt. Earl,
and Melvin Leo
John Fontaine (Fountain), m. Elizabeth Virginia Hawk,
and had John Melvin, and Jas. Alfred.
Fannie Lillian, m. Paul Gill, and had son, James Dwight
Virginia May, m. George Odell Smith, and had Kenneth
Morris, Barbara Joan, and Virginia Gail
Frederick Allen, m. Lunette Dent

Sallie G. Motley, b. Aug. 6, 1869, dau. of John Fontaine and Nannie Sallie Motley, m. Charles Franklin Amos, Dec. 20, 1891, and had issue:

- Ethel, b. July 4, 1894, d. May 30, 1925, m. Dec. 29, 1909, Harvey Wells, and had issue:

    -Valeria, b. Feb. 21, 1911, m. Bill Gammon, Sept. 1930.
    -Beulah, b. Apr. 9, 1913, m. Leonard Wright, Apr. 22, 1934.
    -Audrey L., b. Jan. 20, 1915.
    -Clarence H., b. Nov. 23, 1916.
    -Irma E., b. May 8, 1919.
    -James E., b. Mar. 29, 1921.
    -Harvey C., b. May 27, 1924.

- Sallie Frank, b. Jan. 29, 1898, m. Charles N. Oakes, Dec. 27, 1911, aged 13.
- Annie Lee, b. 1900, m. W. Tosh McCrickard, Apr. 16, 1927, and had 13 children.
- Thelma, b. Dec. 13, 1905, m. Joe Hedrick, and had Doris. Joe d. Dec. 13, 1955.
- Charles Ernest, b. Apr. 28, 1908, m. Lottie Shelton, May 4, 1929, and had 10 children.

George W. Motley, b. Sept. 11, 1865, d. Nov. 29, 1905, son of John Motley, and Geddie Jones, m. First, Martha F. McGuire, (d. Mar. 16, 1865) dau. of Jonathan and Sally McGuire, and second, Missouri F. Lawrence Woodall (widow of Ira Woodall, who was the son of Sam Woodall), and had issue, by the first marriage:

    Sarah (Fanny) m. Daniel J. Motley, Nov. 5, 1867
    Mary S., m. Wm. J. Woodall, Dec. 22, 1880
    John Fontaine, m. Nannie Sally Martin, dau. of Charles Martin
    Joel did not marry
    Lafayette, m. Lula Gilbert

By his second marriage he had issue:

    Henry Clay Motley, m. Mary Fuller. He was b. June 13, 1866
    Virginia, m. William Terry
    Benjamin Franklin, m. Ola Brandon

Henry Clay Motley was murdered June 29, 1907, 3 miles from McDowell's Store in Franklin Co. Henry Adams held Motley while forcing his Negro hired man, Dudley, to shoot him. Adams was sent to the insane asylum in Marion. Henry Clay Motley and Mary Fuller Motley had children: Martha, George, William, Lonnie Curry, and Ben. Martha married Claude Tate. George was killed by a run-away horse. William died a soldier in World War I. Lonnie Curry was killed by a car. Ben lives in Ohio.

Benjamin Franklin Motley and Ola Brandon Motley had children: Mildred, who m. R. S. Dameron of Lynchburg; Virginia Frances b. 1912, m. W. H. Young of Buena Vista; Mary Catherine, b. 1915, m. J. P. Williamson; Ola Blair, b. 1918; Virginia May, b. 1920, m. H. A. Cox; and Elizabeth Claiborne, b. 1926.

James Motley, m. Sarah, dau. of Wm. Allen, and Ann Motley, Issue: Ernest, Edward, Mercer, and Raleigh.

Ann Motley, wife of Wm. Allen, was sister of George W. Motley, who was father of John Fontaine Motley.

Susan Motley, a sister of George W. Motley, m. William Motley, and had issue: John, William, Josiah, Richard, David, Gideon, Doc, Malinda, Polly, Ella, Lucy, and Calla.

THE NAFF (NAEFF, KNAFF) FAMILY

Sebastian Naeff came from the borderlands of Switzerland and Germany in the first half of the 18th century and settled in Franklin County, Pennsylvania. Some time later Jacob Naeff, a younger brother, also came over. It seems that they united their energies in farming and afterwards owned much land in Pennsylvania. Some years later they tired of the rigorous climate of Pennsylvania and moved to Franklin County, Virginia, then a part of the two counties of Bedford and Henry.

Sebastian acquired lands and settled at or near the confluence of the north and south branches of Blackwater River. He had two sons. There is no available account of the subsequent history of his family.

Jacob Knaff made his home in the Maggoty Valley at the junction of the two branches of Maggodee Creek. On March 20, 1788, he obtained a grant of 314 acres from Gov. Edmond Randolph, and on January 23, 1791, he bought 125 acres from Henry McDaniel for 300 pounds. This tract had been granted to McDaniel by Beverly Randolph, June 25, 1787. He, Jacob Knaff, married Eva Flora, whose parents came from Germany. She was born on the Atlantic during their immigrant voyage. Jacob became a minister of the Brethren Church.

The tradition in the family is that Jacob Knaff married Eva Flora in Pennsylvania, where his older children were born. Two children, Abraham and Sarah, evidently remained in Maryland or Pennsylvania. The probable natal order of his children as follows:

(1) Mary, unmarried. Age 94, as recorded in 1850 census of Franklin County, Virginia. She "attained the age of 100". B. 1756.
(2) Abraham, b. ca. 1758, "remained in Pennsylvania or Maryland."
(3) Sarah, ca. 1763, "remained in Pennsylvania or Maryland."

(4) Isaac, b. ca. 1763, married in Franklin County, Virginia, June 1, 1789, Barbara Moyers, step-daughter of John Boon; surety Daniel Barnhart; bond signed Isaac Nave. Isaac Naeff became a minister of the Brethren Church.

(5) Elizabeth, b. ca. 1765, married in Franklin County, Virginia, Feb. 12, 1788, Daniel Barnhart. The consent note to this marriage was signed Jacob Knavem as father of Elizabeth.

(6) Jacob, b. ca. 1769, died 1829, married Elizabeth Stover.

(7) Joseph, b. ca. 1769, married in Franklin County, Virginia, March 7, 1796, Mary Magdelane, daughter of Conrad Hergerdez; surety Daniel Barnhart; bond signed, Joseph Nafe.

(8) Jonathan, b. in Maryland 1771, died Greene County, Tenn., 1853.

(9) Susannah, b. ca. 1773, married in Franklin County, Virginia, Jonathan Fisher, Nov. 10, 1824. Security, David Nafe, signed by mark.

(10) Catherine, b. ca. 1778, married in Franklin County, Virginia, Feb. 7, 1797, John Moyers; security, David Nafe, signed by mark; consent note signed by father, Jacob Naef.

(11) David, b. ca. 1780, married in Franklin County, Virginia, Nov. 14, 1803, Polly Brower; security, Jacob Brower.

His will proven in Franklin County, Virginia, October 6, 1806, names his wife and the foregoing children, excepting Abraham and Sarah. The examination of the records at Rocky Mount, Franklin County, Virginia, did not disclose an administration on his estate.

Jacob Naff, third son of Jacob and Eva Flora Naeff, (b. 1769, d. 1829) married Elizabeth Stover, daughter of Dr. George and _____ (Price) Stover, of Franklin County, Pennsylvania, Dec. 30, 1792. He brought his bride back to Magodee Valley in Franklin County, Virginia in Jan. 1793. They had issue:

(1) George m, Hannah Bowman Dec. 30, 1817.
(2) John m. Sally Howry Jan. 11, 1827
(3) Jacob, m. Susan Webster Feb. 23, 1828
(4) Abraham, m. Hannah Peters Apr. 4, 1830
(5) Isaac, m. Cynthia M. Wysor Jan. 31, 1833
(6) Katherine, m. Daniel Bowman Nov. 14, 1817
(7) Elizabeth, m. Abraham Barnhart Jan. 2, 1826
(8) Hannah, m. Peter Noftsinger Feb. 1, 1827
(9) Mary, m. John Smith Nov. 14, 1822
(10) Rebeccah, m. John Montgomery May 26, 1831
(11) Susan, m. James Montgomery Aug. 27, 1835

Elizabeth (Stover) Naff, d. 1865, aged 82 years. Some

members of this generation moved to Indiana, and some to Tennessee. The spelling Naff, instead of Naeff or Knaff had come
into general use in this generation, although the German language was still commonly used in this family.

David Naff, the youngest son of Jacob and Eva Flora
Naeff, lived at the junction of the two branches of Maggoty
Creek. He had two sons, and probably daughters. The sons were:

> Jonathan, b. Dec. 3, 1810, d. unmarried at an ad-
> vanced age.
>
> Joseph, b. Jan. 18, 1814, m. Emmaline Akers of
> Wythe County, and died at Bristol, Tenn. March 19,
> 1867. They had one son and two daughters:
>
>> Robert J., born Sept. 15, 1852, m. _____ James,
>> and died Oct. 8, 1929. The names of his child-
>> ren are not available.
>>
>> Columbia Ann, b. May 18, 1857.
>>
>> Cora, b. May 6, 1864, m. William Guthrie.

Jacob Naff, third son of Jacob and Elizabeth Stover
Naff, married Susan Webster. They lived in Maggodee Valley,
near the post office called Naff's where a stage relay station
was maintained. Two of his sons were postmasters there. Jacob
and Susan had issue:

> 1. Abraham I., m. Anne M. Turner (Muse), widow.
> 2. Jacob, married, and lived in Kansas.
> 3. Isaac, killed in battle at Chester Station.
> 4. Joseph, died young.
> 5. George, died young.
> 6. Daniel, m. Elizabeth Arthur, and lived in Indiana
> 7. John Warren
> 8. William C., married Charlotte Thomasine LaPrade
> 9. Mary, married William Oxley
> 10. Susan
> 11. Magdalene

Jacob moved to Kansas, and married there. He had a
large family. Daniel went to Kansas in middle life, and reared
his family there.

Abraham Irving, eldest son of Jacob and Susan Webster
Naff, married Anne M. Turner Muse daughter of Gideon and Ruth
Fields Turner, and widow of Charles Muse, who died in the Con-
federate Army. They had issue:

> 1. Josephus A., b. April 5, 1869, married Dec. 31,
>   1895 Edith Elizabeth Naff
> 2. James T., b. March 29, 1871, married Pansy
>   Burckhardt at Denver, Colorado

3. Thomas G., b. Nov. 24, 1874, married Corry M.
   Tench
4. Charles L., b. Dec. 30, 1876, married Julia
   M. Dillon
5. John W. L., b. April 4, 1879, married Bertha
   Nicholson
6. Samuel L., b. April 2, 1882, married Nellie
   Wheeler.

William C., youngest son of Jacob Naff and Susan Webster Naff, married Charlotte Thomasine LaPrade, and had issue:

1. Edward D., married Mary Clay Noell
2. Frederick A., married, first, a Miss Powell,
   who died and left a son Arthur Naff, and, second, name unavailable
3. Mary E., married Walter Montgomery
4. Annie May, unmarried
5. Louisa F., married William Rhoades
6. Maggie D., married Marvin Garst
7. Susie S., married Keith Bussey
8. Rebecca, unmarried
9. Amy G., married Hurley Alley

All of these are living (1935) except the third daughter.

Josephus A. Naff, eldest son of Abraham I. and Anne Turner Naff, married Dec. 31, Edith E., youngest daughter of Rev. Isaac N. Naff and Cynthia M. Wysor Naff, and had issue:

1. Frederick J., b. Sept. 27, 1896, unmarried.
2. Paul M., b. July 9, 1898, married Edith Lucile
   Cline
3. Henry A., b. Oct. 19, 1902, married Ruth Keen
4. Dorothy, b. March 1, 1900, unmarried
5. Ruth E., b. Feb. 2, 1907, unmarried

This family moved out of Franklin County in 1915. The mother died Jan. 25, 1934.

Abraham Naff, second son of Jacob Naff and Elizabeth Stover Naff, married Hannah Peters, and had issue:

1. Joel b. May 20, 1833, married Mary Boon, died
   Nov. 17, 1885
2. Jacob P., b. Nov. 24, 1845, married Mary Naff,
   died about 1905
3. Daniel A., b. June 27, 1848, married Hannah
   Bowman, died Nov. 30, 1924
4. Elizabeth, b. May 28, 1831, married Abraham
   Naff
5. Susannah, b. March 16, 1836, married George
   Flora
6. Sarah, b. March 3, 1839, married David Bowman

7. Rebecca, b. Feb. 20, 1842, married Daniel Hurt

Joel Naff, eldest son of Abraham Naff and Hannah Peters Naff, married Mary E. Boone, and had issue:

1. Benjamin Thomas, b. May 23, 1868, married Flora J. Bowman
2. Josephus A., b. about 1871, married Mary Bowman
3. William L., b. Nov. 21, 1874, married Lilla L. Powell
4. Sarah M., married Daniel Kinsey
5. Hannah E., married B. M. Phelps
6. Mary D., married C. C. Flora

Jacob P. Naff, second son of Abraham Naff and Hannah Peters Naff, married Mary M. Naff, and had issue:

1. George W., married _____ Mills, died in Feb. 1933.
2. David died infant
3. John A. b. July 3, 1876, married Rosa L. Flora
4. Annie married Christopher Grubb, died about 1890
5. Sallie E., married Christopher Boitnott
6. Julia, married John Boitnott
7. Cora
8. Jacob

Daniel A. Naff, youngest son of Abraham Naff and Hannah Peters, Naff, married Hannah Bowman, and had issue:

1. Thomas, married _____ Montgomery
2. Stoner
3. William
4. Emma, married James T. Cummings
5. Ida, married George Cummings
6. Minnie, married Elijah Bowman
7. Mattie, married Enoch E. Bowman

Thomas G. Naff, third son of Abraham Irving Naff and Anne Turner Naff, married Corrie M. Tench, and had issue: Harry Naff of Roanoke.

Charles L. Naff, fourth son of Abraham Irving Naff and Anne Turner Naff, married Julia M. Dillon, and had issue: Bunyan L. Naff of Roanoke.

William L. Naff, youngest son of Rev. Joel Naff and Mary Boon Naff, is a Baptist minister.

Benjamin Thomas Naff, eldest son of Rev. Joel Naff and Mary Boon Naff, married Flora J. Bowman, and had issue: a son, Joel, and three daughters.

John A. Naff, the son of Jacob P. Naff, married Rosa L. Flora, and had issue:

1. Joel Cline, b. Sept. 28, 1902, died Aug. 24, 1918.
2. Wesley W., b. July 4, 1905, married Ethel Jamison
3. Elmer D., b. Oct. 13, 1911, married Ava Hannah Montgomery
4. Eunice R., b. Oct. 22, 1908, teaches science
5. Mary H., b. Sept. 21, 1917
6. Lois K., b. Sept. 12, 1923

THE NELSON FAMILY

Judge Hugh Nelson, son of Dr. Nathaniel Nelson and Lucy Mann Page, was born at "Oakland", Hanover County, October 19, 1821. Thomas Nelson Page's grandfather, Thomas Nelson, was the oldest brother of Dr. Nathaniel Nelson. Dr. Nelson died at the age of 40 years and left a widow with six children. Hugh was the only one connected with the Franklin County. He was sent to a boy's school near Philadelphia, and later graduated from Hampden Sidney College. After graduation, he taught at a boy's school in Halifax County eight years, studying law all the while time under Judge William Leigh, who was one of the signers of his license.

On admittance to the bar, Hugh Nelson settled in Rocky Mount. He was constant student and spent much time gathering information. He had remarkable memory and was a lover of poetry and history. He was called the "walking encyclopedia." His storehouse of information was always at the disposal of those who came for it. Modest, honest, and reserved, he was always a gentlemen. His painstaking, accurate work and his distinctive handwriting may be seen in the county clerk's office. He served as Commissioner in Chancery. He was the first county court judge. His home was the cradle of Trinity Episcopal Church. He read the service when his brother-in-law, the Rev. John R. Lee, found it impossible to come (by horseback) from Leaksville, North Carolina.

Soon after locating in Rocky Mount, Hugh Nelson married Lucy, daughter of Dr. Richard M. Taliaferro and his wife Mary Hale. To them were born: (1) Carter Kinloch, (2) William Leigh, (3) Walter Binford, (4) Mary Hale, (5) Ferdinand Emile, (6) and (7) Richard Taliaferro and Hugh Page (twins), (8) Harold, (9) Lucy Tazewell, and (10) Clarence. Of these Carter Kinloch, William Leigh and Hugh Page died in infancy, and Walter Binford died at the age of 19.

Mary married Parker Worth Strayer of Harrisonburg, and had issue: (1) Mary Nelson, (2) Elizabeth Samuels, (3) Nancy Page, (4) Hugh Parker, and (5) Clare Virginia.

Mary Nelson Strayer married the Rev. W. T. Roberts. No issue.

Elizabeth Samuels Strayer married Robert G. Guthrie, and had issue: (1) Elizabeth, (2) Robert and (3) Lucy Page. Elizabeth Guthrie married Alvin Johnson, a lawyer, of Knoxville, Tennessee. Lucy Page and Robert are not married.

Nancy Page Strayer married Thomas M. Cooper of Kingstree, South Carolina, and had issue: Nancy Page, and Jean, neither of whom are married.

Hugh Parker Strayer married Elizabeth Fique of Texas, and had issue: Elizabeth, who married Harold Hill.

Clare Virginia Strayer married R. P. Dickinson, Editor of The County News of Rocky Mount, and had issue: (1) Robert Nelson, (2) Randolph Strayer, (3) Richard Pendleton, and (4) Lucius Carter. Robert Nelson Dickinson married Genevieve Geisen of Roanoke, and had issue: Genevieve Mann. Richard Pendleton Dickinson married Ruby Walker, and had issue: Anne Nelson.

Ferdinand Emile, son of Hugh and Lucy Taliaferro Nelson, married Martha Clay of Paris, Kentucky, where he lived and died, without issue, at the age of 74 years.

Richard Taliaferro, son of Hugh and Lucy Nelson, married Mary Hover of Colorado. They lived in Missouri. No issue.

Harold, son of Hugh and Lucy Nelson, married May Wiltse of California. Home: California. No issue.

Lucy Tazewell, daughter of Hugh and Lucy Nelson, married Owen H. Price, Clerk if Franklin Circuit Court. They had one daughter, Page Nelson, who is assisant editor, Norfolk and Western Magazine, Roanoke.

Robert Nelson, son of R. P. Dickinson, is advertising assistant of the Norfolk and Western Railway Company.

Strayer and Richard, son of R. P. Dickinson are associated with their father in publishing The County News.

Judge Nelson and his wife lived and died in the home built by Dr. Richard Taliaferro about 1818. Mrs..Nelson was born in this house and it was willed to her by her father before his death at the outbreak of the War between the States. Mrs. Nelson bequeath the home to her daughter, Lucy Tazewell, who married Owen H. Price.

THE PETERS FAMILY

The ancestors of this family came from Germany and settled in the southern part of Pennsylvania. Several members of the family removed to the Valley of Virginia and settled in what was then Augusta County. They later removed to Botetourt County, and from there into Franklin County. There were three brothers who settled in different parts of Franklin where they brought up large families whose descendants are scattered throughout the country.

Many members of this family rendered service in the pioneer days against the Indians. Others held positions of responsibility during the Revolutionary War. Stephen Peters, born in Pennsylvania in 1753, was married in 1773 to Polly Dillman of Botetourt County. They had sons, Stephen, Jacob, and David, and possibly others.

Jacob Peters, son of Stephen and Polly Dillman Peters, married and built a house on Maggotty Creek, in Franklin County, about 1795. The Indians were numerous then and a band of them came when he was finishing his house. They acted so strangely that the family became afraid of them. However, they treated the white family kindly, but no sooner were they gone than the dishes were buried, and the family fled, carrying such things with them as they could.

Stephen Peters, son of Stephen and Polly Dillman Peters, was born in Franklin County and removed to Indiana, near Indianapolis, when the Northwest Territory was being settled. Through thrift and industry he became wealthy. He never returned to Virginia. About 1889, his son and daughter, Daniel and Katie, came to Virginia for the first time to visit their cousin, Mrs. Catherine (Peters) Webster and other relatives.

David Peters, one of the sons of Stephen and Polly Dillman Peters, was born May 19, 1783, and died April 28, 1864. He was married, April 1, 1809, to Christina Brubaker, who was born May 9, 1791, and died July 25, 1861. They lived on Blackwater about three miles northwest of Dillon's Mill and are buried there. They were among the best educated persons in the community. They were members of the Brethren Church. For a great many years the Brethren meetings were held in the homes of the members and their home was often open for service. The house was an old-fashioned log building with partitions that could be hooked to the ceiling thus making the several rooms one. They were familiar with the German language. Christina Peters, wife of David, was the daughter of Jacob and Ann Brubaker, whose home was near Peters Creek Brethren Church. She had fair complexion, light blue eyes and was very vivacious. Their nine children were:

(1) Polly Peters, born February 26, 1819, died in infancy.

(2) Katherine Peters, born January 11, 1812, died June 12, 1897. She married John R. Webster, May 4, 1839. Their seven children were: John Henry, William David, George Stephen, Joel Lee, Sarah Elizabeth, Mary Ann, and James Franklin.

(3) John B. Peters, born October 29, 1815, died December 18, 1888. He was married first, to Mary Brown, and, second, to Catherine Johns, widow of Carey F. Johns and daughter of John and Catherine Brubaker Eller. She was born January 8,

1841, in Roanoke County, and lived for many years with her daughter, Mrs. Mollie Johns Plunkett, Tippecano City, Ohio. Her mother and her husband's mother were sisters. John B. Peters was educated at Virginia Collegiate Institute. He was a member of the Brethren Church; he taught school when a young man, and in later years he was a merchant. He died without issue and was buried at the Peter's burying ground.

(4) Henry D. Peters, born October 9, 1817, died May 1, 1901. He married Mary Gravely. He taught school when young, studied medicine, graduated with honors from the University of Virginia in 1846, and became a practicing physician. He was a member of the Methodist Church and lived and died at Leatherwood in Henry County. He had four children who lived to be grown: Robert, George, Alice and Herbert.

(5) Stephen M. Peters, born July 8, 1820, died, unmarried, November 24, 1852. He was educated at Virginia Collegiate Institute and was employed by Barney Pitzer, a merchant at Salem. His travels were extensive for one of his day. He died in Montgomery, Alabama, and is buried there.

(6) Ann Peters, born September 18, 1823, died September 5, 1893. She was married on January 16, 1851, to Andrew J. Saunders, and had seven children. Of these, Milton Jefferson, J. David, and Emma lived to maturity. Ann Peters Saunders and her husband were members of the Bethlehem Brethren Church.

(7) David Peters, born July 28, 1826, died in infancy, and is buried at the Peters burying ground.

(8) Daniel G. Peters, born June 19, 1829, died January 11, 1897. He married Tabitha Fralin, and they had three children. He was a member of the Brethren Church. He was exceedingly witty and hospitable. He and his family are buried at the Peters burying ground.

(9) Sallie J. Peters, born February 9, 1833, died without issue, September 20, 1904. She was married March 4, 1865, to Edmund T. Mullens. They were members of the Fairmont Baptist (Missionary) Church. Both are buried at the Peters burying ground.

Dr. Henry D. Peters of Leatherwood, Henry County, was the only son of David and Christina who perpetuated the Peters name. Robert, the oldest son of Dr. Henry D., died in early life, after completing a course of training at Roanoke College. George, his second son, was an attorney-at-law and became Judge of the County Court of Franklin County, holding the office as long as he lived. His wife was the widow of A. L. Edmundson of Rocky Mount. Alice, the only daughter, married Jesse B. Lavinder. Herbert G., the doctor's youngest son, was born September 10, 1859, and educated at Roanoke College and the University of Virginia. He represented Henry County in the Virginia Legislature when only twenty-four years old. He was later elected State Senator

for Patrick and Henry Counties. He was Presidential Elector from
the Fifth Congressional District in 1888. He removed to Bristol,
in 1890, where he was a leading memver of the bar. He married
Electra Smith of Martinsville in 1894. His son, Herbert G. Peters,
Jr., was associated wtih his father in the practice of law until
his father's death in 1925.

THE PINKARD FAMILY

Capt. John Pinkard married May Waller, and had issue:
(1) Bailey, (2) Elias, (3) Lucinda, (4) Robert, (5) Benjamin,
(6) Billy, (7) Charles, and (8) Anna.

(1) Bailey Pinkard married Rebecca Smith, and had
issue: William, Fletcher, and Nannie.

(2) Elias Pinkard. No record.

(3) Lucinda Pinkard married Jessie Prunty. No issue.

(4) Robert Pinkard married Jane Belcher, and had issue:
Benjamin, and Julia who lived in Missouri.

(5) Benjamin Pinkard married Julia Hunt and had issue:
Thomas, Billy, Mary, John, and Charles.

(6) Billy Pinkard married Emeline Cooper, and had
issue:

- (a) Walter Leak, m. Lucy Neff
- (b) Charlotte Temple, unmarried
- (c) Mary Anne, m. Peter Stockton
- (d) Emma Augusta m. William Stafford
- (e) Lucinda Wise, m. William O. Jamison
- (f) Nancy Cooper, m. first Charles F. Pinkard;
  second, Henry Hayner and third, Frank Pinkard
- (g) John William, m. Nannie Taylor
- (h) Charles Washington, unmarried
- (i) Eliza, m. George T. Pearson, Oct. 4, 1891
- (j) Minnie

(7) Charles Pinkard married Lucinda Hensley, and had
issue: Alice, Nannie and John.

(8) Anna Pinkard married William N. Copeland. No issue.

Eliza Pinkard married George T. Pearson, and had issue:
(1) Billy, (2) Louise, (3) Kathleen, (4) John, (5) Emeline, (6)
Minnie, (7) George, (8) Doris and (9) William.

(1) Billy Pearson died in childhood.

(2) Louise Pearson married Walter H. Cobbs and had

issue: Walter, Billy, Cabell, Carrington and Johnny of Rocky Mount.

(3) Kathleen Pearson married Leon D. Hetrick, and lives in Pittsburgh. No issue.

(4) John Pearson married Maude Bright, and lives in Charlotte, North Carolina. No issue.

(5) Emeline Pearson married Skinnell, and lives at Rocky Mount. No issue.

(6) Minnie Pearson married Samuel Emlar, and had issue: Louise, and Doris. Home: Pittsburgh.

(7) George Pearson married Agnes Austin and lives in Pittsburgh. No issue.

(8) and (9) Doris and Bill Pearson, live in Pittsburgh.

THE POWELL - PAYNE FAMILIES

Robert Powell died about 1811, according to Inventory of his estate made August 15, 1811, and of record in Franklin County Will Book 2, page 4. He had issue: (not listed according to age).

1. William, who married Sophia Hancock, December 26, 1804.

2. Jane T., who married Phillip Thurmon, October 22, 1807.

3. Elizabeth, who married Henry Smith, May 10, 1790.

4. Sally, who married _____ Craighead

5. Nancy, who married Robert Craighead, November 18, 1792.

6. Charles, who married Lucinda Hancock, April 30, 1809.

7. Robert Jr., who married Polly Sutherland, January 17, 1803.

8. Frances, who married Thomas Payne, January 14, 1799.

Thomas Payne, who married Frances Powell, daughter of Robert Powell, on January 14, 1799, had issue: (not listed according to age)

1. Catherine, who married William Hatcher, March 3, 1819.

2. Jane, who married William Baker, December 2, 1822.

3. Robert Powell, who married Elizabeth Payne, March.
30, 1829.

4. Charles H., who married Rebecca _____.

5. Mary, who married Charles Holland.

6. Thomas A., who married Mary A. Spencer, December
20, 1819.

7. Elizabeth, who married John Frith, November 16,
1840.

8. William, who married Sarah Payne, December 3, 1828.

Robert Powell Payne, son of Thomas and Frances Powell Payne, was born in Franklin County, October 10, 1808, married (about 1829) his cousin, Elizabeth Payne. She was born August 10, 1810, and was the daughter of Floyd Payne and Elizabeth Pollard, whose marriage bond is dated October 13, 1790.

The children of Robert Powell and Elizabeth (Payne were:

I.   Patrick Flayle
II. Frances Jane
III. Mariah E.
IV. Sarah Catherine
V.   Caroline Celesta
VI. Anna Leslie
VII. Nancy Virginia
VIII. Mary Elizabeth
IX, John Austin
X   Emily Electra
XI. Robertella

In 1839 Robert Powell and Elizabeth Payne moved from Franklin County to Callaway County, Missouri, where he died on July 5, 1847 and she on November 29, 1902.

I. Patrick Flayle Payne, son of Robert Powell and Elizabeth Payne, was born December 27, 1830 in the eastern part of Franklin County near the junction of Blackwater and Staunton Rivers. He married first, Elizabeth Catherine Richie in Callaway County, Missouri, December 19, 1854, and second, Mary Frances Lynes, daughter of Harrison and Angelina McBride Lynes on October 9, 1872. The children of the first marriage were: 1. Robert Newton, who married Mattie Hume; 2. John Baxter, who married Lillie Booth; and 3. Ella Frances, who married Lewis Abraham Kirkpatrick.

The children of the second marriage were: 4. Eanie

Harrison; 5. Charles Jackson, who married Frances Hatton Mc-Cracken; 6. William Oliver, who married, first, Lillian Wise, second, Mary Rice; 7. Edward Scott, who married Maude Conner; and 8. Jacob Allan, who married, first, Anna Bartley, second, Ethelene Rice Tullock.

Patrick Flayle Payne died at Ham's Prarie, Callaway County, Missouri, February 18, 1904. His first wife died Nov ember 13, 1864, and his second wife died on March 27, 1920.

1. Robert Newton, son of Patrick Flayle and Elizabeth (Richie) Payne, born September 22, 1855, in Callaway County, Missouri, died August 16, 1910. He was a minister of the Christian Church. He married Mattie Hume, and had issue: 1. Katherine Ercel, who married James Gregory; 2. Frances, who married Elmer Landman; 3. Frenchie, who married C. S. Johnson; 4. Hume, of whose marriage no record is availabe to the author; 5. Robert, who died in youth; and 6. Temple, who died in youth.

2. John Baxter, son of Patrick Flayle and Elizabeth Richie Payne, was born in Callaway County, Missouri, and now lives in Fulton, Missouri. He married Lillie Booth, and had issue: 1. David Ralph, who married Marie Gregory, May 6, 1916; 2. Silas Booth, died in youth; 3. Virgil Frances, who married Wilsie Elizabeth Burnett on June 5, 1917, and has three children: John B., Mary E., and Marciedine (He is an instructor in Transylvania College, Lexington, Kentucky); 4. Robert Paul, who married Minnie West, November 15, 1924; 5. Patrick Maurice, who married Ruth Hurd of Kentucky, on November 13, 1931; and 6. Anne, who married Amanuel Jackson Overton, of Fulton, Missouri, on May 15, 1926, and had issue: A. J. Jr., and Anne Caroline.

3. Ella Frances, daughter of Patrick Flayle and Elizabeth Richie Payne, was born in Callaway County, Missouri, married Lewis Abraham Kirkpatrick, and had issue: 1. Baxter Nixon, who died in youth; 2. Lois, who married Byno Morgan, May 5, 1919, and had issue: William, Robert, James, and Jack; and 3. Gladys, who was married in Ohio June 12, 1926, to George Rooks, of Carrollton, Georgia, and had issue: Donald Dean.

4. Eanie Harrison, son of Patrick Flayle and Mary Frances Lynes Payne, was born in Callaway County, Missouri. He lives, unmarried, at the old home place near Ham's Prarie.

5. Charles Jackson, son of Patrick Flayle and Mary Frances Lynes Payne, was born in Callaway County, Missouri, educated in Harvard, and is an instructor in Southeast Missouri State T achers College at Cape Girardeau. He was married, November 6, 1903, in Polk County, Missouri, to Frances Hatton McCracken, daughter of William Thomas Jewett and Mary Ava Childers McCracken, of Hickory County, Missouri, and had issue: Mary Charline, born in Atlanta, Georgia, and married Stanley Lender Brown of Riverside, California, on July 20, 1931.

6. William Oliver, son of Patrick Flayle and Mary

Francds Lynes Payne, was born in Callaway County, Missouri, and married Lillian Wise, daughter of Horace Benton and Evaline Nichols Wise of Callaway County, Missouri, and had issue: 1. William Maxwell, and 2. Frances Evaline. He practices medicine at Ham's Prairie. His first wife died November 1918, and he married, second, Mary Rice, daughter of William and Frances Lynes Rice. No issue.

7. Edward Scott, son of Patrick Flayle and Mary Frances Lynes Payne, and a merchant at Ham's Prairie, married Maude Connor, adopted daughter of William and Malissa Sanford Connor, and had issue: William Connor.

8. Jacob Allen, son of Patrick Flayle and Mary Frances Lynes Payne, married in Callaway County, Anna Bartley, daughter of Robert and Cora Stucker Bartley, and had issue: Mildred Allene, and Anna Bartley. He married, second, Ethlene Rice Tullock, daughter of William and Frances Lynes Rice, of Callaway County, and had issue: Mary Frances, who died in infancy.

II. Frances Jane, daughter of Robert Powell and Elizabeth Payne, was born in 1831 in Franklin County. She married Isaac Oliver Craighead, son of John R. Craighead, of Callaway County, Mo., and had seven children:

1. Meadora A., who married David Harley Howe, and had issue: Ethel, Merle, and Jewell.

2. Edwin Boone, born in 1860, and served as president of Central College Fayette, Mo.; State Normal at Warrensburg, Missouri; Tulane University, New Orleans; and University of Montana. He married Catherine Johnson, daughter of Benjamin Franklin and Catherine Wheeler Johnson, of Fayette, Mo., in 1889, and had issue: Edwin, Barclay, and Catherine. He died in Missoula, Montana, about 1919, and was buried at Ham's Prairie, Missouri.

3. Annie, who married _____ Hill and had issue: Ditchler, and Dochska.

4. Mollie, who married Newton Gingrich, and had issue: Oliver Newton, and Bernice.

5. Mariah, who married John Lincoln Gingrich, and had issue: Earle, who married a Miss Lindsey.

6. Jacob Ditchler, who married Allie McDonald of South Carolina, and had issue: Catherine.

7. Virginia, who married Earnest Forest Bush, teacher in St. Louis schools, and had issue: Hazel.

III. Mariah E., daughter of Robert Powell and Elizabeth Payne, was born in Franklin County: November 25, 1832, and married John Staub of Callaway County, Mo., and removed to California.

IV. Sarah Catherine, daughter of Robert Powell and Elizabeth Payne, was born in Franklin County, November 2, 1834, and married James William Craighead of Callaway County, and had issue: 1. Charles, who married Lizzie Maertz; 2. Woody; and 3. Bertha, who married a Mr. McCall.

V. Caroline Celesta, daughter of Robert Powell and Elizabeth Payne, was born in Franklin County, August 28, 1836, married Mark Craighead, of Callaway County, Mo. and had issue: 1. Patrick; 2. Samuel; 3. Winkard, who married Etta Haynes; 4. Mallie, who married Thomas Williamson; and 5. Sophia, who married a Mr. Creecy.

VI. Anna Leslie, daughter of Robert Powell and Elizabeth Payne, was born in Franklin County, June 1, 1838, and married James Muir of Callaway County, Mo. and had issue: 1. Della, who married Kem Stucker; and 2. George Payne.

VII. Nancy Virginia, daughter of Robert Powell and Elizabeth Payne, was born April 29, 1840, near Ham's Prairie Mo. married Richard Miles, and had issue: Marvin Payne who married Willie Bell.

VIII. Mary Eliza, daughter of Robert Powell and Elizabeth Payne, was born October 1, 1841, at Ham's Prairie, Callaway County, Mo. She married Robert Henry Taylor, born March 4, 1838, Callaway County, son of John L. and _____ Taylor, and had issue: 1. Britton Payne, 2. Eulah, 3. William Robert, 4. Bruce Holland, and 5. Baxter.

1. Britton Payne Taylor, born June 1, 1871, in Callaway County, Mo., is a minister of the Methodist Episcopal Church. He married Carrie Elizabeth Turner, born August 15, 1876, daughter of William F., and Mary E. Fulkerson Turner of Boone County, Mo., and had issue: Iris S., born November 18, 1903 in St. Joseph, Mo., married Julian A. Parvin of Kansas City, Mo.; Mary C., born May 30, 1905, married Howard C. Beers of Rochester, New York, and had issue: Carol Ann, born December 23, 1931, and Barbara, born August 2, 1933; Britton Morton, born in Richmond, Mo., July 29, 1909; William Robert, born in Richmond, Mo., September 14, 1911; and George Evans, born October 12, 1917, in Kansas City, Mo.

2. Eulah E. Taylor, born September 8, 1872, married J. Lee Kempp, and had issue: Mary Alice, Maud Lee, and Nelle.

3. William Robert Taylor, born March 31, 1875, married, first, Nellie Bradley, and second, Maud Davis.

4. Bruce Holland Taylor, born June 25, 1877, married Susan Wagoner.

5. Baxter Taylor, born January 18, 1884, died in July 1901.

IX. John Austin, son of Robert Powell and Elizabeth Payne August 21, 1843, in Callaway County, Missouri, unmarried, died in 1865.

X. Emily Electra, daughter of Robert Powell and Elizabeth Payne, born November 27, 1845, in Callaway County, Missouri, married John W. Davis and had issue:

1. Samuel Oscar, who married Belle Pinet.

2. Veda, who had a daughter named Roberta.

3. Vera, twin of Veda, who married Samuel Faulker, and had issue: Paul.

4. Flayle

5. Boone

6. Kate, who married John Smith, and had issue: Pauline, and others.

7. Karl, twin of Kate.

8. Mabel, who married Earle Miller, and had issue: Earl, and Payne.

XI. Robertella, daughter of Robert Powell and Elizabeth Payne, born November 10, 1847, in Callaway County, Missouri, is now living with her eldest son in Fulton, Missouri, married James A. Payne, and had issue:

1. Daniel E. Pollard, who married Alpha Lynes, daughter of A. J. and Louisa White Lynes, and had issue: Margaret, who married A. W. Griffith; Andrew Pollard; and Mary C., who married Martellus Staples.

2. Robert Earnest, who married Stella Sneathen, and had issue: Robert H., Howard, Raymond, and Elizabeth Ellen.

3. Elizabeth Ellen, who married Jerome O'Neal, and had issue: Lila L., Ellen L., (twins), and Ruby May.

4. Rufus Thomas, who married, first, Addie Kemp, and, second, Era Simms, and had issue: Orville Thomas.

5. John Smith, who married Bessie Custard, and had issue: Lenrow, Darwood, and Doris Deane.

THE PRICE FAMILY

Joseph Shores Price was the first of the family to come to Franklin County. His birthplace was probably in New Kent County, since he was baptized there in 1740. His parents, Joseph and Ann Price lived and died in Cumberland County.

Joseph Shores Price served in the French and Indian War, and received a grant of land in Buckingham County for his services. He was married, according to tradition, to Charity Bagby. During the Revolution, he lived in Henry County and furnished supplies to the army. He obtained grants on Blackwater River, May 15, 1794.

Showers Price, a son of Joseph Shores Price, also received a grant of land in Franklin County, on the Forks of Blackwater Nov. 16, 1798. Joseph Shores Price died Oct. 20, 1801. He left a large family of sons and daughters.

Showers Price was born April 27, 1763. He married Elizabeth Hill. He was Major, of the 110th Regiment, Virginia Militia, 1809. He was Sheriff of Franklin County from 1816-17, and 1844-45. He left a family of fourteen children.

Cyrus Price, son of Showers Price, was born August 28, 1800. He rode horseback from Franklin to Chester, Pennsylvania, stayed two years at school, and rode back to Franklin. Another brother rode the same horse to Pennsylvania for his two years of school. When the next brother was ready to go, he insisted on a new horse.

Cyrus Price married Elizabeth Boone, daughter of John Boone and had issue: (1) John W. Price, who married Rhoda Abiah Taylor; (2) Susan Price, who married David Campbell Cobbs; (3) Shores LaFayette Price, who married Emma Taylor; (4) James T. Price; (5) George W. Price, who married Jennie Shaver; (6) Henry Clay Price, who married Mary E. Hopkins; and (7) Sallie A. Price, who married Henry S. Deyerle. All sons save the youngest (who was only fourteen when the war ended) served in the Civil War. One died from severe wounds received at Gordonsville.

Henry Clay Price was born and died in Franklin. He married Mary E. Hopkins of Franklin, and had issue: (1) William H. Price, who married Bettie Deyerls, and lives in the ancestral home in Franklin; (2) Annie Lee Price, who married Graham M. Ker, and lives in Washington D. C. (They have one daughter Annita Melville Ker) (3) Estelle Price, and (4) Mildred T. Price. The family has but few members in Franklin today.

Owen Henry Price, son of Peter Price and Louise Carper, was born near Callaway on February 21, 1843, and died February 22, 1910. He was named for his grandfather who married _____ Guerrant. His father died when he was quite young and his grandfather reared him. His education was begun in the

neighborhood school, and continued at a military academy at
Christianburg. He returned to the easy-going farm life but
answered the call to arms at the outbreak of the Civil War and
was assinged to Company K, 42nd Virginia Infantry. He and four
other Franklin men were captured and sent to Fort Delaware where
they were in prison eight months. On January 6, 1864, he got
a furlough and during his stay in Franklin married Lucy Taliaferro, daughter of Tazewell Taliaferro and Amanda Callaway.

After the war he returned to the farm life thought not
to the comforts of former days. Like other Confederate soldiers.
he had to "make a new start in a new era". Within a few years
he sought election as Sheriff of the county, won, and held his
office several terms. His genial nature won him a host of friends.
He was a great fox hunter, and always kept fine dogs and good
horses.

To Owen Henry Price and Lucy Taliaferro were born:
(1) Corbin Reynolds (died in infancy), (2) Louise Carper, (3)
Charles Callaway, and (4) Lucy Taliaferro.

Louise Price married John R. Meadows and had issue:
Lucy, and Rose. Lucy died young. Rose married Clarence Griffith
of West Virginia, and had issue: Howard, and Louise. Howard
married Lucy Allen of Charlottesville. Louise married Daniel
Duvall Holliday of West Virginia.

Charles Calloway Price was educated at V. P. I., Washington & Lee, and received the degree M. D. from the Medical
College of Virginia. He removed to Arkansas where he married
Ruth Kiteley, and had issue: Charles Calloway, Jr., and Al-
fie Taliaferro.

Lucy Taliaferro Price married George Cabell Greer.
Both were great-grandchildren of Dr. Richard M. Taliaferro.
No issue.

In 1900, Owen Henry Price was appointed Clerk of the
Circuit Court to fill out the term of J. C. Carper, deceased.
At the expiration of this appointment, he was elected to the
office, and held it until his death.

On the death of his wife, Lucy Taliaferro, Owen Henry
Price was married on April 26, 1905, to Lucy Nelson, daughter
of Judge Hugh Nelson and Lucy Nelson, and had issue: Page Nelson, a daughter.

THE PRILLAMAN FAMILY

Jacob Prillaman, Sr., wrote a will, July 19, 1796, which
was proved in Franklin County Court in September 9th that year.
He mentions in it his wife, Waltpurgia, and the following children: Jacob Prillaman, Jr., Anne Sowder, John Prillaman, Daniel

Prillaman, and Barbara Martin.

According to David E. Johnston's "Middle New River Settlements", Barbara Snidow, daughter of John and Elizabeth Helm
Snidow, married Jacob Prillaman, of Franklin County, Virginia.
This refers to the above-mentioned Jacob, of Franklin County,
had a wife Sarah, in 1790, and in all probability it was Sarah
Snidow who married Jacob Prillaman, as Sarah is a very common
name in the early days of the Snidow family in Virginia, a
family very persistent in the use of family names, while Barbara occurs only later, and apparently only in the branch descended from another Prillaman line.

Barbara Prillaman, daughter of Jacob and Walpurgia Prillaman, married in Henry County, Virginia, February 14, 1782,
Phillip Snidow, son of John and Elizabeth Helm Snidow. Phillip
Snidow died in 1791 or 1792, and his widow married, June 17,
1793, Christian Martin.

Phillip and Barbara Prillaman Snidow has four children as follows:

1. Nancy Snidow (1783-1860), m. March 3, 1803, Jacob
Prillaman (1778-1859), of Franklin County. He served as lieutenant in the War of 1812. They had eight children:

    (a) Mary Ann Prillaman, m. January 6, 1823, John
        Burnett

    (b) George Prillaman, b. 1806

    (c) Elizabeth Prillaman, b. 1808; m. March 12, 1828,
        Fleming Helm. Issue, at least four children:

        (1) Nancy Helm, b. 1835
        (2) Malinda Helm, b. 1845
        (3) Thomas F. Helm, b. 1848
        (4) James W. Helm, b. 1853

    (d) Samuel Prillaman, b. 1810; m. Permillia ____
        b. 1810. Issue ten children:

        (1) Stephen H. Prillaman, b. 1830
        (2) Lucinda Prillaman, b. 1832
        (3) Elizabeth Prillaman, b. 1834
        (4) Jane H. Prillaman, b. 1836
        (5) John Prillaman, b. 1838
        (6) Ann A. Prillaman, b. 1840
        (7) George Prillaman, b. 1843
        (8) Samuel Prillaman, Jr., b. 1845
        (9) Phillip Prillaman, b. 1848
       (10) Mary B. Prillaman, b. 1852

    (e) Barbara Prillaman, b. 1814, m. January 1, 1844,
        Lewis Jamison (b. 1807) of Franklin County,
        son of Samuel and Winnie Bird Jamison. Issue
        six children:

    (1) Mary E. Jamison, b. 1845, m. Thomas Helm
    (2) Nancy C. Jamison, b. 1847 m. Rev. Taylor
         Turner
    (3) Elizabeth E. Jamison, b. 1848, m. D. Lee
         Ross, Captain, C. S. A., of Franklin County
    (4) Ruth Frances Jane Jamison, b. 1850, m.
         George Ross, a nephew of D. Lee Ross
    (5) Susan Jamison, b. 1852, m. Marshall Pril-
         laman
    (6) Thomas Fleming Jamison, b. 1854, m. first,
         Snug Ingram; and, second, Allie Whitlock.
         They resided in Roanoke.

(f) Fleming Prillaman, b. 1816

(g) Daniel Prillaman, b. 1818

(h) Ann Prillaman, m. September 23, 1858, Granville
     R. Connor

    2. Christian Snidow (May 1, 1787-December 31, 1861);
m. Sarah Turner (December 21, 1788-April 27, 1874), of Henry
County. They resided at Pembroke Giles County, Virginia.

    3. William Melvin Snidow (May 31, 1788-December 3,
1864), m. October 13, 1822, Chloe Ann Freel (November 1, 1804-
June 23, 1848), of Cabell County, now West Virginia. They re-
moved in 1837 to Madison, Missouri. Their daughter, Barbara
Ann Snidow (1837-1909) m. James D. Helms, of Franklin County,
Virginia. They had the following children:

    1. Chloe Ann Helms, b. 1851, m. Moses Overfelt
    2. John Helms (1853-1927), m. 1866, Miranda N.
       Carter
    3. Warren Helms (1855- 1889)
    4. Fleming Busby Helms, b. 1857, m. 1888, Rosa
       Lee Carter
    5. Jennie Helms (1859-1891), m. Frank Owings
    6. Rosa Helms (1860-1861)

    4. George Snidow (April 24, 1790-February 16, 1866),
m. May 12, 1814, Elizaface (April 1, 1793-October 31, 1882),
daughter of Michael and Catherine Nosler Surface. They resided
in Giles County, Virginia.

    According to J. P. A. Hill's "History of Henry County",
George Prillaman of that county was born in 1790, and married
Dicie Ross, a sister of Capt. Lee Ross. He is said to have been
a son of Daniel Prillaman. He was, in all probability a son of
Jacob and Nancy Snidow Prillaman, a grandson of Daniel, and a
great grandson of Jacob and Walprugia Prillaman. In 1850, George
Prillaman and his wife Dicey were listed in the census beside
Jacob and Nancy Snidow Prillaman, and the will of this Jacob men-
tions his son George. The census shows that George was born,
not in 1790, but about 1806.

    Issue of George and Dicey Ross Prillaman, eleven children:

1. Christian S. Prillaman; b. 1828, Lt. C. S. A.;
died at White Sulphur Springs; m. Sarah _____ (b. 1840)

2. Exonia Prillaman, b. 1830; m. January 14, 1850,
George C. King

3. Gabriel Prillaman, b. 1832; m. Elizabeth T._____
(b. 1835)

4. Martha E. Prillaman, b. 1834; m. August 1852, Andrew H. Turner

5. Fleming M. Prillaman, b. 1836; m. Drusilla Turner,
a daughter of Marshall and Sallie A. DeShazo Turner

6. Isaac Prillaman, b. 1840

7. Caroline M. Prillaman, b. 1841; m. John T. Cannady

8. Lydia A. Prillaman, b. 1843; m. Bailey Cannady

9. George A. Prillaman, b. 1844; m. _____

10. Nancy J. Prillaman, b. 1846; m. John W. Bowlin

11. Peyton A. Prillaman, b. 1849; died young

THE PRUNTY FAMILY

The first person of record in Franklin County bearing
the name Prunty was Thomas (Robert?) Prunty, who was granted 354
acres of land "on the waters of Snow Creek, adjoining the land
of Jeremiah Morrow" on October 20, 1779. This grant is of record in the Land Office at Richmond, Land Book A, page 14.

Land Book D, page 160, shows that Robert Prunty, presumably a son of Thomas, received a grant of land "on the waters
of Pigg River" on September 1, 1780. James Prunty (whether a
brother or son of Robert is unknown to this writer) received a
grant of 400 acres "on both sides of Ditto's Creek on Snow Creek,
adjoining Caldwell's line" on December 2, 1785. This grant is
of record in Land Book U, page 572.

The land records of Franklin County, in the Virginia
State Library at Richmond, show that Robert Prunty owned 711 acres
of land in Franklin, when the county was formed in 1786.

Robert Prunty, born 1750 and died about 1824, married
Frances _____, and had nine children. Robert Prunty was the
son of Thomas, presumbably.

1. John Prunty, m. Carpathia Clardy, Sept. 21, 1816
2. Sarah Prunty, m. Philip Carter, Jan. 9, 1804
3. Robt. Prunty, Jr., m. Judith Faris May 6, 1816
4. James Prunty's marriage record not available
5. Jane Prunty's   "   "   "   "
6. Polly Prunty's   "   "   "   "
7. Jesse Prunty, m. Nancy Finney, Mar. 18, 1802
8. Frances Prunty, m. Joseph Rives, Feb. 15, 1814
9. Thomas Prunty, m. Sally Rives, Aug. 10, 1804

These children are named in Robert Prunty's will of record in Will Book 2, page 616, at Rocky Mount. The will was made on May 19, 1823, and probabed in November 1824, which is indicative of the time of Robert Prunty's death. The children of Robert and Frances Prunty are not neccessarily named here in the order of their age.

Jesse Prunty, son of Robert and Frances, had by his wife, Nancy Finney, seven children.

1. John Prunty, m. Lucinda Pinckard, Mar. 25, 1828
2. Thomas Prunty married and removed to Missouri, via Kentucky. He was a minister of the Gospel.
3. Robert Prunty III, m. first, Anne E. Finney, May 17, 1845, and, second, Rebecca S. Neblett
4. Jesse Prunty, Jr., m. first, Charlotte Temple Pinckard, Jan. 18, 1845, and, second, Sallie Hunt.
5. Jane Prunty m. Frederick R. Brown, Oct. 1, 1837
6. Elizabeth (Betsy) Prunty m., first, William Wingfield, Oct. 4, 1824, and, second, her cousin, Amos Finney.
7. Frances Prunty, m. Isaac Montrief, Mar. 2, 1835.

Jesse Prunty, b. ca. 1780, married in 1802, Nancy Finney, daughter of John and Elizabeth Prunty Finney. For a time he was a Deputy Clerk of Franklin County, and issued his own marriage license. His will was written Feb. 20, 1856 and is of record in Will Book 12, at Rocky Mount.

Robert Prunty, son of Jesse and Nancy Finney Prunty, was born in 1811 and died in 1898. He was married, first, to, Anne E. Finney, daughter of Peter Finney, on May 17, 1845, and, second, in 1856, to Rebecca S. Neblett, daughter of William S. Neblett. By his first marriage, he had one son, Robert A. Prunty, born about 1850, who married Kizziah Draper, and died in 1931 without issue. By his second wife (b. 1837d. 1917), he had six childern.

1. Roxie Prunty (b. 1856, d. 1885), m. Raleigh Younger, and had issue: Bruce and Lawson
2. Millard Prunty (1859-1884), d. unmarried
3. William Prunty (1866-1934), m. Ida Ramsey
4. Nannie Prunty (1868-1928), m. Thomas Belcher, and had issue: Myrtle, who married George Brodie; Ben-

jamin; Ruby, who married Jack Bouldin; and Andrew.

5. Maggie Prunty, m. Richard Silas Williamson, and had six children:

    (a) Doris, who m. H. Clay Turner
    (b) Mary, who m. Clifford Goode
    (c) Charmian
    (d) Mildred
    (e) Bernard
    (f) Nancy

Richard Silas Williamson was the son of William S. and Mary Lucinda Bernard Williamson, both representatives of distinguisged Franklin County families.

6. Love Prunty, m. James T. Ramsey, and had issue: Robert, William, and Burton.

NOTE: Anne Finney's father, Peter Finney, was one of the four members of the Finney family who came to Franklin from Amelia about 1790

Jane Prunty, daughter of Jesse and Nancy Finney Prunty, married Frederick R. Brown in 1837, and became the progenitor of a long and illustrious line of descendants. She was the mother of John R. Brown.

Elizabeth (Betsy) Prunty had two children by her first husband, William Wingfield: Ann Hudson, and Jane Mallory.

Ann Hudson Wingfield, b. ca. 1825, married Thomas H. Barnes in Estill County, Kentucky, June 2, 1848, and had issue: Betty, Sidney M., Willie, Jennie, Paul, and Thomas Jr.

Jane Mallory Wingfield, b. ca. 1827, married John O. Grubbs in Kentucky on Nov. 26, 1846, and had issue: Thomas W., Annie, Mary E., Sidney, Amanda, and John O. Jr. Thomas probably was the Thomas Grubbs who married Mary Eliza Jarman, April 12, 1866. Annie married Albert Easter of Estill County, Kentucky. Mary Elizabeth married Albert Simones of Franklin County, Virginia. Amanda married William Cook of Franklin County, Virginia. John O. Jr., was a physician, and lived in Oklahoma.

William Wingfield, the first husband of Elizabeth (Betsy) Prunty was the son of William and Elizabeth Wingfield. His parents were cousins. His brothers and sisters were: Lewis, Christopher, Charles, Austin, Jerusha, Polly, Lucy, and John.

Lewis married Elizabeth Parberry; Christopher married Nancy Stockton; Austin married Nancy Cook; Jerusha married William M. Bowling; Polly married George Cooper; and John married Lucy Hill.

Elizabeth Prunty Wingfield's second husband, Amos Finney,

was her cousin. They were married in Franklin County, Jan. 6,
1834, and left shortly afterward with a considerable caravan of
Franklin County people for Kentucky. Thomas Prunty, a Methodist
minister and brother of Elizabeth's mother, performed the ceremony, according to family tradition, though this writer has been
unable to find any evidence that he became a minister before leaving Virginia. And, it is certain that both of Elizabeth Prunty's
marriages took place in Franklin County.

The Robert Prunty homestead, in the upper Snow Creek
Valley, remains in the Prunty family. William and Ida Ramsey
Prunty lived there until 1934 when he died and the widow removed
to her brother's home near Henry Station. The homestead was noted
for its hospitality and was the scene of many happy festivals.
The home of Captain W. F. H. Lee was nearby. The Lee and Prunty
families were related by ties of kinship. Rebecca Neblett Prunty
was an artist in needlework as well as with a brush. Some of
her pictures are in the possession of her descendants. She was
a lover of flowers, and her garden was one of the show places
of Franklin.

The following members of the Prunty family should fit
into the foregoing genealogy, but the writer has been unable to
make the proper connections:

Nancy Prunty, who married Peter Hammock, January 26,
1788

Elizabeth Prunty, who married William Carver, March
5, 1794

Nancy Prunty, who married Squire Fleming, January 26,
1828

James Prunty, who married Martha Wimmer, June 26, 1794,
service performed by Rev. Randolph Hall

THE ROSS FAMILY

Thomas, John and Daniel Ross, brothers, settled in
Louisa County about the middle of the eighteenth century.

Thomas Ross, probably the eldest of these brothers,
pruchased of James Buchannan, on March 25, 1750, 200 acres for
25 pounds in the Parish of Fredericksville, Louisa County, on
the branches of Rocky Creek, adjoining the line of Alexander
Glaspy and Mumford Robertson. Both Ross and Buchannan are styl-
ed residents of this parish. (Louisa Co. D. B. "A" p. 379).
Thomas Ross disposed of this land in 1769. At a Court held July
10, 1769, a deed was made by Thomas Ross and his wife, Judith,
conveying the property to George Taylor. This deed was proved
by Walter Mouzly and John Smith (Louisa O. B. 1765-1772, p. 331).

The second of these brothers, John Ross, owned land in Louisa in 1752. In a patent granted to Joseph Crenshaw, for 758 acres on South Anna River, it is stated that the land adjoins James Crenshaw, John Ross, Thomas Crenshaw, and others (P. B. 32, p. 663). On Sept. 10, 1755, John Ross received a Patent for 400 acres in Louisa County on both sides of Rocky Creek, adjoining John Price and John Ragland (P. B. 31, p. 594). On this same creek, Thomas Ross owned land adjoining the lands of John Garth and John Ragland. At a Court held for Louisa County, Sept. 8, 1777, John Ross was recommended to the Governor for appointment as Ensign, under Capt. Samuel Richardson, in the Virginia Militia; but the Governor's approval was not awaited, and the oath of office was administered to him that very day (Louisa Co. O. B. 1772-1782, p. 175).

On April 10, 1778, John Ross conveyed to William Lipscom 557 acres for 250 pounds, said land being on both sides of Rocky Creek, adjoining John Raglands' line (Louisa D. B. "E", p. 254).

John Ross, after selling his land, removed to Henry County, where he received a grant of 184 acres (as shown by a survey dated 10th of May, 1780) on the South Side of Smith River (Grant Bk. "D", p. 893). By the formation of Patrick County, in 1791, John Ross, whose lands were on the South Side of Smith River, became a resident of the new county. He soon sold this land, however, and moved to South Carolina.

Daniel Ross, apparently the youngest of these three brothers, bought, on April 28, 1761, 100 acres on the North Side of South River in the Parish of Fredericksville, County of Louisa, adjoining John Pulliam (Louisa D. B. "C", p. 90).

Daniel Ross I moved from near Charlottesville and married a Miss Garth of that vicinity. His wife's name was Betty, the daughter of John Garth, Senior, formerly a resident of Spottsylvania and Orange Counties. By Will dated July 29, 1780, and probated Sept. 11, 1786, John Garth bequeathed his wife all his lands on the South side of Roundabout Creek. He directed that the rest of his property, after the death of his wife, be divided among his children: Thomas, David, John, Betty Ross, Mary Ann Lobbins (or Sobbins), and Sarah Mouzby (Louisa W. B. 3, p. 153). By an Act dividing the counties of Albemarle and Louisa, and Parish of St. Anne, March, 1761, that "part of the said County of Louisa that lies above a line, etc.," was annexed to Albemarle County, which accounts for the presence of Daniel Ross and his brother-in-law, Thomas Garth, in Albemarle County. At a Court held for Henry County, in June 1780, Daniel Ross I was appointed a Second Lieutenant, under O. Rubell, in the Virginia Militia (Va. Militia in the Revolutionary War, McAllister, p. 210). He rendered further assistance by furnishings foodstuffs for the army. (P. S. C.C., Va. Archives, State Lib.)

In 1781-82, Daniel Ross received a grant of 260 acres

on the north side of Smith's River, crossing Beard's Creek to a Sycamore on Nicholas Creek adjoining his own land. (G. B. "D", p. 930 and G. B. "G", p. 250). By the formation of Franklin, Daniel Ross became a resident of the new county, where he received another grant of 66 acres on June 19, 1797, on Nicholas Creek and Smith's River, adjoining his own line.

Daniel Ross I, born in Scotland ca. 1740, settled in Louisa, later Albemarle, married Betty Garth, daughter of John and Elizabeth Garth, moved to Henry, later Franklin County, from whence, in old age, he accompanied his son William to Missouri. Some of his children remained and left descendants in Franklin County. The children of Daniel and Betty Ross, given without respect to their ages, are:

(1) William Ross, born ca. 1764, appeared on the tax lists of Henry County, with his father, Daniel, in 1782 to 1784, and in his own name in 1785. On Jan. 3, 1799, William Ross received a grant of 307 acres in Patrick County, on the south side of Smith's River. He moved to Missouri about 1800.

(2) A daughter who m. Abel Pedigo of Patrick County,

(3) A daughter, who m. a Ransdell, and moved to Tennessee.

(4) Another daughter, who m. a Ransdell, and moved to Tennessee.

(5) Robert, who m. a Miss Turner

(6) Daniel, b. 1776, d. 1861, m. first, Nancy Ingram, and, second, Joyce Harper

(7) James

(8) Joseph, who moved to Missouri

(9) Rachel, who m. a Turner

(10) David, who m. a Miss Anderson

(11) Benjamin, who never married

(12) Louis, who moved to Kentucky

(13) Sally, who m. a Cox

(6) Daniel Ross, son of Daniel lived in Henry and Franklin Counties. By his first wife Nancy Ingram he had issue:

I William, who m. Mahala Burnett of Franklin County.

II Onie, who m. William Conner of Patrick
County.

III Kizzie, who m. James Connor of Patrick
County.

IV Charles, who m. Louvenia Foster of
Franklin County.

V   Burrell, who m. Miss Lester, and moved
to West Va.

VI Dicie, who m. George Prillaman of Franklin County.

VII Martha, who m. a Mr. Kinley, and moved
to Tennessee.

VIII Susan, who m. Crawford Turner of Patrick County.

IX Malinda, who m. Edward Jefferson of Patrick County.

By his second wife Joyce Harper, Daniel Ross had
issue:

X   McDaniel, who m. first, a Miss Williams,
and second, a Harper.

XI Daniel Lee, who m. Bettie Jamison

XII Betty, who m. Dr. George Clark of Patrick County.

William Ross, I. ca. 1801, eldest son of Daniel and
Nancy Ingram Ross, married Mahala Burnett. She was the grand
daughter of Charles Burnett, an early settler of Henry County,
and received a grant of land there in 1781 (G. B. "D".). He
lived in Patrick County, but after his death, prior to 1860,
his family moved to his farm at the confluence of Town Creek
and Smith's River in Henry County, known to this day as "Ross
Bottoms".

The 6 children of William and Mahala Burnett Ross were:

(1) Abram Burnett, who m. Catherine James.

(2) Louisa, who m. Marshall Jamison of Franklin Co.

(3) Harden, who m. Martha Conner of Patrick Co.

(4) Mary, who m. Jake Clark of Patrick Co.

(5) Amanda, who m. Wiley Smith of Franklin Co.

(6) Thomas Jefferson, who m. Eleanor Frances Lemon of Franklin Co.

Charles Ross, son of David and Nancy Ingram Ross, b. Jan. 17, 1810, m. Louvenia Foster, b. June 13, 1813, and had issue:

(1) Thomas D. Ross, b. Aug. 5, 1840

(2) James Ross, died in War Between the States

(3) Charles Ross, m. Fannie Jamison

(4) Lucinda J. Ross, b. March 22, 1844, m. Sam R. Akers

(5) William L. Ross, b. Dec. 12, 1845, died a rich bachelor in California.

(6) Martha Ross, b. Sept. 30, 1849, m. J. A. Nowlin

(7) George C. Ross, b. June 6, 1852, moved to California, and died unmarried.

(8) John Abe Ross, b. Dec. 29, 1855, m. Ida Hooker of Patrick County.

(6) Dicie Ross, daughter of Daniel and Nancy Ingram Ross, m. George Prillaman, of the southwestern part of Franklin County, and had issue:

(1) Christian ("Chris"), who m. Sally Canady.

(2) Flem, who m. Lucilla Turner.

(3) George Jr., who m. Anne Turner, daughter of Meshach Turner

(4) Gabriel, who m. Jane Lesseur of Franklin Co.

(5) Isaac, who m. Betty Via of Franklin Co.

(6) Nannie, who m. John Bowling.

(7) Martha, who m. Andrew Turner, son of Meshach Turner

(8) Onie, who m. George King of Franklin Co.

(9) Caroline, who m. John Canady of Franklin Co.

Abram Burnett Ross, eldest son of William and Mahala Burnett Ross, was born in 1826, and married Catherine James, daughter of Catlett and Elizabeth Thompson James of Franklin Co. in 1856. He became owner of the Ross Farm at the confluence of Smith's River and Town Creek. He served as Magistrate and Commissioner of the Revenue in Henry County, and was in the Confederate Army, receiving the rank of captain. In 1868, he bought land on Little River in Floyd County, where he died in 1874. Issue:

(1) Mary Elizabeth, b. 1858, d. 1894, m. a Mr. Dobyns of Pulaski. Issue: Two children

(2) Augusta Ross, b. 1862, d. 1935., m. Wm. H. Ward of Albemarle County and had issue:

   (a) Al - Willie Ward m. Lockhart, and had 2 children, Jane, and Ward.

   (b) Daniel Henry Ward, m. Elizabeth Wall of Montgomery County and has one child, Daniel Braxton.

   (c) Phoebe Ward, m. Otto Meybery. They live in Richmond and have two children: Anne Ross, and Braxton.

(3) Pocahontas Ross, b. 1863, d. 1885, unmarried

(4) Fannie Mildred Ross, b. 1865, m. Benjamin Meshach Goode

(5) Catlett Ross, b. 1867, d. 1898, unmarried

Charles Ross, son of Charles and Louvenia Foster Ross, b. Feb. 8, 1843, d. June 24, 1932. On Oct. 18, 1869, he m. Fannie Jamison, (b. Mar. 24, 1850), and had issue thirteen children:

(1) Susan Cassie Ross, b. Dec. 18, 1870, m. on Feb. 5, 1896, J. J. Wright, Postmaster and merchant at Dodson, and had issue: Nell Wright, graduate of the University of Richmond, and teacher; Mary Wright of Mount Airy; Frank Wright, m. Ethel Frith and lives at Rocky Mount; Loila Wright, m. Frank Smith; and Eva Ross Wright.

(2) Walter Lee Ross, b. March 26, 1873, m. Nannie Ingram, March 23, 1898, and lives near Ferrum. Their children are: Curtis Ross, m. Mary Mullins, and lives at Akron, Ohio; George Ross, m. Eva Mullins, lives at Akron, Ohio; Harry Ross; and Cove Ross, who m. Luther Burnett, lives at Nola, and has five children: Charles, Truman; Lena, who m. Clifford Prillaman; Annie; Alice; and Roy.

(3) Minnie Lou Ross, never married.

(4) Martha Ann Ross, b. April 5, 1876, m. Hampton Ramsey of Sydnorsville, and had issue: Lolene Ramsey.

(5) George William Ross, b. Jan. 11, 1879, m. Lera

Goode, b. June 5, 1885, daughter of William Gardner and Callie Bettie Goode. He served as rural carrie at Dodson for 30 years. Retired from service, he lives at Ferrum. Issue:

- (a) Archie L., b. Oct. 1, 1906. Graduate of the U. of Va.

- (b) Gertie, b. June 8, 1908, m. Curtis O. Roberson.

- (c) Inez, b. Feb. 18, 1910.

- (d) Migno, b. Oct. 7, 1913.

- (e) Cristobel, b. Sept.. 20, 1915,

- (f) William Ross b. Apr. 10, 1922.

(6) Thomas D. Ross, b. June 28, 1880, m. Daisy Prillaman, lives at Ferrum, and has two children: Park Ross, m. Glenna Nunley; and Bernice Ross.

(7) Mary Jane Ross, b. Apr. 5, 1882, m. Philip Hay of Winston-Salem, and engineer on the N. & W. Ry.

(8) Emma Ruth Ross, b. March 1884, m. Finwich Dickerson.

(9) Barbara Ella Ross, b. Sept. 30, 1885, m. B. G. Beard.

(10) Fannie Lillie Ross, b. Jan. 18, 1888, m. C. K. Lemon of Franklin Co. and had issue: Marvin, Glen, C. K., Helen, Ruth, William, snd Ross Lemon.

(11) Charles Louis Ross, b. Oct. 21, 1889, m. Kate Smith, and has two children: Mary Frances, and Charles III, who is bank cashier of Ferrum.

(12) Annie Lessie Ross, b. Nov. 19, 1892.

(13) Posey Franklin Ross, m. first, Eleanor Wells, issue: Owen, Margaret and Anne Ross. He m. second, Eva Ross Prillaman, daughter of Thaddeus and Dameron Turner Ross.

David Ross, son of Daniel Ross I, m. a Miss Anderson. Pedigo's "History of Patrick County" states that his sons were: Peyton, Robert, Lewis, Joseph, Wiley, Nathaniel, Ben, James, Jefferson, and Samuel. Samuel Ross married Esther Harbour and lived near Elamsville. His daughters were: Jane Ross Loudy (probably Lundy); Polly Ross Anderson, who went to Grayson County to live; and Docia, who died young.

Peyton Ross' children of his first marriage were:

Ruth Ross Pedigo, wife of Rufus Pedigo of Draper; Pencie Ross
McGhee, first wife of Green McGhee of Bassetts; Annie Ross Wright,
wife of Washington Wright of Vinton; Augusta Ross Nowlin, wife
of Joseph Nowlin of Franklin Co.; and Joseph Ross. Issue of
his second marriage were: Lizzie Ross of Vinton; Ada Ross Cox
of Dodson; Patie Ross Turner, deceased; and Ben P. Ross of Draper.

Capt. Daniel Lee Ross, son of Daniel and Joyce Harper
Ross, II, lived and died near Elamsville. He served as Captain
in the Army of the Confederacy, Co. "D" 51st Regiment. He married
Bettie Jamison.

The children of Capt. Daniel Lee and Bettie Jamison
Ross were: (1) Brewster Ross, married a Miss McKenzie of Patrick Co., and lives at Martinsville; (2) Mrs. Loula Tatum, Elamsville, who has one daughter, Cornelia, a teacher in the Spartansburg, S. C. public schools; (3) Flem Ross, who m. Miss Tatum,
and lives at Stuart; (4) Guy Ross, who lives at the Old Ross
home at Elamsville; and (5) Erie Ross, a teacher in the Spartansburg, S. C. public schools.

Issue of Samuel R. and Lucinda Ross Akers, of Buffalo
Ridge: (1) C. W. Akers; (2) Lou Akers, of Buffalo Ridge; and
(3) Mrs. P. G. Wright, of Bassetts.

Issue of J. A. and Martha Ross Nowlin: (1) G. L. Now-
lin, of South Boston; (2) Cove Nowlin, South Boston; (3) J. A.
Nowlin, Roanoke; (4) C. K. Nowlin, Stoneville; and (5) Mrs. C.
E. McKenzie, Buffalo Ridge.

Issue of John Abe and Ida Hooker Ross of Buffalo Ridge:
(1) John Ross, Madison, N. C.; (2) Bertie Hopkins, Draper, N. C.;
(3) Lucy Clark, Stuart; (4) S. L. Ross, Buffalo Ridge; and (5)
Beatrice Ross, Roanoke.

Louisa Ross, daughter of Abram Burnett and Catherine
James Ross, m. Marshall Jamison, who lived seven miles east of
Henry, and had issue:

(1) Charlie Jamison, m. first, Alzie Wade, and had
one daughter, Cora Jamison, who married Will
Scott of Franklin Co. He m. second, Sallie Simms,
and had issue:

(1) Marshall Jamison, m. Maude Ellis, and lives
at Spartansburg, S. C.;

(2) Caroline Jamison, who m. a Hundley;

(3) Hattie Jamison, who m. Tom Finney, of Snow
Creek;

(4) Lee Jamison, who m. a Miss Lovell, of Franklin Co.

Harden Ross, b. ca. 1833, son of William and Mahala Burnett Ross, m. Martha Conner of near Elamsville, and had issue:

(1) Ella Ross, who m. a Rakes of Franklin Co.

(2) Alice Ross, who m. William C. Hooker, and had issue: Alice Hooker, who m. Horace Brown, lives at Martinsville, and has two children: Catherine, and Billy.

(3) Jefferson Ross.

(4) William Ross, M. D.

(5) Charles Ross, M. D., whose widow and children live in Washington D. C.

(6) Creed Ross.

(7) Burwell Ross.

Amanda Ross, daughter of Abram Burnett and Catherine James Ross, m. Wiley Smith of Snow Creek, and had issue: (1) William who lives in Roanoke; (2) Anna, who m. J. L. Wade; and (3) Alberta, who m. M. L. Kirks.

Thomas Jefferson Ross, son of Abram Burnett and Catherine James Ross, m. Eleanor Lemon of Franklin Co., and had issue: Thaddeus, Marcia, Fletcher, Oren, and Webster.

(1) Thaddeus Ross, who m. Dameron Turner, daughter of Andrew and Martha Prillaman Turner of Franklin Co., lived near Ferrum, and had 6 children: Le Roy, m. a Canady; Eva, m. Posy Ross, Chester Ross, m. a Martin; Mamie; Viola; and Laine.

(2) Marcia, who m. an Akers, has several children, and lives at Philpott.

(3) Fletcher Ross, deceased.

(4) Oren Ross, m. a Davis, and lives near Salem.

(5) Webster Ross, m. a Kirks, and has several children.

Issue of George Prillaman, Jr., son of George and Dicie Ross Prillaman, and Anne Turner Prillaman, daughter of Meshach Turner:

(1) Wilton Reed, has several children, and lives six miles west of Henry.

(2) Sally Bettie, who m. Robert Prillaman, lives six miles, northwest of Henry, and has several children.

(3) Turner, deceased.

(4) Callie, deceased.

(5) H. Nicholas, who m. a Burnett, has several children, and lives at Nola.

(6) Pattie, m. and lives in W. Va.

(7) Homer.

Issue of Isaac Prillaman, son of George and Dicie Ross Prillaman, and Betty Via Prillaman: (1) Christian; (2) Peter, m. Winnie Thornton, lived near Henry and had children; (3) Flem (4) Gabriel; (5) Maggie; and (6) Emma.

Issue of George King and Onie Prillaman, daughter of George and Dicie Ross Prillaman: (1) Green, never married; (2) Bettie; (3) Louise, m. George Helms, lived near Henry, and had several children; (4) Arnold; (5) J. Lee, m. Octavia King, lives at Henry, and has issue: (a) Harry Lee King, m. Vida Hurt; (b) Edna King, m. C. J. Shelton; (c) Virgie King, m. a Mr. Pamplin of Winston-Salem; (d) Diuguid King, married, lives at Norfolk and works for the Virginian Railway; (e) Annie King, m. a Moorefield of N. C.; (f) Irene King, m. O. T. Kittinger of Rocky Mount; (g) Alfred King of Rocky Mount; (h) Emmett King, who m. a Miss Holland of Franklin County and has two sons: Thomas and Roger.

THE SAUNDERS FAMILY

The will of John Saunders of York Co., probated Feb. 24, 1700, named Christabel, wife of Samuel Waddow; John; Edward; Robert; George; Hargarve; Peter; Sarah; and Susannah. There is a deed recorded in York Co. in 1707, from John and Edward Saunders, disposing of land to William Barbour, "inherited from their mother, Mary Risle, dau. of John Risle." but reserving "the burial place of their mother and father, forty feet square."

John Saunders, son of John whose will was probated in 1700, m. Mary Susannah Hyde, dau. of Robert Hyde. He removed to Goochland where his will, dated Oct. 2, 1736, is of record. He had issue: 1. Mary (who m. Daniel Johnson), and 2. John Hyde.

John Hyde Saunders lived in Cumberland Co. In a deed of record in York Co., from John Hyde Saunders to Samuel Hyde Saunders for land in Goochland Co., patented 1690, the former is described "as son and heir to John Saunders." His will, dated Feb. 2, 1768, was proved Mar. 29, 1768, and he names as executors William Fleming, Archibald Buchanan, and his son John Hyde Saunders. Issue: 1. Samuel Hyde; 2. Robert Hyde; 3. Chancellor; 4. Jesse Hyde; 5. John Hyde; 6. Peter Hyde (to whom he gave 195 acres in Pittsylvania County; 7. Rebecca; 8. Patty; and 9. Marianna.

Robert Hyde Saunders, son of John Hyde Saunders, b. Nov. 9, 1761, served in the Revolution, practiced law, and was a member of the Virginia Senate in 1799. He m. Nov. 6, 1799, Marianna Barbara Hunter, dau. of John Hunter and Susannah Jones, and had issue: Robert, Mary, and John. Mary died at 16.

Robert Saunders, son of Robert and Marianna Barbara Hunter Saunders, b. Jan. 25, 1805, educ. in College of William and Mary, and was later President of same, m. Lucy, dau. of Gov. John Page, June 17, 1828, and had issue: 1. Marianna Barbara, who m. Rev. George T. Wilmer; 2. Margaret; 3. Lelia; 4. Robert Page; and 5. Lucy Page.

John Saunders, son of Robert and Marianna Barbar Hunter Saunders, m. Lucy Galt. He was for years customs officer in Norfolk. His son, William Turner Saunders, an Episcopal minister, had 4 children: Robert, William Lawrence, Jennie, and Walter.

John Hyde Saunders, son of John Hyde Saunders, was a student at William and Mary in 1762, was dismissed for insubordination, went to Europe, was ordained a minister there, returned in 1772, served St. James Parish, Cumberland Co., and was a member of Cumberland's Committee of Safety in 1775.

Jesse Hyde Saunders, lived in King William Parish, Cumberland Co., m. Mary, dau. of Anthony Lavillion, a French Hugenot. A deed of record in Cumberland, dated Oct. 22, 1764, refers to his property.

Peter Hyde Saunders, son of John Hyde Saunders and _____ Fleming, b. Sept. 20, 1748, in Powhatan Co., d. Nov. 25, 1790, m. Oct. 31, 1767 to Mary Sparrel, at the home of her uncle, William Branch Giles, Gov. of Virginia. Soon after marriage, they moved to a point fifteen miles southwest of Rocky Mount, on the headwaters of Pigg River, then embraced in Pittsylvania Co. The property is no longer in the names Saunders, and no original building is standing. The will of John Hyde Saunders, probated in Cumberland Co., Mar. 29, 1768, left to his son Peter Hyde, "195 acres in Pittsylvania County, a negro fellow named Humphrey, one feather bed and furniture, a pair of hand mill-stones, two iron pots and one frying pan, all lent to him during his life, and to the heirs of his body forever." He seems to have been "cut off," not with the traditional shilling, but with such homely household articles as were suitable for the pioneer life he had to lead in the wilds of Franklin. The estate on Little Deep Creek, Cumberland Co., was left to his brothers, John and Jesse.

Peter Hyde Saunders, served with Col. Abram Penn, as co-Justice of the Peace in the first court ever held in Henry Co., Apr. 20, 1778. He served Henry Co., as tax collector and also in the Virginia Legislature in 1781. He was a member of Pittsylvania's Committee of Safety in 1775, and Lt. Col. of Militia in 1782. He was the first Saunders to settle in Franklin.

A family tradition has it that the wife of Peter Saunders often had to shut herself in for days against the wolves which infested the forests around the pioneer cabin in Franklin.

Peter H. and Mary Sparrell Saunders had issue: 1. Judith, b. 1768, m. Col. Samuel Hairston, was the grandmother of Gen. Jubal A. Early; 2. Lettie, b. 1770; 3. Elizabeth, b. 1772, m. John Ingles; 4. Peter, b. 1776, d. in Pittsylvania Co., unm.; 5. Fleming, b. 1778; 6. Robert, b. 1781, d. unm.; 7. Samuel, b. 1783, m. Mary Ingles; 8. Theodocia, b. 1785, m. John A. Hale (a grandson of hers was killed at Chapultepec in the Mexican War.); and 9. Mary ("Polly"), b. 1787, m. Capt. Wiley Wood.

Fleming Saunders, son of Peter H. and Mary Sparrell Saunders, b. 1778, in the area which became Franklin Co., m. Alice Watts, dau. of William and Mary Scott Watts, of Campbell Co., May 19, 1814, and had issue:

1. Mary Elizabeth, b. Mar. 31, 1816, d. Dec. 8, 1825.

2. Sarah b. July 16, 1817, d. Nov. 6, 1818 (?)

3. William, b. Jan. 18, 1820, d. May 24, 1821.

4. Edward, b. Nov. 4, 1821, d. 1843.

5. Peter, b. Oct. 1823, d. Aug. 13, 1906, served in the General Assembly, m. Betty Dabney, was father of the late Judge E. W. Saunders.

6. Ann Maria, b. Oct. 19, 1825, m. Col. Thomas L. Preston, lived in Charlottesville, had no issue, but adopted Ann Preston Davis.

7. Robert Chancellor, b. May 26, 1827, m. Caryetta Davis, lived in Campbell Co., was an officer in the C. S. A., d. Sept. 22, 1902.

8. Fleming, b. July 18, 1829, m. Mary Gwathmey, was Capt. in C. S. A.

9. Louisa Morris, b. 1833, m. Oct. 4, 1855 to Rev. Richard T. Davis, son of Prof. A. G. Davis of University, and had issue: (1) Anna Preston Davis who, at her mother's death, was adopted by her aunt, Mrs. Thomas L. Preston. She m. George R. Lockwood, St. Louis lawyer, and had issue: (a) Richard John, of St. Louis; (b) Louisa, m. G. C. Stribling, lives in California, has 2 daughters: Anna Preston, and Rebecca Marshall; (c) Angelica Peel, of St. Louis, and (d) Thomas Rhodes scholar, and New York lawyer, who m. Mrs. P. G. Frances.

(2) John Andrew Gardner Davis; (3) Lucy Landon Davis of Leesburg; (4) Alice Watts Davis of Leesburg; (5) Mary Jane Davis;
(6) Caroline Davis of University; and (7) Caryetta Louisa Davis,
b. 1867, principal of St. Peter's Episcopal Mission School in
Franklin Co., since 1906. The Rev. Mr. Davis, m. second, Louise
Taliaferro, and had issue. (8) Louise T., (9) Eugene F., and
(10) Elizabeth Carter.

Howe's "History of Virginia" states that no decision
of Judge Fleming Saunders was ever reversed. He owned much
land in Franklin and Floyd. His wife, Alice Watts, owned much
in Campbell Co. The old Watts home, "Flat Creek", near Evington railroad station, is now (1935) owned by Mrs. J. Sinkler
Irvine, granddaughter of Judge Fleming Saunders.

Judge Fleming Saunders lived in Franklin Co., at "Bleak
Hill" 10 miles west of Rocky Mount on the Floyd Turnpike. The
house was burned in 1830, and he then removed to "Flat Creek"
in Campbell Co. Educated at Chapel Hill, N. C., he was made
Judge of the 10th Judicial District under Gov. John B. Lloyd on
Apr. 20, 1831. It is recorded of Judge Saunders that he knew
nothing of his appointment until one of his friends returned
from Richmond and addressed him as "Judge". He held the office
for many years. When remonstrated with for resigning while his
mental vigor was unimpaired, he replied, "I want to resign while
I have sense enough to do it."

Peter Saunders, son of Judge Fleming and Alice Watts
Saunders, b. Oct. 6, 1823, d. at "Bleak Hill" in Franklin, Aug.
13, 1906. He m. Sept. 27, 1855, Elizabeth Lewis Dabney, dau.
of Rev. John Blair Dabney and Elizabeth Lewis Towles, of Campbell Co. Educated at Washington College (now Washington and
Lee, he inherited "Bleak Hill". He built on the site of the
house that burned in 1830, the house which is now standing, and
in it he died. He did not serve in the C. S. A. due to ill
health, but he did serve in the General Assembly during the war,
and also from 1883-1887, when Virginia repudiated the Readjuster
Party. He was a lawyer, senior warden in Trinity Episcopal Church
at Rocky Mount, and lay reader at Ascension Chapel on his estate.
His children were: 1. Maria Louisa, d. infant; 2. Edward Watts,
b. Oct.20,1860, d. Dec. 16, 1921; 3. William Dabney, b. Sept.
3, 1863; 4. Agatha Lewis, b. May 6, 1865, d. Jan. 11, 1918; and
5. Alice Lee, b. Apr. 27, 1867.

Robert Chancellor Saunders, son of Judge Fleming Saunders, d. May 26, 1827, educ. in the University Major in C. S.
A., m. Caryetta Davis, dau. of Prof. A. G. Davis of the University, and had issue:
>   1. Alice Fleming Saunders, m. J. M. M. Davis, had
>   two daughters, (a) Lily Heth, who m. Prof. Heath
>   Dabney of the University, and had a son, Virginius,
>   who m. Douglas Chelf, and (b) Alice Chancellor,
>   who m. John White.
>
>   2. Eugene Davis Saunders, m. first, Flora Lemmon,
>   and second, Laura Barelli. Issue by second m.
>   (1) Marguerite, who m. Eugene Davis, and had

Marguerite and Terrell; (2) Robert; (3) Laura,
who m. Stuart Landry, and had Cynthia, Stuart,
Laura, and Anne. (4) Eugene, who m. Mae ____,
and had 2 children; (5) Caryetta, who m. Dabney
Langhorne, and had William, and Susanne; (6) Nat-
halie m. Marion Smith; (7) John; (8) Alice Watts.
Eugene Davis Saunders practiced law in New Orleans,
taught law in Tulane University, and served as
District Judge of Louisiana.

3. Edward Watts Saunders, educ. in University College of Medicine, practiced in St. Louis, founded
   the Bethseda Homes, and specialized in diseases
   of children.

4. Robert Chancellor Saunders, d. in infancy.

5. Mary Saunders, lives at Evington.

6. Elizabeth Gardner Saunders, m. William Hickson,
   and had issue: (1) Marion, who m. Charles Prince
   of Cheraw S. C. and had issue: Charles, William,
   Lawrence, and Marion; (2) Phyllis, who m. H. G.
   Carrison, and had Phyllis, Dan, Betty, and Henry;
   and (3) Edward Watts, who m. Mildred Morehead,
   and had James Sinkler.

7. Caryetta, d. infant.

8. Robert Chancellor, educ. in the University, practiced law in Seattle, Wash., m. Nannie Monk, and
   had issue: (1) Chancellor, who m. Ruth Bass;
   (2) John Monk, Rhodes Scholar, aviator, writer,
   author, playright, who m. Fay Wray, lives at Hollywood, Calif.; (3) Edward Watts; (4) Richard; (5)
   Eugene; (6) Nannie; (7) Virginia; and (8) Alice
   Cary.

9. Louisa Scott, d. infant.

10. John Staige, educ. at the University, lives at
    "Caryswood."

11. Walter Hyde, m. Louise Keyser, and had issue:
    George, who m. Roberta Donham; Walter, who m.
    Kathryn Lunt; William; and Edward Watts.

12. Lucy Davis, m. Dr. Cuthbert Gilliam.

13. Susan Richardson, lives at "Caryswood."

Fleming Saunders, 2nd. son of Judge Fleming, b. July
18, 1829, Capt. in C. S. A., m. Mary Gwathmey, had issue: 1.
Eva Smith, who m. Dr. J. Sinkler Irvine, had issue: (a) Mary
Fleming, (b) William, (c) Meade, and (d) Anne; and live at
"Flat Creek", Evington. Mary Fleming m. Frank Hampton and had

(1) Eva Gwathmey; (2) Fleming, III, educ. in V. P. I., m. Frances B. Brown, lives near Evington, has 2 children, Fleming, and Frances; (3) Carter Temple, m. Polly Bowles of Lynchburg; and (4) Mary Elsie, who m. Fenton Day of Danville, and has issue: Fenton Jr., and Elsie.

Samuel Saunders, son of Peter Hyde and Mary Sparrell Saunders, b. 1783, m. Mary Ingles, and has issue: 1. Margaret, 2. Elizabeth, 3. Virginia, 4. Crockett, 5. John 6. Fleming, 7. Robert, 8. Mary, 9. Sallie Ann, 10. William, 11. Peters, 12. Samuel, and 13. Shields.

1. Margaret, dau. of Samuel and Mary Ingles Saunders, m. J. S. Hale, and has issue: (a) John S., who m. Willa Noell, and had Mary, Margaret, Norbonne, and Stafford; (b) Mary D., who d. unm.; and (c) Janie, who m. Dr. Carter Berkeley.

2. Elizabeth, dau. of Samuel and Mary Ingles Saunders, m. Robert Hairston, and had issue: (a) Mary Lou, who m. H. M. Darnell, and had Mary, Elizabeth, Harry, and Tom; and (b) Elizabeth, who m. E. D. Graveley, and had William, Robert, and Sallie.

3. Virginia, dau. of Samuel and Mary Ingles Saunders, m. Peter Hale, son of J. S. Hale, and had issue: (a) Robert E., (b) Mamie, and (c) John. Robert E., m. Mary Callaway. They had 7 children: Samuel, John, Sallie, Tubal, Howard, Mamie, and Jane. John m. in Oregon and lives there.

4. Crockett Ingles, son of Samuel and Mary Ingles Saunders, m. Doshia Callaway, and had 6 children: Peter, Mary, Elizabeth, Sallie, Virginia, and Augusta. Elizabeth, m. Victor Hunton, and had Eppa and Isabella; Sallie m. _____ Robinson; Virginia m. Hugh Cooper, and has William and Patsy; and Augusta m. _____ Gorton.

5. John, son of Samuel and Mary Ingles Saunders, m. Anne Booth. They had 5 children: John B., Wm. C., Mary, Margaret, and Josephine. John B., m. a Miss Ferguson, and had John, and Sallie; William C., m. Sallie Booth, had Chancellor, Howard, Ruth, and Margaret; Mary, m. Robert Saunders, had Robert H., John, Sarah, and Annie; Margaret, m. William Ferguson; and Josephine m. _____ Joplin, and had Joe, Annie, and Eva.

6. Fleming, son of Samuel and Mary Ingles Saunders, m. Sallie Lou Hairston, and had 5 children: George, Mary, Margaret, Maud, and Annie. Mary, m. a Mr. Parkins; Maud, m. a Mr. Sydnor; and Annie, m. a Mr. Bolton.

7. Robert, son of Samuel and Mary Ingles Saunders, m. Sarah Claiborne, and had 3 children: Robert, Peachy, and Sallie Willie. Robert, m. Mary Saunders; Sallie Willie, m. R. A. Lovelace, and has Sallie, Robert, Peachy, Tom, and Mary.

8. Mary, dau. of Samuel and Mary Ingles Saunders, m.

James S. Callaway.

        9. Sallie Ann, dau. of Samuel and Mary Ingles Saunders, m. Peter M. Guerrant, and had issue: (1) John R., a physician, who m. Katharine Lee and had Elizabeth and Marie; (2) Samuel S., physician and apple grower.

        There was a Saunders family in this area at an early date, though not connected with the foregoing family. This Saunders family came from Holland, settled first in Pettsylvania, then came on down the Valley with the Brethren and Moravians.

        William David Saunders was the first member of this family in Virginia. He settled in Bedford. His son, Daniel Green Saunders, b. 1776, married Frances Davis. They built their home on a precipice on the south side of Staunton River, and called it "Ivy Cliff".

        Daniel Green and Frances Davis Saunders had issue:
1. Elizabeth, 2. Susan, 3. Frances, 4. Henry, 5. Margaret, 6. Daniel Green Jr., 7. Louise, 8. Thomas, 9. Catherine, 10. Ardena, 11. George, and 12. William.

        1. Elizabeth married Thomas Morgan of Bedford County, and had issue: Thomas Jr., John, Daniel, Flora, Margaret, and Susan. John, married Emaline English. Daniel, married Betty Cunningham, and moved to Missouri. Thomas Jr., married Mary Burroughs, and had issue: 1. Nicholas, who married Meta Saunders; 2. Lucian who married Janie Moorman; 3. Beulah who married Silas Overstreet; 4. Moses; 5. Flora; and 6. Estelle. Flora Morgan married, first, Edward Garrett, Lt., C. S. A., and had issue: 1. Sallie, 2. Thomas, 3. Samuel, and 4. Edward. Her second husband was James Pleasant McCabe. They had issue: W. O. McCabe, who married Rosa Newman; J. P. McCabe of Martinsville, who married Sue Ella Martin; and Mary McCabe, who married Luther Scott.

        2. Susan, daughter of Daniel Green and Frances Davis Saunders, married John Morgan of Bedford, and had issue: John, William, Victoria, Sarah, and Missouri. John married Cleopatra Morgan; Sarah married Henry Creasy; William, married Rebecca Shann; Victoria married John Overstreet; and Missouri married Samuel Fizer.

        3. Frances, daughter of Daniel Green and Frances Davis Saunders, married George Helms of Franklin County.

        4. Louise, daughter of Daniel Green and Frances Davis Saunders, married Lodwick Cunningham, and had issue: Frances, Laura, and Belle. Laura married Chris Musgrove; Belle married Davis Franklin; Frances married James Saunders, and had seven children: (a) Laura married Harvey Dudley; (b) Leslie married Tyree Watson; (c) James married a Miss Watson; (d) Oscar married Pearl Saunders, (e) Mahlon married a Miss Ramsey.

        5. Daniel Green Jr., son of Daniel Green and Frances Davis Saunders, founded the town of Bedford, Missouri, and named

it in honor of his old Virginia home. He was a lawyer and Senator.

6. Henry, son of Daniel Green and Frances Davis Saunders, married Mary Kasey, and had issue: Daniel, Callaway, George, Green, Thomas, Jesse, and Fannie. He married second, Liza Ann Musgrove by whom he had, Ursula, Christopher, and Elvira. Daniel, Callaway and George settled in Missouri; Jesse died in C. S. A.; Green and Tom were also in C. S. A.; and Tom married Mildred Morgan. Tom and Mildred Morgan Saunders had seven children: Sam, who married Pattie Watson; Jesse, who married Annie Nicholas; Mary, who married J. W. Morgan; Hamlet, who married Lucy Smith; Robert; and Penn.

Fannie married Milton Cunningham, and had eight children: Oscar, Thomas, Maybelle, Hattie, Ida, Estelle, Herbert, and Ernest. Oscar married Pearl Allen, and had Earl, and Randolph; Earl married Lucille Woolwine. Thomas died in 1906. Maybelle married Otto Cunningham, and had three children: Winfred, who married Homer Nowlan, and had Homer Jr., and Doris; Verna, who married Emma Lazenby; and Mabel, who married Robert Brady, and had Mary, and Virginia. Hattie married Herbert Saunders, and had Gladys, and Boyd. Gladys, married William I. Nicholson. Boyd married Freddie Little, and had three children: Elizabeth, Billy, and Dorothy. Ida married James R. Kirby, and had three children: (a) Lee, who m. Carietta Little, and had issue: Louise; (b) Annie Mae, who m. Paul Croft; and James who married Ruby Childress, and had issue: James Jr. Herbert, m. Maude Dixon, and had 3 sons, Gordon, Charles, and Milton. Ernest, m. Myrtle Hughes, had issue: Ernest Jr., and Frances Jane. Ursula, m. John Blankenship, had 10 children: Walter, Muade, Christopher, Robert, Moses, Florence, Thomas J., Aaron, Christopher, and Elvira.

Walter, m. Cammie Ferguson.

Maude, m. First, John Musgrove, and second, Add Dillon.

Christopher, m. Mary Tony, and had 2 children: Ethel, who married Chas. Meadows of Durham N. C., and Pauline, who m. Walter Dunnington of Hopewell.

Robert, m. Reva Morgan, and had a dau. Mabel.

Florence, m. E. W. Martin (police office of Hopewell), and had 5 children: Elbert, Archie, Ursula, Douglas, and Marie.

Moses, m. Sue Divers, and had 4 children.

Thomas J., (Trial Justice of Hopewell), m. Marguerite Johnstone, issue: T. J. Jr.

Aaron, m. Ruth Thompson.

Christopher, m. Puss Saunders.

Elvira, m. Steve Musgrove.

7. Margaret, dau. of Daniel Green and Frances Davis Saunders, m. Millard Hatcher of Patrick Co.

8. Thomas, son of Daniel Green and Frances Davis Saunders, m. Sabre Burnett, and had 11 children: Daniel G., James, John H., Thomas Jr., William, Edgar, Frances, Nancy, Mary, Margaret, and Susie. Daniel, John H., and Thomas settled in the west. James was in the C. S. A.

    (a) Daniel G., m. first, Lucy Parker, and had 3 children: Mary F., Lucy, and Tom Davy. He m. second, Fannie Leftwich, and had 4 children: Don, Boone, Richard, and Eva May.

    (b) James m. Mattie Dudley, and had issue: Ola, who m. W. H. Cook; Ida, who m. C. E. Allen; Tempie who d. young; Kheda, who m. A. J. Osborne; Joab, who m. Nina Campbell; and Sabre, who m. James H. Palmer.

    (c) John H., m. Callie Williamson, and had issue: 7 sons and 7 daughters

    (d) Thomas Jr., m. Willie Mitchell, issue: 3 children.

    (e) William m. Celia Fitzpatrick, issue: 4 children: Dr. W. H. who m. Colie Lovell; Frances, who m. first, Mr. Watts, and Mr. Godsey; Luna, who m. Mr. Engle; and May, who m. B. Deyerle.

    (f) Edgar, m. Kate Arthur, and had issue: Henry, and Edgar.

    (g) Frances, m. John Gray.

    (h) Nancy, m. Frank Turner, and had issue: Samuel, John, James, Dell, Annie, Virgie, and Ruth.

    (i) Mary, m. John Allen, and had issue: Maude, who m. Sam Ragland; Pearl, who m. first Mr. Thomas, second, Oscar Cunningham, and third, C. A. Shaner; Cliff, who m. W. H. Keister; and Edgar, who m. Rosetta Roberts.

    (j) Margaret, m. Alex Eanes, and had 5 children: Oakie, who m. Emma Critcher; Fleta, who m. Walter Stone; Margaret, who m. Fred Helbig; May; and Fannie.

    (k) Susie, m. George Cunningham, and had 4 children: Otho, who m. Maybelle Cunningham; George, who m. Mattie Cliver; Dan, who m. Inez Ely; and Frank, who m. Ruby Lawrence.

9. Catherine, dau. of Daniel Green and Frances Davis Saunders, m. Vincent Bird of Bland Co.

10. George, son of Daniel Green and Frances Davis Saunders, m. Martha Cunningham, dau. of Randolph Cunningham, officer in the War of 1812, and had 6 children: Martha, Angie, Bettie, Frances, George Jr., and Herbert.

    (a) Martha, m. Robert Garrett, and had 4 children: George Jr., who m. a Miss Lester; Robert, who m. Saphronia Thaxton; Beulah, who m. Charles Roby; and Alma, who m. Robert Burton,

    (b) Angie, m. John Hancock, and had 2 children: Effie, who m. Willis Tinsley, and had Lena, who m. Judge Clifton Woodrum.

    (c) Bettie, m. John Garrett, had 3 children: Reginald, who m. Lula Walker; Blanche, who m. Taylor Price; and William, who m. Emma Simms.

    (d) Frances, m. Wm. Fitzpatrick, and had 6 children: Angie, William Jr., Hubert, Nellie, Ruby, and Walter. Angie, m. Robert Elliott. William Jr., m. Pearl Creasy. Hubert, m. Beatrice Manyette. Nellie, m. Blackburn Jordon. Ruby, m. Eugene Maddera.

    (e) George Jr., m. Betty McGhee, and had 7 children: Lucy, Ruby, Pauline, Margaret, Frances, William, and Jack.

    (f) Herbert, m. Hattie Cunningham, and had issue: Gladys, and Boyd.

11. Ardenia, dau. of Daniel Green and Frances Davis Saunders, m. William Cunningham of Franklin, and had issue: George, Alpha, Jefferson, Margaret, and William.

    (a) George, m. Susie Saunders.

    (b) Alpha, m. Richard Martin, and had a son, Richard, who became a physician.

    (c) Jefferson, m. Mary Kasey and had 6 children.

    (d) Margaret, m. Theodore Dellis, and had 5 children.

12. William, son of Daniel Green and Francis Davis

Saunders, b. 1814, m. Florentine Kasey, dau. of Col. Thomas Kasey.
His sword and uniform of War of 1812 are still in the family.
He had 8 children: Jemina, Thomas, James, John, Mary, Cephas,
William Robert, and Frances.

(a) Jemima, m. Bruce Turner.

(b) Thomas, m. Neron English, and had 7 children: Landon, Tilden, Tabitha, Albert, Pearl,
and Thomas Jr.

(c) James, m. Nannie Kate Newbill, and had 4
children: William, who m. Jacquiline Irby;
Flora, who m. George Meyers; Annie, who
m. Frank Woodhouse; and James Lee.

(d) John, m. Sarah Dickerson, and had 6 children: Vera, Bank, Birdie, Sonnie, Hugh,
and Alva.

(e) Mary, m. Chris. Saunders, and had issue:
Oscar, and Lillian.

(f) Cephas, m. Minerva Fitzpatrick and had 4
children: Abbott, who m. a Miss Hawkins;
Lawrence, who m. a Miss Tibbs; Joe, who
m. a Miss Wright; and Maude.

(g) William Robert, m. Pike English, moved,
in 1900, from Franklin to Bedford City,
and had 3 sons and 6 daughters: Frank,
Jack, Richard, Neva, Willie, May, Lena,
Blanche, and Florence. Frank, m. Charlotta Maupin. Jack, m. Alice Burnett.
Neva, m. a Mr. Powell. Willie, m. F. X.
de Souza Netto, lives in Rio de Janeiro.
May, m. O. S. B. Yates of Chatham. Lena,
m. J. B. Bernard. Blanche, m. H. L. Rucker. Florence, m. Frank Johnson. When William Robert Saunders died in July 1918 his
3 sons, Frank, Jack and Richard, and a grandson, Ranson Powell, were soldiers in World
War I.

(h) Frances, m. John Franklin, and had 2 children: Davis, and Mattie.

THE SWANSON-MUSE FAMILIES

William Swanson, Sr., b. 1720, d. 1808, in Oglethorpe
Co., Ga., m. Mary McGuire (b.ca. 1725, d. in Ga., 1811), in
1747.

Among the earliest settlers in Franklin were William Swanson, his wife, Mary, and their 8 children. They lived in that section of Henry which became a part of Franklin when the county was formed. A few years after the formation of Franklin, William Swanson, Sr., with Nathan and John, two of his three sons, and all of his daughters and their families, except Sarah Ryan, removed to Wilkes Co., Ga. His son, William, Jr., remained in Franklin till 1792, at which time he removed to Pittsylvania, where he reared a large family, and died May 25, 1827. He was the great great grandfather of Claude Augustus Swanson, Gov. of Virginia, United States Senator, and Secretary of the Navy.

The earliest Swanson record in Virginia is of Robert Swanson, who came from England with John Dannis, Oct. 15, 1649, and patented 350 acres on the Wicomico River (Book 2. p. 177, Richmond Land Office.) In 1691, John Swanson was a juror in Northumberland Co. The name appears frequently in Northumberland records from 1645 to 1785. The family in Franklin and Pittsylvania claim descent from the Northumberland Swansons.

The first record of William Swanson, Sr., is the record in Goochland Co., showing his marriage to Mary McGuire in 1747. In 1750-1752, he bought 1,000 acres in Goochland (D. B. pp. 115, 268. In 1761-1762, he sold his lands in Goochland (D. B. 6 pp. 268, 217, D. B. 7, p. 217, D. B. 8, pp. 194, 296), and in 1762, he bought 607 acres in Bedford from John Haynes and George Walton (D. B. 2pp. 108). In 1763, he patented 320 acres in Bedford on Little Otter River (Book 35, p. 449, Richmond Land Office). He sold a part of this land, and in 1768, bought 500 acres from Jeremiah Shrewsberry and William Haynes, in that part of Franklin in 1768.

When the oath of allegiance was being administered in Virginia, William Swanson, Sr., age 57, Nathan McGuire Swanson, 29, and John Swanson, 20, were on Sept. 13, 1777, listed in Henry Co. In 1780, Nathan, John, and William Swanson, as citizens of Henry Co., took the oath of allegiance to the new Commonwealth of Virginia.

When Franklin Co., was formed, William Swanson, Sr., with 114 acres, William Swanson, Jr., with 189 acres, and Nathan McGuire Swanson, with 175 acres, became citizens of the new county. They also had lands in Henry, but their residence was in Franklin according to personal property tax records. On Mar. 24, 1787, William Swanson Sr., and Mary, his wife, conveyed to John Davis 175 acres on both sides of Bull Run (Franklin D. B. 1, p. 169). The same year he and his wife, Mary, and his son, Nathan M., sold their Franklin land and removed to Wilkes Co., Ga.

William Swanson, Sr., left will of record in Oglethorpe Co., Ga., (dated Mar. 5, 1801, pro. Jan. 6, 1809).

Issue of William and Mary McGuire Swanson given in order named in his will:

(1) Nathan McGuire Swanson, b. in Goochland Co., in 1748, d. in Greene Co., Ga., ca. 1805, m. Mary (probably Graves) ca. 1770. She d. after 1805. He removed from Goochland to Bedford; thence to Henry with his father, William Swanson, and, in 1786, was living in Franklin where he owned 175 acres. In 1787, he with his father, removed to Wilkes Co., Ga., later to Greene Co., Ga., where he died, leaving several children.

(2) Sarah Swanson, b. ca. 1749, m. William Ryan, an early sheriff of Franklin.

(3) Mary Swanson, m. a Mr. Wilson prior to 1801.

(4) William Swanson, Jr., b. ca. 1750, d. May 25, 1827, in Pittsylvania; m. Ann (Nancy), probably Ann Graves, who d. July 25, 1830.

(5) Ann Swanson, m. a Mr. Maxey prior to 1801.

(6) Frances Swanson, b. Apr. 15, 1760, baptised June 8, 1760, in Goochland Co., m. Humphrey Edmundson in Henry Co.; Nov. 22, 1779.

(7) John Swanson, b. in Goochland, Oct. 7, 1757, d. prior to 1801, m. Polly. It is probable that he also moved to Georgia, as many of his descendants are there in Morgan Co.

(8) A daughter, m. a Mr. Dunn.

II (4)

William Swanson, Jr. lived in Franklin, where he owned 1700 acres, from 1786 to 1792, at which time Peyton Smith and his wife, Judith, of Georgia, conveyed him 600 acres in Pittsylvania. On Feb. 14, 1817, James Patterson and Margaret, his wife, conveyed him 784 acres on Chestnut Creek. On Oct. 11, 1828, William and Frances Swanson, his executor, conveyed this land to Henry Lawson Muse, who married his daughter, Elizabeth Swanson. This property was owned by his grandson, William Leftwich Turner Hopkins, till his death in 1935. William Swanson, Jr., left will of record in Pittsylvania, (W. B. 1, p. 12, dated Jan. 23, 1827, pro. July 10, 1827) bequeathing property to his wife and children. Issue as shown by his will and other records:

(1) Co. William Graves Swanson, b. May 11, 1777, in what is now Franklin Co., d. June 13, 1840, in Lowndes Co., Ala., m. Elizabeth Muse (b. May 21, 1779, d. July 16, 1836), dau. of John Muse, June 15, 1801, in Pittsylvania.

(2) Francis Swanson, d. (Inv. 1852, Book 18, pp. 301, Pitts. Co.); m. Frances Chattin Muse, dau. of Thomas and Elizabeth Tidwell Muse, Nov. 21, 1803, in Pitts. Co. She left will (W. B. 2, p. 468, Pitts., Co., pro. July 26, 1856), devising property to her dau. Mary A. S. Finney; gr. son Francis W. C. Finney. The deed dated Feb. 25, 1873, (d. B. 30, p. 374, Franklin Co.) is from Dudley S. Muse and Mary A. Muse, his wife, to

"F. W. C. Finney, S. R. Finney and Mary A. Finney, infant children of Sanford R. Finney, Dec'd...being the land heired by children aforesaid from the estate of Zachariah Finney."

(3) Mary Swanson, m. a Mr. Tuggle prior to 1827.

(4) Sarah Swanson, m. Thomas Pinckard, July 20, 1801. In Pittsylvania.

(5) Dorothy Swanson, m. Samuel Allen Muse, son of John Muse, Jan. 17, 1803, in Pittsylvania. Issue: John Allen Muse, who m. his cousin, Elvira Muse, dau. of John Muse, Jr.

(6) Elizabeth Swanson, b. June 3, 1790, in Franklin, d. Apr. 11, 1866, in Franklin; m. Henry Lawson Muse (b. Dec. 2, 1788, d. Mar. 7, 1845), son of Thomas and Elizabeth Tidwell Muse, Dec. 5, 1816 in Pittsylvania. Issue: (a) Elizabeth Tidwell Muse, b. in Franklin Mar. 21, 1821, d. July 6, 1886, m. her cousin, Henry Lawson Muse, Jr. Dec. 23, 1841, and had issue: John Henry b. Jan. 10, 1843, and William T., b. Jan. 19, 1846, both of whom died without issue; and (b) Julia Ann Muse, b. Jan. 2, 1824, d. Feb. 22, 1916, m. William Leftwich Turner Hopkins, M. D., Dec. 24, 1850. Issue: (1) William Henry, b. Aug. 13, 1852, d. Sept. 24, 1857; (2) Mary Elizabeth, b. Aug. 28, 1854, d. Sept. 21, 1913, m. Henry Clay Price in Franklin Mar. 29, 1877; (3) Julia Sarah, b. Jan. 3, 1857, d. June 22, 1863; (4) Harriet Burr, b. Dec. 31, 1858, d. Oct. 30, 1875; (5) William Leftwich Turner, b. Sept. 30, 1860, m. first, Mary Ella Hancock, dau. of Col. Abram Booth Hancock, Dec. 26, 1882, m. second, Mary Ann Rebecca Smith, dau. of Samuel Southerland Smith, June 4, 1895, and m. third, Sarah Kathleen Stone, dau. of Capt. William Dickerson Stone, Sept. 9, 1916; and (6) Mildred Turner Hopkins, b. Jan. 9, 1862, d. Dec. 10, 1899, m. Abram P. Hancock, Oct. 20, 1882.

(7) Frances Swanson, d. 1858, m. Joel Muse, son of John Muse, Nov. 18, 1805, in Pittsylvania. She left will dated Mar. 20, 1858, pro. Apr. 5, 1858, of record in Franklin Will Book 10, p. 254. Issue: (a) John Crenshaw Muse, b. May 2, 1807, d. unm. and (b) William Swanson Muse, b. Dec. 24, 1808, d. 1839, (W. B. 5, p. 328, Franklin Co.) m. Judith Glass, (b. Sept. 2, 1815) dau. of Capt. John Glass of Halifax and Franklin. Issue:

(1) Frances Ann Muse, b. May 10, 1832; d. Apr. 4, 1858, unm.

(2) John Crenshaw Muse, b. May 25, 1834, d. Dec. 22, 1894, unm.

(3) Dr. William Henry Muse, b. July 6, 1836, m. Mary Abiah Helm, Apr. 4, 1878, in Franklin. Issue: (a) William Roscie Muse, dentist, Roanoke, b. Feb. 16, 1880, m. Annie Wilton Dickerson of Richmond; and

(b) Ernest Helm Muse, M. D., Roanoke, b.
Sept. 10, 1881, unm.

(4) Dudley Stearn Muse, b. July 2, 1839, m. Mary
Ann Swanson Finney. Issue: (a) Fanny Henry
Muse, b. 1872; (b) John Crenshaw Muse, m.
Mrs. Annie Walker, no issue: (c) William Ca-
bell Muse, m. Annie Hedrick, issue, Walter
Muse, b. 1905, and Ethyl Muse, d. 1907; and
(d) Ida Muse, m. William Steel.

(5) Martha Muse, d. in infancy.

(7) (c) Lucy Muse, b. Jan. 20, 1811, d. unm.; (d)
Mary Ann Muse, b. Feb. 12, 1813, m. her cousin Alfred Lemuel
Harvey Muse, son of Thomas Muse; (e) Sarah Elizabeth Muse, b.
Apr. 8, 1815, unm.; (f) Emily Frances Muse, b. July 19, 1817,
m. Thomas Robbins, issue: John William and Lucy; and (g) Doro-
thy Stearn Muse, b. May 18, 1819.

(8) Nancy Swanson, m. John Muse, Jr., son of John
Muse, Sr., and brother of Samuel Allen and Joel Muse, who m.
Dorothy and Frances Swanson, respectively, prior to 1827.
Issue: Elvira Muse, m. her cousin, John Allen Muse; and Ma-
tilda A. Muse, m. Tilgham A. Pullen, Jan. 15, 1830, in Pitt-
sylvania.

(9) Clary Swanson, m. George Hutcherson, Dec. 3,
1815 in Pittsylvania. Marriage bond is of record in Pittsylvania.
Issue:

(a) Frank Swanson Hutcherson, m. Elizabeth C.
Hunt, Apr. 3, 1867, in Franklin. Issue:

(1) Almira A. Hutcherson, b. 1868, d.
Oct. 15, 1886.

(2) Thomas J. Hutcherson, m. Kate L.
Cooper. Issue: (a) Ruby Hutcherson,
m. Guy Amos; (b) Mary Hutcherson, m.
a Mr. Gravely; and (c) Helen Hutcherson, m. Jesse Amos.

(3) Clary Hutcherson, unm.

(4) Sallie B. Hutcherson.

(5) Nathan B. Hutcherson, m. Sallie Holland Divers, dau. of P. D. Divers, treasurer of Franklin Co.

(6) George Hutcherson, d. at 24.

(7) Madison D. Hutcherson, m. Beulah Jamison, in Franklin. He is now (1935) a

member of the Board of Supervisors, and
for many years was a member of the Franklin School Board.

8. Julia Hutcherson, m. M. L. Arrington, of
Franklin.

(b) Elizabeth Hutcherson.

(c) Robert Hutcherson, m. Permelia Turner, in
1867. Issue: 1. John Reese, who m. Lula
Dudley; 2. Admire, who m. Josie Dudley; 3.
Frank, who m. Leona Dudley; 4. Oscar, who
m. Gertrude Dudley; 5. Robert, who lives
in Minnesota; 6. Lucy, who d. at 33, unm.;
7. Jennie, who m. Robert Hardy; and 8.
Bertha.

(d) John D. Hutcherson, killed in Picketts'
charge at Gettysburg.

(e) Almira Hutcherson.

THE TALIAFERRO FAMILY

The first member of this family in Franklin County
was Dr. Richard McCulloch Taliaferro. Upon his graduation from
a medical college in Philadelphia, his father gave him the con-
ventional medical outfit; two horses, and a Negro man servant.
Thus equipped he set out from Amherst for the county seat of
the newly formed county of Franklin. Soon after crossing the
Staunton River at Hale's Ford, night overtook him. Seeing a
light in the distance he rode toward it, and was soon asking
for a night's lodging at the home of John and Theodosia Saunders Hale. The usual hospitality was extended. The Hale family,
already large, was increased that night by the arrival of another
daughter. The young doctor played the dual role of guest and
physician. The baby was christened Judith, and about twenty
years later became the wife of Walter Callaway. Within a year
or two the eldest sister of this baby, Mary Hale, became the
wife of the young physician.

Franklin's first physician spent a long and useful
life in Rocky Mount. He practised his profession over an area
so large that modern physicians wonder how he covered the territory on horseback. He was highly regarded for his cultured
mind and for his integrity of character. In addition to his
professional duties, he served as Justice of the Peace for many
years. He was a public spirited gentlemen and his civic pride
had much to do with the upbuilding and development of the new
community. He had behind him the spur of splendid ancestry.
His father, Col. Charles Taliaferro, served in the Revolutionary
War. His mother was Lucy Loving of Amherst. His grandfather

was Richard Taliaferro, who built and bequeathed to his daughter, Elizabeth, and to her husband, George Wythe, the house in Williamsburg which is known as the Wythe House.

Dr. Richard M. and Mary Hale Taliaferro had issue:
(1) Henry, (2) Landon, (3) Richard, (4) Mary, (5) Tazewell, (6) Emily, (7) Susan, (8) Lucy, (9) Whitmell, and (10) Celestia.

(3) Richard, married a Miss Leftwich, and had issue, a daughter, Nannie, who married H. G. Wadley, and died without issue.

(4) Mary, married Dr. Henry Dillard, and became the mother of several children.

(5) Tazewell, married Amanda Callaway, and had issue: John, James, Mollie, Rosa, and Lucy. James was killed at Gettysburg.

(6) Emily, married Ferdinand Claiborne and, second, Col. C. F. Suttle. She died without issue.

(8) Lucy, married Judge Hugh Nelson, and had ten children.

(9) Withmell, married _____ in New York, and had issue, one son, Whitmell.

(10) Celestia, married Dr. Thomas B. Greer, a famous physician, and had issue: Charles Callaway, Emily Nelson, Thomas Campbell, Crockett Saunders, Norborne Taliaferro, Robert Edward Lee, Bessie, and Mary Celestia.

Emily Nelson Greer married, first, Andrew Lewis Edmonds, and had issue, a son who bore his father's full name; second, Judge George D. Peters, and had issue, Malcolm Taliaferro, and Alice Wadley.

Thomas Campbell Greer married Etta Willis, and had issue: Mary, Sarah, Thomas, Marion, Charles, Gladys, Susan, and Alice. Only Thomas and Susan have issue.

Crockett Saunders Greer married Sallie Menefee and had issue: George Cabell, Edwin, Edith Taliaferro, Walter M., and Flora. George Cabell married Lucy Taliaferro Price. Edwin married Clare Scott. Edith Taliaferro married T. W. Carper. Walter M. married Nell Parker. Flora married Beverly Parrish.

Norborne Taliaferro Greer, son of Dr Thomas B., married Eva Wade, and had issue: Lydia, Kitty, Bailey, and Norborne. Lydia married William Dripp. Bailey married Ruth Colman. Kitty married Harold W. Ramsey. Norborne married Gladys Pleasants.

Bessie, daughter of Dr. Thomas B. Greer, married Herman Moseley, and had issue: Bessie, Nannie, and Mary Dillard.

The last named married J. N. Montgomery, Jr., for many years, Treasurer of Franklin County.

Mary Celestia Greer, daughter of Dr. Thomas B., married Herbert N. Dillard, attorney, and had issue: Mary Adela, Betsy, Celestia, and Herbert N. Jr.

. THE TATE FAMILY

Henry Tate was in Louisa County in 1743, when he and John Davis processioned their precincts of Frederickville Parish (see Frederickville Parish Vestry Book, 1742-87, p. 4)

In 1755 he was a resident of Bedford County as attested by the following references in "History of Bedford County" by Rev. R. G. Buford, p. 10-11.

During the next two decades Henry Tate acquired much property in Bedford and Campbell Counties. When Campbell County was formed in 1782, some of the Tate lands fell into the new County, hence many comtemporary records are found in both counties.

Henry Tate made his will on the 7th day of August 1784, committing his soul to God, his body to the dust, etc.", requesting his funeral sermon to be preached from the first verse of the last chapter of Ecclesiastes, or the 48th verse of the 89th Psalm.

Wife, Sarah Tate, to have home place, mill, plantation house, land on Goose Creek, for the duration of her life, and after her death to the two oldest sons, Edmund and Caleb. Will probated in Campbell County, Sept. 5, 1793.

Issue of Henry and Sarah Tate:

I. Mary Tate, m. Chesley Davis, and emigrated to District 96, South Carolina.

II. Sarah Tate, d. prior to 1777, m. Nov. 24, 1756, Col. James Calloway, (b. 1736, d. Nov. 1809). After the formation of Campbell County, Col. James Calloway was the most prominent county officer within it's borders, and was made County Lieutenant, having held the same office previously in Bedford and being highly recommended for that position in the new county; served in the French and Indian Wars; member of the Bedford County Committee of 1774; held several military offices; built and operated the Oxford Furnace; owned and operated lead mines; suppressed a comspiracy against the Government in 1780, etc.

Issue of Sarah Tate and Col. James Calloway:

(1) Elizabeth Calloway, m. 1775, Harry Innes, son of Rev. Robert and Katherine Richard Innes. He was superintendent of the Oxford Iron Mines, which operated during the Revolution, supplying the Continental army with munition; served

as an officer in the Bedford County Militia; was the first lawyer admitted to the Campbell County bar; and removed to Kentucky
in 1784, where he became a judge.

Issue of Elizabeth Calloway and Henry Innes:

(a) Elizabeth Innes, d. 1851, m. Col. Gerard
Alexander (b. 1771, d. 1851), soldier of
the war of 1812. One time president of
New London Academy.

(2) Mary Calloway, m. 1781, Daniel Brown of New Yorʌ.

(3) Frances Calloway, b. 1762, m. 1781, James Steptoe (b. July 16, 1850, d. Feb. 1826,) Clerk of Bedford County
for 54 years. Issue of James Steptoe:

(a) James Calloway Steptoe, b. Dec. 10, 1781,
d. Oct. 24, 1827.

(b) Dr. William Steptoe, m., first, Nancy Brown;
and second, Mary Dillon.

(c) George Steptoe, m. Maria Thomas.

(d) Robert Steptoe, m. Elizabeth Leftwich.

(e) Thomas Steptoe, m. Louise C. Yancey.

(f) Elizabeth Steptoe, (by James Steptoe's
second wife), m. Hon. Charles Johnston of
Sandusky.

(g) Frances Steptoe, m. Henry S. Langhorne of
Lynchburg; among their descendants are the
famous Langhorne sisters, all noted for
their beauty and intellect; one of them,
Lady Astor, is a member of the British Par-
liament.

(h) Sallie Steptoe, m. William Massie of Nelson County.

(i) Lucy Steptoe, m. Robert Penn of Bedford County.

(4), (5), (6), (7), (8) all died young.

(9) James Calloway, m. Miss Green.

(10) Robert Calloway, educated at William and Mary,
m. Miss Garrant.

(11) Henry Calloway, educated at William and Mary.

Issue of Col. James Calloway and Elizabeth Early (second wife):

(12) Jeremiah Calloway, died young.

(13) William Calloway, m. Miss Crump.

(14) John Calloway.

(15) Edward Calloway.

(16) Dr. Geo. Calloway, m. Mary Elizabeth Cabell.

(17) Abner Calloway, m. Miss Lewis, and moved to Missouri.

(18) Rev. Thomas Calloway, m. a Miss Anderson, and moved to Missouri.

(19) Katherine Calloway, m. William Langhorne. A daughter of theirs, Mary Langhorne, m. George Plater Tayloe of Botetourt Co.

III.   Tabitha Tate, d. prior to 1784, m. March 8, 1758, John Calloway (b. 1738, d. 1821). He was High Sheriff and Treasurer of Campbell County, and was one of the Trustees of the town of Lynchburg.

IV.   Jesse Tate of Russell Parish, oldest son, d. 1805, m. Aug. 27, 1771, Margaret Miller. Will recorded in Bedford County, April 27, 1805. Legatees:

1. Daughter, Sallie Anthony.

2. Son, Henry Tate - land on Ware Spring Branch, etc.

3. Son, John Tate - land near Wares.

4. Son, Caleb Tate - 875 pounds (bonds on Thomas Wyatt).

5. Daughter, Polly Tate - land purchased of William Harris on Hall's Spring Branch.

6. Son, Waddy Tate.

7. Daughter, Euphan Tate.

V.   Charles Tate, 1809. Will recorded in Bedford County, Feb. 10, 1809. Division of estate and names of Legattes, no relationship given.

Lot. 1. Caleb Tate.

Lot. 2. Joel Preston Tate.

Lot. 3. Pamelia Tate.

Lot. 4. Nancy Tate.

Lot. 5 Obadiah Tate.

Lot. 6 Henry Tate.

Lot. 7 Edmund Tate.

Obadiah Tate, m. Dec. 12, 1798, Nancy Goggin

Pamelia Tate, m. Nov. 23, 1810, William Goggin.
Nancy and William Goggin were brother and sister.

Issue of Stephen Goggin Jr., and Rachael Moorman Goggin:

(a) Pamelia Goggin, m. Oct. 29, 1797, Samuel
     Clemens:

(b) Nancy Goggin, m. Dec. 12, 1798, Obadiah
     Tate.

(c) Mary Goggin, m. Nov. 17, 1801, Alexander
     Gill.

(d) Pleasant Moorman Goggin, b. 1777, d. 1831,
     m. July 31, 1806, Mary Otey Leftwich, (daugh-
     ter of Rev. Williams ("Blackhead") Leftwich.

(e) William Goggin, m. Nov. 23, 1810, Pamelia
     Tate.

(f) Stephen Goggin, m. Dec. 29, 1808, Janet
     Robertson.

(g) Thomas Goggin, m. Dec. 13, 1812, Mary Wal-
     den, dau. of John Walden.

Pamelia Goggin and Samuel Clemens were married Oct.
29, 1797, in Bedford County, by Rev. John Ayres. Their son,
John Marshall Clemens, was born in 1798. He went first to Florida,
then to Hannibal, Missouri, where he became a Justice of the
Peace. He married Jane Lampton, and their son, Samuel Lampton
Clemens, was "Mark Twain". In Mt. Olivet Cemetery, Hannibal
Mo., is an old flat table tombstone bearing the single inscription, "Passed on, John M. Clemens, born in Campbell County, Virginia, August 11, 1798, died in Hannibal, Mo., Mar. 14, 1847."

VI.   Elizabeth Tate, born Aug. 18, 1746, d. May 30, 1834,
was married Apr. 28, 1764 to Mathew Harris (b. Sept. 25, 1737,
d. May 17, 1805). Issue:

     1 Schuyler Harris, b. 1765, d. 1803, m. 1787, Fran-
ces Blaydes.

     2 Mary Harris, b. 1766.

     3 Sarah Harris, b. 1768

     4 William H. Harris, b. 1770.

(5)   Mathew Harris, b. 1771.

(6)   Elizabeth Harris, b. 1773.

(7) ·   Polly Harris, b. 1775.

(8)   Fannie Harris, b. 1777.

(9)   John H. Harris, b. 1778.

(10)   Matilda Harris, b. 1780.

(11)   Sophia Harris, b. 1781.

(12)   Permelia Harris, b. 1783, m. John Tate, her
1st cousin.

(13)   Benjamin Harris, b. 1785.

(14)   Nancy Harris, b. 1785.

(15)   Henry T. Harris, b. Mar. 26, 1787, d. Mar. 8,
1845, m. Apr. 16, 1811, Mary Woods Harris, (b. Aug. 24, 1788,d.
March 3, 1874).

(16)   F. F. Caroline (b. 1789).

Issue of Henry Tate and Mary Woods Harris:

(a)   Mary Harris, m. Dr. Daniel Watson.

(b)   Henry St. George Harris, m. Mary Frances Glenn.

(c)   Margaret Evelina Harris, m. first, Daniel Scott,
and second, Albert Harris.

(d)   Cornelia Rebecca Harris, b. Aug. 11, 1826,
d. Apr. 13, 1909, m. May 5, 1850, Dr. William
Daniel Boaz (b. Jan. 6, 1821, d. Aug. 3, 1883).

As far as can be ascertained Dr. William Daniel Boaz
was the first physician to advocate cold treatment for fevers.
He was the man in Albemarle County to plant an Albemarle Pippin
orchard for commercial purposes.

VII.   Ann or Nancy Tate, moved to Georgia between 1787 and 1789.

VIII.   Nathaniel Tate, d. 1805, m. first, Rhoda Terry, Feb. 22,
1770; and, second, Susanna Gilliam, Jan. 26, 1778 (Bedford County
Marriage Records). His will, probated in Campbell County, July
15, 1805, mentions the following Legatees:

1. Son, Henry F. Tate.

2. Son, Richard H. L. Tate.

3. Daughter, Sallie Walden.

4. Daughter, Polly H. Davis.

5. Grandaughters Betty Walden, Matilda Davis, and Susanna Davis.

6. Grandson, John Tate.

7. Brother, Charles Tate.

IX. Col. Edmund Tate, b. 1760, d. 1823, m. Lucy Barksdale (b. 1766, d. 1857) dau. of Thomas Claiborne and Sarah Goode Barksdale of Amelia Co. Issue:

    (1)   Sallie Makerness Tate.

    (2)   Harriet Claiborne Tate, m. Dec. 18, 1849, Col. John M. Harris of Buckingham Co.

    (3)   Lucy Alice Tate, m. David Gamble Murrell of a New Jersey family.

    (4)   Calvin Tate, lived in New Orleans. Very wealthy.

    (5)   Grief Barksdale Tate.

    (6)   Garland Tate.

    (7)   Edmund Tate, Jr.

Issue of Lucy Alice Tate and David Gamble Murrell:

    (a)   John William Murrell of Bedford County, m. Ann Hart, granddaughter of Bishop Channing Moore. Issue:

        1.   Lucy Alice Murrell, m. Major John B. Brokenborough, son of Judge John W. Brokenborough of Lexington.

        2.   Mary Murrell, m. Thomas David Evans of Lynchburg.

    (b)   Edward H. Murrell, b. July 31, 1825, m. Oct. 9, 1849, Almira Halsey, a daughter of Seth and Julia Peters Halsey. Issue:

        1.   Julia Elizabeth Murrell, m. United States Senator, John W. Daniel.

X. Caleb Tate, d. 1814, Inventory of estate given in Campbell County Record Books in 1814. Very wealthy. Netherland Tate, administrator.

XI. Euphan Tate, m. _____ Rucker.

XII. Sarah Henry Tate, m. May 24, 1795, Mark Anthony, and settled in Wilkes County, Georgia, soon afterward. The marriage
is of record in both Bedford and Campbell Counties.

⌐ Col. Caleb Tate, grandson of Henry and Sarah Tate,
son of Jesse Tate and Margaret Miller (who were married August
27, 1771), was born in 1774. He was the third Clerk of Franklin County. His tenure of office was from 1813-1838. He served as District Clerk from 1797 to 1805, in place of James Steptoe, the noted Clerk from Bedford who had resigned. Colonel
Tate also served as Clerk for the Circuit and Superior Courts
of Law and Chancery from 1809 to 1845.

Descended from a family of wealth and culture, he was
a gentlemen of courtliness, graciousness, dignity and pride.
Selecting the hill of greatest elevation in the village of Rocky
Mount, from which was a splendid view of the surrounding hills
and valleys, he built his residence. The structure was of brick
and followed the English architectual lines so popular at that
time. It was built in the shape of the letter T, and was flank-
ed on each side by low wings. Well-proportioned chimneys stood
at the ends of the wings, and large ones rose from the main portion of the building. Beautiful woodwork adorned the interior.
The yard was shaded by fine old trees, and the walks were box
bordered. A profusion of magnolias, lilacs and the old fashion-
ed flowers graced the lawn and garden. A spring at the foot
of the hill supplied the home with water. It was the task of
the children of the Negro servants to "tote" the water to the
"big house on the hill." The house was burnt but was rebuilt
on the same foundation and by the original plan.

⌐ Colonel Tate was a man of strong character and command-
ing personality. Strong in his convictions, candid, loyal to
his friends, dignified in bearing, resembled closely the old
English Baron depicted in history and romance. He was a prominent figure in his community, honored and respected by those
of every walk in life. Colonel Tate died December 1, 1857.
His property passed from the hands of his heirs by sale on April
17, 1877, to Jesse Prunty. For several years a school was conducted there, presided over by Miss Hattie Doniphan of Lynchburg. The property later became the home of Judge John P. Lee.

THE TINSLEY FAMILY

This family came from Hanover County, Virginia, and
later lived in Amherst County before coming to Franklin. Reubin Tinsley, the first to live in Franklin, was the son of Wyatt
Tinsley. He was born in 1766, and died Dec. 3, 1831, age 66
years. Tombstone in Tinsley graveyard is on the west side of
the highway near Willis Lewis Tinsley's home. He married Frances
Tyree, (the marriage bond is in Courthouse in Amherst County)
who lived to be 104. She was bitten by a red spider, says her
granddaughter, Mrs. Fanny Fishburn. The children of Reubin Tinsley and his wife Frances are:

Reubin, lived at Sydnorsville. His will is in Rocky
Mount Courthouse

Elizabeth, born 1787

Polly, born 1798

Willis Lewis, born 1790

John, born 1792, Amherst, married Jane Jacob Tyree

Jacob Tyree, born 1801

Stewart, born 1804 in Franklin County. He is the
grandfather of Dr. Tinsley of Bent Mountain, Franklin

Issac, born 1806. Issac and Jacob were two of the
original 14 young men composing Richmond College.
He died 1881.

Willis Lewis Tinsley, son of Reubin Tinsley and Frances Tyree Tinsley was born Jan. 3, 1790, and died August 16, 1862
of typhoid fever, in his 73rd year. He moved to Franklin about
1794 and with his father built a home two miles north of Sydnorsville. The home was noted for its quantity of boxwood. Willis
Lewis Tinsley married in Sept. 1809, Amarilla Goode (born March
20, 1783, d. June 2, 1875) who was the daughter of Benjamin Goode
and Elizabeth Camden. Willis Lewis Tinsley was a prominent farmer and tobacco manufacturer of Franklin County. Their children were:

Reubin, who went west

Benjamin, b. 1813, d. 1880, married Emeline Sydney
Trent of Appomattox County (daughter of Thomas and
Martha Holland Trent) in 1844.

Tipton, married Elizabeth Calhoun, and lived at Catons-
ville, Md.

Willis

James

Fannie, married Sam Fishburne of Franklin County.

Lizzie

Benjamin Tinsley and Emeline Sydney Trent lived in
Richmond, Va. They later moved to Roanoke. Their children were,
Mrs. E. T. Kindred of Roanoke, d. 1936, at 92 years; W. H. Tin-
sley of Salem, d. 1931, at 82 years; and Mrs. W. M. Taylor of
Roanoke and Washington, d. 1923, at 92½ years.

THE TURNER FAMILY

The Turner Family Magazine, Volume I and II, states: "Prior to 1748 were living in Virginia three brothers Shadrach, Meshack and Abednego Turner. Shadrach was the owner of 4400 acres of land in Halifax County. The first patent was in 1748. He was active in his county, being overseer of roads and processioner of lands. He lived next in Pittsylvania County, then in Henry County, where he died according to his will made in 1783." That Shadrach Turner's wife was Ann Turner, and he had five sons: Larkin, Jeremiah, William, John, and Josiah, and three daughters: Elizabeth, Mary and Excony. Will Book I, Henry County.

The Turner Family History, April 1916, gives the following record from Henry County records: "In Henry County October 1777 John Turner renounced his allegiance to Great Britian and on the 30th of August 1777 John Turner took a similar oath." Meshack Turner married Rebecca Robinson, February 6, 1760, in Halifax County, Virginia. Again the Turner Family Magazine: "William Turner, a son of Shadrach Turner was born in 1753 and was in the Revolutionary War in 1777. He married Jane Hunter daughter of William Hunter. For 72 years they were members of the Baptist Church. William Turner was the father of a large family and a remarkable thing was their longevity. Twelve of his sons and daughters averaging 83 years of life." William Turner's will and the will of his son, George Turner, (Franklin County Virginia records) has an interesting clause relative to the disposition of slaves. It was their desire that all of his servants be sold in the family, and that the executors suffer them not to be sold otherwise.

William Turner died in Franklin County, December 11, 1845, aged 93 years. His wife, who was Jane Hunter, was 88 years of age when he died. They had lived in wedlock 72 years. To them were born 9 sons and 5 daughters. Of his eight sons who lived to manhood, six held office, two in Franklin, one in Henry, one in Patrick, and two in Overton County, Tennessee. Two of his sons served as officers in the Civil War.

At his death his progeny numbered 363, many of whom were of the fifth generation.

Jane Hunter Turner, wife of William Turner, died May 20, 1851, aged 92 years, 11 months and 13 days. George Turner, the oldest of the fourteen children of William and Jane Turner, was born October 17, 1776, and died August 13, 1884. He married Milly Stone who was born March 3, 1780, and died March 6, 1864. Milly Stone was the daughter of Stephen Stone (died 1835), and his wife Basheba Stone (died May 15, 1852). The twelve children of George and Milly Turner were: Obadiah, born December 24, 1802; Elizabeth Turner King, born August 19, 1804; Stephen Turner, born September 6, 1806; Jane Turner Helmes, born October 3, 1808; Basheba Turner Davis, born October 18, 1810; Ruth

Turner Hoy, born July 6, 1812; George Clinton Turner, born December 14, 1814; Milley Ann Turner Cannaday, born March 6, 1817;
Martha Turner Cassaday, born May 3, 1819; William Creed Turner,
born March 1, 1821; Sarah Hunt Cassaday, born December 30, 1823;
and James Marshall Turner, born April 14, 1827.

The brothers and sisters of George Turner son of William Turner, were:

James Turner, married, three times, a James, a Philpot,
and a Woods.

John Turner

Martha Turner, married Philpot

Betsey E. Turner, married an Ingram

Josiah Turner, married

Adelpha Turner, married LaShores Turner

Sally Turner, married a Snyder

William Turner, married

Jane Turner, married a Stone

Andrew Turner, married Frances Holland

Meshack Turner, married Nancy Martin, sister of Lucinda
Martin Pyrtle (wife of Barton Pyrtle).

Elkanah Turner, married a Wingfield

The children of Adelpha and LaShores Turner were:
(1) Wilson Turner, (2) Owen Turner, (who married a Nash) and,
(3) Nancy Turner, who married William Thomasson.

The children of Nancy Turner Thomasson and William
Thomasson were:

(1)   Jane, married William Dyer

(2)   Adelphia, married Thomas Draper

(3)   Wilson Owen, married Julia Beach

(4)   Martha, married Benjamin Stultz

(5)   Nancy, married Joseph Hardy

(6)   Alked, married Elizabeth Brown

(7)   Elvira

(8)   Emma, married Joseph Nunn

The children of Wilson Owen Thomasson and Julia Beach Thomasson were:

(1) George William, died 1907

(2) Owen Turner, married Elizabeth Nunn

(3) Archer C., married Minnie Nunn

(4) Orin, married, first, Martha Metz, and second, Nancy Mason

(5) Frank, married Cassanda Metz

(6) Nancy E., married George F. Carter

(7) Annie, not married

(8) Julia M., married William Craig

(9) Adelphia Jane, not married

(10) Elsie Fountain, married George Metz

The children of Meshek Turner and Nancy Martin Turner were:

(1) Lucinda, married Bob Ross, and had 9 children. Rev. Lee Ross of Bassett is a son

(2) Andrew H. Turner, married Martha E. Prillaman, and had 9 children. A son, C. M. Turner, lives on the original William Turner Plantation two miles from Henry, Va.

The children of Mary Turner Goode and Dave Goode were:

(1) Peter, married in West Virginia

(2) Gardiner, married Callie Bet Williams

(3) Fanny, married Tom McGee

(4) Louise, married Pleasant Mason

(5) Nanny Bet, married Wiley Woody

(6) Florence, married Ernest Scott

(7) Benjamin, married Fannie Ross

(8) Joseph L., married Martha Jane Eggleston

(9) Solomon, married Lulu Davis

The children of Benjamin Goode and Fannie Ross Goode were:

(1) Catherine, teacher in Henry County

(2) Beatrice, teacher in Henry County

(3) Mabel, teacher in Henry County

(4) Virgil, teacher in Henry County

(5) Clifford, County School Superintendent in Henry County.

(6) Maury, married Grace Ramsay

The children of Hershey Turner Gardiner and James Gardiner were:

(1) Edwin, married Cicely Ramsay--large family

(2) Texas, married Ed. Frith--six children

(3) Emma Jane, died at six years of age

(4) Iowa, married, first, Ferd Cook, and, second, Ezekial Bondinand

(5) Alberta, married Eliza Gardiner--four children

(6) Anna Laura, married William Ramsay--nine children

(7) Betty, married Jess Copeland--six children

(8) J. S., married Nora Shelton--one child

The children of Texas Gardiner Frith and Ed. Frith are:

(1) James, married Cassie Frith--eight children

(2) Lee, married Willia Mason

(3) Lulu, married Wesley Ramsay--six children

(4) Luce, married Burlie East--seven children

(5) Mary, married, first, Tobe Love, and, second, Harry Mills--seven children

(6) Uel, married Ada Nunn--two sons: Burness, and Coy.

Basheba Turner, daughter of George Turner and Millie Stone Turner, was born October 18, 1810, and married Sampson J. Davis in 1836.

Captain George Turner was born in Franklin County,

October 17, 1776. He married Millie Stone, born March 3, 1780, and had five sons and six daughters.

Obadiah Turner, born September 24, 1802; George Turner, born in 1814; Stephen Turner, born in 1806; and James Turner, born in 1827, all married and reared families. Creed Turner went to Texas.

Betsy Turner married Solomon King, and reared a family of five children. The oldest son, Allen King, went to West Virginia. His wife was an Oxley. One daughter was Emma King, who married a May.

Martha King married Harvey Turner, and went to Iowa. George King married Ona Prillaman. Lizzie King married Creed Lemon, and lived at Ferrum, Franklin County.

Jane Turner married Dan P. Helms

Millie Turner married Peter Kennedy

Basheba Turner married Sampson J. Davis, 1836. They lived in Franklin County, and reared a family of eight children. (1) Adeline, (2) Louvica, (3) Elizabeth, (4) Solomon, (5) Loutisha, (6) Benjamin, (7) James Davis, and (8) Ruth Davis. Basheba Turner Davis died September 21, 1885, and is buried in Davis graveyard on the Davis plantation in Franklin County.

Sallie Turner married Jas. A. Kennedy. They moved to Lee County, Virginia.

Martha Turner married Jas. Kennedy and moved to Missouri.

Capt. George Turner had brothers: (1) Josiah, (2) Meshek, (3) John, (4) William, (5) Andrew (grand father of Morton W. Turner and (6) Elkanah. John and Elkanah were Primitive Baptist Preachers. Elkanah's son, Z. T. Turner, was pastor of the Primitive Baptist Church at Reed Creek, Virginia. He died July 28, 1911.

Capt. George Turner's sisters were: (1) Jane, who married Mr. Fifer, a veteran in the War of 1812; and (2) Delphi, who married Le Shores Turner, another veteran of 1812.

John Turner was a brother of Elkanah Turner. His grandson, A. B. Philpott, is a Primitive Baptist Preacher at Philpot, Virginia.

Morton W. Turner, son of Callahill Turner and Julia Anna Menefee Turner, grandson of Andrew Turner and Frances Holland Turner, great-grandson of William Turner and Jane Hunter Turner, and great-great-grandson of Shadrach and Ann Turner, resides with his wife and daughter in Roanoke, Virginia.

THE WALKER FAMILY

Elisha Walker, b. 1746, d. 1841, in Franklin Co., m. Judith Kirby (b. ca. 1757, d. ca. 1835), dau. of John Kirby, Jr., of Pittsylvania Co., ca. 1779. John Kirby Jr., b. 1726, d. 1795, left will dated Mar. 11, 1795, pro. Sept. 1st. 1795, of record in Pittsylvania, naming his wife, Sarah; sons: Nathaniel and Moses Kirby; daus.: Judith Walker, wife of Elisha Walker, and Susanna Crenshaw, wife of William Crenshaw.

John Kirby, Jr., served in the Revolution. (John Kirby, m. H. D. Oct. 1793, 36, and Eight Annual Report of the State Librarian, 1910-1911, p. 256.) In 1840, Elisha Walker, then 94, lived in Franklin Co., and was receiving a pension for services in Revolution. He lived near Dickinson's Store, and at the settlement of his estate, his farm was bought by John Brown, who manufactured tobacco thereon.

The first record of Elisha Walker is a deed to him for 300 acres in Pittsylvania, dated Apr. 16, 1779, from Peter Field Jefferson. On Oct. 16, 1779, Peter Field Jefferson conveyed him 321 acres in Pittsylvania. Under date of Nov. 4, 1773, John Justice and Mary, his wife, of Pittsylvania Co., conveyed Joseph Walker of Goochland 100 acres in Pittsylvania. Joseph was probably his brother. In 1743, George Walker, was granted 6000 acres on Pigg and Irvin Rivers in that part of Brunswick Co., which is now Pittsylvania. In 1767, 1768, and 1769, David Walker was granted 4200 acres in Pittsylvania Co. The relationship of George and David Walker to Elisha Walker is unknown. He left a will dated Nov. 11, 1839, pro. in Franklin Sept. 5, 1841, appointing his son, Nathaniel Walker, grandson, Thomas Walker, and son-in-law, Lewis Potter Jr., executors.

Elisha and Judith Kirby Walker had issue:

(1) John Walker; (2) Susannah Crenshaw, wife of William Crenshaw; (3) Sally Aaron; (4) Polly Aaron; (5) Judith Thomas; (6) David Walker; (7) Nathaniel Walker, served in War of 1812, with his brother, Moses, and his widow, Susan, was pensioned and granted land warrant No. 1504 by agents at Knoxville, Tenn.; (8) Cassa Potter, who m. Lewis Potter, Jr., and lived near Union Hall; and (9) Moses Walker, b. 1793, d. at Dickinson's Store, 1833, m. Frances Elizabeth Glass, (b. in Halifax Co., 1807, d. in Franklin Co., Aug. 8, 1897) dau. of John Glass, Apr. 20, 1831.

Moses Walker's will, dated Jan. 24, 1833, pro. Mar. 4, 1833, is of record in Franklin Co., gives property to his wife, Frances, dau. Martha Elizabeth, father Elisha, mother Judith, brother Nathaniel and sister Cassa Potter. He served in Capt. Samuel Lawson's Co., Va. Militia, Sept. 1, 1814, to Dec. 1, 1814, was paid to Dec. 18, 1814, to include 340 miles of travel. The Muster Roll shows his residence as Pittsylvania Co., place of rendevous; Beavers; discharged at Ellicott Mills

340 m. from home. His widow, Frances Elizabeth Keen Walker,
received Warrant No. 114859 for 160 acres. They had a daughter
Martha Elizabeth Walker, b. Sept. 8, 1832, d. June 28, 1881,
in Franklin, m. Col. Abram Booth Hancock (b. Oct. 29, 1825, d.
Dec. 1, 1903), Nov. 3, 1847, in Rockingham Co., N. C.

THE WEBSTER FAMILY

William Webster, the first to settle in Virginia, was
named in a charter granted by King James, the first.

Rodger Webster, and his wife, Alice came to Virginia
about 1622. He was a member of the House of Burgesses in 1632.
The Virginia Colonial Records show that Maj. Richard Webster
came October 13, 1635, on board the "Amitic," George Downes,
Commander. He was a resident of James City County, and represented the county in the House of Burgesses in 1658. The
Colonial Records recite the will of John Webster, and mention
his sons: John, Joseph, Benjamin, and Daniel. His son, John,
made his will recording his sons as John, Samuel, Richard, James,
and Henry. The sons of James are also mentioned as John and
James, and his daughter as Anne Webster.

The Webster family of Virginia, gave soldiers for the
protection of the frontier settlers against the Indians. Joseph, John, David, Thomas, Henry and Peter Webster served Virginia in the Revolution.

John Webster, son of Richard Webster, born in Virginia
about 1730, served in the Indian Wars. He saw service in the
Revolutionary War as a Private in Captain's Morton's Company
of Virginia Militia. He also served in the third Troop of
Virginia Light Dragoons, First Regiment, commanded by Col. The-
odorick Bland. He was fond of hunting and pressed west, choo-
sing a location on the north fork of the Blackwater River in
Franklin County, then Bedford, where he found game in abundance.
This rich and romantic region had not long been occupied by
white men when John Webster came. He was granted many acres
and became a prosperous planter. The settlement was annoyed
by Indians on numerous occasions. At one time Mrs. Polly Hun-
derson, Jesse Webster's mother-in-law, and a Mrs. Picklesiner
were carried away by the Indians. An Indian squaw, who was
friendly to the whites, told them how to escape. After many
hardships they finally reached home. John Webster was married
four times. One of his marriages was on June 28, 1779, to
Maggie Walker, daughter of James Walker. He moved to the Northwest Territory about 1800, to a place in the present state of
Michigan. Those of his children who continued to reside in
Virginia were: Nancy Webster Arthur, Daniel Webster, John Rob-
in Webster, and George Webster. His son, Dave Webster, went
to Michigan a few years later.

George Webster, one of the sons of John Webster and
Maggie Walker Webster, was born on Blackwater, near the present

Dillon's Mill in Franklin County, on January 7, 1783. He grew
to manhood here, and married Peggy Ricard of Botetourt in 1802.
She was born in England, April 2, 1782, and came to America with
her parents about 1796. George frequently joined his friends
deer hunting in this section and occasionally his oldest son,
John R. Webster, joined the party. There were a great many deer
around the Big Lick, where Roanoke now stands, so called from
the number of deer that frequented this place. In 1824 they
were hunting and stopped to see their old friend Charles Johnston, at Botetourt Springs. Mr. Webster and son made the ac-
quaintance of General LaFayette who arrived while they were
there. Mr. Webster, who died June 14, 1829, was survived by
his widow and ten children as follows:

(1) John R. Webster, oldest son, born November 7,
1804; died June 3, 1891. He married first, Deborah Webster,
a daughter of John Robbin and Jennie Webster. She was his
first cousin. After her death, he married Catherine Peters
in 1839. She was born January 11, 1812, and died June 12, 1897.
She was the daughter of David and Christina Brubaker Peters.

(2) Betsy Webster, born September 10, 1806; died
January 24, 1885, in Franklin County.

(3) George Webster born 1808; died in Franklin
County.

(4) Daniel Webster, born June 10, 1810; died May 15,
1863. Married Batsy Marsh, born March 10, 1811; died September
29, 1893. Lived at Greenville, Tennessee.

(5) David Webster, born December 4, 1811; died in
the fall of 1860 in Franklin County.

(6) Louis Webster, born January 13, 1813; died
September 11, 1872. Married December 1, 1836 to Katherine
Jamison, born March 27, 1816; died May 15, 1890. She was
a daughter of John and Katherine Boone Jamison. Their home
was near Boone's Mill.

(7) Nannie Webster, born May 2, 1818; died June 27,
1877. Married October 1, 1851, to Henry Wilsie Carr, who was
born January 19, 1809; died February 20, 1876; lived in Floyd
County.

(8) Reuben Webster, born January 1, 1820; died February 22, 1865. Married, first, Elizabeth Sowder, born June
1, 1825; died May 16, 1859. Married, second, Ellen Hill, on
December 18, 1860. She died February 4, 1891. Their home was
near Alleghany Springs.

(9) Polly Webster, born January 21, 1823; died October 18, 1889. Married Joe Aldridge, and lived at Copper Hill,
Floyd County.

(10) Adam Webster, born September 19, 1824; died
March 24, 1874. Married Susan Akers, daughter of "Bunker Jim"
Akers. They lived in Virginia, Kansas, and Oklahoma.

John R. Webster (1804-1891) was born on the north fork
of Blackwater, near Dillon's Mill, Franklin County. He bought
the Quigley Place near the foot of Clemmon's Bald Knob and here
he and his widowed mother and other members of the family lived
for a short time. He had one child, Nancy Webster (1838-1903),
who married John Q. Saunders and moved to Mexico, Missouri.
Soon after Mr. Webster was married, he bought the Gray Estate
of about six hundred acres, three miles west of Dillon's Mill,
then John Robbin Webster's Mill. Here he built a new residence,
"Ravenrest," and made it his permanent home. His wife died
in the fall of 1838, when Nancy was an infant. He then married
a neighbor girl of his childhood, Catherine Peters (1812-1897),
second daughter of Davy (1783-1864) and Christina Brubaker Peters
(1791-1861), and to this union seven children were born.

(1) John Henry, (2) William David, (3) George Stephen, (4) Joel Lee, (5) Sarah Elizabeth, (6) Mary Ann, and (7)
James Franklin. Peggy Ricard Webster, grandmother of these
seven, died on May 3, 1876, at the age of 94 years.

John R. Webster. had a friend, Col. Andrew Lewis, who
was prominent in the annals of Franklin. They were frequently
hunting companions and some marvelous stories have come down to
their descendants of these hunting experiences. He was a brick-
layer by trade, and built the first Court House at Rocky Mount,
Franklin County. In the early days, the people of the area which
became Franklin County, attended court at New London, first the
county seat of Lunenburg County, later the county seat of Bedford. John R. Webster loved adventure and was afraid to lease
his own fireside for excursions near and far. When Daniel Webster spoke in Richmond he went to hear him. He walked across
the mountain to Monticello to see his friend Thomas Jefferson
with whom he had become intimately acquainted during Jefferson's
summer visit to "Poplar Forest" in Bedford. In the early 1800's,
he dediced to take a trip out through the Northwest Territory,
and persuaded a friend Ed. Akers, to go with him. Some of his
Webster relatives had moved to Berrien, Michigan, a few years
before. They walked and carried with them six hundred dollars
in gold, and spent many weeks on this trip. They had many ex-
citing experiences to tell, of rivers crossed, people met, and
the reception received at taverns and homes. On one occasion
they came late in the afternoon to where lived a man by the
name of Hull. He and his family were rugged and rough in ap-
pearance, and with only the coarsest accomodations available.
However, the travelers were very tired and settlements were
far apart, so they asked for lodging. After some consultation,
they were granted permission to stay. They did not like the
looks of their host and were anxious concerning the safety of
their persons and purses. They watched their host every moment
and were especially alarmed when, looking through a knot-hole
of their room, they saw him go out and bring in an ax. Still
watching, they saw him knell down with his wife and ask God's

protection on their household and guests. Then their anxiety
vanished and they slept in peace. Mr. Webster did not seek
public office and did not hold any beyond serving on the local
school board, though he was self-educated in law, and acquainted with the political questions of his day. He was of Dunkard
faith and would not own slaves. He did not believe in secession
and made speeches pleading with the people not to secede. The
struggle came and though he was too old for service. He had
three sons in the Confederate Army; John Henry (1840-1862),
William David (1842-1862), and Joel Lee (1846-1918).

Catherine Peters Webster, wife of John R., was born
at the Peter's homestead on Blackwater River in Franklin County,
January 11, 1812. She could speak and write German, and was
a very quiet Christian woman and a devoted member of the Beth-
lenem Dunkard Church. She died on June 12, 1897. After the
death of her husband, June 3, 1891, she went to live with her
oldest daughter, Sarah Webster Jamison, where she spent about
six years. The seven children of Mr. and Mrs. John R. Webster
were:

(1) John Henry Webster, the oldest son, born March
27, 1840, near Dillon's Mill, Franklin County. He was educated
in the private schools of the community, and at Emory and Henry
College. He devoted much energy to the dause of temperance.
At the outbreak of the War between the States, he enlisted in
the Confederate Army, Company "A", Sixth Virginia Regiment, and
went to Norfolk Virginia. He died soon after his enlistment
and was brought home and buried at the Peter's burial ground
on Blackwater.

(2) William David Webster, the second son, born February 20, 1842. Enlisted April 3, 1862 in the same company with
his older brother. He was forced to go to the hospital at Norfolk, where he remained for months and was finally given a furlough. His father brought him home, but he never recovered,
dying in the fall of 1862.

(3) George Stephen Webster, died in infancy.

(4) Joel Lee Webster, was born June 22, 1846. He
served in the Confederate Army the greater part of the war,
and returned home uninjured. Afterwards he devoted his attention
to farming and fruit growing. He was for a long period of years
on the school Board of Franklin County. He was married on January 25, 1869, to Hannah Catherine Jamison, born June 26, 1853
daughter of John and Elizabeth Akers Jamison. They had twelve
children: John William, Henry L., James Wyatt, Elma Alonza,
Hazel, Herbert, Minnie, Fields, Newton, Elizabeth, Berkley,
and Allie.

(5) Sarah Elizabeth Webster was born September 14,
1849. She married John William Jamison, April 4, 1878. He was
born January 22, 1849, and was the son of John and Elizabeth
Akers Jamison. They had two sons: John Ernest, and Edgar Forest
Jamison.

(6) Mary Ann Webster, born April 2, 1852, in Franklin County, died in Roanoke, Virginia, August 2, 1917. She
married Daniel S. Webster, her first cousin, son of Adam and
Sue Akers Webster. He was born August 14, 1850, and was killed while attempting to arrest a desperado, May 3, 1891. They
were the parents of eight children: Ammon, Edward, Walter, John,
Bennie, Fred, Cassie, and Alice.

(7) James Franklin Webster, died infant.

Peggy Ricard Webster wrote the most vivid description
of the meteoric shower of November 12, 1833, that has come to
the attention of the author of this volume. She stated that
there was no noise connected with the phenomenon, but that the
display was more spectacular than any of the four (1797-1831-
1833) "Star-falls" which she had witnessed. The blazing flash-
es fell like plummets, darted horizontally, and crossed and re-
crossed one another in great confusion. The shower continued,
she wrote, "until it seemed that the celestial pyrotechnist
would exhaust the supply of sideriol flakes, but the real stars
shone on in undiminished number. To form an accurate idea of
the magnificent display one would have to imagine a snow-storm
with every flake a star. If the celestial visitants had been
solid substance the earth would have been covered with a sheet
of glowing fire."

THE WINGFIELD FAMILY

The Franklin County family traces descent from Thomas Wingfield great grandson of Sir John Wingfield of Lethering-
ham, England. According to the Register of St. Peter's Parish,
this Thomas Wingfield settled in York County, Virginia, in 1636.
His son, Thomas, married Mary ____, who died in 1714. They
had 6 children. Ruth, bap. Oct. 18, 1691; Thomas, b. ca. 1693,
m. Sarah Garland; John, b. ca. 1695, m. Mary Hudson; Robert,
b. ca. 1696, m. Ann ____; Mary, bap. Feb. 25, 1699-1700; and
Elizabeth, bap. July 12, 1702. Thomas m., second, Mary ____
and had a son, Owen, b. Sept. 23, 1719. (See Virginia Magazine
April 1952, article by Dr. John G. Herndon.)

Of the six children of Thomas Wingfield and Mary ____
John, b. ca. 1695, m. Mary Hudson in 1720, and spent his life
in Hanover County. John d. before 1762. They had only one
proved child, named Charles, b. ca. 1720, and d. 1803 in Albemarle County, Virginia. Charles m. Rachael Joyner in 1741,
and had 11 children. These children are listed in Dr. Herndon's
article and also in Wood's "History of Albemarle." This Charles served in the American Revolution, according to Auditor's
Accounts, Vol. 18, p. 462.

The 11 children of Charles and Rachael Joyner Wingfield were:

1. John, 1742-1814, m. Robina Langford in 1764.
Issue 12 children.

2. Charles, m. Mary Lewis. He died 1819. No issue.

3. William, served in the militia company of Sept.
1758.

4. Christopher, d. 1821, m. Elizabeth _____ and
had 4 children.

5. Joseph, Capt., 1st Militia Co.

6. Frances, m. his cousin Elizabeth, dau. of Thomas,
and had 6 children.

7. Mary, m. John Hamner.

8. Ann, m. John Harrison.

9. Sarah, m. a Mr. Martin.

10. Jemima, m. Samuel Barksdale.

11. Elizabeth, m. Henley Hamner.

Mary Hudson Wingfield, dau. of Charles Hudson, and
wife of John Wingfield, of Hanover, conveyed to her son Charles,
in 1762, a part of the 500 acres which she had received from
her father. This place on which Charles was living when his
mother conveyed it to him, was situated in the Biscuit Run Valley of Albemarle County, near the north fork of Hardware Creek,
a locality long occupied by the Wingfield family. Charles was
a signer of the famous Albemarle Declaration of Independence.

Charles Wingfield, a son of Charles and Rachael Joyner Wingfield, was long known as Charles Jr. He was appointed
a magistrate in 1794 and served as sheriff in 1819, but died
a month after taking office. His home was at Bellair, on Hardware Creek. In 1783, he m. Mary Lewis, daughter of Charles
Lewis Jr., of Buck Island, and widow of Col. Charles Lewis of
North Garden. In his will he mentioned generally his wife's
relatives as well as his own. He left no children.

John Wingfield (1742-1814), m. in 1764, Robina Langford, and had 12 children:

1. John Moore, b. May 6, 1765, m. Ann Buster, dau.
of John Buster, and had 5 children.

2. Edward, b. 1767, m. Nancy Hazelrig, Dec. 27, 1790,
and had 8 children. He d. 1806.

3. Robert, d. 1825. He had 7 children.

4. Matthew, m. Martha Buster, and had 2 children.

5. Rebecca Gilham, m. William Wingfield, her cousin, and had 9 children.

6. Mary.

7. Martha.

8. Reuben, b. ca. 1780, m. Mary Anderson, and had 6 children.

9. Elizabeth

10. name unknown.

11. name unknown.

12. Joseph Benjamin, m. Susan.

There were 12 children in all, although his will dated July 8, 1804, says, "if more than one of my sons should be desirous of keeping the said land I desire that they should cast lots for it, and whichever of them gains it by lot shall pay to the other eleven the above mentioned sums." Strangely, he mentions only 6 of his children, as does the article by Dr. Herndon. That Reuben was one of John Wingfield's sons is proved by a deed which he signed Apr. 7, 1842, in which Reuben sold to Thomas F. Wingfield (a nephew) his interest in the "real estate of John Wingfield (my father) Senr. deceased, in Albemarle County". Deed Book 42, p. 446.

Reuben, b. ca. 1780, d. Apr. 1842, m. Mary Anderson. He lived in Hanover County, Va. They had 6 children.

Another Charles Wingfield came to Albemarle from Hanover in the early 1800's, m. Cary Ann, dau. of Lewis Nicholas. He died in 1864. His children were:

1. Frances, m. Waddy Roberts

2. Mary, m. John Mosby

3. Sarah, m. John Morris

4. Miriam, m. Robert Thornton

5. Julia, m. John Roberts

6. Edmonia

7. John

8. George

9. Charles L.

I

James Lewis Wingfield, b. ca. 1790, d. 1840, m. Elizabeth Parberry, dau. of James and Ann Parberry, b. ca. 1794, on Dec. 15, 1807, and had issue:

    1. Gustavus Adolphus Wingfield, b. ca. 1808, m. Charlotte Griffin, and had issue:

        a. Mary, m. Col. William Allen, who was killed at Gettysburg.

        b. William Lewis, who succeeded to Allen's command, m. Jerusha Kasey.

        c. Charlotte, died unmarried.

        d. Kate, d. unmarried.

        e. Samuel G., b. Oct. 17, 1846, m. Sallie Alexander, Oct. 17, 1887, and served as Clerk of Court and Mayor of Lynchburg. He had a son, among others, named Samuel, who edited a magazine for Dupont, called Splinters, at Hopewell, Va., during World War I.

        f. Sarah, d. unmarried.

        g. Nannie, died unmarried.

        h. James F., m. Lucy Dillard, and had issue: Martha (Daisy), William Lewis, and Gustavus A., who was a lawyer in Roanoke.

    2. Anne Elizabeth Wingfield, m. Capt. Sam Morgan and had issue:

        a. Samuel, who died at Martinsville. He had a son Ben.

        b. Lewis, died at Rocky Mount.

        c. Charlotte, m. C. M. Zeigler of Dickinson's Store.

        d. Frank.

    3. Susan Lewis Wingfield, b. 1816, d. 1899, m. Jan. 16, 1844, Maston Jackson Ayers, 1817-1857, and had issue: 6 children:

        a. Sarah Charlotte E. Ayers, b. Nov. 23, 1844, d. Aug. 12, 1903, m. Henry C. Barr, b. June 8, 1845, d. Mar. 10, 1892, on July 18, 1867, and had issue:

(1) George Roy Barr, b. June 25, 1868,
d. Mar. 16, 1910, unmarried.

(2) Lillian (Leila) Wingfield Barr, b.
Oct. 14, 1872, m. Charles F. Maddox,
June 6, 1899; issue: Charles Kellog
Maddox, b. Jan. 14, 1902, m. Ruth Skin-
ner, June 12, 1927; and Harry Barr
Maddox, b. Apr. 19, 1906, unmarried.

(3) Henry C. Barr, b. Oct. 12, 1876, m.
Aug. 6, 1901, Kate C. Cardoza, of
Philadelphia, b. Dec. 31, 1879, and
had issue: Cameron C. Barr, b. Aug.
17, 1903, m. Anne Bomberger, b. Apr.
9, 1904, on Mar. 3, 1928, and had
Cameron Jr., b. Aug. 31, 1929; George
Roy Barr, b. Dec. 20, 1906, unmarried;
and Sarah Lewis Barr, b. Feb. 3, 1916.

(4) Mary Lewis Barr, b. Apr. 13, 1887, d.
July 5, 1888.

b. Ann Jane (Nannie) Graves Ayers, b. Mar. 29,
1847, m. Albert B. Eaton, of Bristol, and
had 6 children:

(1) Alice Lelia, m. Prof. R. H. Sheppe,
and had Robert, who m. Mary Kent Haw-
ley.

(2) Ethel J., unmarried

(3) Bessie, m. Norton F. Smith and had
Norton Jr., and Jane Elizabeth Smith,
who m. Edward N. Backus

(4) Sarah Albert (Roberta) unmarried

(5) Victoria, m. Embree Potts, and had
Mary Victoria and Embree Jr.

(6) Hugh H., m. Julia Parkey, and had Julia
Wingfield, and Hugh Jr. Hugh Sr., d.
Apr. 10, 1934.

c. Rufus Adolphus Ayers, b. May 20, 1849, d. May
14, 1926, m. Victoria Louisa Morrison, and had
5 children:

(1) Kate Lewis, m. L. O. Pettit; and had
a large family

(2) Henry Jackson, unmarried

(3) Maggie L., dead.

(4) James B., m. Julia Bullitt, and had several children.

(5) Rufus Wingfield, who was attorney general under Gov. Fitzhugh Lee.

d. Mary Lelia Lewis Wingfield Ayers, b. June 11, 1851, d. Oct. 1, 1905, m. Arthur Joseph Eaton, b. July 18, 1849, d. June 19, 1929, on Feb. 1878. Issue:

(1) Sophia Peebles, b. Feb. 14, 1879, m. Wilbur Egbert Pettus, who d. Dec. 29, 1933.

(2) Joseph Jackson, b. Sept. 1882, m. Lucy Lykes Downey, Nov. 14, 1912, and had Joseph Jr., b. May 25, 1918, and James A. Downey, b. Sept. 30, 1920.

(3) Arthur Josephus, Jr., b. Jan. 7, 1884, unmarried.

e. William Alexander Ayers, lawyer and judge, b. Aug. 17, 1853, d. June 26, 1914, was twice married: First he m. Margaret J. C. Fickle, b. Jan. 20, 1860, d. May 14, 1883, on May 11, 1877, and had issue:

(1) Nannie Estelle, b. May 20, 1878, d. Nov. 11, 1880

(2) Susan Lewis, b. Aug. 8, 1879, d. same day

(3) Bettie Lewis, b. Oct. 12, 1880, m. Lynn Wood Haskins, b. Jan. 4, 1874, on Sept. 16, 1903, and had issue: Mary Margaret, b. Dec. 22, 1904, m. Dr. Graeme A. Canning, b. Oct. 5, 1900, assistant professor of Zoology at the Univ. of Tenn., on June 22, 1931; Betty Lynn, b. July 30, 1910, unmarried; and Lynn Wood Jr., b. Jan. 19, 1925.

(4) Margaret, b. May 8, 1883, m. Abner Lunsford, b. Dec. 6, 1873, d. Apr. 12, 1926, on June 21, 1906, and had Julia Lewis, b. Mar. 21, 1908.

William Alexander Ayers, m. second, Mary A. Gilmer, b. Mar. 16, 1860, d. Mar. 14, 1923, on Feb. 11, 1885, and had issue:

(1) Eula Ayers, b. Feb. 24, 1887, d July
     22, 1896

(2) William Rufus Ayers, b. Dec. 10, 1888,
     m. first, Willie Glenn Shomaker, b.
     Mar. 15, 1892, d. Mar. 29, 1915, on
     June 29, 1915, and had issue: Mary
     Elizabeth, b. Mar. 20, 1915, m. Wil-
     liam Callaway, June 6, 1933, and had
     Betty Glenn.William Rufus, m. second,
     Mrs. Mattie Lee Morgan, b. June 18,
     1891, on June 22, 1921, and had Betty
     Mae, b. Jan. 11, 1923, and Wm. Rufus
     Jr. b. July 2, 1925

(3) James Morgan Ayers, b. May 7, 1889,
     m. Virginia Elizabeth Gilmer, b. Mar.
     29, 1892, on June 30, 1915, and had
     issue:
               Eula, b. May 11, 1916
               Virginia, b. June 7, 1917
               James, b. May 16, 1919
               Ann Gray, b. Nov. 26, 1920
               William Alexander, b. Nov. 21,
                    1922
               Charlotte Marie, b. Aug. 18, 1924
               David Lewis, b. Jan. 13, 1926
               Richard Wingfield, b. Apr. 22,
                    1927
               Hugh Allen, b. July 18, 1931, d.
                    Dec. 1934

(4) Mary Sue Ayers, b. Dec. 7, 1890, m.
     Clarence R. Painter, b. Nov. 4, 1892,
     on Sept. 10, 1924, and had Mary Alice,
     b. Aug. 2, 1933

(5) Esther Pauline Ayers, b. Jan. 6, 1893,
     m. Ira R. Gray, b. Mar. 17, 1883, on
     Sept. 22, 1914, and had Reynolds Ayers,
     b. Aug. 30, 1915; Maston Lewis, b.
     Aug. 17, 1916; James Morgan, b. Feb.
     14, 1918; and Wm. Howard, b. Jan. 26,
     1921

(6) Alice Jane Clarice Ayers, b. Nov. 4,
     1895, m. Felix P. Heald, b. June 25,
     1892, on July 7, 1919, and had: Felix
     Jr., b. Dec. 3, 1921; and John Ayers,
     b. Feb. 9, 1922

(7) Sarah Wingfield Ayers, b. Jan. 2, 1899,
     m. Joseph E. Duff, on July 29, 1924,
     and had : Mary Catherine, b. June 6,
     1925; Sammy Lewis, b. Oct. 12, 1926;

Joseph Eugene Jr., b. June 27, 1930

f. Thomas James Ayers, b. Jan. 13, 1857, d. Oct. 16, 1859

NOTE: In the fall of 1933, Mrs. Gustavus Wingfield Lovell, wrote the author: "Judge Wm. Alexander Ayers' second wife was my half-sister, Alice Gilmer. It was my uncle, T. J. Gilmer, and his wife who took Bob Schuler, a noted Methodist preacher, upon the death of his mother, and kept him for several years, until his father remarried. The second Mrs. Schuler was Miss Mary Ketron. My uncle died when he was 54. The widow then married George Ketron, a brother of Bob Schuler's stepmother."

4. William A. Wingfield, m. Elizabeth Prunty, dau. of Jesse and Nancy Finney Prunty, Oct. 4, 1824, and had 2 daughters: Ann, and Jane. After the death of William, his widow, m. her cousin, Amos Finney, Jan. 6, 1834, and moved to Madison County, Kentucky.

5. James Lewis Wingfield

6. John Graves Wingfield

7. Paulina Wingfield, m. William Jackson Bernard, and lived at Glade Hill. Their sons, Peter and William, lived in Roanoke.

8. Sarah Jerusha Jane Wingfield, m. John Pinckard Lovell, b. 1827, and had:

    a. James Lewis, b. 1860

    b. John William, b. 1863, m. Betty McDermid

    c. Gustavus, b. 1866, m. Sarah Jane Taylor of Russell County, and had : Sarah Gilmer, Mary Katherine, and John Taylor. Sarah, m. Ernest L. Becker, and 2 children, Gustavus Wingfield Lovell was an esteemed friend of the author. He died in Cincinnati, Ohio, in 1934

    d. Mary Eliza, m. a Mr. Doyle

    e. Joseph Pinckard, m. Allie McDermid

    f. Samuel Francis, m. Ada Crouch

II.

Christopher Wingfield, m. Nancy Stockton, dau. of Richard, Feb. 1, 1815:

1. William H., m. Sarah V. Bondurant, Oct. 1853, and had issue:

    a. Edward, m., first, Nellie Trent, and, second, Myrtis Coleman, and had: Thomas, Kathryn, Edwin, and Janie.

    b. Copeland, m. Lula Copeland of Snow Creek, and had Lottie, and E. B. Both Edward and Copeland served as high constables of Roanoke.

    c. William L., no record.

    d. Alice, m. Thompson Minter, and had: Virginia, J. W., Ella, and Eva. Alice, died in 1891.

    e. Bonner, m. Thomas B. Stultz, and had Jesse. Bonner died in 1929.

    f. Mary Elizabeth, m. W. L. Draper, and had: Jesse, Ben, Harry, Janie, Helen, Edna, Ruth, and Margaret.

2. John Spotswood, m. Harriet Bondurant, Feb. 11, 1847.

3. Copeland, d. unmarried.

4. Lewis died in the Army.

5. Matthew Madison, b. on Snow Creek, Dec. 12, 1831, m. Martha J. Salmon, of Henry County, in 1853, and moved to Indiana in 1867. His daughters are unknown to me. His sons were:

    a. James C.

    b. John B.

    c. Lewis

    d. George C.

Matthew d. Sept. 30, 1918. His wife died Jan. 17 1909.

6. Charles, d. unmarried.

7. Susan, m. John R. Martin, Aug. 5, 1840.

8. Sally, m. Henry Ivey, and had Henry and Sally.

    Note: Some say she m. Peter Stockton, and had Sally, Susan, and Charles, but this marriage date is June 1, 1812, and so is questionable.

9. Elizabeth C., m. Elder Elkanah B. Turner, Oct.
27, 1840, and had Zachary Taylor Turner, a primitive Baptist
preacher. There were other sons, but I do not have their
names. Zachary was a son by the first wife.

III.

William Wingfield, m. Mary (Polly) Tench Wingfield,
dau. of Henry and Patty Tench, on Jan. 6, 1817, and had issue:

1. Oliver Pinckney Wingfield, b. 1819, m. Delilah
   Smith, dau. of Mark, Apr. 3, 1843, and had:

   a. William L., b. 1844

   b. Frances Marian, b. 1846, d. Apr. 26, 1913

   c. Nancy M., b. Feb. 18, 1852, d. Jan. 16, 1916,
      m. a Mr. Snyder

   d. James F., b. 1852, d. Nov. 7, 1926

   e. Virenda, b. 1855, m. Charles Townsend

   f. Susan (Lottie) b. 1857, m. William Conner

   g. Ann E., b. 1857, d. 1929, m. Milroy Oliver,
      in 1877

   h. Perry Wyatt, 1860, migrated West

   i. Frank

      These children moved to Indiana.

2. Parthenia (Athenia) Wingfield, d. unmarried.

3. Dolly Wingfield, b. 1825 or 1833, m. James Atkins
and had issue:

   a. Alice, m. John Stegall

   b. Anna Eliza, m. Tarleton Carter

   c. Henry, m. first a Miss James, second, Lelia
      Hicks

   d. William, m. Nannie E. Winn

   e. Emma, m. John P. Brock

   f. Mary, unmarried

   g. Caleb, m. Julia Cole

  h. Octavia, m. Calvin Stultz

  i. Rebecca, m. Ferdinand Hough (Huff)

  j. Mattie, m. William Hall

  k. Susie, m. Joseph Stultz

   4. William Henry Wingfield, b. Jan. 2, 1826, d. Dec. 26, 1907, m. Letitia Bennett, b. May 1, 1830, d. July 24, 1907, dau. of Preston S. and Mary Beheler Bennett, Jan. 10, 1854, and had issue:

    a. Mary Ann, b. Dec. 24, 1854, m. Granville Stratton Jones, Aug. 25, 1874, and had 12 children:

     (1) Letitia Clark, b. June 1875, m. Garland Y. Bailey, Oct. 28, 1904.

     (2) Margaret Lois, b. Mar. 23, 1878, m. Stephen Boray, June 30, 1820.

     (3) Robert Oliver, b. Feb. 20, 1879, m., first, Minnie Trent, May 30, 1904; second, Eva Ward, July 12, 1914; and had Aubrey, b. Mar. 3, 1905; and Ann b. Jan. 16, 1907.

     (4) William Stratton, b. Feb. 18, 1882, m. Carrie Smith, Dec. 25, 1913, and had 6 children: Mary Elizabeth, b. Oct. 23, 1914; Sallie Clark, b. Aug. 28, 1917; Evelyn Thornhill, b. May 5, 1919; Margaret Boray, b. Apr. 26, 1921; William Stratton Jr., b. Feb. 18, 1926; Frank Grandison, b. Oct. 19, 1931

     (5) Frank, b. Dec. 15, 1884, m., first, Sallie Teague, and had Frank Jr., b. 1929. Married, second, Lena Dutton.

     (6) Wyatt Willard, b. Aug. 1886-7, m. Lottie Jefferson, Nov. 25, 1911, and had 5 children: Rachael, b. May 27, 1916; Wyatt, Jr., b. Aug. 19, 1917; Leah Clark, b. Feb. 12, 1920; Laurice A., b. Sept. 5, 1922; and Alpha, b. Dec. 28, 1925.

     (7) Warner, b. Aug. 8, 1888, m. Margaret Stiles, Oct. 22, 1916, and had Virginia, b. July 20, 1917-18.

     (8) Gordon Bennett, b. May 5, 1895, m. Nell Jefferson, Oct. 1, 1916, sister of Wyatt's wife, and had Gordon Jef-

ferson, b. Jan. 18, 1930, and Beverly Gail.

(9) Lillie Mae, b. July 15, 1892, m. John
Whitmyer, Apr. 30, 1919, and had:
Betsy Ann, b. Dec. 9, 1920; John Jr.,
b. Mar. 11, 1922; Lewis Searing, b.
July 14, 1927; Nancy Lou, b. Sept.
1931.

(10) Eugene, b. 1897, m. Debra McCann, and
had son Jack Michael, b. Oct. 13, 1930.

(11) James Mart, unmarried (1935)

(12) Brother Braxton, died when 2 years old.

b. Sarah Virginia, b. July 10, 1856, d. May 19,
1900, m. Edgar Moore, Dec. 12, 1878, and had
5 children:

(1) William Ludwell, b. Sept. 10, 1879,
m. Sarah E. Evans, and had William
Jr., b. Dec. 21, 1905

(2) Sue

(3) Minnie

(4) Walter Henry

(5) Grace

c. Robert Calvin, b. Jan. 10, 1858, m. Judith Va-
sti Scott, and had issue:

(1) Charles W., b. Nov. 28, 1883, m. Nannie B. Asher, Jan. 31, 1906, and had
4 children: Carlton A., b. May 2,
1909; Evelyn E., b. Mar. 26, 1912;
Mallen H., b. May 31, 1918; Jonsy E.,
b. July 8, 1921.

(2) Elsie S., b. Sept. 5, 1889, m. Tanner
Asher, Oct. 4, 1905, and had 3 children: Edith W., b. Feb. 2, 1909; Ken-
dall C., b. Mar. 23, 1911; and Kathleen V., b. July 1, 1913.

(3) Olive Hudnall, b. Oct. 3, 1892, m.
Herbert A. Matthews, Feb. 4, 1928
and had son, Stuart Gray, b. Jan. 28,
1930.

d. Frances Eleanora, b. Dec. 3, 1859, d. May 4,

1948, m. John Robert Gilchrist, Dec. 12, 1878,
and had 11 children:

(1) Charles Henry, b. Dec. 27, 1879, m.
Nellie Frances Trent, Dec. 24, 1902,
and had 2 children: Clyde Herbert,
b. Mar. 12, 1904; and Cornelia Florence, b. Dec. 22, 1905.

(2) Eleanora Holmes, b. Dec. 3, 1880, d.
Jan. 15, 1919.

(3) Earl, b. Apr. 1, 1882, d. May 17, 1905

(4) Edward Hobson, b. Apr. 1, 1882 (twin
of Earl) m. Feb. 2, 1905, Ruth Harvey,
and had 2 daughters: 1st d. an infant,
2nd Charlotte Temple, d. Dec. 21, 1909.

(5) Willie Lewis, b. Dec. 23, 1883, d.
Mar. 17, 1884.

(6) Walter, b. Feb. 24, 1885, m. Nannie
F. Wright, Apr. 15, 1906 and had 3
children: Robert Braxton, b. Feb.
23, 1907; Mollie Virginia, b. Sept.
28, 1908 and Frances Alease, b. Feb.
20, 1915.

(7) Virginia Frances, b. Feb. 11, 1887,
m. Herbert H. Cochran, Feb. 12, 1908,
and had 3 children: Sedorah M., b.
Apr. 29, 1910; Anita R., b. Mar. 30,
1916; Herbert Jr., b. Sept. 13, 1924.

(8) Ida Lillian, b. July 5, 1889, who is
a registered nurse in Lynchburg.

(9) Florence, b. Dec. 10, 1891, d. Apr.
25, 1892.

(10) Raymond, b. Feb. 13, 1893, m. Mary
Virginia Myers, Mar. 12, 1924 and had
Raymond Jr., b. Aug. 16, 1926.

(11) James Valentine, b. Feb. 14, 1895, m.
Bessie I. Bryant, Nov. 7, 1921, and
had 4 sons: James Jr., b. Aug. 2, 1922;
John Robert, b. Feb. 16, 1924; Curtis
Wilson, b. Mar. 24, 1926 and Edwin
Earl, b. Feb. 6, 1928.

e. William Preston, b. July 2, 1861, d. Jan. 19,
1931, m. Nannie Bob Elder (b. 1862) and had
7 children:

(1) Ella Frances, b. Nov. 26, 1885, m.
Raymond Viar (b. 1883) Mar. 1, 1910,
and had 5 children: Everett R., b.
Dec. 18, 1910; Earl R., b. Aug. 8,
1912; Evelyn F., b. Apr. 16, 1915;
Elwood Pershing, b. Oct. 7, 1917; and
Emmett M., b. May 11, 1920.

(2) Gertrude Holmes, b. Sept. 5, 1888, m.
Daniel H. Hubbard, Jan. 26, 1911

(3) Flora Samuel, b. Dec. 6, 1890, m. William D. Holt, Oct. 31, 1919, and had
2 children: Daniel Stockton, b. May
11, 1921; and Fred Calvin, b. May
25, 1925.

(4) Conrad Barksdale, b. Dec. 3, 1892,
m. Carrie Walton, Dec. 20, 1913, and
had 3 children: Virginia Alice, b.
June 14, 1915; Leighton Walton, b.
May 11, 1917; and Conrad Jr., b. Nov.
22, 1919.

(5) Ralph, b. Apr. 18, 1895, m. Alice R.
Monaghan, Aug. 7, 1915, and had 2 children: Ralph Gabriel, b. May 15, 1917;
and Muriel Cecile, b. Sept. 28, 1917

(6) Ardie, b. Jan. 19, 1899, m. Herbert
O. Cox, and had Nan Catherine, b. Sept.
28, 1929

(7) William, b. Nov. 9, 1901, m. Beatrice
Johnson, and had Robert Terrell, b.
Jan. 19, 1925.

f. Emma Lee, b. July 10, 1866, d. Sept. 23, 1917,
m. Walter H. Woodall, Dec. 3, 1884, and had
6 children:

(1) James Henry, b. Aug. 7, 1885, m. Lillian B. Echols, Oct. 16, 1911, and
had 7 children: Torina Virginia, b.
Aug. 5, 1912; Mildred Alice, b. Apr.
11, 1914; Edna Grace, b. June 14, 1915;
Mary Joyce, b. Feb. 13, 1913; Audrey
Echols, b. Feb. 1, 1920; Dorothy Lee,
b. Sept. 14, 1921; and James Henry
Jr., b. Oct. 26, 1922.

(2) Thomas Richard, b. Aug. 7, 1887, m.
Minnie M. Hackworth, June 19, 1913,
and had 7 children: Herman Richard,

b. May 14, 1914; Myrtle Lee, b. Mar.
10, 1916; Etna Gail, b. July 27, 1918;
Margaret Louise, b. Aug. 4, 1920; Ethel,
b. Nov. 22, 1922; Eleanora Virginia,b.
Jan. 11, 1925; and Thomas William, b.
Dec. 10, 1927.

(3) Ida Lillian, b. Oct 21, 1889, m. Jesse
F. Capps, Oct. 26, 1910, and had Jes-
se Maxwell, b. Dec. 31, 1911; Randolph
Perrow, b. Dec. 11, 1913; Calvin Cau-
lease, b. July 8, 1915; and Walter
Lee, b. Nov. 19, 1917.

(4) Willard, b. Dec. 10, 1891, m. Josephine Brown, June 19, 1916, and had
2 children: Emma Elizabeth, b. Jan.
15, 1923, and Frances Virginia, b.
Jan. 10, 1925.

(5) Lillian Frances, b. Jan. 9, 1894, m.
William Edgar Owens, Aug. 5, 1920,
and had 3 children: Lois Helen, b.
Sept. 27, 1921; Martha Price, b. Sept.
10, 1923; and Lillian Frances, b.
Sept. 14, 1928.

(6) Lucy Hazel, b. Mar. 29, 1897, m. Percy
V. Kirby, Sept. 10, 1919, and had Percy Victor Jr., b. July 29, 1920.

g. Mattie Burton, b. Apr. 8, 1868, m. John Wesley
Evans Jr., Feb. 22, 1888, and had 8 children:

(1) Hubert Hearn, b. Dec. 11, 1888, m.
Frances N. Ware, Sept. 12, 1942. They
adopted a son, John Ware, b. Oct. 2,
1942, adopted Sept. 7, 1946

(2) Herman, b. Aug. 31, 1890, m. Ethel
Sowell, Nov. 24, 1915, and had 7 child-
ren: May, b. Sept. 16, 1916; Kathryn,
b. Nov. 7, 1917; Robert Preston, b.
June 29, 1920; Nancy L., b. June 21,
1931; Shirley Grey, b. Apr. 26, 1933;
Herman, Jr., b. Aug. 30, 1939; and
James Malcolm, b. Aug. 11, 1941.

(3) Georgie, b. Dec. 4, 1892, m. William
R. Davis, Jan. 31, 1910, and had 4
children: Minnie Ruth, b. Feb. 11,
1911; Nannie William, b. Jan. 17, 1913;
Ella Elizabeth, b. July 12, 1915; and
John William, b. Jan. 31, 1920.

(4) Florence Elizabeth, b. June 5, 1895,

m. Edward G. Minnix, Jan. 31, 1915,
and had 4 children: Edward Irvin b.
Nov. 26, 1915; Vivian Marie, b. Oct.
3, 1917; Edith Mae, b. Nov. 23, 1919;
and Carl Haywood, b. Dec. 23, 1921.

(5) Paul, b. Oct. 4, 1897, m. Bessie E.
Carwile, Dec. 3, 1926, and had Mildred Pauline, b. Dec. 27, 1927.

(6) Elna, b. Apr. 15, 1901, m. Willie Cyrus, Dec. 23, 1924.

(7) William, b. June 12, 1904, d. Jan.
17, 1934.

(8) Marguerite, b. May 28, 1908, m. Russell B. Elder, Dec. 23, 1926, and
had son Reginald Burns, b. Nov. 20,
1929

h. Ada Lillian, b. July 20, 1870, d. Nov. 26, 1912
(one of twins) m. John Phillip Davis, Dec. 18,
1895, and had 5 children:

(1) Eva Ludwell, b. Jan. 18, 1899, m.
Sandy Sowell, and had Martin Phillip,
b. Aug. 25, 1915; and Wingfield, b.
Jan. 24, 1916.

(2) James Russell, b. Feb. 26, 1901, m.
Jessie M. Tilley, June 20, 1924, and
had 4 children: Russell Edward, b.
May 6, 1925; Wesley Earl, b. Nov. 1,
1926; Shirley Agnes, b. Aug. 24, 1927;
Jessie Winfred, b. Feb. 2, 1929.

(3) Robert Braxton (Braxter) b. Jan. 17,
1904, m. Ellen Alice Tilley, July
16, 1932, and had 5 children: Carol
Ann, b. Sept. 4, 1933; John Robert,
b. Feb. 4, 1936; Barbara Ellen, b.
June 2, 1938; Phyllis Jean, b. June
28, 1942; and Dennis Richard, b. Jan.
5, 1947.

(4) Innis Earl, b. May 2, 1906, m. Jeanette M. Druschell, July 31, 1927; m.
second, Jessie Morgan Martin, Dec. 7,
1934, and had son Innis Jr., b. Oct.
3, 1935.

(5) Infant son lived only a few days.

i. Ida Leonard, b. July 20, 1870, d. Feb. 28, 1911,
m. James Henry Marshall, Dec. 18, 1895, and had
4 children:

(1) Layton, b. Jan. 30, 1898, d. Aug. 22, 1916.

(2) Iva, b. Sept. 5, 1899, m. George Lee Moore, D c. 22, 1928

(3) William Robert, b. Apr. 6, 1904, m. Nora May Williams, Jan. 31, 1935, and had Elizabeth Collins, b. June 21, 1940.

(4) Virginia Elizabeth, b. Apr. 19, 1908, m. Henry Walden Davis, Jan. 28, 1927.

5. Pinckney Green Wingfield, b. July 7, 1827, m. Harriet Cooper, b. Oct. 28, 1829, dau. of Gideon and America Law Cooper, Sept. 6, 1850. He m. second, Lucy Lovell Woody, Feb. 1897. Harriet d. Aug. 1893. Issue:

a. William Jasper, b. June 20, 1851

b. Emily Mandeville, b. Aug. 3, 1853

c. Mary Catherine, b. May 31, 1855

d. Tazewell Tarleton, b. Oct. 4, 1858

e. Victoria Ann, b. Aug. 3, 1862

f. Martha Victoria, b. Feb. 12, 1866

6. Lewis Franklin Wingfield, b. Nov. 12, 1831, d. May 20, 1907, m. Virginia Elizabeth Wingfield, daughter of Charles and Lucy Hicks Wingfield, d. Nov. 1856, and had issue:

a. George, b. Sept. 11, 1857

b. Sarah Elizabeth, b. 1859

c. James L., b. Apr. 15, 1865

d. John, b. Mar. 12, 1867

e. Ida Emerson, d. Nov. 1903

f. Florence, b. Sept. 11, 1873

g. Mary Eliza, b. Apr. 7, 1878

h. Robert Lee, b. Oct. 31, 1880

Lewis Franklin Wingfield, m. second, Letitia Brock, dau. of Lorenzo Dow and Mary Kidd Brock, and had second, son, Charles T., b. Apr. 17, 1887.

Pinckney Green Wingfield, b. July 7, 1827, d. Apr.
28, 1908, son of William and Mary Tench Wingfield, m. Harriet
B. Cooper, b. Oct. 28, 1829, d. Aug. 1893, dau. of Gideon and
America Law Cooper, Sept. 6, 1850. He m., second, Lucy Lovell
Woody, Feb. 1897.

1. William Jasper Wingfield, b. June 20, 1851, d.
Jan. 31, 1929-30, m. Quintina, dau. of Samuel Woodall of Mountain Valley, and had 13 children, listed below. Quintina d.
Apr. 20, 1901. He m., second, Ella Trent, b. Dec. 25, 1914,
d. 1937.

a. Betty Marcelle, b. Nov. 27, 1881, m. George
Lewis Brodie, Dec. 1902 and had issue:

(1) Dewey Clifford Brodie, b. 1903, m.
Geneva Owen, Sept. 2, 1933. Betty,
d. May 1905

b. William Tell, b. Mar. 12, 1883, d. Dec. 9, 1955
(?), m. June 7, 1909, Sallie Allen, b. Aug.
3, 1881, and had issue:

(1) Juanita, b. July 8, 1910

(2) Allen, b. Sept. 12, 1911

(3) Sallie Rainey, b. Dec. 16, 1912

(4) Mary Marcelle, b. Oct. 16, 1918

(5) William Tell, b. Jan. 12, 1921

c. Berta M., b. Aug. 26, 1884, d. unmarried in
Nov. 1896

d. Patrick Green, b. May 20, 1887, m. Ena L. Turpin of Rockbridge County, July 6, 1914 (Ena
d. Aug. 31, 1944). He m. second, Henrietta
Child, Feb. 25, 1947. Issue:

(1) Elizabeth, b. Oct. 12, 1916

(2) Nancy Pope, b. Oct. 9, 1917

(3) Patrick Green, Jr., b. Mar. 3, 1922

e. Ella Kate, b. Jan. 12, 1886, m. William B. Turner, Dec. 27, 1911, and had issue:

(1) Samuel b. Oct. 18, 1912

(2) Mary Quintina, b. Dec. 12, 1914

        (3) Jasper DeShazo, b. July 7, 1916

        (4) Virginia Rainey, b. Nov. 28, 1921

        (5) Mildred W., b. July 28, 1925

f. Samuel J., b. Dec. 25, 1888, d. Dec. 22, 1961, m. Essie D. Jones, Apr. 8, 1912, and had issue:

        (1) Georgia Helen, b. Jan. 27, 1913, m. Lloyd Richardson, July 15, 1932

        (2) Quintina Louise, b. Dec. 4, 1914, m. Jesse Draper, Sept. 2, 1933

        (3) Nancy Beatrice, b. Oct. 23, 1918

g. Thomas Otis, b. Mar. 30, 1890, m. Bessie Davis, Mar. 27, 1912, and had issue:

        (1) Fred D., b. Dec. 22, 1912

        (2) Della F., b. Apr. 19, 1914, m. Henry W. Barbour, Apr. 16, 1932

        (3) Lewis W., b. Jan. 9, 1917

        (4) Lottie V., b. May 18, 1918

        (5) Henrietta, b. Feb. 27, 1920

        (6) Fairy, b. May 30, 1922

        (7) Russell R., b. Oct. 29, 1926

        (8) Nancy W., b. Feb. 18, 1930

h. Beverly Fulton, b. Aug. 1891, d. Aug. 1960, m. Argie Bateman, Apr. 20, 1919, and had issue:

        (1) Mary E., b. Sept. 25, 1920

        (2) Anna Lee, b. July 28, 1922

        (3) Nancy Ruth, b. Dec. 3, 1925

        (4) Clara, b. Dec. 20, 1927

i. Sallie F., b. Apr. 25, 1893, d. July 1909

j. Luther Alfred, b. Nov. 27, 1894, d. Jan. 14, 1958, m. Margaret Cahill, Feb. 9, 1921, and had issue:

        (1) Melton, b. Aug. 14, 1922

(2) Rives, b. Dec. 10, 1923

(3-4) Twins Madie and Marie, b. Mar. 30, 1925

(5-6-7) Triplets: Ina. Ivey and Iris, b. Nov. 7, 1926

k. Lottie Harriet, b. Apr. 12, 1896, m. Waddy T. Allen, died without issue in Feb. 1916

l. Rainey Maud, b. 1899, d. Nov. 3, 1929, m. Waddy T. Allen and had issue:

(1) Lottie Thompson

(2) William Darling

(3) Jettye

m. Fletcher Pinckney, b. Nov. 25, 1897, d. unmarried in 1948

2. Emily Mandeville Wingfield, b. Aug. 3, 1853, m. Jesse Carter and had issue:

a. Sallie, m. James Metts

b. Emma, m. Joseph Wilson

c. Mary)Polly), m. Henry Overton

d. Rose, m. first, John McDowell, and second, John Eiler.

e. Peachy, m. Elizabeth Petty

f. Hetty, m. Bruce Stone

g. Annie, m. first Charles H. Bell, and second, Stirling Carter

h. Posie, m. Susie Bell

i. Thomas Cody, m. Hope Bell

3. Mary Catherine Wingfield, b. May 31, 1855, m. Daniel Barrow, and had issue:

a. John, b. ca. 1880, disappeared when young, and never heard from

b. Ellen, b. ca. 1882, lived in West Virginia

c. Watt Green, b. Jan. 26, 1885 in Franklin County m. first, Nannie Lee, and, second, _____ Barrow

    d. William Oren, b. June 4, 1886, m. Mary (Mollie) Yates (Yeates), and had 4 children

    e. Robert D., b. 1889, m. first, Minnie Manns, and second, Ella Bream, and had 7-8 children

    f. Joseph B., b. 1893-4, m. first, Nannie Burnett, and second, Maud Spicer, and had 5 children

    g. Charles S., b. Nov. 11, 1895

    h. Harrison F., b. Dec. 24, 1897, m. Ollie Prewitt (Pruitt), and had 2 children.

4. Tazewell Tarleton Wingfield, b. Oct. 4, 1858, d. Mar. 30, m. first, Alice Mitchell b. June 29, 1863, d. July 19, 1891, dau. of Franklin, Dec. 16, 1866, and had issue:

    a. Mary Belle, b. Jan. 10, 1888, d. July 13, 1891

    b. Lelia Clare, b. Nov. 24, 1890, d. Aug. 10, 1891.

Tazewell Tarleton Wingfield, m., second, Mary Susan Motley, (b. May 20, 1873, d. July 2, 1945), Jan. 21, 1892, and had issue:

    c. Henry Marshall, b. Feb. 19, 1893, ca. May 7, 1961. He dropped the name Henry in early youth. He m. Marie Kerfoot Gregson of Cincinnati, Oct. 11, 1927. No issue He is the author of this volume.

    d. Willis Roy, b. June 10, 1894, d. Dec. 21, 1894

    e. Nannie Rebecca, b. Oct. 3, 1895, m., first, Beverly A. Davis, Jan. 1, 1918, and, second, J. Richard Eggleston, Sept. 19, 1923. Issue by 1st m.:

        (1) Randolph, b. Dec. 31, 1918 By 2nd m.

        (2) Spottswood Fisher, b. June 18, 1924

        (3) Mary Elizabeth, b. June 7, 1925, d. Dec. 24, 1925

        (4) Phillip Gordon, b. May 26, 1926

        (5) James Thomas, b. May 18, 1927

        (6) Julia Johnsie, b. June 19, 1928

        (7) Berneice Rebecca, b. Sept. 22, 1929

        (8) Josephine Motley, b. Nov. 13, 1931

f. Lucy Marvin (Marvene), b. Sept. 19, 1897, m. Benjamin Giles Craig, Sept. 24, 1919, and had issue:

    (1) Benjamin Burton, b. Aug. 31, 1920, d. Nov. 19, 1921

    (2) Herman Marshall, b. Dec. 6, 1921

    (3) Catherine, b. Jan. 17, 1924

    (4) Frances Lucille, b. June 6, 1926, d. Mar. 20, 1928

    (5) Naomi, b. Aug. 18, 1932

    (6) Philip Wayne, b. Aug. 21, 1935

g. Elsie Frances, b. May 3, 1899, m. J. Byron Lavinder, May 18, 1921, and had issue:

    (1) James Shelton, b. Aug. 1, 1922, d. Nov. 18, 1925

    (2) Elsie Wingfield, d. Mar. 20, 1925, and her infant son was buried in the casket with her.

h. Ada Lillian, b. Jan. 25, 1901, d. July 8, 1941, m. John Robert Heflin, July 16, 1918, and had issue:

    (1) Mary Iciline, b. Apr. 23, 1919

    (2) John Robert, b. Sept. 19, 1920, d. July 26, 1939

    (3) Ada Myrtle, b. May 20, 1922

    (4) Marshall, b. Nov. 12, 1924

    (5) Edna Violet, b. Mar. 23, 1926, d. Oct. 19, 1931

    (6) Rachael Virginia, b. Oct. 14, 1928

i. William Pinckney, b. Oct. 24, 1902, d. Dec. 22, 1949, m. Esther Cahill, Sept. 1, 1923, and had issue:

    (1) William Rudolph, b. July 5, 1924

    (2) Lorena, b. Aug. 28, 1925, d. Nov. 9, 1931

    (3) Douglas, b. Oct. 18, 1926, d. May 28, 1928

(4) Robert Earl, b. Dec. 5, 1928

j. Stuart Edward, b. Oct. 24, 1904, d. Dec. 5, 1929, m. Dessie Boitnott, Jan. 3, 1924, and had issue:

    (1) Marie Grace, b. Dec. 9, 1925

    (2) Stuart Gordon, b. Apr. 4, 1928

k. Richard Lafayette, b. Dec. 5, 1906, m. Mary Hessie Parks, Oct. 16, 1926, and had issue:

    (1) Mary Jane, b. Aug. 7, 1927

    (2) Richard L. Jr., b. Aug. 22, 1929

    (3) Edward Ashley, b. Sept. 18, 1936

l. Rachael Harriet, b. Dec. 24, 1908, m. Benedict R. DeAngelo, July 11, 1931. No issue.

m. Mary Motley, b. June 24, 1912, m. Harry Fontaine, and had issue:

    (1) John Robbin, b. Mar. 4, 1952

n. Helena Virginia, called Virginia Lee, b. Oct. 6, 1914, m. July 23, 1940 Robt. Luchars Urban, and had Susan, b. Apr. 3, 1944; and m., second, Milton Noyes, June 12, 1954. Robt. d. Mar. 6, 1947

5. Victoria Anne Wingfield, b. Aug. 3, 1862, m. John Henry Woodall, son of Samuel Woodall of Mountain Valley, and had issue:

a. Henry, who m. Elizabeth Watson in 1911

b. George who was killed in World War I

c. Lelia, who m. Pigg Cousins

d. Roy, who m. Ora May Gilbert

6. Martha Virginia Wingfield, b. Feb. 12, 1866, m. first, John Kidd (b. 1865, d. July 16, 1906), and had issue:

a. Mary, b. Aug. 2, 1884, m. Robert Frazier in 1906

b. Edward Pinckney, b. July 17, 1887, m. Maud Barts Love (Lucy) d. unmarried, July 29, 1906

c. Anna, m. first, Charles Jones, and, second, Daniel Butler

Martha Wingfield Kidd, m., second, John H. Wilson, of Axton, Jan. 19, 1913

V

Children of William Wingfield and Rebecca Elizabeth Wingfield, dau. of John and Robina Wingfield, of Albemarle.

1. Lewis, m. Elizabeth Parberry, Dec. 15, 1807.

2. Christopher, m. Nancy Stockton, Feb. 1, 1815.

3. William, m. Polly Tench, Jan. 6, 1807.

4. Charles, m. first, Rebecca (Sally) Marshall, Dec. 10, 1821, and had issue:

   a. William, m. Jennie Frith

   b. Louisa, m. John Cheshire, and had Rufus and Charles.

   c. Mary, m., first, Joseph Stultz, and second, Charles Stockton.

   d. Jane, m. Anderson Stultz.

   e. Ann, m. Peyton Gravely.

   f. Frances, m. William Beheler, and had Elmira Jane, who m. C. C. Lavinder.

   Charles, m. second, Elizabeth Wingfield, dau. of Francis Wingfield, Jan. 10, 1854, and had issue:

   g. Hallie, m. William Buchanan Wade.

   h. Sally, m. Jabez Gravely.

   NOTE: This Francis Wingfield, m. his 1st cousin, another Elizabeth Wingfield, and so the confusion.

5. Austin, b. ca. 1800 m. Nancy Cook, Dec. 23, 1826, and had issue:

   a. Caroline Cook, m. Thomas D. Frith, Nov. 1853, and had: Mary C., Ann Eliza, William O., Florence L., and Lee.

   b. Mary, m. Jacob Frith, and had: Edward, Emma, and Jacob Austin.

c. Nancy is listed in some records.

6. Jerusha, m. William M. Bowling (Bouldin), Nov. 1, 1817, and had Gabriel, who m. Catherine Lavinder, Oct. 15, 1849.

7. Mary (Polly) b. shortly after the turn of the century, m. George Cooper, Sept. 23, 1824, and had issue:

    a. George, m. Susan Williamson

    b. Morgan, m. Haseltine Parker

    c. Charles, m. Pauline Orvis

    d. William, m. Julia Williamson

    e. Mary Ann, m. Greene Gravely

    f. Eliza, m. Calvin Martin

    g. Nannie, m. Chrisopher Law

    h. Emaline

8. Lucy, m. _____, and had issue:

    a. Elizabeth, m. Frederick Cook, Mar. 6, 1843, and had Eliza, Lucy, who m. Charles Carroll Brodie of Snow Creek, and William Horseley.

9. John H., m. Lucy Hicks, dau. of Howard and Sallie Hicks, Jan. 7, 1828, and had issue:

    a. Elizabeth, m. Lewis Franklin Wingfield

    b. Letitia, m. Anderson Kingery, Aug. 16, 1845, and had: Fontain, Geroge, William, Sarah and Jenny.

    c. Julia, m. Elbert Quinton, and had: Tyler, Lewis, and others.

    d. Thomas, m. Dolly Wells, and had: Thomas, Charles Wooten, and Lucy.

    e. Charles

    f. Wiley

    g. Hutts, m. in Floyd County. Issue: Richard, and older brother.

    h. Thalos, removed to Pennsylvania.

    i. Almira, m. Creed Scott.

    j. Sally A. H., m. Joseph Hodges, Oct. 10, 1848

and had 8 children

NOTE: In "Marriage Bonds of Franklin County," 2
        others are listed, as daughters of John H.
        and Lucy Hicks Wingfield:

    Sally, m. Peter Stockton, June 1, 1812.

    Polly, m. Charles Stockton, Dec. 5, 1814.

VI

Children of Lewis Franklin Wingfield.   He m. twice.
His first wife was Virginia Elizabeth Wingfield, m. Nov. 1856.

    1.   George W. Wingfield, b. Sept. 11, 1857, m. Mary
O. Kidd, in 1877, and had issue: he m., second, Annie May Ford,
June 29, 1933.

        a.   Oren, m. Connie Payne, and had: Bonner, Ruby,
             George, and Charles.

        b.   Belle, m. Conrad Gentry, and had: Thomas, Lay-
             ton, George, and Gordon

        c.   Alonzo, m. Laura DeLancy, and had Simona, Eliz-
             abeth, Alonzo Jr., Dorothy, Barbara, Benjamin,
             and Virginia.

        d.   Benjamin, d. after service over seas-World War
             II

    2.   Sarah Elizabeth Wingfield, b. 1859, m. John Car-
ter, and had Jack, and Stirling.

    3.   James Lewis Wingfield, b. Apr. 15, 1865, m. first,
Lou Emma Beale, and Feb. 12, 1885.   Issue:

        a.   Annie, b. June 10, 1887, m. John Poe, and had:
             Elizabeth, James, and Rudolph

        b.   Leonard, b. Sept. 15, 1890, m. Annie Miles,
             and had Tiny, Ethel, Virginia, and Louise

        c.   Mamie, b. 1892, m. Arthur Poe, and had Beulah

        d.   Gladys, b. 1896, m. Wm. Martin, and had Robt.,
             Francis, Barbara, and Beatrice

        e.   Clyde, b. 1899, m. Lottie Johnson, and had Jam-
             es Cecil

    f. Irene, b. 1903, m. Otho Miles, and had Ray

    g. James Jr., b. 1906, m. Mattie Shaw, and had Christine and James

James Lewis Wingfield, m. second, Hattie Johnson, Dec. 24, 1918.

4. John Wingfield, b. Mar. 12, 1867, m. Anna Elizabeth Hatcher, and had:

    a. Plummer, m. Minnie Perdue

    b. Lawson, m. Daisy Billings

    c. Frank, m. Margaret Compton

    d. Webb, m. Pearl Raikes

    e. Fairy, m. Bruce Campbell

5. Ida Emerson Wingfield, b. in 1869, m. J. P. Gearheart, and had:

    a. Osa

    b. Lewis

    c. Elizabeth

    d. Bruce

    e. Linnaeus

Ida Emerson Wingfield lived at Twelve Mile, Ind., and died Nov. 1903.

6. Florence Wingfield, b. Sept. 11, 1873, m. James W. Smith, Dec. 31, 1891, and had:

    a. Ernest, a Methodist Preacher, who m. Florence Doyle, and had Aaron, Ruth, and Howard

    b. Arthur, m. Minnie Kidd, and had Harry, Hazel, Elizabeth, Grayson, Lawrence, Maurice, Audrey

    c. Minnie, m. Jesse Wood, and had Raymond, Margaret, Jesse Jr., Carneal, and Rebecca

    d. Stafford, m. Agatha Moore, and had Virginia, and James

    e. George, m. Dora Norman, and had George Jr.

    f. Clarence, m. Elsie Trusler, and had: Edna, Elizabeth, and Clarence Jr.

g. Blanche, m. William John Lawless, and had William Jr.

h. Elizabeth, m. Dennis E. Wilson.

7. Mary (Molly) Elizabeth Wingfield, b. Apr. 7, 1878, m. William M. Kidd, d. Aug. 27, 1914) and had:

a. Waller, b. Sept. 10, 1896, m. Mrs. Frances Purcell

b. Minnie, b. July 17, 1898, m. Arthur Smith.

c. William Harold, b. Dec. 18, 1900, m. Emma Martin.

d. Robert, b. Mar. 22, 1904, m. Hester Wilson, and had Edward, Robert, Otis, Mildred, and Irvin.

e. Herbert, b. Dec. 21, 1906, m. Mildred Holcomb.

f. Milton, b. Aug. 14, 1911, m. Ursa Isley, and had Bobby Ray.

Mary Elizabeth Wingfield Kidd, m. second, Henry Lee Laprade, Aug. 16, 1931.

8. Robert Lee Wingfield, b. Oct. 31, 1880, m. Susan Kate Gilbert, dau. of William Gilbert of Henry County, May 17, 1905, and had:

a. Mabelle, m. Noel Griffin, and had: Hubert Lee, and Noel.

b. Layton, m. Ella Estelle Gilbert, Dec. 23, 1931.

c. Isaac

Robert Lee Wingfield is a Baptist Preacher.

9. Lewis Franklin Wingfield, m., second Letitia Brock, dau. of Lorenzo Dow Brock and had:

a. Charles Thomas, b. Apr. 17, 1887, m. Sue Miles in 1909, and had: Doris, Revell, Hazel, Vivian, Garland, and Alton.

INDEX

A.

273

J. S.	200
James T.	40
Jane	200
John 56, 155, 200,	210
John A.	197
John S.	200
Judith	210
Maggie	155
Mamie	200
Margaret Saunders	200
Martha Mongtomery	155
Mary 168,	210
Mary Callaway	200
Mary D.	200
Mary E.	53-54
Mary Margaret	200
Mollie	155
Norboune	200
Peter	200
Polly	92
Robert E.	200
Sally	40
Samuel	200
Shields	200
Stafford	200
Theodocia Saunders	197
Theodosia Saunders	210
Tubal	200
Virginia Saunders	200
Willa Noell	200
William	155
Hall, Dr.	37
Mr.	82
Ann	97
Elizabeth Wade	37
Matilda	82
Mattie Atkins	240
Randolph 1,	186
Richard	97
Sarah	30
William	240
Halley, Earl	55
Ethel	55
Fannie Craghead	40
Henry Clay Dean	55
Henry Clay Dean, Jr.	55
Olivia Dudley	55
Thomas H.	40
Thomas Peyton	55
Halsey, Almira	217
F. L.	84
Julia Peters	217
Seth	217
Nannie	84
Sena	84

Ham, Maria F.	130
Hamilton, Charles	55
Charles Atley	142
Jane	147
Laura Pasley	55
Lucy	55
Martha Woodson Hill	142
Victoria	55
Hamlet, Sally	4
Hammersly, Annie Ray	114
John W.	114
Lorina Thelma	114
Lorina Thelma Etter	114
Nancy Elizabeth Hancock	114
Russell	114
Hammock, Nancy Prunty	186
Peter	186
Hammond, Mary	9
Hamner, Elizabeth	
Wingfield	231
Fannie Dudley	54
Henley	231
Mary Wingfield	231
Richard	54
Hampton, Carter Temple	200
Eva Gwathmey	200
Fleming	200
Fleming III	200
Frances	200
Frances B. Brown	200
Frank	199
Mary Elsie	200
Mary Fleming Irvine	199
Polly Bowles	200
Hancock, Major	95
Abram	110
Abram Booth 74, 99, 108,	
	208, 226
Abram Oscar	109
Abram Oscar, Jr.	109
Abram P. 100, 127,	208
Ada	59
Ada Nye	100
Agnes Booth 13,	99
Alice M.	105
Angie A. Saunders	104
Angie Saunders	204
Ann Nancy	117
Anna Oren Garland	104
Anna Spencer	110
Anne	99
Anne Spencer	110
Annie 100,	102
Annie Sue	113
Annie Melville Gwaltney	114

324

|---|---|---|
Robert Richard, Jr.		143
Sallie Moorman	61,	143
W. F. H.		186
W. P.		143
W. P. F.		144
William L., Jr.		144
William Ludwell	65,	144
William Peter Francis	65,	143
LeFew, Burah Fay		106
C. B.		106
Leffler, Mary Carr		101-102
Olive Parrish		102
Philip		102
Leftwich, Miss		211
Augustine		125
Catherine Greer		87
Elizabeth		213
Fannie		203
James		87
Mary		60
Mary Otey		215
Miranda Callaway		87
Ralph		125
Sarah		125
Thomas		125
William	87, 125,	512
Leftwichs		64
Leggett, David		147
Margaret McNiel		147
Leigh, William		168
Lemmon, Flora		198
Lemon, C. K.		192
Creed		224
Eleanor		194
Eleanor Frances		190
Fannie Lillie		192
Helen		192
Ida		85
Lizzie King		224
Marvin Glen		192
Minnie R.		109
R. M.		109
Ross		192
Ruth		192
William		192
Lesh, Rebecca		156
Lesseur, Jane		190
Lester, Miss	189,	204
Eliza Jane		103
Elizabeth M.		20
Henry Clay		24
John K.		20
Katherine		20
Lamar B.		103

Lucy Clark Brown		24
W. G., Jr.		20
William G.		20
Lewis	62,	145
Miss		214
Andrew		228
Charles		231
Charles, Jr.		231
Kate		26
Mary		231
Lindsey, Miss		176
Linus, Velie		121
Lipscom, William		187
Little, Billy		202
Boyd Saunders		202
Carietta		202
Dorothy		202
Elizabeth		202
Freddie		202
Lockhart		191
Jane		191
Ward		191
Lockwood		197
Angelica Peel		197
Anna Preston Davis		197
George R.		197
Louisa		197
Richard John		197
Thomas Rhodes		197
Loudy, Jane		192
Love, Mary		65
Mary Frith		223
Maud Barts		252
Tobe		223
Viola		59
Lovelace, Emma		55
Mary		200
Peachy		200
R. A.		200
Robert	29,	200
Sallie		200
Sallie Willie Saunders		200
Tom		200
Lovell, Miss		193
Ada Croach		237
Allie McDermid		237
Betty McDermid		237
Calie		203
Gustavus		237
Gustavus Wingfield		237
Mrs. Gustavus Wingfield		237
James Lewis		237
John Pinckard		237
John Taylor		237
John William		237

328